RAGGED COAST, RUGGED COVES

RAGGED COAST, RUGGED COVES

LABOR, CULTURE, AND POLITICS IN SOUTHEAST ALASKA CANNERIES

Diane J. Purvis

University of Nebraska Press

LINCOLN

Library of Congress Cataloging-in-Publication Data
Names: Purvis, Diane J., author.
Title: Ragged coast, rugged coves: labor, culture, and
politics in southeast Alaska canneries / Diane J. Purvis.
Description: Lincoln: University of Nebraska Press,
[2021] | Includes bibliographical references and index.
Identifiers: LCCN 2021007596
ISBN 9781496225887 (paperback)
ISBN 9781496228505 (epub)
ISBN 9781496228512 (pdf)
Subjects: LCSH: Cannery workers—Alaska—Social
conditions. | Cannery workers—Alaska—Economic
conditions. | Salmon canneries—Alaska—History. |
Salmon canning industry—Alaska—History.
Classification: LCC HD8039.C272 U678 2021 |
DDC 331.7/664942097982—dc23
LC record available at https://lccn.loc.gov/2021007596

Set in Adobe Text by Mikala R. Kolander.
Designed by N. Putens.

CONTENTS

ILLUSTRATIONS

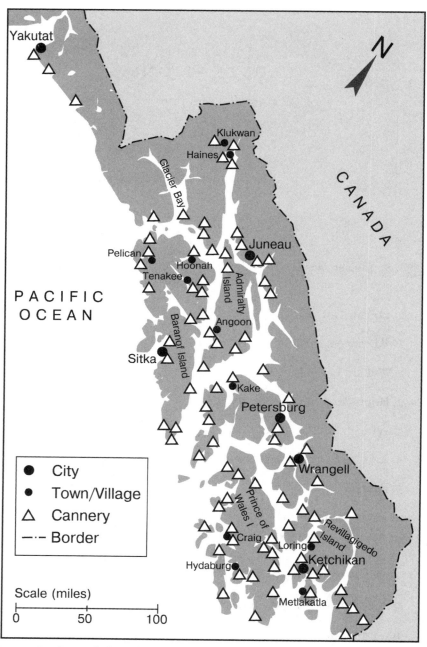

MAP 1. Southeast Alaska with cannery locations, ca. 1930s. Designed by Gabe Emerson.

RAGGED COAST, RUGGED COVES

Introduction

What does the mention of Alaska bring to mind? Perhaps it is the floating icebergs, pioneer log cabins, Native sod houses, or the extremes of wilderness. Often it is thought of as that far away place barely clinging to the North American continent, as if it does not truly belong. When one delves into its history, however, there is a much different tale to be told. Aligning with regional history, Alaska cannot be taken out of the framework of the Pacific Northwest and western Canada. Economic policies, political maelstrom, and social change instigated along the Eastern Seaboard eventually arrived on the western coast, touching the sparsely populated and diverse Alaskan region. Historian Richard White argues that the West is defined by more than geographical parameters; also central is the history enacted in this environment. Geography merely distorts the "nature of the western environment itself by making static what is dynamic. The land and the plants and animals that live on it are not just natural, they are also a result of the past actions of human beings. . . . It limits as well as creates human possibilities, but it simultaneously reflects the actions of human beings upon it."[1]

In considering regional history, Susan Armitage has pointed to the paucity of detail in standard history books regarding ethnic lives, female roles, labor history, and the accompanying lifestyles. Instead, there is more emphasis on great leaders, who are usually part of the dominant society, a sociological term indicating a majority, not a measure of moral superiority. She calls for more emphasis on those groups or communities that make up the "sum total of innumerable small actions and reactions by ordinary people as they come into contact with other people who may seem similar or very different from themselves."[2] Breaking this down, there is a need for a story told by the people who lived it; the laborers operating machinery, not the owners of the operation. In the working culture, people perform their tasks side by side, and despite differences in background, and possibly in political or religious beliefs, they find they have much in common. Those shared traits unify a group, developing into a force for change and equity. Yet Armitage is quick to remind us that the "effect of economic decisions of capitalists" has real consequences for the working people, as it did for cannery workers in the unique environment of southeast Alaska, located on the Alexander Archipelago and bordering Canada.

In tracing the transformation of the West, William Robbins contends that "capitalism is the common factor to understanding power, influence and change in the American West."[3] This conclusion was applicable to Alaska's cannery industrialization as it was financed by capital and investment monies coming from the Pacific Northwest and San Francisco. The influx of money encouraged more technology, leading to increased production and the need for more labor. The companies relied on a steady flow of able workers, both indigenous and immigrant, dependent on their jobs for survival while distant companies controlled wages, working conditions, and the resource itself. Alaska salmon canneries operated much like the original thirteen colonies did, as a manufacturing hub, distinguished by "colonial economic status and absentee control."[4] While other areas of the West grew into major urban centers and organized their own financial centers, Alaska remained chained to Eastern or Pacific Coast mega-companies.

This trend corresponds with corporate colonialism, as these same business interests controlled resource extraction simultaneously with political jockeying for favorable laws, avoiding tax collection, and exerting influence on all aspects of Alaska life. Yet the economic stranglehold was slow to develop at first. The Russian American Company (RAC), a mercantile company specializing in furs, attempted to colonize Alaska and the people but was never fully successful. With Native help, the Russians harvested and exported some fishery products, but they were limited in their attempts, and most of their activities centered on a few salteries in the area. The more enduring transformation from a pioneer market economy to a monopoly empire occurred when the nascent territory was forced to support itself through the exploitation of natural resources, namely minerals, timber, and salmon. This was an expensive proposition, requiring capital investment. San Francisco banks had become rich after the 1850s gold rush and were ready to take a chance on a new form of gold in Southeast Alaska as they financed infrastructure, cannery machinery, and fishing equipment and continued to expand technology. Since these big banks and companies held the purse strings, they made the rules. Provincial politicians, understanding the chokehold the absentee cannery companies had on Alaska, bolstered their platform by assuring Alaskan residents they were qualified to break conglomerate domination and return Alaska to Alaskans, but by the turn of the century, colonialism was deeply entrenched and continued to dig deeper.

In this book, I adopt a multivariate approach in terms of viewpoint and experience among the settlers, cannery owners, and laborers, both immigrant and indigenous. A discussion of this nature is rare in the existing literature. In the few examples when Native Americans were involved in company business, there were unexpected consequences. H. Craig Miner relates in *The Corporation and the Indian* that the "Indians" who were given a share in the corporation experienced an erosion of tribal sovereignty as the corporation rose in power, while the "federal government [was] standing by to watch the direction of the breeze of circumstances. It was a psychologically and culturally disorienting and intellectually twisting experience for Indians, most of whom were unsure where their future happiness lay."[5] The indigenous people were compelled to adapt to new circumstances and modify their traditional socioeconomic and political customs, while the government was determined to ignore the existence of Alaska Native populations.

When speaking of the Southeast Alaska Natives—the Tlingit and Haida, and later the Tsimshian—it is important to understand the social structure and its ancient roots. Although their languages varied, these peoples did retain similar cultural characteristics in terms of social structure, particularly the matriclans and matrilineal organization. The clans were responsible for stewarding culturally determined property, including the hunting, gathering, and fishing areas, oral narrative, and artworks, all inherited through the female line and in direct opposition to the Western economic system, subsequently leading to grave misunderstandings. With the inherent power in a matrilineal society, Native women were accustomed to a more prestigious role as compared to their Western counterparts, and the expectation was unaltered after being employed in the canneries, instigating immediate friction and influencing historical outcomes.

Cannery labor was ethnically diverse. The use of the term *ethnic* is preferred over *race* because both geneticists and anthropologists have discarded the former term as faulty in a biological sense. Race, however, continues to be used as a sociological concept. Michael Omi and Howard Winant theorized that racial classification, determined by society, has a direct correlation with privilege, assigned attributes, and discriminatory behavior. These repressive attitudes set the scene for political struggles and attempts to escape rigid socioeconomic confinement.[6] The Alaska cannery story was marked by ethnic conflict, and as Omi and Winant suggest, these factors impacted labor unions, segregated markets, and motivated exclusionary legislation that worked to perpetuate "the color line within the working class."[7]

Another component of racial formation theory centers on the use of stereotypes to identify ethnic groups. In political discourse there was a tendency to label groups by compartmentalizing assumed human traits, leaving little room for natural diversity or an acceptance of cultural differences. The racial slurs flung against the "other" were not only reactionary but intended as a display of dominance. Many people continued to believe that a "real Indian" wore an eagle-feathered war bonnet and performed rain dances during times of drought, a typecast upheld in the available media. This type of labeling further justified colonizing the indigenous for their own good, reducing the original inhabitants to being regarded as substandard in "civilized" society. Forced to thrive in this new environment, the Tlingit and Haida "pruned elements of tradition and modernity from this struggle and fashioned self-identities that were authentic on Aboriginal terms."[8]

In Alaska the newspaper was a powerful force for disseminating negative images of Native society, but beyond the printed word, sojourners were liable to give their opinions as well. For example, Frederick Whymper, a young English adventurer attached to the 1865 Western Union survey, came across a Tlingit village in his travels and described the scenario he found: "These people dwell in a long line of rude houses. . . . Their dwellings are shanties." Further, he mentioned that the people had a bad reputation among the Russians: "They appear to be more than usually lazy natives, probably from the fact that Nature has been so kind to them."[9] Within this short passage, stereotypes are reinforced that these lazy children of nature live in houses that were apparently not up to European or Victorian era standards. Consumers of books and periodicals formed opinions of aboriginal America based on the writings of wealthy travelers, who reinforced the rigid class system derived from European culture and society, despite the difficulty of realistically comparing those standards to frontier Alaska. In response, a class warfare evolved, and by the 1920s Alaska Native politicians had taken up the fight for the common man as the indigenous people struggled to preserve their lands, resources, and culture.

Asian immigrants, who were as diversified as Native Americans, suffered the same fate. The Chinese were considered disposable "coolie labor," while the next wave of Asian immigrants, the Japanese, were under suspicion from the moment they arrived, based on the alleged militarism of their country. A 1900 societal snapshot would indicate a tendency to generalize about the Asians based on "rumors, half-truths, and emotional fears," with images of evil gambling dens and other scenes of iniquity.[10] These early immigrants coped by keeping their heads down and aspiring for an escape from the fish factories, although there were a few cases of outright defiance.[11] The final wave, the Filipinos, had a completely different status based on Spanish colonialism and their American nationalist status originating from the United States takeover of the islands after the Spanish American War. These three immigration waves were integral to Southeast Alaska's cannery history and are explored in depth in this book.

In the early 1900s the average American looked upon immigrants as a necessary evil that must be controlled. This was the cloud under which the Asians lived, described by historian Ronald Takaki as an atmosphere of racial slurs, discrimination, and exclusion, marked by the entrance of an "industrial reserve army" more multifarious "than Karl Marx had imagined: it was transnational and racial" and supported by capitalism.[12] Immigrants were indispensable to the canned salmon industry, and although there were many willing Native men and women wanting to work, their numbers were not great enough for the hoped-for production, creating a large demand for foreign labor. For the Asians, their reasons for coming to the Pacific Coast were varied, but in the beginning the immigrants were usually young men escaping poverty in their home country.[13]

There were times in China and Japan when certain classes of people were encouraged to emigrate to another country to lessen the burden on their home country, or perhaps a young man saw no future with his peasant family. At other times United States industry actively recruited labor from overseas with promises like California's famous and mythical Gold Mountain, where a young man could make a fortune. On the other side of the equation, and based on racialization, discrimination, competition, and xenophobia, the United States also limited immigration, beginning in the early 1800s through exclusionary efforts. For the most part, individuals left their home country to seek a better life, but the gap between expectations and reality was often vast. Takaki portrayed these early immigrants as "overblown with hope."

Some men hung onto the belief that they would make enough money to return home, despite all indications to the contrary. In their thought process, it was only a matter of finding enough gold, picking enough sugar cane, or butchering enough salmon, but more often than not that dream was dashed, and they were forced to make a life wherever they were at that time. Many became part of a growing fishery community and opened their own businesses, including grocery stores, bakeries, candy stories, and laundries.

Besides the "picture brides," a few women immigrants also found their way to Southeast Alaska. For some it was the only solution to the "poverty, war, or persecution" they faced in their home country. In this foreign land, however, a new hostility was revealed, compelling a reliance on "values compatible with Western ways" to ease the adjustment process into Southeast Alaskan life.[14] Few Asian or European women worked the "cannery line," a job that was populated by local Native women to a much greater degree. For this reason, Tlingit, Haida, and Tsimshian women's labor is highlighted in the following chapters to a greater degree.

Most Chinese and Japanese cannery workers arrived as single men and developed a bachelor society, living in a segregated bunkhouse referred to as the China house or Japan house, but such residences were temporary and seasonal. For those who stayed in Alaska, there was a high prevalence of mixed ethnic marriages since there were so few Asian women. Frequently, Chinese, Japanese, and Filipino men married a Native woman and settled in her village, working both a subsistence lifestyle and a cannery job, and further developing and enriching a complex community.

After the Chinese and Japanese had left cannery employment for various reasons, the central ethnic labor groups were Filipino men and Native women. The Chinese population had declined due to anti-immigration legislation and older Chinese workers leaving the industry, while the "better educated second generation were moving up the socioeconomic ladder to become small business entrepreneurs, tradesmen and professionals. They had no interest in summer employment in Alaskan canneries."[15] Young Filipino workers, educated in Western schools, had assumed a sense of civil rights and acquired leadership skills, which were put to use in fighting against discrimination and eventually organizing powerful unions. At first these unions were exclusively Filipino, but in time they extended their reach outward to other laborers regardless of ethnic background or gender.

In chronicling Southeast Alaska's salmon canning industry, there is no story without the women, particularly the Tlingit, Haida, and Tsimshian.

History tends to marginalize Native American women, who coped with both gender and indigenous status issues, realizing the double prongs of bigotry. Mixed marriages were often viewed with disdain by certain sectors of society, but there was also a positive aspect. When two cultures effectively merged, harmony and strength were a result as blended families became the building blocks for cannery towns. Through social networks, whether at a July 4 celebration, honoring the independence of their new home, or a neighborhood meeting to discuss local matters, the residents worked for shared betterment. From this premise, it was not a large leap to political organization.

Among the women workers a cannery culture was constructed for mutual aid. As they worked in a rough and tough environment, they naturally discovered commonalities and complaints. Women had families and the problems of balancing work and domestic duties, especially childcare. Sometimes they faced foremen or bosses who tried to make their lives more difficult, or perhaps the enemy was low wages or poor working conditions. Whether during coffee breaks (known as "mug up") or walking home after a shift, they discovered their shared experiences and banded together for encouragement. From there, a cannery culture was created that acted as a support group in life and work. Although the term "working culture" has been around for a relatively long time, Vicki Ruiz further refined the concept to refer to the "bonds of sisterhood" and how "collaboration and unity . . . attested to the surprising strength" of the group.[16] Patricia Zavella found a similar pattern among women in northern California when "workers confront, resist, or adapt to the constraints and possibilities of their jobs. Transmitted by oral tradition, work culture encompasses workers' understandings and definitions of work and their sanctions."[17] And this bond could (and did) lead to collective resistance.

In labor history literature a few outstanding works illustrate the working woman's experience, including the struggles for equity while spending lives as breadwinners, community leaders, and mothers. Labor historian Philip Foner stresses that the "history of working-class experience must go beyond emphasis on workers on the job" and address collective organization and actions. For Alaskan women cannery workers, an exchange of ideas occurred during social events and informal affairs where women were freer to discuss their mutual issues. In addition, and Foner echoes others on this thought, "it is impossible to separate the story of working women from that of working men and from major events in social, economic and political history that had profound effects on changes in women's work."[18] In the case of Southeast Alaska cannery workers and the fishermen, their jobs were intertwined, and through expertise they kept the canneries going from the late 1800s into the next millennium in the face of major cataclysmic events such as wars or widespread financial fatigue.

There is a down side to this combined history, however, in that women's studies have often been presented as merely an extension of a male-oriented social system still governed by patriarchy. The women's role becomes subordinate to that of the men, and the identities are lost in what Joan Scott argues is a stereotypical view of women as secondary and weak in a labor history that stresses men as strong and as protectors.[19] Ruth Milkman expands this concept of equality to explain that "profit-maximizing capitalist firms . . . substitute cheap female labor," and it was not until "organized labor and the feminist movement had indeed challenged sex discrimination" that any inroads were made in equality, including in wages.[20] The "pervasive stereotypes" kept women doing what was perceived as women's work, which in the case of the cannery corresponded to menial labor, such as the slime line or labeling cans. These jobs, of course, paid less because the work was considered unskilled, although there was reason to believe it required a great deal of ability. This phenomenon was turned upside down during World War II. When faced with a shortage of male employees, production did not come to a halt; rather the problem was solved by hiring more women to do the heavy work. For Alaska, this was also the time when Tlingit and Haida women emerged as political leaders and labor organizers to defy a multifaceted world of discrimination.

Women faced problems related to preconceived societal constructs, and for Native women this was intensified because of ethnic bias and false notions of lifestyle. Among Native American societies, including the Tlingit, Haida, and Tsimshian, the gender roles are egalitarian and fit together in the spirit of reciprocity—the fisherman and the processor were part of the same organic, holistic circle. The intra-ethnic high respect for women was demeaned by Western societal stereotypes of Native women, which lingered well into the twentieth century, going beyond noble savage to picture indigenous females in vulgar terms tantamount to "squaws," only fit for tedious labor, such as salmon cleaning or packing. In fact, in cannery reports they were often referred to as such, paralleling what Rebecca Tsosie suggested was a type of gender categorization with the tendency to "rank duties into hierarchical layers of status, thereby ascribing notions of inferiority to women's domestic duties and superiority to men's roles. . . . Such value judgments invariably stem from assumptions of the universal attributes of the male-female relationship."[21] Tsosie was speaking of Native women, but to a certain extent her concepts also hold true for women in general. Euro-American gender classification was antithetical to Native ideals of rank and prestige, traditionally determined by the clan system.[22] The indigenous social system defied Western rigid boundaries and was more permeable, allowing women to come to the forefront of political participation.[23] These differences in Native women's influence and authority form a major theme in the cannery story.

Native women who worked outside the home faced an additional set of issues that were not likely worrying non-Native women. The literature concerning female labor continually emphasizes the struggle between employment and domestic duties. For instance, a woman might feel she was neglecting her household tasks while she was at the plant, even when her paycheck was important to the family. Native women had an additional problem in that they were responsible for their part in the maintenance of the customary subsistence lifestyle, dependent on the season and naturally broadening domestic obligations. These factors had to be balanced with childcare in order for women to retain cannery jobs. Often this was solved through kin networks, but not always, leading to a crisis situation or a uniting together to effect change.

Collective action can "arise in complex social orders with class struc-tures that define incompatible interests between owners of capital and workers. Unions can come into existence when those with privileged access to resources hire others to create value the owners can appropriate for their own use."[24] Absentee cannery owners and inside workers are a perfect example of this maxim. As multi-ethnic communities came together they found reasons to organize for better wages, sanitary working conditions, and a modernization of living arrangements. For the women there was no advocacy body available since the preeminent unions were established for fishermen only. In fact, the entire United States labor movement would need to change before there was an appropriate coalition force for Alaskan women, aptly labeled the "feminization of the unions." The change in character and emphasis was stimulated by a "sense of economic rights and women's success in building permanent and influential labor institutions. . . . The new-found rights consciousness and sense of class power emboldened working women to make their own claims . . . a set of conditions existed that allowed for the survival and even success of gender politics."[25] Since the food processing industry employed a large number of women, it was natural that they founded a union of their own, but how did this come about? What were the steps?

As background, it is necessary to establish that women and men have different ways of interacting in communication events. Men might group together on the dock to discuss the salmon runs or perhaps joke about how they spotted some illegal activity going on at one of the company's fish traps. Women found an identity in the community often in tandem with their children's school activities or church functions, and from there it was possible to create community-based alliances around common interests, often aligned with familial and fraternal activism that bolstered the struggle to overcome obstacles. In the case of the cannery, the point of contention might be absentee cannery owners placing severe demands on the employees without compensation. In defiance, concerned workers gathered in numbers and formed an impermeable front. A "culture of solidarity" was built to incorporate the political role of women, who had a "clear, aggressive role that was legitimized in the context of community and family."[26]

The cannery history of Southeast Alaska cannot be divorced from the natural landscape of ragged coastlines, verdant forests, pristine streams filled with salmon, rugged coves acting as protection against the harshness of extremes, and the indigenous reverence for lands and waters. As industrialization increased there was a deep sense of loss. Measures to preserve or conserve the resources were incomplete, resulting in a backlash by Alaska Natives carving out their own indigenous pathway.[27] Despite the patterns of paternalism, legally dating back to early 1800s Supreme Court decisions, the Tlingit, Haida, and Tsimshian stood up against the intruders, although the battles were dichotomous and involved a great deal of cultural dissonance. The clash between village traditions and the enticement of the wage or cash economy created discord and the need for compromise, often resulting in the careless harvesting of fish or timber.[28]

The indigenous fight for land and waters was defined by local laws, racialization, and congressional legislation. Legal scholar Lindsay G. Robertson has encapsulated the state of affairs that applied to all of North America: "Over a succession of generations, Europeans devised rules intended to justify dispossession and subjugation of native peoples of the Western hemisphere. Of these rules the most fundamental were those governing the ownership of land."[29] Without a shot being fired or a sword drawn, the indigenous people were dispossessed of their hunting and fishing territories, even their sacred places. Despite the adversity, the Tlingit, Haida, and Tsimshian acted to regain autonomy and self-determination, and Native leaders were not afraid to politicize the group to gain civil rights and to "reclaim and regenerate relational place-based existence" before the lands and fishing grounds were completely consumed by big business. In the following narrative the Natives' quest to recover their heritage is illustrated from its grass roots level to that of a decisive player on the national scene.

The scope of this book ties economics, immigration, Native sovereignty, and inter-ethnic unity together, including the role of capitalism, wage equity, growing monopolies, and the power of government and regulations. Corporate wealth and domination were the historical drivers that influenced labor immigration and Native politics. In defiance of the monolith, diverse people stood together to shake off the yoke of absentee ownership in what labor historian Eric Arneson describes as a "corporate monopoly that threatened to reduce labor to a pauper status and imperiled the health of American democracy."[30] Even so, unions were characterized by socialism or communism, defaming the American ideal of the free enterprise system. Yet even communal Native villages could not be defined as communistic in pure philosophical terms. Native historians and political analysts, like Ward Churchill, are quick to warn that Marxist references were not appropriate for indigenous communities, although these public theories continued to be manufactured.[31]

Zeroing in on the labor and the cannery industry in the Pacific Northwest and Alaska, the optimal study must be Chris Friday's works: *Organizing Asian-American Labor*. He discusses both Asian and Alaska Native labor and finds that the canneries were as important as any other resource development industry at the time. For Alaska, it was no doubt the prime commercial effort for many years. As is characteristic of monopolies, "the ultimate benefit [goes] to those with the greatest political and economic power. . . . Yet, the history also reveals that immigrants were by no means cogs in the wheel of some larger machinery that ground human lives into insignificant dust." Despite eighteen-hour shifts, communities composed of Natives, Asians, and Europeans found meaning in their life that was not solely governed by their cannery shift or by harvesting fish, even as "the canned-salmon industry epitomized the extractive process so common to the American West . . . through the transformation of nature's bounty into commercial products, of wealth for a relative few and toil for the comparatively many."[32]

The basic themes of social change, economic development, cultural adaptation, and political machination have been introduced, but the organization of this book also encompasses distinct eras in Alaska's history. The period to be discussed, illustrated, and examined extends from 1878 to the late 1950s. Modest fish processing began during the Russian era and escalated shortly after the American takeover of the territory in 1867. The first canneries had to scramble for investment funds, but soon the industrialization of Alaska saw not only the building of new plants up and down the archipelago but also the need for more labor. Since the Alaska Natives could not fill all the positions, Asians were brought from San Francisco, Seattle, Portland, and Astoria on a seasonal basis. Based on commonalities of work life and humanity, there was a bonding between cultures as they realized their standing as marginalized people, eventually catalyzing activities to defeat the reign of cannery bosses, the territorial government, absentee owners, and the federal government by asserting a degree of autonomy. In essence, this was a social phenomenon that has rarely been duplicated and adds to the uniqueness of the human drama. Ultimately, this is the story of people who worked hard, relished holidays and celebrations, attended weddings and funerals, and in their old age regaled their grandchildren with tales of the old cannery days.

1

A Time before the Salmon Cans

In 1741 Vitus Bering, a Dane commissioned to explore the North Pacific for Russia, made landfall on the Aleutian Islands in southwestern Alaska. Before that the crew of the companion ship, *St. Peter*, had been sailing farther south, spotting Mount Saint Elias, a volcano in Southeast Alaska. During a storm Bering had been parted from the *St. Paul*, manned by Alexsei Chirikov and his crew of seventy-five men, who found themselves in the area of Yakobi Island (*Takhanes* in Tlingit), which lies on the western edge of Chichagof Island. In Chirikov's account he tells how he sent Avram Dement'iev and other men out on a long boat to reconnoiter and fetch fresh drinking water, taking gifts of copper kettles, beads, and coins, should they find inhabitants. This party never returned, and so Chirikov sent out Sidor Savel'iev under the same conditions, but apparently he and his party met the same fate. After a while canoes appeared in the distance, approaching the ship and speaking in a language neither Chirikov nor his interpreters understood. The Native men encouraged the Russian ship to come closer, but this proved impossible because of wind conditions. The *St. Paul* turned and headed toward the Kamchatka Peninsula (Russian Far East).[1]

Regrettably, Bering and most of his crew never made it back to the Motherland, dying of scurvy on an Aleutian island in Russian territory that today bears his name, but the men who did make it back were bursting with tales of the great riches that could be found in this new land, particularly marine mammals' furs, "soft gold." When worthy ships were readied, the *promyshleniki*, Russian fur traders, made their way to Alaska, setting up makeshift trading posts along the way with hopes of becoming wealthy. There was one problem, though. The Russians knew nothing of these waters or how to capture sea otters or fur seals, and consequently a cruel plan was devised to enslave indigenous hunters to harvest the animals under threat of their lives, reinforced by superior European firearms. In short order, Russian greed almost wiped out the sea otter population and motivated the Russians to seek new hunting grounds.

By the 1780s six new trading companies stretched from the Aleutians to Prince William Sound in south-central Alaska along the gulf. The largest two companies were Lebedev-Lastochikin, on the Kenai Peninsula, and the larger Shelikhov-Golikov company, headquartered on Kodiak Island between the Aleutian chain and the Alaska Peninsula in southwest Alaska. In 1784 Ivanovich Shelikhov arrived in Three Saints Bay on the coast of Kodiak Island with his family and constructed the first Russian settlement. He petitioned the Russian monarch to sanction his exclusive jurisdiction, but Catherine the Great did not agree with his aspirations. Her view was largely based on her disdainful attitude toward further expansionism in an unknown country at that particular in time. She denied his request. He returned home without a Russian charter, but that did not mean he lost his initial trading center. To solve his management problem, he turned to a most unlikely character, Alexsandr Baranov, a minor businessman in Siberia, later described as having the Machiavellian management style necessary to run a fur trading operation in this unknown land.[2] When the sea otter population showed signs of decline and trade prospects grew dim, Baranov sought to expand the empire from its original base on Kodiak Island.

In the 1790s a lucrative site was located in Southeast Alaska with a perfect harbor at the place the Tlingit called Sheet'ka Ḵwáan, which the Russians pronounced as Sitka.[3] It was here that the Russians built what they considered a magnificent fort, which would surely attract European and American vessels, and thus the Russians would be known as the merchants of the "Paris of the Pacific."[4] Those dreams were never fully realized, and due to the lack of marine traffic there were food shortages and a critical need for essential materials. Moreover, the Tlingit viewed the fort as temporary and remaining under their control, as the area had been from a time before memory. The first dwellers had developed a complex social organization, cosmology, economic system, and political hierarchy completely unlike that of the Europeans. Distinctively, the Tlingit were divided by moieties, the Raven and the Eagle, and then further subdivided into clans based on matrilineal inheritance. Part of the clan's duties included environmental stewardship, which meant taking care of the lands, waters, and resources as delineated in the ancient oral narrative. Given the great divergence in worldview, values, and ethos between the Russians and the Tlingit, there would be troubles in *Lingit Aani*, Tlingit land.

To the north, there were similar Russo-Tlingit interactions. Yakutat, the northernmost Tlingit village, was the location of the first Russian fort in Southeast Alaska and bordered the territory of the Chugach Alutiiq and interior Athabascans. For thousands of years there had been extensive trade routes in this region, extending into Canada, and it did not take long for the Russian intrusion to create disharmony in the region. Native leaders grew angry when their rules and protocol had been broken and argued that the lands and valuable salmon streams had never been ceded to the interlopers. In fact, the Russians were Tlingit guests, and should the privilege be abused they would suffer a justified fate; but the Russians had a different viewpoint, believing the local leaders had given full permission for the establishment of a trading post and settlement without stipulations.[5] Based on this premise, the Russians carried on as if they were now in charge, while assuming the Tlingit were mere lessees of their own territory, a critical error.

In 1805 the Yakutat Russian settlement bore the brunt of these mis-assumptions when the Tlingit reacted to broken rules and unfulfilled promises and burned down the fort. The violations included draining the shores of fish and infringement on ancestral fishing and hunting areas.[6] This particular fort was never rebuilt, and instead efforts were concentrated on the Sitka fort, which had previously endured a similar fate based on the same grievances. In 1802, while Baranov visited the Kodiak location, a skirmish broke out, resulting in the destruction of the Sitka mercantile establishment. Wisely, Baranov bided his time, and after two years he journeyed back to Sitka with an arsenal of canons and the Russian frigate *Neva*. In the end the Tlingit were forced to retreat in what they have named as a survival march, and they established a village on the other side of the island. Even after rebuilding of the Russian operation, it was apparent that Tlingit expertise was necessary, and in 1821 the Russian governor, Malvey Ivanovich Muravyev, summoned Tlingit traders and fishermen. His stated purpose was to keep an eye on the Tlingit, but more to the point, the Russians depended on the Tlingit market, particularly as their own business interests declined, increasing the demand for Native goods.

The first Russian mistake was to underestimate the Tlingit. They were stalwart adversaries, unwilling to give up one inch of their territory to these strangers, and they scoffed at Russian hegemonic attempts. Tlingit leaders leased a promontory to the Russians, an arrangement that would be in effect as long as it proved mutually beneficial. That was the nature of the transaction, and to this day the Tlingit are adamant that no land was ever given or sold to the Russians. As guests in a foreign land, the Russians soon realized another impediment to their potential business interests—they still did not know how to hunt sea otter or other fur-bearing animals. For a short period they commanded the services of Unangan (Aleuts) whom they had brought over from Kodiak Island, but this proved not enough to serve their needs, and so they reluctantly negotiated with the Tlingit for more furs and other valuable items, knowing full well the Tlingit would name their own prices.

This is not to say that indigenous people from the Aleutian chain did not play a role in Southeast Alaska history. As Kyrill T. Khlebnikov, a Russian administrator at Sitka, described it in his journal: "When an Aleut hunting party sets out, the Company supplies the baidarka (large kayak) crew with firearms . . . they are also issued fishing hooks and a pound or two of tobacco." When they worked they were paid one ruble, and if there was no work, they received a cup of vodka. Khlebnikov also records Aleut (Unangan) women as the first fish processors in Southeast Alaska, paid 50 kopecks (half a ruble) per day.[7] According to Khlebnikov, "It took one and half barrels a day in winter to provide food . . . 35 fish are given to the artels in the barracks and 25 go to a general kettle, from which all persons who live in their own dwellings receive a share."[8]

Regardless of whether fishermen were Tlingit or Unangan, one thing was certain—the Russians were not adept at securing food for themselves without help, and those hoped-for foreign ships never arrived in Southeast Alaska, leaving the merchants without necessary supplies such as flour, sugar, potatoes, and distilled beverages, leading to further dependence upon the Tlingit for foodstuffs and other supplies. Not only were they reliant on the Natives for their existence, but it was evident that they were required to treat the Tlingit with the utmost respect, since the Russians were intruders and therefore a hated people for "having seized their ancestral lands, occupied their best fishing and hunting grounds, desecrated their burial sites," in addition to a long litany of further offenses.[9] Under these precarious circumstances and for their peace of mind, the Russians petitioned for status confirmation on this "discovered land" by way of official documentation from the Russian monarchy.

In 1799 the Russian government under Czar Paul I established the Russian American Company (RAC), as a full mercantile company and colonial government of the region, although in reality that could hardly be backed up due to the insignificant number of Russians, the absence of a military, and what Russian officials called "the ferocity of the Tlingit."[10] For a myriad of reasons the Russian company forts were never prosperous and continued to rely upon the Tlingit for supplies, including salmon, for which they developed quite a taste, but again there were problems. Fresh salmon were abundant during the summer months, but there was nothing for the winter months. In answer to this predicament, the Tlingit showed them how to smoke and salt the fish so that it could be stored for use when provisions were low.

By following the Tlingit instructions, the Russians built their first saltery located near the redoubt on the outskirts of Sitka. These efforts, however, met with limited success, and the Russians found it necessary to continue purchasing fish and other goods from the Tlingit in the open market, which added a new dynamic to the Native economic system.[11] The Russian-American authorities were indebted to the Tlingit for sharing their methods and skills, deeming Native preserved salmon of high quality. For example Aleksandr Baranov "admonished the manager of Fort Mikhailovskii" (Fort Michael), claiming he preferred fish "to be prepared by smoking in the same manner" as the Tlingit did it, "by cleaning and cutting and hanging under a shed and outdoors" to be smoked. Baranov went on to lament that any other method ended up wasting the fish and the end product was not appealing.[12] Fish was likened to bread in this new environment as the Russians increased their dependency on indigenous supplies of fish, wildfowl, and snails (marine slugs), while the Tlingit remained shrewd bargainers.[13]

Putting up fish for the winter was a serious matter, and in 1832 Chief Manager F. P. Wrangell warned that without great care, there would not be enough salted fish: "It is very desirable to have more than last year's pack, which, as you know, barely sufficed until spring, despite the continual absence of a considerable number of people on trips."[14] The threat of shortages was ever present, and by 1845 Governor Mikhail Teben'lov calculated the growing colony might not be able to sustain provisions over the long haul, partially due to the unreliable Tlingit market, which now included the English and American buyers. In essence the Tlingit had become business men, shaping a new economy that placed Russian merchants in a weak position.[15] By 1850 the RAC managers were resigned to the fact that the local fishing industry "should be carried out exclusively through natives, for pay commensurate with the sale prices of the fish, in addition issuing them nets and other fishing equipment from the company if it turns out to be necessary."[16]

Since the Russians were inept at supplying for their own needs, it is surprising to note that they managed some salmon product exports. In fact, the RAC shipped salted salmon to St. Petersburg "as a delicacy to be enjoyed by their friends and relatives."[17] Salmon was also sent down to their northern California outpost, Fort Ross, during the California gold rush era (1850s) in the first major shipments outside Alaskan borders, although the efforts were thwarted "because the only method of preservation available at the time was salting (canning was yet to come into commercial use). The market for salt fish was rather limited."[18] To add to the hindrances, transportation was unpredictable, and Native labor costs increased until colonial expenses rose by 91 percent while "colonial revenues rose only 13 percent" in 1831. This type of deficit could not be sustained, and the only reason the Russians were able to keep a foothold in Alaska was because they had no serious competition.[19]

The Russians attempted to get along with the Tlingit as best they could, and when the English Hudson's Bay Company (HBC) entered the scene there was even more to contend with, but nothing threatened the solvency of the Russians more than the independent Americans. The frontiersmen lived by their own rules and took what they wanted, whether it be furs or fish, answering to no one and incensing the Tlingit clans, who believed this was their territory and they owned all the resources of the land and waters. The Russians and the English had been an intrusion on the Tlingit homeland, but at least there had been the pretense of financial and political agreements. When the Americans increased their presence in Southeast Alaska, every aspect of Tlingit life was affected or altered. Who were these "Boston Men" who came into Lingit Aani and stole everything, including the precious salmon, but paid nothing? Yet matters were to deteriorate further when Russia sold Alaska to the United States in a transaction believed to be fraudulent by the Tlingit and Haida to this day.[20]

In October 1867 the Russian flag was lowered in Sitka, followed by the raising of the American flag. The United States Army presumed control over the area, enforced by military law, and soon afterward the missionaries arrived in Southeast Alaska. The Tlingit were suddenly in the midst of a cross-cultural setting and exposed to aggressive demands for change that touched every crevice of the traditional indigenous culture. Further, the abrupt initiation into the Western socioeconomic system diminished their trade dominance and autonomous way of life. Novel goods, such as flour, sugar, guns, and alcohol, became necessities, but under the American system, cash was required to purchase these items rather than using the old traditional methods of bartering. In response, the Tlingit guarded their fishing streams even more fiercely, not only to prevent trespassers but also because these waters were the source for acquiring the money to buy goods in nothing short of a fiscal revolution. This transformation was extended by the company model, eventually making room for corporations.

After Alaska changed hands, the Alaska Commercial Company (ACC) assumed the former dominance of the RAC and was able to secure a twenty-year lease for fur seal industry in the Pribilof Islands of western Alaska. Hayward Hutchinson of Baltimore paid $155,000 for the assets remaining after the RAC left. As they expanded posts throughout the territory, it is safe to categorize the business as the first absentee owner in Alaska. Since it was in their best interests to have as little bureaucratic interference as possible, the company managers were able to convince government agents, such as Henry Wood Elliott, that Alaska was a forsaken place of icebergs and polar bears, and did not require local government.[21] Though it was not quite this barren, it is true there was a certain degree of isolation, and communication with the outside world was almost impossible for years, except when ships briefly docked at harbors to unload or reload. While Alaska was moving at a relatively slow pace, industrialization was occurring much faster in other parts of the Pacific Northwest.

Contemporaneously, along the Columbia River, the four Hume brothers and their partner Andrew Hapgood had found a way to can salmon. In the 1860s these initial canning operations were labor-intensive and each can was hand-soldered, but that did not stop the growth of this endeavor. It did not take long for the canned salmon enterprise to spark the rise of the Pacific Northwest's first great industry, as it "offered tremendous opportunity for a relatively small investment to both fishers and canners."[22] Salmon commerce profits grew and enticed major companies to make investments in plants and machinery, turning the initial plants into "fish factories." Unfortunately, with this much ambitious harvesting, the salmon runs were over-fished, beginning on the Sacramento River, moving to the Columbia River, and then up to British Columbia. In relatively short time, the salmon runs were less frequent and smaller. The blame resided within the cannery men's avarice and the non-regulation of the resource, and in due course it became clear that to continue the canning business there was a need for more abundant fishing grounds.

The hoped-for rich salmon harvest was eventually found in Southeast Alaska against the backdrop of the verdant forest canopy, the ethereal mist that surrounded the shores and hillsides, and the milky turquoise glacial streams. The rapidly built canneries stood out as starkly steel-gray, mechanized, and intimidating structures in this otherwise pristine setting. The Southeast Alaska Natives, who had fished in a wilderness setting from time immemorial, were now part of an industrial environment that was divorced from their ancient rapport with the water and land. The inorganic nature of the cannery routine was without the spiritual connection that had once been part of daily life, and the cacophony of grinding gears was deafening, while the oily wooden floors challenged the abilities of the most agile.

Native fishermen brought salmon to the cannery docks in scows and offloaded the catch in bins that were forwarded to the women for cleaning and cutting under rather crude conditions. Despite increased technical innovations, most of canning methods were done by hand, starting with the butcher table and then on to the slime table. Women descaled the fish and removed any leftover blood and offal, and then whisked the fish into a saltwater bath.[23] After the gang-knife filleting and piecing was accomplished, the cans were filled to the proper weight, and sent along to the patchers, who "weighted it and if necessary, topped it off with small fragments of fish. Another worker spread salt . . . that added one-quarter ounce" to each can. From there the cans were wheeled to the pressure cooker or retort for a final cooking, followed by the re-cleaning of the cans, labeling, and placement into shipping crates, constructed with local timber.[24]

The canners, of course, were concerned about the proper sealing of cans as it would be bad business to poison your customers. The final tester "gently tapped each can with a small hammer or a tenpenny nail, listening for the appropriate sound to signify an airtight can."[25] These workers had to be highly skilled to turn out the best product efficiently, which throughout history, even with the entrance of Asian immigrants, meant Alaska Native women continued to be employed because of their expertise. The women labored on "the line" for up to twelve or thirteen hours a day when the runs were plentiful, leaving little time or energy for customary subsistence activities and proving disruptive to family and village life. When fish were not put up or berries, seaweed, or other staples went uncollected for the winter, there was an increased demand for Western goods to make up the difference, coupled with the irresistible enticement of novelties that could be acquired with a regular paycheck, ultimately generating a dual economy.

The southeast salmon cannery evolution went from small businesses to conglomerates in a short period of time, influencing every aspect of Alaskan life. According to labor historian Chris Friday, "Canned salmon produced in Alaska between 1880 and 1937 had a greater value than the total value of minerals mined in the territory in the same period."[26] Salmon was the real gold and the only means for Alaska to fill its meager coffers, leading to political confrontations from Juneau, Alaska's capital (after 1906), to Washington DC. Continuing battles were waged over the management of Alaska's natural resources while the territory irretrievably slipped further into colonial status, but what were the effects on the labor force?

The early roots of colonization can be traced back to Russian hegemonic exploitation of marine animals, precious metals, timber, and other commodities of value. The Russians, however, could not control the Southeast Alaska Natives. Historians and ethnographers conclude that although the Russians were capable of showing force, the Tlingit maintained their place in Lingit Aani, and underwent far less disruption as compared to indigenous people in other areas on the continent. The Russian American Company argued the Natives were colonial subjects, but this claim falls short in light of contemporary eyewitness reports. Councilor of State S. A. Kostlivtsev made it clear that the Natives were not dependent on the company, and instead the Russian settlements on the American shores were so reliant on the Tlingit that if there was a disturbance in Sitka, the

Russian residents would be "deprived of fresh food and the possibility of stepping some score of paces outside the fortress."[27]

Russian ethnologist Andrei Grinev offers a modified observation of history as he concludes that this era was characterized by politarism, or a government with unlimited authority and direct control over production, rendering the workers as dependent on the government. This description appears to be a grave misrepresentation of the Tlingit, who could more accurately be portrayed as merchants. Grinev, however, layers this initial theory by highlighting Native "political independence," adding, "European colonization did not change the economic base or social structure of Tlingit society." Some Russian innovations were adopted, and produced cultural alterations, but not the destruction of traditions.[28] It stands to reason that when two diverse cultures meet there will be change, but that does not translate into domination for either side.

In the ukases or charters issued by the czar, Russian fur traders and governors were warned to treat the Natives with care and to preserve their independence. Unfortunately, the language used in the 1867 Treaty of Cession did not emulate this previous language or the historical relationship between the Russians and the Alaska Natives. The Russian charter had designated groups: dependent, semi-dependent, and independent. According to the Russian American Company, dependent people had been Russified and joined the Russian Orthodox Church, perhaps even been married to a Russian, and were to enjoy all privileges under Russian citizenship. The others were considered uncivilized and received no guarantee of protected rights. These terms were incorporated in the Treaty of Cession, appearing in Article III, largely due to the efforts of Russian Ambassador de Stoeckl and his attitude of distinguishing only between "Russians" and "savage tribes." For the latter category he added that it "was impossible to stipulate anything in their favor."[29] In the end Russia's mixed legacy was bestowed on all Alaska Natives without remedy or further explanation, stimulating debate for years to come.

Senator Charles Sumner, one of the proponents for the sale of Alaska, was more focused on the commercial aspects of the territory than on any civil rights for the indigenous people, and his dismissive attitude was clear in the final document. It is thought that Sumner was most likely influenced by Professor Louis Agassiz, a Swiss-American scientist, who subscribed to Charles Darwin's theories and then added his own conclusions regarding racial designations. In Agassiz's opinion there were separate species of humankind that were relatively ranked, and the so-called "savage natives" were at the bottom.[30] Once this dogma was instilled in the American imagination, it was difficult to dispel.

Despite stereotypes and racialization, there was active trade between all groups and Southeast Alaska Natives possessed superior bargaining skills, yet trade was accompanied by massive sociocultural modification, particularly when the United States assumed control over the territory. To understand the dramatic shift from a barter system to a wage or cash economy it is necessary to see the steps leading to industrialization. Southeast Alaska Natives possessed a complex socioeconomic system that encompassed prestige, status, culturally determined wealth, and a class system. For these reasons, the introduction of the Western economic system did not entail a total realignment of values and practices. In cannery work, however, there were necessary adjustments in terms of traditional hierarchy and rank standards based on the position of the cannery supervisors. More distressing was the fact that companies came into the Natives' ancient territory and used their land, salmon, and forests at will based on the perceived right to conquer the wilderness, assisted in this pursuit by the attitude that the original inhabitants were inferior. The Southeast Alaska Natives took notice, and it did not take long for their political network to address these circumstances and the perceived theft. Alaska was colonized for its resources and to a certain extent so were the indigenous peoples through enforced assimilation, but they were not defeated and refused to be victims.

2

The Tin Can Men

Harsh talk, anger, fervent questions demanding answers—all coming from the fishing waters outside Sitka on that summer day in 1878 and revolving around the fact that without permission, the Americans had constructed a building on Tlingit land. If this was not bad enough, a further insult occurred when the company's steamer *California* arrived with foreigners; there was going to be trouble. Who were these people who looked so different and spoke an unfamiliar language? The ship's captain called them "China Men" and told the Tlingit crowd they were there to make cans. What? Make cans? If there were cans to be made, we will make them; we are capable, the Tlingit men insisted, and these strangers must be sent back to where they came from at once![1]

The Cutting and Company officials attempted to subdue the disturbance by repeating their plea: the Chinese would be on these shores only for a short duration, and they would teach the Tlingit how to make cans. That is, if the Tlingit cared to know in the first place; after all, there appeared to be little benefit from this undertaking. An eyewitness from the federal Treasury Department, William Gouverneur Morris, explained that the Tlingit were quieted only by the reassurance that the Chinese would not be fishing in their waters, and he conceded: "It was their country and John Chinaman should not come. A very strong argument, it must be admitted."[2] Nonetheless, this encounter altered Southeast Alaska forever—the cannery companies and the Asian tin can makers were there to stay.

After this controversial start, the cannery company had further problems to contend with, particularly transportation between the remote Sitka location on Baranof Island in Southeast Alaska and the market, but in time a routine developed whereby the Chinese crew did make those crude tin cans and processed the salmon harvest, while Tlingit supplied the fish. In those early days a few Tlingit men and women even worked at the cannery, but not for long because the Cutting and Company plant was short-lived. After two annual packs, the owners decided to shut down because the "bosses" could not control the conflicts between the Chinese and Tlingit on top of the problems associated with the capital-intensive nature of the business. Without guaranteed backing from big investment firms, the operation could not be sustained.[3]

The rudimentary tin can was invented in Europe in the early 1800s and refined for Pacific Coast salmon shortly after the Civil War, but from the beginning the largest problem thwarting productivity was not technology or transportation but the need for a stable labor force. The early cannery man Robert Hume reminisced that in those days they employed vagrant men, and "it was months before we got sight of any womankind, except my mother."[4] It would not be long, however, before women were a common sight at the canneries, regardless of the massive Chinese immigrant influx to the Pacific Northwest and Alaska after California's railroad construction projects were completed. By 1874 there were dozens of "fish factories" in Oregon between Astoria and Portland, and according to 1883 records, the number increased to fifty-five canneries on or near the Columbia River, stretching from Oregon to Washington, often dependent upon local Native help.[5] When the large companies decided to invest in more salmon harvesting, the plants moved north to take advantage of the larger fish runs, until reaching the Southeast Alaska coast. It was a time of "breathless growth . . . frequently accompanied by rivalry, exploited labor, and prodigal waste."[6] An observant tourist remarked that the fledging Alaskan canneries maintained activity "in spite of government neglect," and commerce increased while tin cans were assembled to hold up to one pound each.[7] Another traveler was not optimistic about the future: "The canneries drain the country of their natural wealth . . . spend almost nothing of their profits in the Territory; and are a fruitful source of trouble and corruption among the native people."[8] Inevitably these forecasts proved true, but new plants continued to mushroom along Alaska's coast, coves, and rivers, similar to the early Klawock cannery on Prince of Wales Island.

Several salteries had been established in Southeast Alaska during the Russian occupation, and this pursuit was further taken up by the Americans who now ventured into the region's Alexander Archipelago from the eastern United States or Europe, including George Hamilton, one of the first non-Russians to build a successful saltery and cannery site. It was near the Native village of Klawock. At first it was only a small operation, but it was capable of salting up to 830 barrels of salmon a year.[9] He supplemented his income by selling fish and seal skins to San Francisco firms, yet was anxious to find methods for further expansion, which led to his fortunate meeting with Charles Vincent Baranovich.[10] Baranovich had come to Alaska with gold fever and started the first trading post in Southeast Alaska, but like Hamilton, he had entrepreneurial ambitions. Subsequently, Baranovich and Hamilton went into business together and built a new and bigger trading post on Prince of Wales Island that sold smoked and dried salmon, among other items. After marrying a Haida woman, Hamilton shifted his priorities and dissolved the joint business venture to strike out on his own, but soon found it to his advantage to form another partnership. In the 1870s Hamilton paired up with John Peratrovich, a Croatian immigrant, who had brought his European fishing skills to Southeast Alaska. The working relationship was solid, and they were eager to increase their sales, but were thwarted by the lack of funds until their entrepreneurial dreams were made possible through a sizable outlay from Sisson, Wallace Company. In short order the cannery was then sold to a San Francisco firm, the North Pacific Trading and Packing Company.[11] San Francisco had developed into a prominent business hub after the 1850s gold rush period, inevitably casting a net of influence on Alaska's resources and economy.

The significance of these financiers went beyond the necessary cash flow; this interaction marked the beginning of absentee mortgagers—a dynamic that shaped Alaska's political economy and international labor migrations. In essence, this was Alaska's introduction into a corporate colonialism status that would follow the territory's history into the next several decades. Because small entrepreneurs were without significant capital to set up packing plants they had to enlist the help of larger firms willing to extract resources at a profit, and in the process, the Alaska cannery entrepreneur was tethered to a loan that must be repaid with interest, or the entrepreneur risked foreclosure and bankruptcy. Despite these dangers, future hopes were not dimmed, and cannery plant expansion was simultaneous with industrial growth in Pacific Northwest cities. Above all, there was now the ability to invest in new technology.[12]

After securing the necessary capital, the Klawock plant was renovated with new machinery, capable of packing up to 350, 000 tin cans a season.[13] John Peratrovich and his wife Mary, a Henya Tlingit woman, demonstrated their family and community ties with their first 1900 salmon can label, "Family Brand Salmon," picturing the entire family. Unfortunately one of the daughters died in 1915, and out of respect the label was never used again.[14] Despite the family's personal setback, their cannery business grew into one of the most important packing houses in the region, and in the future the Peratrovich name would be synonymous with territorial, state, and national political life.

As more canneries spread northward, the increased labor needs were filled by Chinese immigrants from San Francisco and the Pacific Northwest, but the Klawock facility was unique in that most of the workers remained either from the Henya Tlingit ḵwáan,[15] or were Kaigani Haida, and by the late 1880s there were seventy-five Native men and thirty women on the payroll.[16] The number of women employed at the cannery steadily grew as they took on the more tedious tasks while the men ran the heavy machinery. In the Tlingit and Haida culture, women occupy a significant position based on the matrilineal system, whereby all property is owned through the female line, a status associated with a certain degree of power in their society. With this rank, the women would not abide slights or substandard wages. In 1896 one example of defiance took place when the Native women complained that they had not been fully compensated for their labor. Faced with a halt in production, the Klawock managers shipped Chinese workers to the cannery to take the women's place in the tense standoff.[17] The Native crew, incensed when forty-six Chinese workers arrived, responded by demanding higher wages, citing their experience and expertise. Management was undeterred and told the women to go home. But the cannery routine did not go ahead smoothly, and the woman were grudgingly invited back and received a raise over their usual one dollar a day.[18] Women found out early that they had a certain degree of clout based on their skills and proximity to the resource, and cannery bosses were willing to make concessions to keep the operation running smoothly. Owners expected a certain volume of packed salmon, and it was the foreman's responsibility to make sure the quotas were filled or be fired, signifying the corporation's ultimate influence over labor and management.

This Klawock cannery experience exemplified dual trends, which developed further over the next two decades: Native disputes would arise over poor wages, and more Asian immigrants were sent to process the salmon. Cheap labor was critical for the profit margin, and although women could be paid less, often business owners wanted more production cuts. Conversely, Native women were not afraid to ask for higher wages, and if not satisfied, they walked off the job. In 1900 a Treasury Department agent visited Klawock and mentioned that the recent increase in Chinese labor was due to the "indifferent and intractable native labor" who were allegedly given to "insolent and domineering" behavior; but the truth was that the Alaska Natives were self-sufficient without the cannery.[19] As their ancestors had done for generations, the women followed the seasonal subsistence lifestyle, which was misinterpreted by outsiders. Ernest Lester Jones, deputy commissioner of the United States Fish and Wildlife Service, recorded that the superintendent had observed the absence of at least eleven "Indian women who cleaned the fish and found that they were going off in a party for four or five days vacation." He noted further that it had taken persuasion and bribing to keep these women in their places and prevent the loss of fish.[20]

This "vacation" referred to the traditional hunting, fishing, and gathering cycle that sustained life, physically and culturally.[21] The women managed their own schedules to assure a balance between the Native lifestyle and cannery work in a blended economy. Their lack of adherence to a clock did not undermine the demand for their proficiency in processing, especially if the Chinese were not available and canning had to be done immediately to preserve freshness. Throughout history, despite the immigrants, the Tlingit and Haida held their positions in the canneries and fisheries: "At the pioneer Klawock cannery on the coast of Prince of Wales Island, Tlingit were employed as fishermen and as 'inside workers' and weathered all intruder advancements."[22] Vincent Colyer, an agent for the Office of Indian Affairs, reported that the Tlingit were quite willing workers and often accepted lower wages.[23] Colyer's assessment, however, did not take into consideration that unlike the Chinese, the Alaska Natives did not need to spend money on housing or food due to local resources, so a lower wage was actually ample, but for the enticements of the cannery store. Despite the women's consistent employment at a set rate, frequent visits to the cannery store allowed the management to make a profit off its workers. According to a government account, labelers struck for higher rates: "25 cents was paid for 12 cases; they demanded 25 cents for 10 cases and got it. It is said that it now costs the cannery 60 cents a case to make the pack; one half is paid in coin and the other in store checks" or script. When prices were raised at the store and the customers paid in script, those apparent losses were recouped by the cannery owners.[24]

The cannery store was an economic revolution, further transforming the Native value system. The Tlingit and Haida workers were tantalized by Western goods, such as tobacco, firearms, white flour, sugar, and alcohol; consequently the stores did a brisk trade. After the cannery season, those store-bought items were no less desired, and the temporary lack of funds was not a problem because the store extended a credit line until the salmon were once again ready for canning, which, of course, elevated the need for steady earnings and introduced the concept of debt. Without the buyers' full realization, corporate colonialism manipulated spending habits by offering novel goods at exorbitant prices, ultimately separating the workers from their money one way or the other.

Wages were directly related to purchasing power, and the lure of Western goods motivated the Alaska Natives to hold out for more money per pack, which in turn encouraged the cannery men to import more Chinese workers, who accepted lower pay and would not gripe or leave work to go out fishing. For immigrants, Alaska was the perfect place to hide away from exclusion laws and violence.[25] Nonetheless, in spite of the Chinese availability, the cannery employers remained dependent on Native workers, particularly the fishermen with their knowledge of Southeast Alaska's turbulent waters and narrow passages between islands. At an increasing rate, the symbiosis between fisher and processor was intensified. In a cannery operation, all the cogs must be working for the assembly line to function optimally, and this analogy also applied to the fishermen, who were as important as the processors.

As Sheldon Jackson, the head of the Presbyterian mission program in Southeast Alaska, explained: "All the operations from the catching of salmon to the boxing of cans ready for market, were carried on by Indians."[26] Jackson also noted how much the Tlingit and Haida enjoyed shopping at the company store. As had been done along the Pacific coast, cannery scrip was negotiable only at the cannery store, deepening the already captive consumer market. Even so, the indigenous subsistence lifestyle remained imbedded in the culture, and store merchandise never fully took the place of those products harvested from the land. Frequently, the Native cannery workforce named their own hours in order to pursue their traditional subsistence hunting, fishing, and gathering, while cannery management was forced to adapt or risk losing the local work force.

Nonetheless, drastic social transformations occurred, producing clashes between the old and new ways. An early 1900s observation from the Klawock cannery described this: "The women more easily adjusted to the radical changes required of factory employment. They worked as labelers, fillers, cappers, and washers" and reconciled life's demands between the artificial confines of a cannery and village life. U.S. Fish Commissioner Jefferson Moser reported: "For a season a woman might make from $80 to $100 with the men earning $200."[27] Yet, regardless of wages and even as Westernization altered Native institutions, Tlingit and Haida families lived close to the land and their traditional waters, as their ancestors had. A prime example of this dissonance could be observed through the potlatch event (its Western name) or "giving away ceremony," the socioeconomic and spiritual bedrock of Southeast Alaska Native culture.[28] In Southeast Alaska Native society the clan's culturally defined wealth was established by the amount and type of goods "owned" by the clan. At the potlatch these goods were displayed and ritually gifted to the guests as a gesture of generosity and to confirm the host clan's prestige and rank in the region, ultimately creating a sense of harmony, reciprocity, and spiritual renewal.

Traditional gifts ranged from the treasured ceremonial robes (Chilkat blankets) to decorated copper shields, and although these ritual items remained part of the ceremony, now Western goods were also introduced in nothing short of a material and economic revolution.[29] Cloth, rifles, tobacco, and the like were purchased with cash, and at times, money itself was presented to guests or clan heads.[30] Ethnohistorian Victoria Wyatt explains that after the Tlingit were employed in the canneries, potlatch gifting was modified to reflect the modern material wealth, and to demonstrate this point she cited Governor John G. Brady explaining he had observed one potlatch in 1901 held in a Chilkat village where an enormous amount of money was exchanged.[31] Clearly, American money was necessary to host more potlatches, producing a critical need for steady employment in the canneries. Later, in 1909, a missionary in Hoonah reported that the custom persisted there and, in his view, because great sums of cash were given away, the hosting clan was rendered destitute, although this definition relied on a Western lens. He went on to advocate for a halt to potlatches, not necessarily based on the perceived financial chaos but rather because the events, in his view, discouraged the absorption of Western civilization, which was the prime missionary goal.[32]

Presbyterian missionary Caroline Willard in Haines lamented that "potlatching had been going on for several weeks and the Indians had probably spent all their wages from summer cannery work."[33] Although she believed this custom should be stopped, she also understood how engrained the ceremony was in the independent Chilkat area. Even later in the twentieth century, "hundreds of thousands of dollars' worth of food and other gifts" were distributed at potlatches, indicating not only the dependence on wages, but the persistence of the custom.[34] The essence of the potlatch centered on "identity, community, and cosmos," and while the missionaries or other outsiders focused on monetary values, they did not realize that the potlatch, although modified by the American financial system, remained the bedrock of indigenous community.[35] This reality, however, did not stop government officials from trying to control Alaska Natives or their lifeways.

The goal of Alaska's nascent government was to increase revenues, while the cannery companies wanted to see profits rise, and both were dependent on labor and production. This was one of the reasons there were attempts to manipulate Native events so that they would not coincide or conflict with cannery work. When a large salmon run was harvested, the workers had to be on call and not involved in other activities that could prove detrimental to the economic goals of the territory or the growing influence of absentee cannery owners. The 1904 Sitka potlatch, financed by Governor John G. Brady, was the definitive instance of this sentiment. Careful planning went into the event, and clans from all over the archipelago were invited to make sure there was full representation. In Brady's mind this would be the final potlatch. It is hard to know whether he was arrogant or naïve, but in retrospect these actions were intended to stop what Brady thought were wasteful Native proceedings and to synchronize workers to the cannery clock. In the end the Native workers exerted their autonomy and the potlatches did not end.[36] In a power play, Native labor was pitted against business interests and Native resiliency and independence won out this time, but there was more at stake.

As the Tlingit and Haida were swept up in the factory mode, life's tempo had to be adjusted, but like the potlatch, traditional activities were not neglected. "The height of summer was dominated by commercial pursuits—purse-seining for men and cannery work for women," and yet there was an overwhelming need to return to the land and waters on their own terms and cling to the old ways.[37] The Tlingit and Haida never forgot a certain sense of place as "a cultural geography of salmon streams, fish camps, Native villages, and canneries."[38] Thomas Thornton illustrated how the concept of "place" was at the heart of Native culture even though Alaska's rapid growth as a resource colony sent out shockwaves that subordinated and dismantled the indigenous world, marring a "Native vision of the landscape."[39]

Through the upheaval, there was an adherence to the ancient foundations, enabling cultural persistence regardless of "colonizers seeking to claim new lands for possession, pioneers venturing to tame the wilderness."[40] Alaska Natives did not view their home as a backwoods wasteland fit only for industrial development, and this was one of the glaring divides between Western commerce and indigenous cosmology. Lingit Aani was more than the Tlingit name for their combined clan territories and transcended the notion of legal title or deed. In the words of Tlingit fishermen Gabriel George: "These lands are vital not only to our subsistence, but also our sense of being as Tlingit people."[41] Yet transformation was inevitable. The ancient ideals had to be managed against the rules and laws of the government, missionaries, and business, all three threatening to usurp a way of life. By 1900 Southeast Alaska was experiencing land dispossession at an alarming rate as corporate imperialism overwhelmed the resources. Unlike other areas of the United States, this loss was not by way of wars, treaties, or reservations, but rather the integration of Southeast Alaska Natives into the business of canning and fishing for corporations, increasing a colonialist hold on the political economy. With monetary clout and the blessings of the territorial government, more and more companies moved in and took over traditional clan regions. Stuart Banner, in his study of Native American dispossession, likens this process to "Indians" turning into occupants when they were once owners.[42]

For centuries, Native social roles had been defined, whether elder, child, female, or male—with the introduction of factory work, wages, and Western goods, the matrix had been flipped on its side. Native women carried on a processor role whether inside the canneries or out at fish camp, yet when confined within the cannery walls, there was not the same fulfilling and organic outcome as when putting up fish for their family. This attitude developed into an unresolved conflict for women "who worked the line" and were increasingly dependent on a cannery paycheck.[43] To understand this struggle fully one must be aware of the necessary transformation in traditional and modern roles and the need for balance. When hardships occurred on the fishery grounds, whether brought on by the depletion of salmon runs, corporate fish traps, or later government regulations, there was an increased necessity for cash to purchase goods.[44] At times a fisherman could not make a living, and it was a woman's cannery employment that sustained the family through the winter. In addition, there was an interdependence between the fishermen and the canneries for which they worked, especially on a contract basis. "Indian labor proved instrumental to industrial development and would remain so until the mid-twentieth century."[45] Acceptance and adjustment on the part of the Tlingit and Haida did not negate the sense of loss for their land, waters, or old way of life, but if they protested, they were replaced by immigrants arriving on the next steamer, eager and ready to work.

Beginning in the 1800s Chinese immigrants were shipped to wherever they were needed, whether Hawaiian sugarcane fields, Pacific Northwest orchards, logging camps, or California railroads. When these jobs dried up many decided to try their luck in Alaska. The initial rise in Chinese immigration stemmed from the poor economic environment in China during this period, particularly for farmers, who were not only being pushed off their lands by larger landowners but also experiencing a devastating drought. In Chinese peasant society only the first son had a chance of inheritance, leaving other children without means to live. In these circumstances, immigration appeared to be the only option, but it was not without obstacles. The would-be immigrants were limited by anti-foreign attitudes against the backdrop of an eager capitalist desire for cheap labor that tended to outwit sociopolitical constraints. If an immigrant was successful in making the trip, that was not the end of the barriers. The first wave of immigrants, the Chinese, were employed in the most undesirable jobs and viewed as a threat, leading to legislation for the purpose of controlling the flow of immigration.[46] Coupled with racial stereotypes, the

Chinese, and later other Asians, were to be plagued for the duration of their stay by disdain, ethnic slurs, and at times outright violence.

Yet cannery bosses preferred transitory Asians over the obstacles associated with Native autonomy—a people accustomed to following their own rules. Although the Tlingit and Haida continued to be in demand, they were reluctant to work in an industrial setting where someone else set their hours, and they "were confident that a small amount of money will supply them with the few necessities which money alone will purchase," even as villages were "increasingly dominated by assembly line speed" and the territory became more colonized by outside interests.[47]

Eliza Ruhamah Scidmore, an Alaskan tourist and journalist during the late 1800s, left a description of cannery operations that not only depicts the importance of Chinese labor but also offers a rare glimpse into the factory setting:

In the skillful manipulation of the cans and machines within doors, neither (the Indian) nor the whiteman can approach the automatic dexterity of the Chinese, who being paid by the piece, take no account of a day's working hours, and keep the machinery moving as long as there are fish in the cannery. The fish are thrown from the arriving scows in a latticed floor or loaded directly into the trucks and rolled into the cannery. The cleaner seizes a fish and in two seconds trims and cleans it—beheading, detailing, and rending it with so many strokes of his long, thin knife. It is mashed, scraped, cut in sections the length of a can, packed, soldered, steamed, tested, vented, steamed again, resoldered, lacquered, labeled and boxed. The tin is taken up in sheets, and an ingenious machine punches, rolls and fits the covers to the cans, which roll down an inclined gutter of melted solder, which closes the edges. The experts can tell by the tap of a finger, if each can is air-tight.[48]

In this way Chinese workers provided the low cost and capable labor that was needed to expand output and increase revenues while cannery bosses controlled plant operations, increasingly enhanced by advances in technology and transportation, chiefly steamships, that were often owned by the absentee companies. San Francisco's dominance went unchallenged as the mega-companies enjoyed a monopoly on trade. One outstanding example was the northern California–based Pacific Coast Steamship Company, later reorganized in the Puget Sound area as the North American Transportation and Trading Company, which demonstrated that the efficacy of the fleet could not be beat. The fully loaded vessels brought trading goods up to Alaska along with well-to-do tourists, who probably had no idea the bottom of the vessel was crammed with immigrants in the infamous China Hold.

Based on racial stereotypes, the Southeast Alaska settlers perceived the immigrants as an inferior class that should not be mixing with them, resulting in xenophobic actions. Both the mines and canneries displayed these same human dynamics. In the *Alaska Mining Record* of November 1888 an article chronicled this sense of outrage, painting a grim picture of the so-called Chinese problem: "They [the Chinese] have arrived in our territory under the guiding hand and protecting care of avaricious salmon canning corporations. The government officials should keep a vigilant watch and see that none of these Chinamen steal aboard the steamship while lying in British ports. Last season many Chinamen worked their way into Alaska from British Columbia in canoes. The canning corporations should be compelled to employ white labor."[49]

Given such vehemence, there were bound to be legislative attempts to curb the alleged menace and address the concerns of white settlers. In the spring of 1882 a Chinese Exclusion Act was passed by Congress and signed by President Chester A. Arthur. This act provided a ten-year moratorium on Chinese immigration, and for the first time federal law banned entry of an ethnic working group on the grounds that the good order of certain localities was endangered by the loose moral standards of the immigrants. For those allowed into the country, the Chinese Exclusion Act required Asian immigrants to swear they were not laborers. Based on this premise, the men were allowed entry into the United States with the proper documents, verifying that they had met the Chinese government specifications. Obviously, exclusion legislation hampered Alaska employers' need to hire immigrant workers, particularly since the 1882 act prohibited "skilled and unskilled laborers and Chinese employed in mining," leading to inevitable civil disobedience and other methods of skirting the law.[50] With no oversight agency, smuggling an illegal workforce was as simple as transporting bootleg whiskey, and both occurred with steady frequency.

Further, the 1882 exclusion act also placed new requirements on Chinese already in the country, and if they left the United States, they had to obtain certification to re-enter. In addition state and federal courts were not allowed to grant citizenship to Chinese resident aliens, although these courts could still deport them. When the exclusion act expired in 1892, Congress extended it for ten years in the form of the California-initiated Geary Act, followed by the McCreary Amendment.[51] This extension, made permanent in 1902, added restrictions by requiring each Chinese resident to register and obtain a certificate of residence. Without a certificate, an immigrant faced immediate deportation.

The exclusion acts were a product of the manufactured fear of the "yellow race," and when legislation proved unable to hold down the number of immigrants, vigilante types sought to rid themselves of the menace or at least keep the Chinese segregated and out of sight in company bunkhouses, never coming into town.[52] Realistically, the small "white" populations would be hard-pressed to do anything that might permanently alter the circumstances, and the prominent salmon industry management wanted no part of turbulence that might stop the machinery from running continuously. If the Chinese had understood the language and the circumstances better, they might have held the upper hand in a "workers' market," regardless of the public hate campaign, but instead they were severely disadvantaged from many sides.

The Chinese found themselves living in desperate times, and although they were promised a prescribed payment per pack according to the manager's calculations, they were paid only at the end of the season, after their room, board, and transportation had been subtracted. The cannery companies gave the excuse that this was to protect the men from gambling away their money. It was true that this activity was widespread, even aboard the transport ships, but the company's reasoning was faulty, exaggerated, and meant to cheat the men.[53] Although games of chance were a traditional pastime for Asian men, a tradition carried over from their home country, the lack of cash or credit frequently curtailed gambling.

When Chinese workers finally did receive their seasonal pay, they were frequently further swindled out of their money, one way or another. The most corrupt system to affect Asian labor involved the contractors. Contractors, frequently based in San Francisco or Seattle, were responsible for recruiting the cannery work force and making sure they were dispatched to their destination. These labor suppliers, more and more often Chinese themselves, developed a type of pidgin English-Chinese to communicate with immigrants, but of course there were problems with translation, often favoring the contractor's agenda.[54] Canners and contractors bargained between themselves for the best labor at the cheapest prices, which more often than not ended up fleecing the workers in this alien environment. The cannery owners grew wealthier, while the Chinese tolerated horrendous situations and conditions to maintain their existence, hoping to send a portion of their wages back to China.[55]

Little is known about these first Chinese, chiefly because of language barriers and lack of documentation in cannery records, but there were a few reports from ship captains and scientists, who conveyed a picture of workers treated like machines running at a non-stop pace. Jefferson Moser, in command of the *Albatross*, described the Chinese as "weary" and how the men seemed "to drag along as though they would drop in their tracks."[56] Many workers lacked sufficient training and were unprotected from hazardous machinery and forced to stand an entire shift (sometimes over thirteen hours) in cold water up to their knees.[57] One of the most dangerous tasks was at the lye tanks, "with the hot sputtering lye splashing over them," indeed "no sinecure."[58] Who would advocate for these disadvantaged men? They were invisible, simply cogs on a wheel.

Suffice it to say that the contractors had a genuine racket. They were, however, indispensable because they understood both cultures, their needs, and the transportation system, and though condemned in many circles, including the cannery administration, these labor suppliers provided "stability to an unordered chaotic labor market," enabling employers to fill the seasonal labor quotas.[59] Contractors played the game well among diverse actors in a volatile market and exploited the anxious and inexperienced "just off the boat" immigrants while scamming the employers, neither of whom knew better. Everybody was out to make a buck, and for a while the contractors enjoyed a sweet deal.

One 1894 episode stands out as representative of how the Chinese depended upon contractors for their final pay while illustrating the naïveté that made these men an easy mark. Since the workers relied on the cannery transportation between Alaska and the West Coast cities before and after the season, they were at the mercy of whatever the ship's crew told them, including when they would be paid. Contractors promised the workers would be paid in full after they returned to their home base, but for the poor unfortunate cannery workers in one particular case, Tong Yoong and Company, based in San Francisco, made off with more than $40,000 dollars in back wages and left 240 Chinese men stranded in a foreign city.[60] The news of this incident and other similar "bad deals" made its way up north, and an Alaskan newspaper opined on what was believed to be a solution to a complex problem: "The men who are employed by the canning companies during the Alaska fishing season are taken back to San Francisco. . . . As soon as they have "loosened" their money in the city front saloons, they once more fall back into the army of the unemployed. Would it not, therefore, be better to pay off the men in Alaska . . . and thereby increase the working population of the territory?"[61]

Chinese resilience was a testament to survival skills as they followed the path of least resistance.[62] These stoic people began their ordeal in cargo holds before arriving on Alaska shores, and though they were anonymously listed by ethnicity and number in government and cannery reports, there were fishery agents who documented the living conditions and offered a graphic portrayal of the scene, as in the following account: "The worker's quarters contained three sleeping rooms. One had three windows and measured 12 by 18 feet, with bunks for 11 men and [one] measured 9 by 9 feet . . . the bunks were stacked three high and in some rooms the windows were blocked with boards. . . . The sleeping rooms were dark and foul smelling as many of them had no ventilation . . . the room was heated by a single oil stove."[63]

If met by a barrier the immigrants scaled it, including sneaking away on cargo ships bound for Alaska and melting into the cannery or mining labor force, a testament to their steadfast determination. George Ramos of Yakutat recalled the stories his uncle told him about the Chinese workers brought up by the local cannery company in spring. Even in the cannery they wore Chinese robes and silk shoes, though the slippery floors demanded boots and full sleeves were an obvious danger around the machinery. One can only imagine the difficulties these naïve Chinese men encountered, including Native bitterness. According to Ramos, the company occasionally employed Chinese workers as "beach gangs" to fish offshore, which cut into Native business and was, of course, not welcomed.[64] For a while, however, the Chinese met all obstacles thrown in their path, which was more than could be said for the salmon. After the harvesting technology had been refined for mass production, including the voracious fish traps, the salmon runs grew smaller and smaller.[65] When the government got involved, the problem was not alleviated, but instead increased as processing salmon was more efficient, resulting in larger profits, the sacrifice of a finite resource, and corporate colonialism digging its talons in deeper.

The commercial fish trap played a significant role in Alaska economics and politics. The trap and its usefulness went unquestioned in the industry, although much of the catch was wasted by overharvesting and throwing the excess off overladen boats.[66] Whole salmon runs were captured along their migratory routes, leaving nothing for the critical escapement that allowed the migration of fish returning to natal streams to spawn, thereby ensuring a new crop of salmon for the future. In a 1909 journal the author, a fisheries agent, described the proficiency of the fish trap: "The catch is dumped unceremoniously into waiting scows. The capacity of the scows used in Alaska is about twenty thousand fish, and it is not uncommon to see two of these coming from one trap completely filled with flapping, gasping salmon."[67]

The resultant harvest reduction had to be blamed on something, and angry political battles brewed between residents, nonresidents, local fishermen, and distant federal bureaucrats. Independent fishermen believed they had the exclusive rights in the fisheries based on Alaska residency and declared that absentee companies were simply thieves. From the early 1900s on, there was an all-out citizens' effort to ban the fish traps, but the cannery companies, convinced the waters and fish traps were their property, fought back, and frequently the law was on their side. Court cases were decided in favor of the large outfits that had publicly accused fishing crews of unloading company traps into their own boats with intent to sell.[68] It was well-known that such piracy occurred, and the suspects were thought to be frustrated local fishermen, angry about the cannery traps monopolizing the waters. These same fishermen were trying to eke out a living, and they justified the robbery as the only way to even the odds. Consequently, trap piracy evolved into a survival tactic, while the "fish-trap owners and legal authorities grew increasingly concerned over the constant theft from traps, most of which were untended and unguarded while fishing 24 hours a day, seven days a week."[69]

Historian Robert DeArmond was a court reporter during these tumultuous years and recalls that many an accused pirate was brought before the courts in Sitka and Juneau to face charges. DeArmond recalled there was no one type of defendant and that ethnic background or residency had little importance. What was consistent were the nightly raids on unguarded fish traps in southeast Alaska.[70] To make matters worse, the fishing industry was almost completely unregulated, creating a scene comparable to the Wild West frontier, with everyone claim jumping. The federal government wrestled with the problem, but had no viable solutions. In the end, profit was prioritized ahead of ecological vigor, largely motivated by the territory's struggle to maintain its solvency.

The Tlingit and Haida believed they had a better understanding of the issues, based on their conservation ethic and long-time proximity to the waters, but their traditional outlook was reshaped by capitalism and the market economy. Succinctly, there was a radical departure from customary lifeways with the entrance of a competitive atmosphere, redefining the fishery. Clan rights were ignored as the waters were opened to big companies possessing the advantages of more sophisticated technology and greater financial means. And if that was not enough, outside fisherman claimed certain rights based on the ideal of a common fishery, a model recognized by early ecologist Garrett Hardin, whose writings depicted how American fishermen believed all waters were public and open without restraint for those skillful enough to maximize profits. From the premise and reality, Hardin then traced how these actions resulted in the "tragedy of the commons," whereby these avaricious pursuits resulted in stock depletion to the point where the continuation of species was in jeopardy.[71] The combination of a common fishery and corporate control created the situation where "at times one cannery will catch and destroy tens of thousands of fish which they are unable to can rather than allow the rival cannery's fishermen to catch them."[72] While few protective measures were in place or enforced, cannery companies reinvested in further innovations, promising increased efficacy and correspondingly more money in San Francisco or Seattle banks.[73] Progress was the byword for expanding industrialists, but the operation could not always be mechanized when humans were involved in the day-to-day work.

With the salmon industry commanding millions of dollars in the market, efficiency was key and the fish trap fit the bill. That did not mean there was not a need for local help to make up for some of the deficiencies with the machinery. The labor force, composed of Alaska women and Asian immigrants, continued to be employed for the tasks of beheading, cleaning, key and sliming the fish.[74] Cannery hours fluctuated, dependent on the unpredictable salmon runs. When the scows laden with fresh salmon were spotted making their way toward the cannery dock, the cannery employees, who often lived nearby in summer camps, were summoned by means of a bell or other type of alarm. A hasty response was necessary since the salmon had to be processed immediately or the company risked a stale (or worse) end product.

Yet if hunters were out in the forest or women were gathering berries, they paid no heed to any alarm. This attitude flummoxed cannery managers, who had a lot riding on the salmon packs going out. According to historian Ted Hinckley, "after making sufficient wages to supply their personal wants and getting a few dollars ahead (the Natives) go hunting and fishing when they are most wanted" by the cannery bosses.[75] When confronted with an apparent disrespect for the Western timetable, the Tlingit shot back that cannery rules were inconsequential to their lives; after all the trespassers were in Tlingit territory, using their land and waters without permission or payment. While the indignation deepened the rift between Native cannery workers and management, the Tlingit and Haida were also in a quandary, caught between the desire for cannery employment and protecting the vital fish supply that was necessary to support their families in this novel and expanding dual economy.

Historian Robert Price documented that "in 1889 there were twelve salmon canneries packing 8,159 cases and up to 136,760 cases in 1899." Further, it was "significant that the canneries packed mainly red salmon . . . the favored subsistence salmon of the Tlingit and Haida."[76] Not only did the canneries prefer red salmon, but other less desirable species were frequently thrown overboard in an act of wastage. Hoonah elder George Dalton gave a first-hand account of what was happening: "Often they would throw away everything but the Reds . . . the whole bay was just full of sour fish. That's the beginning of the dying off of the salmon."[77] Another contemporary observer likened the blatant squandering of fish stocks to the killing of the buffalo for their tongues in the Plains states.[78]

Clearly, the cannery industry had commandeered Native land and resources, diminished the salmon runs, and created grave disruptions in village life. The culture shock was complete. As stewards of the waters, the Tlingit and Haida were appalled by the cannery practice of tossing back what they determined were not money fish, and it was apparent that fish runs were not making it up to the village streams. Across the Alexander Archipelago resentment took on immense proportions, as observed in the following incident. In 1890 the Tlingit from Klukwan and Haines protested the activities of the Pyramid Harbor cannery, whose traps purposely obstructed the salmon migration to the Lynn Canal villages. The cannery management refused to move any apparatus, believing it was their property, and in response, the Tlingit resorted to firearms to destroy the traps, thrusting the fisherman and cannery workers into a tenuous position. The event ended in a standoff and nothing was resolved, but it was obvious the Natives were a force to be reckoned with and they were not backing down.[79]

Regardless of tensions and skirmishes, cannery owners protected their investment while workers were left with a dilemma: they had to choose between complaining, an action that might affect their employment status, or honoring the traditional lifestyle inherited from their ancestors. As the next century approached, this was the setting in Southeast Alaska as the region sank further into a colonized state. In Stephen Haycox's analysis, "The absentee-owned cannery companies were permitted to use their large, efficient traps" with no recourse, and protesters believed the government was "in collusion with the industry to keep Alaska in corporate bondage."[80]

The Tlingit and Haida had fished for salmon from a time before memory, and each clan owned specific fishing sites under their collective stewardship. In these older times there had been no reason to overfish because all their needs were met. Even after the arrival of the Russians, English, and Americans, the trading activities were not detrimental to the resource, if only because of the small population. It took advanced resource extraction with growing private enterprise to transform a way of life that had been held in reverence for centuries. Smaller canneries could hardly survive alongside the out-of-territory mega-companies that controlled Alaska's economy and set fish prices, demolished competition, and shaped the labor force. The monopoly grew to such proportions that it was referred to as the "fish trust."[81]

Inter-ethnic rivalry was intense as Native women, prized for their skills and willingness to work long hours, were pushed to the fringes by the growing number of Asian men. Vulnerable Native fishermen coped with the advent of high-powered fishing gear and had such trouble making a living that women and children were employed in the canneries to supplement family income.[82] When more Native children were employed in the cannery and did not attend school, the missionaries complained to civil government authorities, but child labor continued into the next century despite the paternalistic arm of the missionaries and the federal government.[83]

By 1910 southeast Alaska's population had grown from small indigenous villages to a cosmopolitan arena of European and American settlers and Asian immigrants. The Tlingit and Haida adapted to the intrusion of cannery structures, fish traps, foreigners, and unfavorable Western law, but the adjustment was far from seamless. An 1894 incident demonstrates these competing interests. A cannery superintendent had fired a Tlingit fisherman, who had protested the lack of upstream escapement for his village. He expressed the double-bind dilemma all Native fishermen faced: "We are catching the fish for you. Now you are going to block the creek. That creek is not going to last."[84] There were numerous disagreements like this one along the rivers, creeks, and inlets, and the Tlingit realized they must unify to get their message across in no uncertain terms. It was time for a formal complaint.

The lack of salmon in the steams raised a red flag that propelled the Tlingit to form an interclan council in 1890, and the group hired a lawyer, Willoughby Clark, to draft a letter to President Benjamin Harrison, listing their objections to the growing encroachment of the salmon canneries on Tlingit land and the sabotage of whole runs of fish. The letter promoted civil rights and endorsed property titles while addressing the mounting fishing crisis. Several clans were involved in this effort, but the most active leaders were from the Stikine area, now called Wrangell.

The letter stated that the Tlingit were not infants under the law and their rights to fishing streams must be recognized and not usurped by the newcomers who had sought to build dams and other barriers to the free movement of the fish, cutting off the spawning grounds and the food supply without recompense.[85] President Harrison forwarded the letter to Secretary of the Interior John Noble, but there was no response. Nothing changed; it was business as usual, and more canneries were constructed on the Alexander Archipelago despite the antipathy caused by the Tlingit's territorialism. Clashes escalated as frustrated Native fishermen took matters into their own hands and fought back. But what tools did they have?

Southeast Alaska was void of formal law codes, although the occasional revenue cutters intervened in quarrels from time to time.

A case in point involved Navy attempts to settle troubles at a Chilkat village where it was argued that centuries-old clan lands were being infringed upon, encompassing the Saint Elias mountains and the major rivers flowing into the Pacific, including the Alsek, Tatshenshini, Chilkat, and Taku, in addition to trade networks with the interior Athabascan bands. For years the Tlingit had criticized the canneries and the fishing industry for creating instability in the region, finally resulting in a showdown. Customs Inspector John J. Healy reported that the Chilkat and Chilkoot were complaining about outside fishermen in their territory, and when no action was taken the Tlingit threatened to burn down the canneries. Problems persisted until Healy grew concerned about three canneries in the area and pleaded that Native rights must be observed, calling a halt to the "wanton depredation upon this most important resource by the cannery people." He continued: "It is not only the fish that is caught and canned that the natives are deprived of, but thousands are thrown away as unfit for canning . . . The natives of Alaska never ceded any rights to the United States, nor to the Russian Government before them. . . . Unless some steps are taken by the government to preserve the natural food of these people from destruction they will surely revolt."[86]

The warning went unheeded. Big business and the distant government ignored the opinions of custom clerks, and instead canneries remained unregulated and continued to take over former Native hunting grounds, and in some cases even sacred locations, using timber from the Tongass forest and trapping salmon from the waters. There was no sincere effort to shelter Alaska Native lands from commercialization or to preserve indigenous lands. In 1884 Congress had passed the Alaska Organic Act in order to institute a civil government, and a component of the legislation attempted to protect "Indians or other persons" in Alaska "in the possession of any lands actually in their use or occupation."[87] Because of indistinct language and lack of enforcement, using the Organic Act to decide property disputes had limited results.[88] Ultimately there was nothing to stop the canneries from spreading right across the archipelago, which drove the Southeast Alaska Natives into a deeper adversarial position while the powerful salmon industry permeated every dimension of Alaska life and stood as an oligarchy capable of calculating the economic future and political path. Despite these realities, the Alaska Natives did not abandon their fight.

In the words of Donawak (Dáanaa waak), Silver Dollar Eyes, a highly regarded Chilkoot leader: "When I was a young man, I worked for myself. Before the canneries were built here, I was consulted and told that presents would be given me for the privilege of building canneries in my country. I am sorry to say that the promises were not fulfilled. . . . I am speaking for my people in the Chilkoot Inlet and ask you that some mark be put near the mouth of the river which will stop fishermen from preventing our salmon from going to the river."[89]

Unfulfilled promises were the norm, while disputes between rival non-Native fishermen, selling fish at a cut-rate price, undermined the Native market. In 1890 the famous naturalist John Muir had made his way up the Chilkat River and remarked on how the Northwest Trading Company and Kinney Brothers canneries were paying the Chilkat about ten cents per salmon, but in hopes of an even great profit, a price war began when the cannery owners slashed the salmon price to five cents each. The Chilkat responded with a strike and refused to harvest any more fish.[90] To settle the dispute, the naval ship USS *Pinta* was summoned, and Captain O. W. Farenholt tried negotiation at first, but had no luck convincing the Tlingit fishermen to go back to work and supply the canneries with fish. They were not budging until they felt sure they were receiving adequate compensation for the salmon, motivating Farenholt to threaten the men with a Gatling gun. The standoff continued until the cannery bosses acquiesced to the Native fishermen's demands. This would not be the last time that fishermen or cannery workers stood their ground.

In 1867 the Russian flag was lowered in Sitka and the American flag was raised, signaling a new era. The Tlingit were obliged to accept the American culture and the capitalist economy while their customs were submerged for the time being. Clan houses disappeared and were replaced by single family dwellings. The potlatch went underground to avoid censure. The children were no longer exclusively taught the ways of life from their uncles or elders but were instead required to attend school in buildings constructed from clan-owned timber. In turn, fishing, the mainstay of the Native economy, was modified by the cannery empires and eventually the resource regulators as bureaucracy started to rule the waterways.

For the Alaska Native the cannery became a controlling factor in everyday life, and the once communal life was Westernized, drastically altering the Tlingit and Haida's prestige-oriented society, formerly based on property and rank. From the days of the Russian mercantile period, the Tlingit had known a market economy, but previous autonomy was replaced by set work hours, wages, and taking orders from someone other than the head of their clan. In all of this, the Tlingit and Haida still cleaved to clan ownership and did not waver from their conviction; the land and waters were not a commodity in the indigenous holistic ethical framework, and collective protest was their reaction when their conventions were crushed. Given this cultural milieu, it may appear ironic that the Tlingit and Haida also desired cannery jobs, and they enjoyed the money to buy goods and even luxuries. Human dynamics are never static. Instead societal groups mold their identity and choices in rhythm to changing patterns.

Adopting a changed landscape became a survival skill. Traditional gender roles were modified and women found an enhanced status in their labor, which mixed shift work with subsistence living, all the while striving for a balance and sculpting variations into a new routine. Inevitably, industrialization and commercial interests pitched emerging Native leaders into the sticky mire of politics to act as advocates and to interpret laws that were made on the other side of the continent. Labor, whether Alaska Native or Asian, was subjected to racialization and federal government control, creating friction that called out for resolution. From 1879 to the early 1900s there was vigorous growth in the cannery industry, eventually spreading to Prince William Sound and then to the southwest area of

Bristol Bay. Corporate colonialism was reinforced by advancements in technology and transportation, eventually transforming the landscape and waters, but as the next chapter illustrates, each cannery had its own unique story and variations on the theme. In this case, it was the incorporation of newcomers from bordering British Columbia.

3

Metlakatla and the Tsimshian

The Tlingit and Haida were the first indigenous groups to occupy the Alexander Archipelago, but in the late 1800s another Native group, the Tsimshian, arrived from British Columbia, Canada. All three cultures have similar socioeconomic systems, including matrilineal clans, ritualized ceremonies such as the potlatch, and a livelihood based on fishing. Since the Haida, Tlingit, and Tsimshian languages are dissimilar, there is no doubt they had different origins, although even before Western recorded history, these distinct people were interrelated through marriage and trade relationships. Several Tsimshian clans still occupy their traditional Canadian homes, but in 1887 about eight hundred Tsimshian migrated to Alaska's Annette Island. Their story is valuable for its portrayal of a cannery operation ostensibly run by Natives and the surprising presidential executive orders and corresponding federal legislation that protected their endeavor, attesting to a historic anomaly in several respects. Further, their story serves as an additional perspective regarding the advent of cannery industrialization and governmental directives that orchestrated culture change. Native villages experienced overlapping circles of government, business, and politics, but as part of the adaptive process and as a means to prosper, these Tsimshian found an indigenous pathway, allowing a certain degree of Westernization while retaining parts of the ancient heritage. Above all, the Tsimshian retained their independent spirit and would not be victims of missionary colonization, but it was not without great effort.

From a time before memory, the Tsimshian lived on the mainland and islands around the Skeena and Nass rivers, and Milbanke Sound, alongside their neighbors, the Haida Gwaii (former Queen Charlotte Islands) and the Canadian Athabascan people. By the early 1800s their lives were interrupted by the fur traders, gold seekers, and nomadic fishermen, who brought alcohol and gambling. One of the Tsimshian extended clans, Lax Kw'alaams, moved to Port Simpson when the English-owned Hudson's Bay Company erected a fort at that location to take advantage of the numerous trade opportunities. The Tsimshian were an integral part of the commercial ventures as fur trappers and fishermen, broadening their knowledge of other cultures and the cash economy. Unfortunately, it also increased their participation in alcohol consumption, gambling, and other vices.

Scottish-born William Duncan had been sent by the British Anglican Church Missionary Society in 1856 to minister to the spiritual needs of the Canadian Natives, and gradually he gained adherents to his brand of Christian philosophy. After Duncan realized that Fort Simpson was not a suitable venue for his plans, he and a group of about eight hundred Tsimshian followers relocated south of the fort and started a new community called Metlakatla. Duncan, imbued with self-proclaimed righteousness, was sure he would realize his dream of a theocratic socialism in this "model Indian community," but he underestimated the patience of his church and the defiance of the British Columbian Natives. The deep-seated Tsimshian cultural belief system was modified for the circumstances, but the basics were left intact. In the meantime, the rogue minister faced church scrutiny, as witnessed through several quarrels, while the Canadian government was not happy with his free hand concerning land laws and other standards.[1]

Undaunted and focused on his mission, Duncan promised the Tsimshian a good life through Christian virtue, full assimilation in the Western social system, and a severance of all things Native, including potlatches, the clan system, matrilineal inheritance, and cleavages to ancient customs that thwarted his utopian aspiration. When the church dismissed him and the Canadian government threatened to imprison him, he was motivated to find a new venue for his vision, and his relocation plans were hastened when he received word that the "court in Victoria, British Columbia, ruled that the government of British Columbia and the Anglican Church, rather than Father William Duncan and the Tsimshians, owned the Metlakatla townsite" as absolute sovereigns over the people and their resources.[2]

Duncan sent scouts to the east to look for a suitable site that would sustain the already functioning sawmill and cannery, and it was found among the Gravina Islands at a place called Annette Island, named by American naturalist William Healey Dall. The area was located on the traditional lands of the Tlingit *Taak'w Aan*,[3] and what is infrequently mentioned in the Metlakatla story is that a group of Tsimshian met with the Tlingit leaders to discuss the land transfer. Non-Natives might assume the site was there for the taking if it appeared to be abandoned, but these two Native groups knew a satisfactory deal must be struck concerning the land and waters in question.[4]

William Duncan may have been unaware of the dialogue between the Native groups, but he did understand that this was United States territory. The Tsimshian and Tlingit had been trading for hundreds of years without concern for a border, but now they were faced with the fact they had migrated from British territory into an American-held land base. To square up matters, Native leaders encouraged Duncan to go to Washington DC and with the support of the territorial governor A. P. Swineford and the important political figure of Sheldon Jackson, general agent of education for Alaska, Duncan traveled to the nation's capital to petition for exclusive use of Annette Island for the Tsimshian and their commercial endeavors. Duncan felt sure his wishes would be granted because Congress, after all, had recently appropriated a large sum of money to relocate Icelanders to Alaska, and they were truly foreigners.

Upon arriving Duncan was showered with praise for "saving the Indians," characterized as "victims of an oppression more cruel and shameful than that which drove the Pilgrim Fathers to New England." President Grover Cleveland did not wish to antagonize the British, yet was moved by Duncan's testimony and granted temporary squatters' rights to address the refugee crisis.[5] He was a proponent of "Native progress" and believed the missionaries were the answer to any "Indian problem."[6] Early on Cleveland had been impressed with Presbyterian missionary Sheldon Jackson, and even more so when Jackson took on the role of general agent of Alaska education in 1885, believing he could spread Christianity and keep peace in the northern territory.

In 1887 President Cleveland signed an executive order setting aside land to build a self-sufficient Native community, and by the stroke of a pen the president of the United States permitted Canadian immigrants to find sanctuary under the protection of the federal government. Duncan wasted no time and began the complete exodus out of Canada, establishing the New Metlakatla reserve at Port Chester on the west side of Annette Island with the objective of setting up a civilized Christian community. Though he exerted a certain degree of coercion, the Tsimshian did not give up their customs and instead took their ceremonies, rituals, and artistic symbols underground, unbeknownst to Duncan, and continued to live under the assumption that they were independent people. At times there was outright defiance, as seen in the construction of totem poles in front of houses, which Duncan justified as family history, not idol worship, in an acquiescence to group harmony and unity.[7]

There was, however, one tenet that both Duncan and the people agreed upon—the value of industrious labor and profitable enterprises. In this time period and most likely beyond, there was a tendency for European or American critics to think of the indigenous people as indolent, but as Rolf Knight's British Columbia study concluded, the indigenous people were "hard working" and could not be viewed as "lazy Indians" or "feckless hunters," and those stereotypes should be rejected: "Whatever else they were, whatever distinct cultural traditions they retained, Indian loggers were loggers, Indian longshoremen were longshoremen, Indian cannery workers were cannery workers."[8] The Tsimshian were skilled in carpentry, seamanship, and boatbuilding, a proficiency that had grown out of their previous occupations coupled with an understanding of the forest and waters.

At New Metlakatla the Tsimshian first built a sawmill, using the rich stands of spruce, birch, and hemlock from the Tongass Forest, before constructing a cannery plant to take advantage of the abundant fish supply. Bit by bit the town grew, displaying a cultural mix of English architecture with Tsimshian canoes lining the beach.[9] By 1890 an observer remarked: "Metlakatla boasted an impressive handsomely-crafted wooden church, bordering its streets were picket fences neatly delineating Victorian cottages. Tsimshian villagers also operated its shops and stores. Its citizens worked an industrialized work week, and their own Indian police protected them from liquor traffickers and lecherous miners."[10] But was the community truly this harmonious?

The transition from a clan-based to a market economy was jagged. Although the Tsimshian sought ways to embrace Westernization, they were fully aware of Duncan's attempts to destroy their esteemed ancient roots: socially, economically, politically, and spiritually. Duncan's followers were mostly from the older set, while younger community members had their own ideas and rebelled against a church-dominated atmosphere and Duncan's iron rule.[11] In turn, Duncan sought further authorization from the U.S. government through established property rights.

In 1891 Duncan submitted a petition to formalize the Metlakatla reservation status. Stemming from his appraisal of the circumstances, he declared: "What the Indians need in their new environment are what we all need while we are children, namely protection and education."[12] Despite the dissent from the young people seeking a break from Duncan's paternalism, the federal government agreed with him based on an admiration of his progressive work with the Tsimshian. Subsequently a reserve was established through congressional order under the auspices of the Department of the Interior. Ironically, from that point forward, it was not Duncan who held dominion over New Metlakatla, including the lumber mill and salmon cannery, but the federal government. In essence, the Tsimshian traded off theocratic socialism for bureaucratic colonialism.

Although the status was malleable and fluid, Metlakatla stands as the first statutory reserve established in Alaska, deeming the land and waters for the exclusive and irrevocable use of the Tsimshian. Since reservations were considered a step back in the assimilation process, Duncan must have been persuasive, or perhaps these actions were based on the territory's remoteness and lack of protection. To ensure smooth running, the secretary of the interior retained a "specified and continuing role," extending the long arm of paternalism from the nation's capital to Annette Island to assist "the Indians in their effort to train themselves to habits of industry, become self-sustaining and advance in the ways of civilized life."[13] Commerce and industrialization appeared to hold the key in meeting these goals.

The Metlakahtla Industrial Company was resurrected from machinery the Tsimshian had been able to take with them when they moved, and "all parts and branches of the cannery and the fisheries supplying it [were] conducted by native Indians . . . some 30 to 40 women and girls were making seines and nets for the use of the community and for sale."[14] This revelation highlights the significant role women played in the canneries, eventually leading to indisputable influence in the day-to-day operations. Women were integral workers with a corresponding degree of independence, largely stemming from the traditional egalitarian society. This labor environment, however, conflicted with Duncan's belief that women should only fulfill a secondary role in industrial settings because it was the men's function to protect and provide for the family. In fact, Duncan discouraged women from working outside the home at all and advocated that girls stay in church school until safely married.[15] Whether Duncan knew this or not, his efforts to suppress female authority violated Tsimshian cultural principles, resulting in factionalism between traditionalists, who clung to the ancient system, and ostensible progressives adhering to Duncan's plan.[16] Naturally these two conflicting worldviews resulted in rebellion and defiance against Duncan's authoritarianism, particularly his efforts to destroy the ancient distribution of goods and resources based on the matrilineality. The anger spilled over into the workplace and at community meetings.

Despite Duncan's disapproval, the Native-run commercial enterprises continued to employ both men and women, rousing the more conservative faction to accuse the women of deserting their feminine duties and chastising them for immoral conduct. To punish the women for their perceived haughty independence, several measures were taken to shame them, including dividing their kitchen gardens into patrilineal cooperative units, the membership of which was defined by Duncan. Trade of surplus production was placed in the hands of men, creating increased resentment among the Tsimshian.[17] Isolated from lineage production and thwarted in their attempts to engage in wage labor, the women, many of the esteemed clan leaders, could no longer maintain age-old property claims, and in a domino effect this undermined the prestige and ranking system. Moreover, matriclans were banned from hosting potlatches for religious reasons, yet it mattered little since female heads had been stripped of their material wealth, and there could be no accumulation of possessions necessary for ceremonial gift giving. As the discord in the community grew, a group of leaders confronted Duncan with what they considered abuses, and their charges extended to the management of the fishing and cannery operations. The Tsimshian labor force believed they should be in charge of the plant and did not want Duncan interfering with the day-to-day workings. To add strength to their cause, they were gaining adherents.

One of Duncan's most fervent opponents was the Tsimshian minister Edward Marsden. He had been among the original eight hundred who had left Canada and established the Annette Island community, but because of ideological differences Marsden had broken away from Duncan's church, simultaneously becoming a follower of Sheldon Jackson's Presbyterian mission, and eventually graduating from seminary and assuming duties at his Saxman Presbyterian parish. Although Marsden believed in assimilative measures to a certain degree, he abhorred ward status, stating that "there is a day coming when that special act of Congress that temporarily provides for our exclusive use of the body of lands known as Annette Island must be repealed." He was adamant that barriers to participation in the free enterprise system would doom them forever to second-class status and that genuine ownership of property "by deed as a citizen of the United States" was better than holding title "in common with others and be[ing] isolated on an Indian reservation."[18] Naturally he assumed membership in the American capitalist system would loosen governmental control, but considering American Native status at that time, it was a lofty objective for a people not yet allowed to vote or stake mining claims, among other restrictions.

Edward Marsden was a symbol of the newly emerging identity of Southeast Alaska Natives, a people who had one foot firmly placed in their ancestors' footprint yet who desired a place in the mainstream economy with the accompanying civil rights. Full citizenship appeared to be the key, and the Tsimshian, like the Tlingit and Haida, had petitioned for naturalization with the understanding that they would be the rightful owners of their businesses and home, with legal deeds and titles. In one documented case, a group of Native men traveled from Metlakatla to Sitka, the seat of Alaskan government, to plead their cases, but the magistrates said they had no jurisdiction to grant citizenship to these men, even if they were born in the territory.[19] In fact, Native Americans would not achieve citizenship until 1924.[20]

Nonetheless, Marsden and other like-minded leaders were relentless in their collective move to free the Tsimshian from what they believed was a dependent state that compromised membership in the free market.[21] Sheldon Jackson supported Marsden's ideas and believed the reservation system was counterproductive (even using the term corrupt) because it required segregation, leading to stagnation, instead of allowing American values to permeate the Native culture.[22] Eventually President Theodore Roosevelt heard these disputes, and in a surprising gesture the president sided with Duncan and his firm grip on Metlakatla.[23]

Roosevelt had spoken on several occasions about his mission to break up tribes, but in Alaska, a place he only knew through his friend, the naturalist John Muir, he thought it better to leave the matter in abeyance for a time.[24] Conversely, Marsden could not be dissuaded from his objectives and claimed he "would rather own a piece of property by deed, pay my taxes and vote . . . than to hold in common with others and be isolated on an Indian reservation." Alaska Governor John G. Brady echoed Marsden's sentiments and called the reserve a poor piece of legislation that trapped the Tsimshian in an unresolved state.[25] Yet neither Brady nor Marsden could compete with Duncan's political clout, supported by the president.

In the early 1900s this was Metlakatla's sociopolitical environment as people struggled to maintain their culture and also run a profitable cannery business. Those living at the time have left a record of the tensions, among them William Reynon, a member of the Canadian Gyitlan tribe. He had spent time in Metlakatla and worked in the cannery. Being part of the community, he remembered the anger over having the ancient ways now called demonic, but he also noted that the more oppressive rules concerning land ownership had eased. This meant that the lowest-ranking person in the old system now had a level playing field. Reynon gave Duncan the credit, whether that was deserved or not, by stating that the minister "had established permanent industries which occupied and absorbed the energies of the people" and allowed a community council to run the cannery, which on the outside appeared to signal local control and a modicum of sovereignty. Eventually the workers saved enough money to buy their own cannery, but there was a catch. It was still under government management, and there appeared to be no way to shake off the old missionary paternalism and the new restraints of the Department of the Interior.[26]

In the past Duncan had been blindly focused on an ideal utopian Native community administered by church regulations, but he could not shy away from realities. When a fisheries inspector questioned Duncan about the Tsimshian's rights to water bodies and fish, he replied: "Our answer is, that, pending the Indians arriving at full American citizenship and responsibility, the Government might proclaim all salmon streams, Indian reservations or Government property, and only allow fishing in them to proper persons and under proper regulations." Duncan imagined this umbrella might protect Metlakatlan interests, and "prevent canning companies from taking exclusive control of the salmon streams," and thereby "better the conditions of the natives." The final result would be that fishing and canning would be in the hands of the Natives, "not as employees only, but as vendors of the salmon to the canneries."[27]

At first, Duncan's words sounded as if he thought the Tsimshian were capable of controlling their destiny, but a closer evaluation indicates he was still entrenched in his benevolent monocracy and saw the government as his willing and able aide. He was not, however, unaware of outside competition and feared that the larger fishing fleets he had seen in the distance would eventually get closer and infringe on Metlakatla. In his view, cannery jobs introduced the workers to the various steps of Western economy, and the Metlakatla cannery was "organized as a business corporation with outside investment capital in the spirit of capitalism," the socially approved economic system.[28]

Southeast Alaska Natives had enjoyed profitable trading for hundreds of years, and as economist Robert Price reasoned, the Tlingit, Haida, and Tsimshian had a natural inclination "to participate in the system" influenced by "their acquisition of property whether for potlatch or trade goods."[29] By the turn of the century the Tsimshian had blended Western ways with those of their ancestors as cannery production met the needs of a growing market, and the Tsimshian pursued full independence from the Department of Interior, which continued to oversee operations. At the country's capital, officials relied on fish and wildlife agent reports regardless of possible bias or gaps, to make regulations, and it was this bureaucratic grip that posed the most danger to the resource and harvesters. Without thorough knowledge of the people or the fisheries, rules were made that did not align with reality, but little could be done. The Tsimshian lacked political sway, and their only hope was to band together to fight for the full management of the cannery as a private enterprise.

A Native Council had been formed in the early years of Metlakatla, based on the old traditional form of an elders' council, but it was ineffective since Duncan had the final say in matters. In a furtive manner the council attempted to skirt Duncan, but without success until Marsden took hold of the reins, rekindling the feud between Duncan and Marsden. Based on information from Marsden, Duncan was arrested by the secretary of the interior in early 1916, and when he was released, he was in no mood to forgive and forget. He disbanded the Native Council and formed in its place a town council and a new company, the Metlakatla

Commercial Company. In spite of that, it was obvious that Duncan had lost his strength, particularly because Marsden had the backing of federal officials and a growing number of followers, which allowed him to be elected secretary of the town council with the power to run everything based on his ideal of Native success, not Duncan's theocracy.[30] With the dissolution of church domination, the federal government assumed more control over the reserve, although the Metlakatlans fought against the bureaucracy and followed more closely the precepts within the council's constitution, which read: "The Metlakatla Indian Community shall for all purposes of this Constitution exercise jurisdiction over all the territory and waters" described under the Presidential Proclamation reserving the Annette Island village.[31] In essence the Tsimshian were using the government's own pledge to gain self-determination, but the salmon runs and culture were still at risk.

For the cannery business, the fish harvest had been good from the start. Jefferson Moser from the United States Fish Commission visited Metlakatla in 1897 and described it thus: "In 1890 an experimental pack of 500 cases was made, but by the next year there were 5,834 cases packed."[32] Moser observed that "they were making cans for the season's pack, rebuilding the steam tender . . . 30–40 women and girls were making seines and nets for the use of the community."[33] It should be noted that despite Duncan's attempts to have the women stay close to home and hearth, they were integral employees in the cannery business, and Native fishermen were what Duncan had hoped for: "vendors of the salmon to the canneries."[34] But the government continued to believe in a fiduciary relationship and considered the Tsimshian incapable of managing their own affairs.

Duncan, in his characteristic fatherly role, had consistently warned the cannery managers about the stiff competition from other packing companies, and in 1898, when the federal fisheries inspector interviewed Duncan on the cannery premises, he was quick to interject that laws were necessary to protect the Natives and prevent outside canning companies from controlling the salmon streams. This industrious labor would be an important factor in Duncan's plan to raise the economic level of the

Metlakatlans.[35] As Metlakatla's cannery enterprise grew more profitable, the prophecy proved true, as there was a need to defend the fishing grounds against the cannery conglomerates and—even more important—against the ravenous fish traps, the most physical sign of corporate dominion in Southeast Alaska waters. The intrusions escalated to the point that the Tsimshian found themselves in a courtroom, fighting for their rights. William Duncan died in 1918, but the Metlakatla Natives were still under government ward status, and although they took great efforts to shake it off, in some situations there was an advantage in federal protection.

Alaska Pacific Fisheries v. United States (1918) questioned property rights, cannery interests, and the status of a Native reserve. The dispute was over a private company's fish trap located within the Metlakatla reservation. If it was proven that the fish trap was there illegally, it must be removed and damages assessed, but a large part of the essential evidence revolved around the question of Metlakatla's exact boundaries, requiring a definition of the parameters first established in 1891 and extended in 1916 by President Woodrow Wilson. The latter extension also included the withdrawal of all of the waters within 3,000 feet of the shore for the exclusive use by the Tsimshian.[36] The United States, as trustee (and defender), was forced to sue the Alaska Pacific Fisheries Corporation to ban their encroaching fish traps in these waters, based on the assumed deleterious effects to Metlakatla's fishing and cannery businesses. Because the government had set up the reserve, it must uphold all restrictions, and if this trust was broken, the Native plaintiffs could sue for breach of duty. In the words of the court, the Tsimshian had been allowed "to establish a colony which would be self-sustaining and reasonably free of obstacles which attend the advancement of a primitive people. . . . The fishery adjacent to the shore would afford primary subsistence and a promising opportunity for industrial and commercial development. . . . The conclusion has general support in the general rule that statutes passed for the benefit of a dependent tribe are liberally construed."[37]

The use of "primitive people" and the obvious government influence in the proceedings emphasized that the Metlakatla reserve was far from being considered a sovereign area, but it did authorize vital protection against their fishery being usurped, like so many others along the archipelago, and further upheld the reserve status created through executive order.[38] Since Metlakatla had few resources to depend upon outside the fishery, it was declared that navigable waters were a vital part of the Tsimshian's economic welfare. Therefore the federal government was dutifully safe-guarding and advancing the rights of a dependent people based on the Commerce Clause. In summary: "In 1919 Congress prohibited the creation of future executive order Indian reserves without legislative consent, but the *Alaska Pacific Fisheries* decision confirmed the exclusive status of the previously created Alaska reserves and implied that the legal status of Alaska Natives was similar to other Native Americans."[39] But unlike the lands of many American Native tribes, their reserve was not classified as Indian Country, with all the rights and privileges that standing afforded, including self-determination. While subject to territorial and federal laws, they still could not manage the cannery operation as a private business, reinforcing a ward colonialism.

Under these circumstance, the Tsimshian were left to the whim of the Department of Interior, an issue that was re-emphasized shortly after the conclusion of their legal battle when the government leased out the Metlakatla cannery to the Annette Island Packing Company without input from the Metlakatla council.[40] J. L. Smiley, the lessee, managed or owned several other canneries, particularly in the Ketchikan area, but this was his first stint as a government agent. He was tasked to fully employ the community and to buy fish from their fishermen.[41] Smiley ran the operation the only way he knew how: as a regular profit-making enterprise, and the Metlakatlans were employees only. Once again the goal of achieving economic independence was thwarted in favor of per-petual status quo.

It was not only the government or the environmental conditions that determined what happened in Metlakatla. The Alaska cannery business was influenced by world events, which tended to shake the territory out of its provincial state. World War I affected American industry in sev-eral ways, including increasing demand for canned salmon production.

Exercising wartime powers, federal authorities took over the management of salmon output quotas to ensure the required packs were shipped overseas, particularly to soldiers in the European theater. The government also wanted to modernize the plants, including Metlakatla cannery, which was legislatively required to employ the Tsimshian over "whites."[42] After the war's end, however, there was a significant drop in salmon canning production, coupled with the undisputable evidence of resource depletion, leading to discussions between fishery agents and businessmen concerning resource preservation. Worry over the fisheries escalated simultaneously with President Warren G. Harding entering office and his appointment of Herbert Hoover as secretary of commerce, responsible for the fisheries of the United States, among other things. During Hoover's tenure there was an emphasis on making money versus resource preservation, based on his personal theory that greater efficiency in the fisheries would act as a conservation method. Above all, he aimed to advance domestic and international trade.

Hoover's mindset would color history as he became more and more aware of the potential and profitability of Alaskan fisheries, motivating him to prevail upon President Harding to issue an executive order to institute a fishery grounds reservation policy without specifics.[43] This was a radical departure from the free and common fishery, and in the beginning, the big cannery outfits balked at any talk of restrictive legislation, although in due time, they came to see the advantage as it became clear that they could secure exclusive property rights in the fisheries, including permanent fish traps.

In February 1922 President Harding proclaimed the first such reserve, where "no person was allowed to engage in fishing, canning or preparing salmon in the reserved area without obtaining a permit from the Secretary of Commerce."[44] Of course this would not apply to Metlakatla since it was already reserved for exclusive use by Tsimshian residents. In 1923, however, Secretary Hoover and President Harding had the opportunity to review the Metlakatla situation first-hand as part of a two-week Alaskan visit. President Harding had heard about the flourishing cannery on Annette Island operated by a Native crew, and both he and Secretary

Hoover had a keen interest in appraising the operation. Also, the president had received a plea from the Metlakatlan citizens indicating there were troubles in their cannery business, including the harvesting of salmon.

Mr. and Mrs. Harding| were greeted warmly at Metlakatla, where "Florence (Harding) was startled by accomplished Native Alaskan musicians in their bare feet playing for the presidential couple!" They visited the grave of Anglican missionary Father William Duncan, and Herbert Hoover was personally interested in the history since his uncle, the man who had raised him after the death of both his parents, had been an Oregon Indian agent who later traveled to Metlakatla to study Father Duncan's unique methods with the Tsimshian people.[45]

The Tsimshian residents were eager to display their town, and they had also invited guests from nearby Tlingit and Haida villages. Hoover and Harding met with a delegation from Wrangell, Kake, Kasaan, Hydaburg, and Ketchikan, all cannery towns, who described their villages in glowing terms, paying careful attention to mention how well the fishing industry was doing. Reverend Edward Marsden spoke of the Native quest for full American citizenship and the need for a productive and positive business atmosphere.[46] To punctuate the air of Americanism, the community put on a patriotic demonstration and played the "Star-Spangled Banner" with an accompanying flag salute.

Guided by Metlakatla's mayor, they walked down to the docks and cannery.[47] While listening to the history, Harding remarked that the plant appeared to be in good working order, and before leaving the president and his wife were given "fine silver bracelets." Both Harding and Hoover had been informed of the problems in Alaska fisheries, including the intense competition and piracy that went on.[48] Future legislation could well have been based on this visit, but at the time Hoover showed little compassion for Native-run enterprises. Already there were signs that the secretary tended to favor conglomerates, and as the events played out, it was obvious "the white man companies were the beneficiaries" of congressional and executive decisions, acting to strengthen the "fish trust" in Alaskan waters.[49] For all his bluster, however, Hoover experienced a setback as regards Metlakatla. Since it was already a federal reserve, it could not be further divided into a fishery district, and that ended any genuine authority he might have had on Annette Island.[50]

Before leaving, President Harding promised to look into their concerns when he returned to Washington DC, but he emphasized that Natives were not to turn back to their savage and heathen ways: there can be no "return to primitive conditions because that is against God's law and the best interests of human society."[51] Apparently indigenous capitalism had both presidential and celestial blessings, but it could not be fully played out since the president died a week later.

In the 1920s the Metlakatla Reservation and cannery modernized and increased production. To this day it stands out as an anomaly because it is the only reservation (or reserve) in Alaska, and the federal government on several occasions has protected the status and business interests of these Canadian immigrants. During the Depression era, Secretary of the Interior Harold Ickes visited the Metlakatla village and remarked it was "the best built, cleanest and most prosperous Indian village I have seen in these parts"; at a later date he finished this thought by describing Metlakatla as "probably the most completely self-supporting Native community in Alaska."[52] Contrary to this statement, the paternalism continued, but the oppressive thumb of the Department of the Interior could not halt the community's quest to seek full American citizenship and guaranteed property rights.

Over time the Native culture adapted to shifting circumstances and modified the local market economy to suit people's needs, so that "they could draw on familiar cultural frameworks as a means of negotiating new realities"[53] whether those be fierce competition, the need for advanced gear, converting from a barter system to wage employment, or working around governmental interference. In 1911 Tsimshian leader Peter Simpson had predicted the demise of fish runs, and there was no denying this reality. Because of the resource depletion, Secretary of Commerce Herbert Hoover attempted to regulate the Alaskan fisheries, particularly after the potential for vast profits became obvious, and in due course, he sponsored legislation that impacted every fishing ground and cannery in Alaska.

The idea of the Native American or "Indian" presented special problems for the dominant powers, and they relied on older interpretations of race to defend what they believed were the appropriate actions, which varied from welfare solutions to full assimilation campaigns. When missionaries arrived at indigenous settlements, they assumed they were lifting these men and women from their basest instincts, without acknowledging that the people had lived with the environment for thousands of years. Instead the missionaries were filled with the Rousseauian idea of the "noble savage," tempered by their interpretation of social Darwinism, which contended that the Native American had the ability to rise from an assumed lowly position but never to the level of the dominant society. Within this atmosphere, it was difficult to run a cannery on an autonomous basis. Indigenous efforts were thwarted by limitations placed on fishermen, canners, and managers, and these restrictions were founded "by equating the cultural hierarchy assumed under the idea of progress with the physical and mental traits believed to exist between human groups."[54] This safely allowed stereotypes to flourish in the popular imagination. Racial or ethnic group segregation, as in a reserve or reservation, facilitated the administration of specific laws based on a perceived status of lesser people, thus robbing these once sovereign communities of their self-determination.

The Metlakatlans were not the only indigenous group to enter the private enterprise arena and be reined in through government interference. The Menominee and Metlakatlans were compared and contrasted by Bruce Hosner, who found similar business challenges and the emergence of capitalism balanced with the retention of cultural ways. Both groups also had to find ways to make a living under their own terms. To do so, they needed to be able to rework their identity for the exigencies of the modern world. Monetary rewards provided individual satisfaction, but there was a need for more. "Economic change mandated cultural adaptations, and Metlakatlans and Menominees altered political institutions to fit new circumstances," introducing "novel concepts or sets of relationships" while attempting to maintain a degree of independence.[55]

Against incredible odds, they did not abandon their identities; that was their strength: "Their success in conserving traditions while working with the white-man's market system bears witness to the flexibility of culture" and adaptability.[56]

It was not only Alaska Native communities wanting to start their own cannery businesses. There were many European immigrants, with a background in fishing from their old country, venturing into Alaska to start packing businesses at the turn of the century. The resources were there for the taking, with few restrictions in the early years, but these immigrants faced the same problems as other smaller canneries: the need for financing, semi-skilled labor, and modern cost-reducing machinery. When they successfully resolved these hurdles, as in the following story of the Norwegian Buschmann family, they became part of Alaska's greater cannery history.

4

From Norwegian Fjords
to Alaskan Glaciers

Petersburg's history offers a unique snapshot of Southeast Alaska cannery life in the first half of the twentieth century, particularly the role of European immigrants. Through the story of the Buschmann family, one can view the transactional nature of power and financial authority that dominated the political economy of Southeast Alaska. Where Wrangell Narrows converges with Frederick Sound, a quaint hamlet was founded by a Norwegian immigrant through individual entrepreneurship against the backdrop of American politics and European rivalries. It is important to note that not all Europeans can be grouped as one cultural unit, and in fact, there was a long history of strife between northern, southern, and eastern Europeans, all with different cultures. What did bring them together was an expertise in fishing and a great motivation to find a better life in Alaska. The region's history, however, started much earlier when the region was part of the Kake Ḵwáan, whose territories encompassed the islands of Mitkof, Kuiu, and Kupreanof; Kake Ḵwáan denotes a large region of multiple clans, all with their own special sites.

Before recorded history the Tlingit had established villages up and down the Alexander Archipelago and into the interior toward where the Canadian border now lies. Beyond the permanent winter settlements, summer fish camps were places where families put up fish to take back to the winter village after the fishing season. After a hard day's work, everyone gathered around a fire pit to share the ancient legends passed down from their ancestors—tales of daring adventure with didactic lessons to inspire the present generation and pass on to the next. As was the custom, these camps were "owned," or more aptly stewarded by certain clans, and for the Kupreanof (Kake) Tlingit, their fish camp was located at the north end of Mitkof Island, where remnants of early fish weirs and petroglyphs have been carbon-dated at 2,000 BP.[1]

In the 1800s Tlingit Chief John Lott was an influential leader, although little is known of his life or clan.[2] We can imagine, however, that he witnessed an old world fading and a new one thrust upon him, as did other Tlingit communities adjusting to a modern era and the introduction of foreign fisherman plying a trade on Southeast Alaska waters. By the early 1900s, in Lingit Aani, Tlingit territory, "there was a merging of two cultures—the indigenous and European immigrants."[3] The life and times of the Kake Tlingit and the Norwegians provide a vantage point for witnessing change and persistence as several ethnic groups lived side by side and together built a thriving cannery system in the Alexander Archipelago.

It was the LeConte Glacier that first caught the eye of Norwegian immigrant Peter Buschmann in 1899, filling him with hopes for business ventures. The ice was a perfect medium for packing and shipping salmon to destinations as far away as San Francisco, and Buschmann began by barging supplies up north to build a plant. Upon its completion, he named the facility the Icy Strait Packing Company and also added an accompanying sawmill for his lumber needs, all located on the north end of Mitkof Island, where Wrangell Narrows meets Frederick Sound.[4]

There was a need for ready boats and nets, and after disembarking at Ketchikan in 1894, Peter Buschmann bought a sixty-foot schooner, the *Volunteer*, and used the vessel to scout for promising locations to start processing plants, similar to his already functioning salmon saltery near Taku Point, which was a big enough success to be listed in the 1903 *Congressional Record* as one of the more productive sites in Alaska.[5] But Peter Buschman was a cautious man, and while pursuing other projects, he continued to work for other canneries to increase his savings and the investment capital necessary to expand, and by 1895, he believed he had an adequate labor force to incorporate the Quadra Packing Company. Nonetheless, always concerned about finances, he continued to work as a cannery superintendent at Dundas Bay.[6]

Amid the usual grind and long hours, Peter Buschmann envisioned opportunities for further expansion and with his oldest son, August, a strong partnership was solidified. On a summer day in 1896 the senior Buschmann dropped off his seventeen-year-old son at a place he thought might be a good location for another cannery, giving him and his companion, a Tlingit man named Paul, orders to investigate the island. If the location appeared suitable, he wanted the men to build a cabin to satisfy the trade and manufacturing laws, which required all homesteads or businesses make improvements to the property within a certain timeframe.[7] The fishing grounds appeared to be productive, with a good anchorage point for scows and other boats, and the two men built a modest cannery with minimal and somewhat crude machinery. There are no records of what the Tlingit might have said about these new buildings, but the strip of land located at the north end of Wrangell Narrows was called Gantiyakw Seédi or Steamboat Channel by the Tlingit, so named for the ships that passed through the area.

By 1900 the Icy Straits Packing Company and sawmill were completed on the southeastern shore of Wrangell Narrows, and the town was named Petersburg after the founder, who continued building new canneries and salteries along the coast as funds would permit. According to August Buschmann's later account, his father established a fishing station at Swanson's Harbor, located not far from Point Couvenden at the junction of Icy Straits and Lynn Canal, where he constructed the first pile fish trap, increasing the number of traps in 1902 with the intention of building another large cannery at this location. Unfortunately, Peter Buschmann ran out of cash and was forced to declare bankruptcy, leaving his investors with no returns, many of them family or local men. Racked with guilt, Peter Buschman committed suicide in 1903.[8]

Brothers August and Eigel took over the family business and were forced to navigate a rocky road of start-ups, failures, and stopgap measures to survive. Although rapid turnover in cannery ownership was characteristic for the era, the next time interval for the Buschmann family was particularly shaky, both financially and organizationally, marked by suspicious investment companies and unlucky mergers. Luckily, the salmon industry was entering its heyday with an abundance of capital and chance takers. In 1902 the cannery was incorporated under the Pacific Packing and Navigation Company, but it was closed in 1903, 1904, and 1905 due to poor salmon runs, a common problem in these waters. The Pacific Packing and Navigation Company backed the Buschmanns for a while despite the bad years, until the "eastern capitalists" ran out of patience and the plant was purchased through a property sale by the conglomerate Northwestern Fisheries Company in 1905. Although the Buschmann brothers were ambitious, fate constantly caused stormy waters, and instead of being captains of their ship, they were often marooned and at the mercy of capital bestowed by absentee owners.[9] In 1906 the facility changed hands once again and came under the ownership of the Pacific Coast and Norway Packing Company, which already had a cannery at the well-known and thriving Tonka site on Wrangell Narrows. In 1915 the original Buschmann cannery was leased to the Petersburg Packing Company, composed of stockholders of the old company, who now felt safe to take a risk in the more favorable financial climate.[10] With the stockholders' money the Buschmann family incrementally developed new facilities from Ketchikan to Hoonah, setting up what looked to be a potential cannery empire. The Buschmann brothers, however, never forgot the shaky past and maintained supplemental employment, particularly during those times when the salmon runs were no longer plentiful and predictable.

From the early 1900s there had been a great quantity of money exchanging hands, particularly in the hub of San Francisco, which continued to expand its interests in transportation. Controlling cargo was efficient and increased the ability of the bigger companies to swallow up weaker companies, thereby strengthening corporate colonialism. Although the Buschmann family was successful on several fronts, they were at the mercy of industrialists making the rules, and as hard as they worked, they never truly owned their businesses outright. That was a typical status of the time, however, as even the large companies were in competition with the Alaska Packers' Association (APA), a fierce monopoly controlling the fate of Southeast Alaska's cannery industry.

By the turn of the century, the APA dominated the canned-salmon market on the West Coast and Alaska, intensifying the conditions in which a small group of capitalists competed for a resource, or an oligopoly.[11] The rise of the APA was meteoric. Packers, determined to increase their influence economically and politically, had pooled their sizable assets together to create a monolith. Francis Cutting, who had been connected with the early Sitka cannery, was one of the first directors and members looked to him for his knowledge of the Alaska market. In this capacity Cutting led the way to founding the permanent organization, incorporated in 1893. It quickly became the largest salmon-canning co-operative on the West Coast, with a fleet of ships in the *Star* line that traveled back and forth from their headquarters in San Francisco to Southeast Alaska and later throughout Alaska.[12]

The dominance of the APA cannot be overstated. Alaska natural resource economist Richard A. Cooley provides dozens of examples of the association's greed and ability to pay a minimum in taxes. Looking back at Metlakatla, William Duncan had some inflammatory rhetoric aimed at this organization, which he labeled a syndicate. It was well known that several canneries and fishing fleets were controlled by the APA, and Duncan was convinced that they wanted to "kill" all competitors and their harvest methods threatened future fishing in the area. Duncan charged them with recklessly disobeying the few laws that were in force while fishery agents turned their backs on the worst abuses. He clamored that "backed by their great wealth and emboldened by the lenient application of fishing laws, the APA . . . now was determined to fish without limits or regard for the rights of others." The consequence would be "a calamity" that would result in the end of salmon life in Southeast Alaska.[13]

Despite the absolute tyranny of the APA and the big outfits, the irony was that nothing could be accomplished without labor—workers were indispensable, more than mere cogs in the industrial machine. Buschmann, unlike other packers, hired almost exclusively Scandinavian foremen, who played an important role in the start-up of operations but rarely stayed in the position long. They instead wanted to purchase their own boat and work independently, chasing money and adventure. Conversely, processors, usually Southeast Alaska Natives, were steadily employed but underappreciated. If it were not for their work, salmon would not be processed, packed, and loaded onto the steamers. It should be noted that before the Europeans arrived, Tlingit men were fishing for Buschmann's canneries, yet as the century unfolded the salient point was that all members of the operation were dependent on the continuation of salmon runs if there was to be any business at all. The Buschmann family faced a tricky balancing act to have enough money to run the equipment, afford labor, and manage unpredictable salmon runs.

As early as 1904, fishery officials were alarmed at the unhealthy salmon escapement and attempted to solve the problem through fishing restrictions, which severely curtailed canning efforts. Compelled to diversify, August Buschmann acquired a contract to provide herring for the Killisnoo fertilizer plant, belonging to the Alaska Oil and Guano Company, formerly a whaling station and an ancient Tlingit camp. Unlike other businesses of the time, the Killisnoo plant was doing well, and August remarked that the company had three steamers, four scows, and two fishing gangs composed of "forty-five whites, fifty Indians, and a few Chinamen."[14]

For the time being August made a comfortable living at the Killisnoo plant, shipping oil and other products to San Francisco, Portland, Hawaii, and England, and he also engaged in whaling while it was still profitable. He added freelance trips to the "neighboring bays and brought home a load of fish" to sell locally, appearing to enjoy working on his own and escaping the drudgery of management and the bickering between fishermen and processors at the plants.[15] All the while he was waiting for the time he could rebuild and expand the family business when the financial climate was not so inclement.

The Buschmann story stands out as a variant from the norm. Although many Norwegians and other Scandinavians had plied Alaskan waters for years, it was unusual for an immigrant to start up a business, particularly a risky business like labor-intensive canneries. European fishing in Alaska, however, can be traced back to the early Russians and later those from eastern Europe, such as Croatians and Slavs. Norwegians were relative newcomers to these fishing grounds. Scandinavian immigrants had first settled in the Midwest and only a few headed toward the Pacific Coast, but by 1910 Norwegians and Swedes made up a large proportion of the fishing fleet around Kodiak and Prince William Sound, where many found the landscape much like the home they had left. Some were lured by Buschmann's advertisements, which boasted that Petersburg was a Norwegian oasis, and as more people settled in the small hamlet, a Nordic revival took place, particularly when they gathered to celebrate holidays amid the glaciers and hills so reminiscent of Norway. In the large cannery facility, the town participated in traditional dances like the Hambo and Springar, taking breaks to sample the familiar fish and potato dishes as the town became known as "Little Norway," with a prominent fishing fleet and culture.

As Buschmann's business interests grew, there was a corresponding need for more labor, and although Asian workers were available, it was the local Tlingit who remained a vital part of the cannery workforce, dividing their time between subsistence needs and cannery work in a mixed or dual economy. Native women were able to bring home cash for the family and still keep up the traditional gathering of food sources for winter survival, an activity that reduced but did not stop visits to the cannery store. Beyond purely subsistence activities, women often created "Indian curios" to sell at local shops or even along the street, with this becoming more lucrative as the tourist trade increased along with steamship travel. The Tlingit men performed much of the manual labor associated with the cannery, but the women's contributions were steadfastly important.

The Tlingit workers lived in a nearby encampment during the canning season. In the spring of 1900 the buildings had been completed with a thousand-foot plank walk connecting the Native village to the cannery. In addition, if a Native family decided to settle permanently in the area, they were provided the necessary lumber to build a home and smokehouse.[16] When the *Albatross* docked to make an inspection, Captain Jefferson Moser commented on the attractive surroundings and well-built houses, stating "it was a good advertisement," perhaps for the long existing steamship route. By 1910 the original Kupreanof Island Plant was packing sixty thousand cases of salmon a year and Petersburg was nationally known as a major port, employing the Tlingit, Europeans, and a few Chinese men.[17] Almost from the beginning the Tlingit and the Scandinavians worked together, at times intermarrying and forming blended families and cultures with common threads; yet not all ethnic differences were erased, and there were tensions.

Shortly before his death Peter Buschmann had purchased the Bartlett Cove operation in Glacier Bay and placed his son August in charge. At that time the crew consisted of about fifty employees from Hoonah, a Tlingit village on Chichagof Island. Initially Buschmann had been handicapped by not having modern equipment to make his businesses cost effective, and he concentrated solely on salted fish. Two hundred barrels of red salmon were processed the first season, and the profit was reinvested in the necessary infrastructure and expansion.[18] The Tlingit, who possessed both superior fishing and processing skills, brought their talents to the operation, while the Scandinavians, who had known fishing as a way of life from their mother country, kept the business afloat by any means possible. The Buschmanns prospered with the help of the Tlingit, illustrating not only how expedient alliances were made but also how important both the immigrants and indigenous people were to the industrialization of Alaska.

The Tlingit women were "inside workers," while Scandinavian and Native men fished for both the cannery and their families. Kake fisherman Roy Bean spoke about the changing times back then. When he was out on his boat he stayed at the site of the traditional summer camp, which allowed fishermen to harvest salmon nearby and stay close to their families. Bean, who fished near Petersburg in customary waters, described the setting: "They have a camp they put up there right where they going to fish all the time, you know, and they come in at night, after they come in and live with their family." He spoke of the seiner's camps "around Petersburg, or Mitkof Island, and then Red Bay." Bean remembered that the money was good; fishermen could keep their nets and equipment in good shape and purchase the most modern gear. Bean, who had started seining with his uncle in 1909, was adamant that the Tlingit would "continue on fishing just as long as there is fish to be caught, just as long as the cannery men wants the fish," stressing the economic and social tie between the independent fisherman and processors.[19] It was well understood that fishing remained the center of the Native livelihood regardless of variations in technology, cannery management, or the advent of conservation regulations that were creeping in with more governmental controls on the valuable Alaskan fishing grounds. These new patterns had a decided effect on villages and towns.[20]

The two forms of economy, subsistence and fish factory, merged, as David Arnold aptly described: "To the Tlingit and Haida people, southeastern Alaska was not a virgin wilderness, but a cultural geography of salmon streams, fish camps, Native villages, and canneries."[21] And yet in order not to be left behind, Alaska's original people moved into the industrial age and reconstructed the ancient map of their seascape.[22] While adapting to a new cultural setting, Alaska Natives maintained their ways of life, reaped the benefits of available opportunities, never vanishing as a people, as the assimilators had hoped they would. Instead the cannery business coupled with the continuance of subsistence fishing kept families grounded in indigenous traditions as they continued to offer their expertise on salmon harvesting and processing. The Native fishermen were also the first to observe that the once abundant streams were ecologically unhealthy, much sooner than the canning companies or government would admit. Once the scarcity was undeniable and in the true capitalist spirit, the plan was not to conserve, or reduce harvest limits, but rather to make more fish.

On a cultural level, this overfishing and apparent disrespect for salmon created problems. In the Tlingit and Haida culture, children were taught from a young age to honor all natural resources—fish were not a commodity—but now Native fishermen and cannery workers were asked to exploit salmon runs to fit the needs of an industrial economy. What were they to do? The alternatives were to work for health of the waterways or be a part of the workforce. It was difficult to do both. Fishermen were also wary of fishing in the areas that were traditionally owned by other clans, another tenet of their cultural base. The set of problems come under the rubric of moral ecology or moral economy, which David Arnold defined, in part, as how a group regards the environmental sources (now commodities) and local economy as being bound by "tradition, community standards, and fairness," and specifically where common fishing grounds were "managed informally by local communities rather than private holders, corporations, or distant bureaucracies."[23]

If a genuine moral ecology had been followed, the resource and the fishermen's livelihood might have been sustained, but when self-interest is involved these pathways are shaped by modes of production to increase efficiency and ultimately profit. In the case of the Southeast Alaska fisheries, this meant that new technology—such as fish butchering machines, stronger and larger nets, fish traps, and hydraulic brailing—allowing a quicker, more robust catch to the detriment of future runs and escapement (the ability of fish to "escape" to their spawning grounds). As a consequence, to continue to participate in fishing or canning, indigenous workers had to adapt further or convert their ethics and mores in response to contemporary developments, although the window had been left open for resistance.[24] Yet beyond theoretical presumptions, salmon were finite, and there were numerous quandaries within scientific ecology.

It was not only the Alaska Native harvesters who noticed the decrease in salmon runs. August and Eigel Buschmann understood that some years the fish did not come in at the usual sites, motivating them to set up operations at other locations on a test basis. For example, August explained that at Chatham Strait the runs had been tremendous in 1900, but by 1902 they could only pack 20,000 cases when they were expecting to pack 60,000 using "14 hand seine boats covering Chatham Strait, Icy Strait, Chichagof Island, and Baranof Island," where Sitka is located.[25] Because of the unreliability of salmon stocks, there was a need to diversify beyond the consistent halibut and herring harvest and open new markets, which explains why during the 1904–5 season August was operating a steamer for the Killisnoo fertilizer plant in addition to having a contract to deliver shiploads of the more undesirable dog salmon for distribution to the Japanese government. The mention of the Japanese may sound odd in this context, but in a global perspective, this was during time of the Russo-Japanese War and Japan was unable to acquire salmon from its usual Siberian sources because of the tensions. Alaska was a natural alternative, principally because of its geopolitical location within the region, promoting a further introduction into the world market.

During these difficult times August managed a government-owned hatchery on the west coast of Prince of Wales Island at Hunter's Bay as part of the newly instituted salmon conservation program. It was also at this location the brothers proudly announced they had built the first power seine boat in Alaska, a gear type that would become the mainstay of the Southeast Alaska fishing industry.[26] Eventually the purse seine fleets would come under question because this gear type acted as a wide-ranging net, capable of capturing the major portion of a salmon run. Once the fish were within the net, it was pulled up like the string of an old-fashioned drawstring purse. The political debates centered on this gear type as equivalent to a fish trap and capable of promoting overfishing, but August did not concern himself with this matter since he believed the hatcheries were the answer to any potential problem.

The advent of hatcheries and resource conservation marked a change in oversight management. Beginning in the late 1800s the federal government had noted problems with the fish stock, and there were accusations about the extreme wastage. Scientists, however, assured the Bureau of Fisheries that a hatchery program would be so successful in Alaska that eventually the government would not be involved at all, which pleased both the overstretched federal bureaus and the cannery owners. In May 1900 regulations required "each company taking salmon from Alaska waters to establish a suitable hatchery and to return red salmon to the spawning grounds at the rate of at least four times the number of fish taken the preceding season."[27]

At the Hetta Lake Hatchery, located on the southern edge of Prince of

Wales Island and operating from 1899 to 1917, August acted as an accountant and was also responsible for submitting government reports. Although owned by the Northwest Fisheries Company, the hatchery operated as a non-profit to meet the government's requirements and was funded by a modest fishermen's assessment and cost recovery profits from the fish packing company. What this meant in reality was that the Northwest Fisheries Company could offset any financial losses through the fees earned by operating the hatchery on fishing grounds already well-known for record sockeye harvests.[28] Without the government's knowledge, these hatcheries turned into profitable ventures, particularly when owners manipulated the records to gain further federal subsidies.[29] A hint of these shady dealings was noted by fishery agent Howard M. Kutchin in his 1900 report as he lamented that when he toured the facilities, the hatchery operators would show the agent what they wanted him to see, and any profits could hidden from view through clever bookkeeping.[30]

August did not care for the confines of the Hetta Lake cannery, and after earning his steamer pilot's license, he traveled to other canneries over a wide distance, making stops at the many ports to visit with other cannery men and see what was going on in the industry. During World War I he had the opportunity to share this knowledge when he was appointed as a dollar-a-year man by President Woodrow Wilson, serving as a consultant and advisor on the Alaska salmon industry. He developed a proficiency in problems associated with shipping to the wartime front, and later in the century he was selected as a member of the Fact Finding Board, organized under the United States Department of Labor. The main task was to establish fair salmon prices and labor costs, but he was also called upon to report on fishery conditions.[31] The demand for salmon during World War I had not only expanded competition in the fisheries but also further depleted the resource, leading to a crisis. Simultaneously, federal agencies were gaining momentum, and more fishery agents were making it up to Alaska, which meant the government was getting increasingly involved in the management of the fisheries and canneries, but not necessarily with more understanding of the conditions.

Government agencies often relied on men like August Buschmann to enrich the understanding of northern fisheries, although it was difficult to keep up, due to the changes in the fish stocks and fishing pressure. Simultaneously, population ethnicity was shifting, with more immigrants coming from southern Europe, especially Italy, and making an impact on the cannery scene. San Francisco, Alameda, and Monterey, all in California, supported a large Italian fleet, but many left those waters, drawn by word of Alaska profits. When they arrived on the competitive northern fishing grounds, ethnic tensions escalated, sometimes into brawls.

In the Petersburg area as well as Alaska in general, there was an almost inborn rivalry between the European groups, particularly those from northern Europe versus southern Europe. By the turn of the century there were Germans, Austrians, Italians, Yugoslavians, Croatians, and other immigrants besides the Scandinavians who had made Alaska their home. Many had arrived from the arctic latitudes in Europe and found that the pristine waters and ice caps of the region evoked the image of their homeland. On the political side, the Nordic migrants appreciated the more laissez-faire attitude of the American government, compared to the autocratic regimes from which they had escaped, and they believed they could now control their own destiny and not be held down by poverty.[32] The fishermen were in awe of the liberty they were allowed as frontier fishermen: "Fishing was the free life, the interesting life that saved one from a life in industry and production where the jobs are so darn lackluster."[33] A profit could be made through one's own merits without restrictions; atmosphere and attitude were summed up by Norwegian-born Oscar Otness, who started fishing out of Petersburg in 1922: "There wasn't much money to make, but I think people were just as happy."[34] These were good years fishing for the canneries, but the waters were choppy.

Ethnic hostilities heated up among the Europeans and anger turned into name-calling and outright violence when antipathy reached a breaking point against the backdrop of rigorous commercial fishing and relentless one-upmanship.[35] These attitudes were not left out on the fishing boats but entered the public forum, whether at the bars or on the docks, building an us-against-them mentality, particularly between the Scandinavians and the Italians. Both groups thought they held more expertise on the fishing grounds and possessed superior gear. It was true that Italians had perfected their own type of net, which was adopted by the general industry because of its effectiveness, but to counter those claims, Scandinavians boasted that they were permanent residents, while the Italians were seasonal and had less claim to the local resources, an assertion that appeared plausible.

The Italians had faced discrimination from the moment they set foot on American shores and had struggled with stereotypes in tandem with the red scare phenomenon that singled out suspected Bolshevists, including people from southern or eastern Europe. "Denouncing Slavs, Jews, Italians and Greeks, as racially inferior and inassimilable, American nativists sought to restrict their immigration," even setting up groups such as the Immigration Restriction League (IRL). The IRL had numerous chapters throughout the country and often grabbed newspaper headlines in their efforts to focus on increasing northern European (Scandinavian) immigration while banning other European immigrants. This persuasive propaganda filtered into the public sentiment, and by 1924 crippling legislation restricted these allegedly inferior people and thwarted future immigration, seriously affecting the labor force.[36]

When the fishermen and their families relocated from northern California to Southeast Alaska, conflict persisted and ethnic differences were manifested in "vicious tribalism" that further segmented "the salmon fishery into racial and ethnic categories," recomposing the social construction of the fishery. Yet there was more to this human dynamic. Despite the antagonism between European fisherman, there were times they banded together in a mutual distrust of "Indian fishermen, Asian cannery workers, and women." These targeted groups became further marginalized based on a cultural philosophy that viewed fishing as "white man's work" and superior to the toil of processing fish in a cold, steel environment.[37]

Scandinavians had already grouped together on the Columbia River and in the Puget Sound region, while in San Francisco the Italians had been at the forefront in creating associations and unions, and both ethnic groups carried that sense of solidarity up to Alaska, occasionally creating informal protective units to support their temporary communities and enclaves, and to offer a shield against the disparaging remarks, actions, or bias in the marketplace. These loose associations followed similar group patterns that had been established of organizing situational snag unions (which collectively cleared the fishing grounds of snags) or other protective fraternities.[38] Deterrents, either individual or governmental, were anything that stood in the way of profit. These loosely formed associations did not last long, but in retrospect they were the building blocks for the eventual fishermen's union movement.

One of the largest unions encompassing the entire Pacific Coast and Alaska was the Alaska Fishermen's Union (AFU), founded by Italians in 1902, and one of the most powerful organizations in Alaska's fishing business. When the burgeoning AFU merged forces with the APA, a monolith was produced that firmly tied fishing and cannery operations together, naturally shaping the industry socially, economically, legally, and politically. According to Arnold's assessment, it was a racial hierarchy. Privileged white fishermen received better pay and conditions, while Native fishermen and cannery workers fell another rung closer to the ground. The AFU also protected its members by effectively shutting out others, including Native fishermen, who were deemed unskilled and unable to compete. The AFU "perpetuated racial division" and unwittingly fueled resistance from the ranks of resident Alaskans, Natives, and women, a situation gradually evolving into the stimulus for a grassroots populist movement. Before that time, however, the AFU and APA expanded the "colonial pattern of exploitation where outsiders plundered the region and left locals with the ecological wreckage but none of the spoils."[39] Historically this simmered for two decades until Alaskans, although diverse, realized that absentee conglomerates, lobby groups, and ethnic unions had enveloped their life and well-being.

In retrospect, the human dynamics of us-against-them can be analyzed in many twists and turns, but the ethnic differences remained deeply embedded and did not disappear. As far back as the 1890s Jefferson Moser, captain of the USS *Albatross*, described the situation in no uncertain terms: "The cannery fishermen are nearly all foreigners," the majority from Europe, and some fishing gangs were called "dagoes consisting of Italians Greeks and the like. When these two classes form different fishing gangs for the same cannery, the north country crew is referred to as the white crew."[40] The *San Francisco Daily News* observed that most of the fishermen were "Latins from Monterey and San Francisco bays and Scandinavians from the Columbia River and Puget Sound and they did not mix anymore than oil and water."[41] Alaska was becoming increasingly multinational and in addition to the hard feelings between the European fishermen and the Asian or Native cannery workers, there was also antagonism between European northerners and southerners—the Finns, Icelanders, Russians, Norwegians, Swedes, Danes, and Dutch kept their distance from the Italians, Portuguese, and Sicilians. For the most part this ethnic rivalry was confined to the fishing grounds, but the Tlingit villages and settlements could not remain untouched.

While the Italians and Norwegians were scuffling about in their power struggle, Tlingit fishermen, who often had wives or sisters working for the canneries, felt the sting of discrimination and realized a need to combine their resources to combat "cannery operators that favored Euro-American fishermen over Indian fishermen and Asian cannery workers."[42] Furthermore, as the outside fishermen gained greater status, Alaska Natives could not stand by and watch their lands and rights slip away. From village to village, there was a call to unify, while the Tlingit, Haida, and Tsimshian found themselves unwilling participants in a rapidly moving political scene that set them up as rivals to the immigrants, whether Asian or European. Simultaneously, as Alaska's position in the nation grew more prominent, largely based on industrialization, politicians found they could no longer ignore this place that had been referred to as merely a wilderness, consisting of igloos and mountain men.

Petersburg's cannery history presents a glimpse into a microcosm of the overall industry, but one must be aware that by the early 1900s there were many canneries beyond Southeast Alaska, extending to the south-central region at Cordova in Prince William Sound, and Bristol Bay in southwest Alaska, soon to be the largest salmon fishery in the world. Southeast

Alaska fish factories competed locally and regionally in conjunction with the growing knowledge that the fisheries could provide a source of revenue for the fledging territory. From an indigenous economy, Native communities entered an era of corporate colonialism that entangled and pulsated through every aspect of Alaska life as the territory struggled to sustain its existence and throw off oppressive bondage.

Bureaucratic agencies were the most imposing, yet the least helpful for the struggling political economy. The behemoth was the Bureau of Fisheries, an agency ostensibly created to protect the resources but that instead proved ineffectual for conservation purposes or the needs of the territory. Taxation was a sticking point for all. The territory needed the revenue, but the federal government countered with their evaluation that taxes would "seriously impair the industry by making it unprofitable." E. Lester Jones, the deputy commissioner of fisheries, felt it necessary to emphasize that federal agencies like his own were the only bodies that could adequately monitor the vast fisheries, as opposed leaving this to local control.[43] Clearly, besides ethnic tensions in the fishery, there was friction between the independent fishermen, the cannery owners, and the government—whatever affected the fishermen also trickled down to the cannery workers.

The Metlakatla and Petersburg stories offer exceptional views of how intense competition in Southeast Alaska escalated, amplifying an already stealthy political web. Southeast Alaska had gone from a group of Tlingit and Haida villages to a cosmopolitan region with a diverse immigrant population. Whether Native, European, or Asian, people all labored side by side in the same confines, not so different from their counterparts in Seattle, San Francisco, Monterey, or Salinas, packing sardines or peaches. Despite the obstacles, bridges were built due to the symbiotic nature of the industry, and a sense of cultural pluralism allowed the acceptance of differences in these cannery towns, largely because everyone was thrown together. Each culture kept its foundation as a buoy in turbulent waters, but there was enough overlap to develop a comfortable kinship. European hegemonies might have existed, but they were broken down by the mutual nature of the work, life's challenges, Alaska's isolation, and the social events that brought communities together.

In the early part of the twentieth century immigrants and adventure seekers continued to arrive in Southeast Alaska, many sailing from San Francisco's Golden Gate bridge, and as one old-timer reminisced: "Italians and Swedes swabbing down, stowing shore gear, and settling in for a long haul North with a last jug, a crib board, and soiled decks of pinochle and pan and poker; the gulls wheeling, the ship's bow rising, falling, rising again on the long, slow rollers; the tang of salt and tar, again on the horizon the promise of the season."[44]

5

Salmon and the Politics of Corporate Capitalism

After the first canneries were running in Southeast Alaska it did not take long for the on-site bosses to develop a total disregard for the salmon harvest while the industry was controlled by out-of-territory interests with no regard for the biological conditions in these northern waters. There were few natural resource laws, except the ones built by avarice. Fishermen took as many fish as possible while the canneries processed salmon sometimes for twenty-four hours a day, seven days a week, using only two shifts of exhausted workers. Simultaneously, former Tlingit waterways and forest lands were taken over to build more facilities, infrastructure, bunkhouses, salmon crates, and fish traps. These trends endangered the existence of the first people of the land, obligated to adjust to the circumstances without legal recourse. While Alaska fought to enhance its national standing, Alaska Natives unified to gain civil rights. In this struggle canneries provided the setting for a showdown between local government, resident fishermen, labor, and corporate interests.

In 1905 Alaska had sent its first congressional delegate to Washington DC, but little changed until 1909, when a vibrant leader, Delegate James Wickersham, imbued with Progressive Era philosophy, became the territory's foremost representative, employing an odd combination of business acumen, political finesse, and self-aggrandizement. Alaska historian Stephen Haycox describes Wickersham this way: an "able politician with a nimble mind and iron determination, he emerged as the territory's most effective advocate."[1] With the growing awareness of Alaska's potential wealth, Wickersham jockeyed between the voice of the general populace and the growing number of industrial magnates with names like Rockefeller, Vanderbilt, Carnegie, Morgan, and especially Guggenheim, all interested in increasing their wealth in this era of rapacious corporations and steely trustbusters. Wickersham knew the law; he had served as city attorney in Tacoma, Washington, and in the Washington state legislature before being appointed as Alaska's third district judge. These experiences had built a consummate politician with a flair for the dramatic and the ability to move freely move in diverse circles, which made him the one to be sought out to get things done. During his long career he learned, in most cases, how to compromise without being compromised.

From his early political years Wickersham had been interested in Alaska Native issues, which differed from the Native American problems found in the continental United States. One of the conditions that set Alaska Natives apart from tribal communities in the states was the absence of reservations or treaties, muddying the waters concerning designated land bases or binding agreements. Metlakatla was the closest to the definition of "Indian Country," with corresponding privileges, yet it was an executive reserve, not a reservation, and so did not qualify as a sovereign entity. There was also no organized tribal body that spoke for the people. The established Tlingit, Haida, and Tsimshian social organization was desegregated by clan affiliation and allegiance, without a comprehensive unified force. Moreover, Alaska Natives were village-based rather than tribal and did not fit the parameters of federal Indian policy.

What alternatives were available? In 1884 the first Organic Act had been passed, which instituted civil government. Within the act was a clause regarding indigenous inhabitants, stipulating that they would not be disturbed on the lands they occupied or otherwise claimed, although the exact interpretation of this premise was murky. In 1906 the Homestead Act was modified for Alaska Natives, whereby they could acquire 160 acres of land if they could show they were fully assimilated, but who was to be an impartial judge for this ruling? In most cases the Homestead

Act was unsuitable for Southeast Alaska Native customs that combined village life with summer camps, reinforcing the established land and water use patterns. The situation was further problematic with employment in canneries or as fishermen, which might confuse or mar rights and duties. These issues, however, would be tackled by Wickersham, placing him in an odd situation between the corporate capitalists and emerging Native leaders.

Divergent attitudes in Alaska and Washington DC muddled Wickersham's commitments while he straddled settings and issues to keep the territory afloat by developing the natural resources, yet also defended aboriginal title. Though he had no congressional voting power, he would not be silenced, and one of his highest causes centered on liberating the territory from the strangling monopoly held by the packing companies, dubbed the "fish trust." Without restriction, these industrial complexes were permitted to harvest Alaska's resources with limited taxation, and these revenues were necessary to fill Alaska's governmental coffers and vital for Alaska's growth. Congress and the Bureau of Fisheries had allowed, even encouraged, large outside canning companies from San Francisco and Seattle to run wild in the territory, importing temporary labor and exporting wealth. Wickersham chastised the packers who had enjoyed huge profits but left not a penny for the people. To remedy the lack of power in this provincial environment, Wickersham promoted the ideas of self-determination and local control as opposed to federal oversight, which had proven ineffective and ignorant of the problems.

At the turn of the century, it was evident that the tight-fisted corporations from the Pacific Coast and on the eastern seaboard had enriched their oligarchies by assuming control over Southeast Alaska in every facet of the industry. One of the most effective tools was to block unfavorable regulation, and at the forefront of this movement was the APA, which had already given smaller operations, like those of the Buschmann family or at Metlakatla, quite a bit of trouble. The absentee company owners wanted to dictate every aspect of the canned-salmon market on the West Coast and Alaska.[2] With this authority, the APA exerted a forceful lobbying effort in Congress, and Wickersham was determined to stand up to the monolith, but this would be difficult because "salmon industrialists often perceived themselves as swashbuckling frontiersmen" bringing economic development to the hinterland and lifting the region to a higher level. These sentiments were not unlike those in other regions of the world where corporate colonialism reigned, and the heads of these big companies fancied themselves as heroic.[3] At first the APA was free to expand its authority until pressure mounted, primarily from Wickersham, and the strategy was altered to appease conservation advocates.

In 1906 David Jarvis, the president of the Northwest Fisheries Company, lobbied Congress for a cessation of all taxes on the condition (and promise) that the company, at their expense, would replenish the waters with hatchery salmon fry. They reasoned that this would qualify them for a tax credit of forty cents per thousand salmon fry liberated into the waters. Of course, there was no agent to make sure this "liberation" took place, and the science was as yet undeveloped. In 1908 the Third Division grand jury exposed how it actually worked: "the Alaska Packers Association alone took over 80,000 cases of salmon from the waters of the third judicial division, paying only thirty-two cents, in currency and certificates in the amount of $32,272 . . . for which no adequate proof was made that any court would admit as sufficient evidence."[4]

While Wickersham continued to fight the APA, or Libby, McNeill & Libby, or Booth Fisheries, a contemporary fisheries agent explained, "The canning factories in Alaska are owned by three or four corporations in San Francisco . . . [and] do not add one dollar to the wealth of the young Territory from which they take millions of dollars annually."[5] The workers who made this all possible were relegated to being the tiniest cogs in the machinery and no doubt knew little about the political manipulation from big business or the Washington DC deliberations. Although it was said that Wickersham had the backing of the common people—miners, fishermen, loggers, and shopkeepers, basically pioneer Alaska—he also faced a land divided between resource extractors and those who believed the lands and waters belonged to Alaskans in perpetuity.[6] To effect solutions, Wickersham attacked the advantage packing houses had in Alaska's economic picture, punctuated by their default exempt taxation status. When he spoke out against the inequities, the cannery interests kept a close eye on him to make sure he did not topple their domain, counting on the prominent voices of owners in Seattle, San Francisco, Portland, and Astoria, who all shared a seat at the head of the table, discouraging all others.

Regardless of Wickersham's effort, the status quo was firmly in place, and nothing changed for years, but he would not be deterred and continued to contest the stranglehold the federal government had on Alaskan affairs and the territory's destiny. In his December 1916 "Address to the People," he promised to work for the "passage of laws by Congress for the extension of the powers of the Alaska Legislature over fisheries and fur bearing animals, and the enactment of such laws as will save the fisheries from destruction and encourage the settlement of a population of fishermen along our coast; the enactment of such laws as will require those engaged in Alaska fisheries to pay their just proportion of taxes for the development of Alaska and her government."[7]

While Wickersham pressed for Alaska's autonomy, including the right of taxation, he also championed sound natural resource policy. In his testimony before Congress he argued that long distance oversight did not contribute to fishery longevity, and he carried this message through several appearances before the House Committee on Merchant Marine and Fisheries, reporting on salmon stock devastation and imploring the body to make laws to aid restoration. For any recovery or conservation measures to be effective, however, it would take money and talent. Finally, the House Committee agreed with Wickersham and reversed a clause that previously prevented "the legislature from imposing other and additional taxes or licenses," and now taxes could be legally collected on the cannery harvest and production.[8] Wickersham had scored a small victory, and he wrote in his diary that he was "jubilant" over the bill's passage, but his elation was tempered by the knowledge he might have alienated key political and business allies in the process, possibly affecting his career.[9] In the Progressive Era there was an emphasis on reforms in industrialization and addressing political corruption, but not all politicians bought into this clean-up effort, and it was a tricky calculation to know how to approach such transformations and continue to command influence in Congress and at home. Meanwhile, the cannery owners were forced to take a defensive stance and fight with any tools at their disposal, including the courts.

Wickersham watched the cannery conglomerates ride roughshod over him and Alaska, inspiring him to lead "a scathing attack on the bureau (of fisheries) and the Fish Trust," claiming these monopolies used the legislature to tighten its rein on the salmon industry.[10] Putting pen to paper, he sent a letter to President Woodrow Wilson, charging that the industry and the Bureau of Fisheries were in collusion, and it was a public scandal "without law and quite without aid to the development of Alaska." Wickersham declared that the president was the only one who could turn this situation around.[11] No action followed his protest, and a year later Wickersham was still in combat mode when he testified that the gross fishery products taken between 1867 and 1916 were about $247,363,828, to the devastation of Alaska's fisheries and without benefit to the people. His ire was palpable as he proclaimed he had tried for seven years to change the laws so that revenue could be collected to build churches, schools, and other necessary infrastructure, but instead the fish trust took everything out of the territory without adding anything to the well-being of Alaska, and in essence, they were "robbing the territory."[12]

Undaunted, Wickersham continued his dual fight to save the fisheries and collect taxes from the out-of-territory packing houses, all the while believing a successful resolution to these issues would also help the Alaska Native cause. He had been meeting with Tlingit and Haida leaders, who were talking about organizing and fighting for their civil rights and striking out for land claims. To Wickersham, the Native issues and the problems that were visited upon the Alaskan population as a whole were not separate. If Alaska could collect due compensation for the fish and timber it supplied to the other states and territories, it would result in heightened economic status and a more level playing field. Importantly, Wickersham felt the Tlingit and Haida "were entitled to some remuneration for their fishing and hunting grounds, which had been appropriated by the federal government without a treaty."[13] Reforming Indian policy, a characteristic of the Progressive Era, motivated Wickersham to assist in organizing Southeast Alaska Natives to fight for equality and citizenship while the assimilating forces were muted, to make room for self-determination, local management, and respect for Native property. To do so, there was a suspension of the missionary "civilization" methods and the "vanishing Indian" assumption.[14]

When Alaska's second legislature passed a law taxing cases of canned salmon shipped from Alaska, there was hope that a revenue base could be built.[15] Predictably, the industry responded to the threat of taxation and subsequent dip in their profits by taking the matter to the Alaska District Court, which upheld the tax, but the controversy did not die there. The cannery companies continued to fight and appealed their case through the United States Supreme Court in *Alaska Pacific Fisheries v. Territory of Alaska*, whereby the defendant, Alaska Pacific Fisheries Company, representing the canners, questioned the constitutionality of the law that empowered the Territory "to recover taxes claimed to be due under an act of the Legislature of the Territory of Alaska for prosecuting the business of fishing for and canning salmon for Alaska."[16] The Supreme Court, however, would not fully review the arguments or circumstances since it was not within the court's purview to acknowledge claims brought by "writ of error" and therefore the court could not conclude on the merits of the question. As with several legal cases involving Alaska, the disposition of the argument was settled on a procedural basis as opposed to through laws or the Constitution.[17]

In essence, the Supreme Court had washed its hands of the controversy, claiming the matter was not within its jurisdiction, and by default endorsed Alaska's right to charge the license tax. Wickersham's initial "jubilance" over the passage of the bill permitting taxation was reinforced, but of course, the APA and other wealthy cannery outfits would not admit defeat. In order to make up for the alleged deficit, the cannery owners decreased worker wages or created business losses on their books. Either way the packers continued amassing sizable earnings, carefully secured in Washington, Oregon, or California banks.[18]

The cannery industry had a decided advantage, but that could not deter Wickersham's push for more congressional bills aimed at the protection and conservation of the fisheries. Also, he attempted to tackle workers' rights, believing the Alaska Natives should rightfully have jobs before immigrants.[19] In these endeavors, however, he had an antagonist with nascent fishery unions. In the early 1900s labor alliances were forming, and one of the strongest was the Alaska Fishermen's Union, based in San Francisco. The AFU gained such clout that other smaller alliances could not compete, yet that made little difference when World War I temporarily halted union activity, and the workers' plight was forgotten in the scramble to fill canning production quotas. Prices soared as the focus shifted to the war effort and the needs of the boys overseas. That is, until November 1918, when that market fell away and production came to a screeching halt. The sudden decline in salmon demand produced a glut, further complicated by the competing Japanese-owned canneries in Siberia.[20]

In the aftermath of World War I, revenue raising was inconsequential compared to the issues brought on by the ensuing recession. The industry tried to stay alive, although it was obvious the salmon runs were depleted. The canned salmon production frenzy during the war had temporarily concealed the damage to the fish stock numbers, but the big companies realized they needed to find an answer. Frank M. Warren, president of the Alaska Portland Packers Association, a prominent company in Southeast Alaska waters, spoke to the packers and was forthright with his convictions: "We have been overfishing the country generally, there is no doubt about that, and one main essential that we have to consider . . . is whether we have borrowed from the future, and whether we are going to get the packs of salmon in the future."[21]

The unmasking of the issues prompted a few in Congress to respond to the crisis and recommend safeguarding measures with the assistance of the Bureau of Fisheries. While the cannery owners were scurrying around looking for business, Wickersham and others of like mind proposed fishery regulations, which developed into another thorn in the side of the out-of-territory packing houses, whose owners rejected the idea that there was a permanent problem. To be effective, Wickersham hunted down stalwart allies in Alaska and Washington DC, but he also had to contend with world events and how the war's aftermath filtered into local politics.

During the period 1900–1915 there was an influx of more than fifteen million immigrants into the United States, most from southern and eastern Europe. They did not speak English and had a difficult time fitting into the tempo of American life, creating social problems. Politicians attempted to solve these issues through legislation, but nothing eased the chaos, and anger built up in those who felt their livelihood and way of life were threatened. In Alaska the population dynamics were slightly different in that many of these immigrants worked either in mining or for canneries, and the largest percentage were Asians, not Europeans. For the time being the Asians were seen as necessary and remained carefully cloistered out of sight in bunkhouses. Since Alaska was cut off from the American scene, news of social turmoil was slow to arrive, but with steamer travel and newspapers, Alaska was eventually informed of the growing national attitude.

Historically, the year 1919 is associated with a phenomenon known as the "Red Scare," or the fear of all things related to Soviet communism, alleged German tyranny, or the 1917 Bolshevik Revolution that resulted in the overthrow of the Russian monarchy. When analyzing the Red Scare, author John Higham, who studied the impact of foreigners on the national thinking, concluded: "On Armistice Day, a close observer might have guessed that the anti-radical tradition would make trouble for the immigrants. . . . It is unlikely that he could have predicted the full fury of the Big Red Scare. Who could have foreseen that the emotions stirred up by the war would persist so violently into the postwar era?"[22] The nation's sentiments toward immigrants grew increasingly hostile after World War I, fueled by the need to blame something or someone for the economic woes.[23] Fear of Russians or Germans expanded into a wider hatred for all immigrants, and the intensification of Americanism or that blend of ardent patriotism supported by a quasi-spiritual manifesto, and a belief in one group's innate superiority in a fierce nativism.

Populism and ultra-patriotism were at the core of the Red Scare that targeted foreign labor, with people seemingly unaware that it was these workers who were responsible for production and holding the operations together. Fueled by the xenophobic atmosphere, there was a demand to justify hiring immigrants, who, it was feared, "carried the seeds of radicalism and the brawn to attack the socioeconomic fiber of the nation."[24] Any dissent from immigrants was seen as communist-inspired and dangerous. To all intents and purposes, the "nation that emerged after World War I was less tolerant of ethnic and racial minorities [than at] any time in history."[25] What did this national fervor have to do with provincial Alaska?

One might think that world events or attitudes an ocean away would have had little impact in Alaska, but that perception discounts the lure of yellow journalism, even if only an outdated newspaper arriving on a steamer. Alaskans, feeling isolated, craved the news about what was going on outside their little towns. Beyond the reports coming from San Francisco, Seattle, or Portland, Southeast Alaska residents devoured their own local newspapers from Sitka and Juneau, the territory's capital, along with those from another developing cannery hub, Ketchikan, a site quickly becoming a focal point for the fishing and cannery industry in Southeast Alaska.

Ketchikan is located "on the rocky southwestern shore of Revillagigedo Island" and is the first port of call or gateway city to Alaska. Originally Tlingit country, the town had been populated by non-Native settlers only since the 1880s.[26] Initially attracted by the salmon harvest, the population grew and along with schools, churches, and government buildings; a newspaper was launched, the *Ketchikan Chronicle*. The editor, Edward Morrissey, had begun his career at the *Seattle Post-Intelligencer* before bringing his cosmopolitan worldliness north with him. In July 1919, during the post–World War I recession and Red Scare, Morrissey published the *Chronicle*'s first editorial explaining that the newspaper's "platform" would stress anti-Bolshevism, a square deal for labor and capital, an all-out encouragement of the federal government's regulation and development of the fishing industry, and lastly, a strict adherence to Americanism, "which necessarily involved the repudiation of the so-called red flag wavers, whenever, wherever and however displayed or found."[27]

Morrissey's editorials provided an insight into Alaska's state of affairs, including the slogan-driven rhetoric that was commonplace in the postwar milieu. For instance, it was said that the Bolsheviks, along with "Lenin and Trotsky and their deadly disciples," were responsible for the social predicaments that had beset the territory. Morrissey felt it his duty and that of the *Chronicle* to "expose some of the falacious [*sic*], muddle-mindedness of their Doctrine." That was not where the newspaper's mission stopped, however, for there were "other problems confronting the world today surrounding labor, capital, wages, the cost of living, and living conditions." Crisis resolution was dependent on the capital outlay necessary from "the men in whose power it is to furnish the means" to expand industrial growth in the fisheries and forest, naturally uplifting everyone's financial state in the process. Again this could be accomplished by a vigorous adherence to "Americanism." Anyone who did not believe in these tenets was to leave the country and "seek a land more suitable to his way of thinking," because if dissident factions were allowed to stay they would "poison the minds of others seeking the truth" and "should be dealt with summarily." The final statement in the editorial concluded that the *Chronicle* would "give nothing in the way of encouragement to the followers of the red flag, nor does it want anything from the wavers of the emblem of Bolshevism and Anarchy."[28] Edward Morrissey and others of like mind, such as John Weir Troy, the editor of Juneau's *Daily Alaskan Empire*, carried this theme through the 1920s, using their newspapers as a podium, and striking out at anyone they believed had fallen out of the conventional and appropriate path.

The vitriol stirred up by these stories directly corresponded with the treatment of Asian workers, who were doing their best to keep a low profile. The language barrier undoubtedly kept Chinese immigrants from reading about the hate for their "race," but if they had known it probably would not have mattered, since their circumstances in their home country were little better.[29] Once in Alaska these men did what they could to keep body and soul together in order to survive. Alaska Natives were also treated poorly with the same sting of ethnic bias. At the turn of the century and beyond, it was not uncommon for Alaska Natives to be referred to as savages.[30] When this outrage could no longer be tolerated, the Southeast Alaska Natives, the Haida, Tlingit, and Tsimshian, gathered their resources, including the champions in their corner, and made a pact to fight back. Group discussions centered on achieving empowerment and full citizenship, but to be effective, they would need to form a recognizable organization to speak out for their issues. From the lessons in the Sitka Boarding School, Russian Orthodox Brotherhoods, or Salvation Army meetings, a cadre arose with the goals of wiping out intolerance, discrimination, and poverty. They were also determined to gain citizenship in the country of their ancestors' birth. While the Asians sought support wherever they could find it, Alaska Natives formed the first indigenous civil rights body in North America.

In Sitka and Juneau, flagrant bigotry incensed the Tlingit and Haida. Signs in front of businesses reading "No Indians, No Dogs" were physical evidence of the racialization that rendered Alaska Natives second-class residents. William Beattie, former superintendent at Sitka Industrial Training School, encouraged a Native cadre to rise up and address these insults, and in turn, several Tlingit men, many graduates of the Sheldon Jackson High School or members of the Russian Orthodox Church, met together to discuss the best approach for maximizing their resources. In 1912 the Alaska Native Brotherhood (ANB) was created as an advocacy group to gain civil rights and address the disparities in the Natives' livelihood, both commercially and for subsistence purposes.

The ANB is the oldest Native organization in North America. Members claim they thrived because the founders adhered to the goals of fraternity, equality, and the redemption of Tlingit and Haida lands and waterways. As the elders tell the story, the school and the church were the only avenues for achieving the goals of opportunity. The Brotherhood, it was said, was for "the good of the people, for the grandchildren. We talked of ourselves as one people, not just clans and houses."[31] At first there was an emphasis on Christian pathways; arguments were deflected by singing hymns, most notably "Onward Christian Soldiers," because this was the methodology that graduates of boarding school understood. As the organization developed, religious aspects were retained, but it was obvious that to meet contemporary challenges the ANB had to become politicized, paralleling Western organizations.

The ANB's first president was Peter Simpson, a Tsimshian man from Metlakatla. He was a fisherman and sawmill owner and was involved with the Annette Island cannery before relocating to Sitka. Although he was characterized as soft spoken, he had the ability to rally members together to contest what he and his allies believed was the theft of their aboriginal lands and waters. The fisheries had always been at the core of the Native culture, and the ANB, as a representative of Native villages and fishermen, kept the issues front and center while relying on available expertise, particularly that of Territorial Delegate James Wickersham, who was committed to the promising organization, its goals, and its members.

For many years the Tlingit and Haida had been dominant in the fisheries. According to a 1913 report by *Pacific Fisherman*, a journal for professional fishery interests, there were only 384 white men engaged in fishing for Southeast Alaska canneries, as compared to 1,137 Indians.[32] There was much to protect, and Peter Simpson did his best, but by 1920 it was apparent that another type of leader was necessary. It must be someone aware of the issues and with abundant energy to wrestle with local authorities, corporations, and Congress if need be. That man was Tlingit attorney William L. Paul Sr., who opposed ethnic discrimination, the loss of land rights, and the devastation of Alaska fisheries brought on by the cannery industry, overfishing, and mechanization. While Congress fecklessly attempted to keep the balance against the clamor of interest groups yearning for an increase in their share of the annual harvest, concerned Alaskans, whether Native cannery worker or European fisherman, demanded protective laws against the number one enemy to their livelihood—the fish trap, a vestige of corporate colonialism, and capable of harvesting whole runs of fish. This device alone rallied people together under common cause for decades to come.

William Paul Sr. was a formidable politician. After joining the ANB at the urging of his brother Louis, a respected member, William Paul jumped in with both feet and worked on the problems the fishermen and cannery workers were coping with in a "David versus Goliath" situation. As a fishermen himself, he was close to the waters, and his reverence for the seascape made him detest the wastage he saw around him. Paul's background was humble. He was the son of a widowed Tlingit woman who was both missionary and teacher in Wrangell, Haines, and Sitka. He graduated from a Washington college in 1905 and then went on to Presbyterian Theological Seminary at San Anselmo, California, for one year. His first job, as a manager for a large commissary store, taught him what would become a guiding principle in his life, and he recalled the "rough European class of workers" and how he had received his "first insight to the heartlessness of big corporations who grind out their profits from the blood of men and women."[33]

After returning to Alaska, Paul entered the contentious ring and started throwing punches. Some cautioned him to "keep his powder dry," but he never heeded those words. It did not take long for him to become a marked man for what some termed abrasive forcefulness, but above all, it became obvious that he would seek justice for the Tlingit and Haida and would settle for nothing less. Since salmon were the heart of the Tlingit and Haida culture, he and his brother centered their energies on the fisheries, yet they quarreled over methods of attack. William pushed through like a bulldozer, leveling all impediments in the way, while Louis tended to adhere to ancient precepts and the words of the elders, which he believed would be effective and keep the peace.

The influence of Louis F. Paul, William Paul Sr.'s brother, has been understated in the few history books that even mention his name. He was an integral part of every aspect of the ANB and often served as an officer for his local camp in Wrangell or the Grand Camp. Louis Paul was the more guarded of the two brothers and was forced to vacillate in his role as both supporter and apologist for William Paul, but what might be less known was that Louis Paul was fluent in both English and Tlingit, which would serve to unite both young and old Alaska Natives, building strength through deep cultural traditions. He also had the temperament, patience, and diligence to establish solid intermediary relationships between industry and Native villages. On those infrequent occasions when Louis lost his temper out of frustration, people took notice, not only because it was unusual but because even in anger he was eloquent. These brothers were destined to make a significant difference in the struggle for justice, but they also realized the ANB was incomplete without the women's voices.[34]

The Paul brothers along with other ANB members encouraged the start-up of a women's auxiliary to the ANB, and in 1915 the Alaska Native Sisterhood (ANS) was set up by a group of Wrangell women, soon becoming a force in its own right. From the beginning the organization worked to support women's needs, including the problems within the canneries, and since women were highly respected in their communities people listened to their ideas and opinions. The formation of the ANS enhanced the Native voice, and without hesitation the ANB acknowledged that "the Alaska Native Sisterhood was the backbone of the Brotherhood."[35] Whether within the cannery walls, working the line, or on the fishing grounds, the ANB and ANS worked hand-in-glove to support their members in the quest to achieve equality in the land of their birth.

In sum, these two organizations were vital during the cannery era and later formed alliances with other ethnic groups in mutual solidarity, but there was a need to move local political prowess to Washington DC.[36] When the funds could be found William Paul testified before congressional committees, similar to his 1922 experience concerning the deleterious effects of fish traps in Alaska.[37] His testimony was extraordinary on many levels. Not only was he the first Alaska Native to represent the ANB during a congressional committee session; he also spoke out for non-Native fishermen, emphasizing that these issues did not solely affect a small enclave but impacted the whole of Alaska, declaring that he had been "endorsed by the white fishermen of Wrangell, Petersburg and Juneau so that I think I am safe in saying that I represent the resident fishermen of southeastern Alaska." Further, resource depletion had "resulted in driving out the white families . . . and terrible hardships on the natives of the Territory. Over 5,000 in southeastern Alaska depend on fishing for their bread and butter." Although standing up for the livelihood of the fishermen, he also mentioned the terrible conditions Alaska Natives were living under and how "they are obliged to take the native children out of school and put them to work in order to be able to make a bare living. . . . The remedy is to abolish the trap."[38]

Even before Paul's testimony it had been well established that the fishermen and cannery workers were tied together in mutual effort to overcome obstacles. For instance, in the early days the "APA at Wrangell employed 40 to 60 crews, supporting from 200 to 300 people. Today they use nothing but traps," resulting in a loss of employment to the detriment of the community.[39] Without the fishermen's income, cannery employment became more important than ever. In 1923 Paul returned to Washington DC with the same message, but Congress "disregarded the opposition of the ANB as well as other anti-trap Alaska groups."[40] For Congress there was not enough at stake, and wealthy lobby groups had a more dominant voice. The traps caught fish and fish made money. Although disheartened, William Paul Sr. rolled up his sleeves and looked for another strategy.

Paul was convinced he could organize the "Indian vote" in Southeast Alaska. Although the American Native could not legally vote until 1924, it was not always enforced by Alaskan officials, and Paul reasoned that he could gather "a reliable bloc of voters," thereby effecting change in the status quo and the balance of power.[41] From this vision, the so-called "canoe vote" was launched, supported by the few Native voters who had qualified under the 1915 Alaska Citizenship Act, a piece of legislation meant to enforce assimilation.[42] In late 1923 Paul campaigned for a seat in the territorial legislature and the unthinkable occurred—he won.

The campaign had been riddled by acerbic rhetoric, drawing sharp lines between the Native and non-Native population and demonstrating high levels of malicious name-calling, as witnessed through newspaper headlines, particularly in Juneau's paper, the editor of which was John Troy, Paul's archenemy. This was an era when no holds were barred; in other words, "political correctness" was unknown. The Paul brothers were called upon to defend their position and to counter the attacks, and they started their own newspaper—the *Alaska Fisherman*—which not only became the mouthpiece of the ANB but also raised awareness of the overall decline of the fisheries and the role of big business in colonizing the territory and its people. The paper targeted the fish trap for its role in Alaska's demise, and editorials were guided by the mission statement displayed prominently on the front page of each edition. This was the first time the slogan "Alaska for Alaskans" appeared in print, but shortly thereafter it would become the rallying chant for a growing grassroots populist movement in Southeast Alaska.

William Paul was now regarded as a significant player in Alaska's political matrix, and that increased his target value for those who characterized him as an enemy of economic progress and of the elevation of Alaska to its appropriate place in the United States. To counter these criticisms, Paul refuted the yellow journalism that called him everything from unpatriotic to a fish pirate, using his own newspaper to tear down the blatant racism. His method was to reprint the original derisive articles and then pick apart the lies. For instance, one paper accused him of stirring up trouble when the Natives had previously been satisfied with their lot and he had taught them "they are just as good as the whites. You know well enough that this is not true. We don't want the Indians to try and govern us. This is white man's country."[43]

In opposition, Paul shot back that this was not "White Man's Country," and if the legal realities were uncovered, it would show that the Alaska Natives were entitled to their aboriginal land and waterways, including some of the cannery sites. Paul used his expertise to advance the arguments against racism and to also draw attention to the waning health of the Alaska fishery, which was the number one mainstay of Alaska's economy, besides being the primary livelihood of the Tlingit and Haida. Paul would not compromise, but given the milieu of the day he was continually obstructed by incendiary rhetoric accusing him of trying to put the canneries out of business so that only Natives could fish. At least one editorial displayed a degree of desperation: "If the canneries quit where are we going to get money to run this Territory?"[44]

Accusations went on to depict Paul with a derisive agenda, such as the

Ketchikan Chronicle calling him "a Bolshevik and menace."[45] Paul let no character defamation go unanswered and shot back, "On account of my present views, Cannerymen, Trapmen, Capitalists and their dependents call me a Dangerous Man, a Radical, a Boss. My so-called radicalism is nothing more than the application of the golden rule to the practical affairs of government."[46] The insults continued, and so did the control of the packing houses over Alaska government, business, and consequently, the political economy, while territorial leaders were afraid to be forceful lest they scare away commercial firms that might bring revenue to Alaska. Meanwhile, the fish traps were harvesting full runs of salmon without consideration of any conservation methods. The resource would not survive without drastic measures.

The traditional stewards of the land and waters in Southeast Alaska, the Tlingit, Tsimshian, and Haida, were without defense but never forgot their ancient birthright, while their champion William Paul continued to fight for civil rights, Native enfranchisement, and labor justice. But even he seemed to be exhausted at times, forlornly stating: "In the course of a very few years there will be no fish in Alaska for which to legislate. I cannot put the danger of depletion too strongly."[47] Yet he would not give up. During the 1920s William Paul continued to voice his concerns at ANB assemblies and through the *Alaska Fisherman*, arguing for the protection of the salmon fishery by eliminating the use of the fish traps that "catch every fish that swims, for salmon follow the shore. When the cannery floor is so loaded with fish that they lie around to a height of 3 or 4 feet, still the cannery tenders and scows will come to their canneries loaded with thirty to eighty thousand salmon, and if they can not be used they are dumped into the bay."[48]

The threat was real. Cannery scows were consistently overloaded and the fish were pitched back into the waters in an endless cycle of disregard for a finite resource. William and Louis Paul took their message not only to Juneau but to the Native villages, where they barnstormed to any crowd that would gather, sending out their message concerning the threats to Southeast Alaska waters, and persuading others to join the cause. It was not until 1924 that these complaints prompted legislation with the promise of being the panacea of all troubles. Early conservation measures had centered on the hatchery programs, but they were not well monitored and were therefore ineffective. William Paul was convinced the hatchery problem was based on one significant error: "the reason why hatchery fish don't come back is because they can't find the box in which they were born," referring to the salmon's natural life cycle of returning to their natal stream to spawn; artificial fish farms made that impossible.[49] Despite the obvious failings of the hatcheries, Herbert Hoover boasted that his refined plan would restore Alaskan fisheries to their former glory.

After Hoover had returned from his 1923 Alaskan trip, he met with the newly sworn-in President Calvin Coolidge, who had ascended to his executive role after the death of President Harding. Hoover and Coolidge developed an Alaska fishery reserve bill that appeared to have elements that might prove effective, but only time would tell. The White Act, as it was called, was enacted to conserve fish stocks by limiting the number of fishers and amount of caught fish in designated reserves. After it was implemented, it was found that the reserves acted to tie up prime fishing grounds in the hands of commercial interests, mainly due to their superior gear. This situation had the effect of nudging out the smaller fishermen and independent cannery operators, who could not compete. Angry independent fishermen accused Hoover of catering to corporate interests, but he "denounced" any ties with big business and swore he was looking out for the little man.[50] In reality, the cannery outfits were now forced to buy their fish from the industrial fisherman, who had every advantage, including great amount of capital to invest. On paper the White Act had established fishery reserves for conservation purposes and ostensibly prohibited establishment of exclusive fishing privileges for any class of people.[51] In the world of politics and revenue, however, paper promises were flimsy.

Nonetheless, the federal government was convinced the White Act was capable of turning around the Alaska fishery situation. The secretary of commerce was authorized to limit or prohibit fishing in Alaska waters at his discretion, including designating the appropriate type and size of gear. Fishing was only prohibited until 50 percent of the fish had been allowed to escape to their spawning grounds, although this was not monitored due to the lack of personnel.[52] From the beginning the system favored the non-Native fishermen and boosted the pocketbooks of the out-of-territory cannery conglomerates, which viewed the White Act as permission for exclusive fishing and the permanent establishment of fish traps as a form of property.[53] In other words, this solution deemed to preserve the salmon only escalated the injustices on the fishing grounds.

News of this disparity caught the ear of James Wickersham. At this time he was only marginally within inner political circles, but he held a reputation as an elder statesman and was not without a degree of earned authority. He had been grooming another man with similar views to pass the torch to as the next Alaskan delegate to represent the territory's interest in Washington DC. Dan Sutherland, Wickersham's former campaign manager, entered the national arena to play hardball politics. Based on his former occupations as a miner and fisherman, Sutherland's friends described him as a man with his roots planted in the ground. Indeed he was a champion of the common man and railed against wealthy business men who were increasing their monopolies over a finite resource. Sutherland opposed fish traps and had the support of independent fishermen and the ANB. In his unifying words, he proposed that "those fishermen who are attached to the land of Alaska, who live there, who intend to remain there when the cannery men are through and gone, should have full consideration."[54]

As a delegate, Sutherland spoke to Congress concerning the cannery workers' plight and that of the independent fishermen. They were caught in the middle between the cannery monopolies and government: "Whenever efforts are made to bring relief through legislation two elements come into conflict, the cannerymen and fishermen. I say that adequate relief will not be afforded until both sides make fair and equal concessions."[55] Further, resident fishermen were being "starved out" and "natives were forced into low wage jobs at the very canneries that stole their fish."[56]

After a period of serious discord, Sutherland and William Paul partnered to fight against corporate interests and destructive government measures. In 1923, for instance, Sutherland telegraphed Paul and the ANB, asking for their help in busting the fish trust, and he charged that the current fishery regulations, including the then proposed White Act, were without merit. In support of his argument, he cited the case of a well-known cannery company that had devised a way to get around regulations. He claimed that "the whole scheme was framed by the Alaska Packers and Libby, McNeill & Libby. If we do not take action in the Territory, the fisheries are lost to us forever."[57] Together Paul and Sutherland took their message to Washington DC and spoke to congressmen and legislative committees, but they were talking to people who considered Alaska "Icebergia." Others denied there was a problem because the White Act was going to take care of everything, but in truth, the legislation created a more craggy political mountain.

Dan Sutherland was popular in Alaska, except with the cannery companies or, as William Paul called them, the "fish barons." He had the support of Alaska residents in his responsibilities as delegate and protector of resident interests, and he continued to introduce congressional bills to abolish the fish traps, but Congress and the Bureau of Fisheries could not be budged on this matter. According to Louis Paul, "Hoover listens to the voice of the big interests and tells the world that our 'Fighting Dan' has exaggerated the situation and this was not the genuine will of the people."[58] Louis Paul lamented:

> Proof as to who misrepresents—Hoover or Sutherland, the Packing Trust or the fisherman is self evident. Hoover, three thousand miles away, turns to lobbyists of the Packing Trust, the Bureau of Fisheries and Henry O'Malley. Sutherland turns to the people who are most directly benefited or hurt by any proposed legislation. Consider the memorial presented to Congress by the Territorial Legislature; the petitions and protests of the Alaskan Native Brotherhood in fourteen towns . . . and the thousands of other Alaskans who are outspoken against the legislation proposed by the Packers. Against these we have a mere statement from Hoover that the facts are misrepresented.[59]

Widespread protests continued, but what could they do to convince the federal government that this was wrong for the fishermen, the cannery workers, and Alaska? Apparently nothing, since the White Act proponents were able to push the independent fishermen out of business in favor of big outfits like Nakat Packing or Libby, McNeill & Libby while manipulating Alaska's political economy. In later years Fred Paul, son of William Paul Sr., characterized the White Act as a method of putting "all Alaskan fish under the control of the US Government with the blessings of President Hoover and the Department of Fisheries for the sole use of the cannery business" and locking out Natives from their ancestral waters.[60] These circumstances angered Sutherland and the ANB, and in their frustration they realized it was not Washington DC or Congress that was making the rules, it was bureaucracy, which had furtively taken on a life and command of its own.

In Congress, Delegate Sutherland introduced evidence to show that the White Act was not only discriminatory but could never fulfill its intended purposes of fishery conservation and equality of access for all fishermen and gear types. In reality, the regulation obstructed resident fishermen from the pursuit of their livelihood because they could not compete with the bureaucratic hold of the Department of Commerce, the Bureau of Fisheries, and those fishing fleets and fish traps with a technical advantage.[61] The *Alaska Fisherman* expressed how the White Act shut out Native fishermen by excluding purse seine boats, the preferred gear type for the Tlingit and Haida, while continuing to approve industrial fish traps. "The traps are starving you slowly, but the House of Representatives would starve you at once. . . . Perhaps the Senators will find out that the Indians of Alaska are human; they have wives and little children. And they will find out about the heart of the trap he is talking about, a 'shark's heart,' and not a human heart."[62]

The purse seine method was controversial and was blamed for the overharvesting of salmon, with some people asserting that it was no different than a fish trap.[63] On several occasions William Paul had countered that these allegations unfairly targeted Native fishermen and had been cooked up by the fish barons to eliminate competition. The big companies were not the only foe of the seine fisherman. There were other clashes on the local level, particularly coming from Ketchikan's trolling fleet, members of which found the White Act favorable to their needs since it guaranteed them a space on the cutthroat fishing grounds. Up north in Wrangell, located on the Stikine River, the "citizens" denied Ketchikan's complaint. For them, it was the fish trap alone that was responsible for the low salmon runs, and not a specific fish harvesting method. The struggle was discussed in a *Ketchikan Chronicle* editorial in which Edward Morrissey inculpated the Native fishermen and the purse seine fleet as inefficient and rudimentary, while praising the out-of-territory companies, believing that greater encouragement should be given to these men "who by their work and thrift have accumulated means greater than the majority of us."[64] According to Morrissey, any undue legislation or regulations served as an impediment to both Ketchikan and, by extension, Alaska, in reaching their economic potential.

In answer to this editorial opinion, Wrangell residents once again disagreed and found allies from neighboring towns and villages. Together they stood up for local fisherman, avowing that "the depletion of our fisheries has not been due to purse seines" but rather to traps.[65] These collective opinions not only drove the ongoing clashes over gear types but also aggravated the factional stances between those who sought to develop Alaska, thereby producing a large revenue base, and those wanting to preserve Alaska's resources for future generations—a growing and divisive concern dominating regional politics.

In sum, the White Act favored big business interests and was prejudicial in its enforcement, as witnessed through the arrests and fines inflicted on small fishermen. In a 1924 issue of the *Alaska Fisherman* William Paul Sr. reported on one case of regulatory agency abuse where the Bureau of Fisheries had hired its own watchmen for a Booth Fisheries fish trap. Allegedly, the plant had "caught about $30,000 worth of fish" using what Paul deemed was an illegal trap. That fall an action was filed against the trap owners, who pleaded guilty, and the court "fined them $400 and costs. BUT THE TRAPMEN KEPT THE FISH."[66]

Who benefited from the fish laws (such as they were) was no secret, and those in power did not want the boat rocked, but that did not stop the dissent coming from William Paul Sr. and the ANB. It was, however, difficult to wage war with a foe like Washington State's Senator Wesley Jones, one of the leading proponents for keeping Alaska in a subservient position in tandem with a desire to keep his constituency happy, including a number of cannerymen. He was a powerful man and was chairman of the Senate Committee on Fisheries, responsible for mandating future legislation for Alaska's fisheries. Previously he had been instrumental in realigning stipulations within the White Act to eliminate any possibility of handicapping big business, and he had well-placed allies and others of like mind.

Before the passage of the White Act, California Representative Arthur Free voiced his ethnically biased resolution declaring that without the White Act, Alaska's bountiful fishery would be put in "the hands of a few Indians in Alaska."[67] Free's statement was typical of the prevalent attitudes, bolstering Jones's maneuverings of legislation to increase federal control over Alaska's fisheries, and with the urging of the packers, Jones made sure that the wording in the final bill would effectively reduce the number of fishery closures, which were countering full production. Further, there was an effort to uphold the use of fish traps in opposition to Delegate Sutherland's plea calling for restrictions on the traps. Although it was difficult to stand up to Senator Jones and come out winning, Sutherland was not about to give up.[68]

The Washington senator had a long record of promoting bills that were unfavorable to Alaska's ultimate well-being in order to keep Alaska a colony of Washington State. Senator Jones had been the author of the controversial 1920 Merchant Marine Act, commonly referred to as the Jones Act, which as part of a protectionist effort mandated that all commercial ships running between United States ports be American-owned and manufactured in the United States. Because Alaska was an international port, these requirements crippled Alaska's economy and hit the fishermen especially hard since the shipping lanes were under federal control, ultimately shaping global trade.[69]

William Paul Sr. had problems with Senator Jones from the beginning, and in the spring 1924 issue of the *Alaska Fisherman*, he condemned the senator and accused him of turning a blind eye toward the wastage. Paul recalled that when Jones was investigating the fisheries and dining with the Ketchikan Chamber of Commerce and "cannerymen," the same companies had "dumped over 100,000 pounds of trap caught fish within 100 yards of Carl Strong's wharf and the Ketchikan cold storage."[70] Although this was but one example, Paul was sure these issues were endemic. Senator Jones, however, was a well-respected member of Congress and remained unscathed by his critics. He continued his legislative pursuits, which were not always favorable to Alaska's overall interests.

Absentee monopolies and the fish trust thrived while William Paul Sr. blamed duplicity on class warfare. He attacked Hoover, accusing him of being "a special interest man whose friends are among the packers, not because he is bad or corrupt, but because he belongs to that class; he thinks like they do, he likes them. He cannot understand us, the little fellow, who has never been able to earn more than a couple of thousand dollars per year. He understands money, millions of it and power, plenty of it."[71]

Whether intentionally or not, the White Act granted a monopoly to the packing houses and left the fishermen restricted to relatively small designated fishing grounds, and simultaneously cannery workers were without the necessary clout to ask for better conditions or pay since they could easily be replaced. The colonization of Alaska was complete. Delegate Dan Sutherland, a rising star in progressive circles, fought against the tyranny of the White Act, which, in his words, merely "consolidated the victory of efficiency and rational exploitation over social equity as the defining parameter of federal conservation in the 1920s."[72] Meanwhile cannery activity soared due to high-speed production lines and nationwide advertising campaigns to increase canned salmon sales.[73] Regulation was scant and further undermined by pressures to "curtail the already slender enforcement capability in Alaska."[74] Residents and workers alike railed against the worst abuses of the industry, from unsafe cannery conditions to the lack of respect for their labor, but no action would be taken in this decade.

Regardless of the slow strides, the cannery environment was an incubator for ethnic tensions while nativism rose to epic proportions. Foreigners and Native Americans were placed in a subordinate category to justify preferential laws, lower wages, and a lack of equality. Paul, however, imagined a new class rising that opposed the Hoovers of the world, and he vowed to rally people together to condemn privilege and oligarchies that depleted the territory. In this maelstrom, Asians faced crowds of jeering enemies, calling for their deportation, and using them as scapegoats. While the Tlingit, Haida, and Tsimshian were finding unity in organized groups, the Chinese and Japanese navigated a path of least resistance against the backdrop of the Great Depression.

6

The Immigrants Are Necessary
but Unwelcome

In 1882 President Chester A. Arthur approved a federal law restricting the free immigration of Chinese laborers into United States and thereby reinforcing public attitudes toward foreigners. At first, the Chinese workers had been welcomed on Hawaiian sugar plantations, for California railroad construction, and at logging camps in the Pacific Northwest because they worked for low wages and caused few problems. Under these conditions it was easy to identify and eliminate troublemakers—those demanding better working conditions and larger paychecks. The exclusion policy, motivated by aggressive anti-immigration attitudes, was a reaction to the perceived notions that livelihoods and American values were in jeopardy. This stance was one of the characteristics of the 1920s—a paradoxical decade of clinging to the old and embracing urbanization. As industrialization grew, so did globalism until countered by a national fervor against the perceived bombardment of foreign cultures who appeared to be the antipathy of Americanism, and instead clung "tightly to the familiar moorings of traditional custom and values."[1] For all the mythology surrounding the "roaring twenties," it was a time of uncertainty as the nation tried to reinvent itself after ending the war that was expected to end all wars.

Because of its position on the North American continent, Alaska was semi-isolated from a changing world, yet soldiers had fought overseas, and newspapers like the *Seattle Post-Intelligencer* and even local newspapers from Wrangell, Juneau, Sitka, and Ketchikan reported on what was going on in other parts of the world. Journalism, based on the editor's ideology, was no stranger to outrageous headlines, yet readers accepted the printed word with little question in this land of Native villages, remote home-steaders, bucolic settlements, fishing fleets, cannery plants, and logging camps. Further, the population was too small to meet the increased labor demand, encouraging more Asians to come for work in the territory, with the accompanying escalation in anti-foreigner rhetoric.

In Southeast Alaska the anti-Chinese resentment erupted into several episodes with perhaps the best known—the mine riot—dubbed the "Douglas Island Incident." In 1886 a white inciter from Seattle provoked a Juneau mob to drive out eighty-seven Chinese miners.[2] As one can imagine, this turned out poorly for the Chinese. After being paraded through town they were set adrift in small boats without food and water. After ten days they miraculously surfaced over two hundred miles away in Wrangell at the head of the Stikine River. The starving and weary Chinese refugees were taken in by the Tlingit and spared a watery death at sea. Afterward this confrontation was condemned "in the most bitter terms, the inhumanity and barbarity that compelled the defenseless Chinamen to quit their labors and risk their lives in small and unseaworthy boats."[3]

This had not been the first anti-Chinese event, however; in 1885 a Juneau building filled with Chinese immigrants was dynamited.[4] Although this was a violent confrontation, there were relatively few ethnic altercations in Alaska during this era despite provocative yellow journalism. Undaunted, albeit sometimes desperate, the Chinese survived by any means possible and were often stowaways on steamers bound for Alaska. Once stowaways got there, the cannery bosses had no incentive to send the cheap labor away, and eventually the resentment died down due the relative isolation of Chinese workers and to exclusion policies.[5]

Nonetheless, the idea of the Yellow Peril, a metaphor for the alleged existential threat Asians posed to the Western world, coupled with the 1919 Red Scare, had catapulted xenophobic rhetoric to new heights. Regardless of the frenzy to protect Americanism from foreign intrusion, canneries needed workers as the industry expanded, with some towns having as many as five fully operating canneries. As the Chinese labor population dwindled due to exclusion policies, a new wave of immigrants from Japan arrived, and the social color palette was extended. By 1910 a noticeable influx of Japanese had entered Alaska, though the Chinese were still the preferred workers since they accepted lower wages without transportation costs: "Remember we do not pay any fares on Japs, as there are lots of unskilled labor at Ketchikan."[6]

Finally, it came to a point where the cannery bosses had no choice but to employ the Japanese, and subtly the wages were raised to a slightly more equitable level. In the 1920s Japanese numbers grew in Southeast Alaska canneries to become an "important contingent in the labor market" as "Chinese and Japanese struggled with each other for preeminence while other ethnics and Native Americans supplemented the crews."[7] It must be remembered that once the Japanese arrived in Southeast Alaska, they only stayed where there was work. With the building of more and more canneries along the coast and the growth of Bristol Bay, Asians spread over the territory to the west and north, yet the largest percentage of Japanese tended to stay in Southeast Alaska, never returning to their homes, although they kept their cultural ties, which concerned politicians and provided fodder for journalists.

Newspapers articulated concerns about Japan nationalism, a worry that deepened after Japan's victory in the 1904–5 Russo-Japanese War, creating uncertainties about building militarism that surely must have an outlet. Rumors abounded that the West Coast would be attacked at any second and that "Japan was growing more aggressive and hostile."[8] Anti-Japanese pamphlets were distributed to editorialize against Japanese Americans. A prime example was Valentine McClatchy, the California newspaper tycoon. He led an anti-foreigner crusade based on the theory that the Japanese intended to colonize California and impose Japanese ways on American society, thereby destroying civilization.[9] In congressional testimony McClatchy declared: "Of all races ineligible to citizenship, the Japanese are the least assimilatable (sic) and the most dangerous to this country. . . . With great pride of race they have no idea of assimilating in the sense of amalgamation. They do not come to this country with any desire or any intent to lose their racial or national identity."[10]

However absurd it appears in retrospect, this small immigrant population was considered capable of uprooting American culture. Baseless fear was reinforced by portraying the Japanese as "sneaky, treacherous agents of a weapon-toting country seeking to control the country in an indictment of the people and their culture without merit."[11] There was, however, a kernel of truth in McClatchy words: the Japanese were a homogenous population ethnically, linguistically, culturally, and spiritually. This made it easier to racialize the Japanese into a perceived inferior group, yet the effects of bigotry strengthened cleavages to ancient social manners and philosophies, acting as a buoy in a turbulent storm. This stability was sustained for years and kept the Asian population not only unified but also reluctant to join other ethnic groups or any protest movement that might draw attention. Given all the difficulties with immigration and living in a foreign country, it is of interest to understand why these people would leave their homes and families to venture to an unknown place.

After the Meiji Restoration in 1868,[12] Japan experienced rapid urbanization and industrialization, producing economic disruption and a decline in agricultural production. Farmers were forced to seek work in the cities. Many had heard of America and a place called "Gold Mountain," where an ambitious man might become rich. These factors led to a desire to leave their country, but that was no simple matter, considering the cost, red tape, and the Japanese government's stance toward emigration. Through persistence, however, more than 400,000 men and women left Japan for the United States between 1886 and 1911, after having maneuvered through the bureaucratic maze.[13] The Japanese officials, desiring to display the country's integrity in all matters, only gave permission to candidates deemed of ethical merit, who could not be confused with the Chinese. As Japanese Consul Takahashi Shinkichi claimed: "It is indeed the ignominious conduct and behavior of the indigent Chinese of inferior character that brought upon the Chinese as a whole the contempt of Westerners," resulting in exclusion legislation.[14]

From the moment they arrived on Western shores, the immigrants faced disapproval and hardship, but with the decline of available Chinese workers, Japanese men were hired to fill the gap as the rapid industrialization along the Pacific Coast and Alaska continued at an increasing rate. The residual Chinese population resented the incoming Japanese and "found themselves in intense competition for jobs with other racialized people."[15] Bitterness within the confines of the cannery accelerated, forcing the bosses to segregate the Chinese and Japanese into their own bunkhouses and dining facilities to alleviate clashes. But there was more to this strategy. Over the course of time and in spite of everything, management feared Asian workers might unify and start riots, resulting in chaos and endangering the power pyramid. Meanwhile, cannery owners had no desire to stop the immigration flow; it was necessary for production, though there were a few in influential positions who had other ideas.

During the 1920s the numbers of Japanese immigrants increased, and politicians thought they might have a problem. There were those who looked back to the early 1900s to recall how the immigrant problem had been handled in the past, when the Japanese and the United States governments had discussed limiting new arrivals in the Pacific region.[16] President Theodore Roosevelt had been impressed and shocked by Japanese military power, and during his time in office he walked a fine diplomatic line to keep relations harmonious, but after his term his true colors came through as he stated that since Japan and America had followed different lines of development, any mixing of people would culminate in "points of two such lines of divergent cultural development [that] would be fraught with peril."[17] As convoluted as this theory appears, it fueled racist thought and lingered for decades afterward, setting a precedent in legislation and public opinion.

In 1907 the international problem had been settled through a "Gentleman's Agreement," which attempted to halt the flow of young Japanese into the United States and to ease tensions for Japanese immigrants already in the country.[18] An agreement was not a law, and so it was not surprising that between 1908 and 1924 over 120,000 Japanese immigrants arrived on the Pacific Coast, leading to legal tenure cases to block foreign ownership of property. In 1909 alone seventeen anti-Japanese land bills were introduced, and one California assemblyman declared that the ground should remain a wilderness before "the foot of these yellow invaders, who are a curse to the country, a menace to our institutions, and destructive of every principle of Americanism" set foot on it. In comparison to the West Coast turmoil, Alaska appeared to be more liberal, a situation bolstered by the isolated nature of the region and lack of legal enforcement. Some may even have heard about the Alaskan legal case when a Japanese man, not a citizen, was allowed to engage in a retail liquor business, fully licensed.[19] That was far from the status quo.

Exclusion legislation was instituted through the 1924 Immigration Act, which restricted European and Asian immigrants, but even so, the Japanese remained a mainstay in the canneries and were sought after for their processing prowess, as the following account explains: "Japanese cannery workers had to race furiously and frantically against the machinery. After the boats brought in the catch of salmon, conveyor belts carried as many as two hundred salmon per minute up to the deck. The men, holding hooks in both hands, had to sort this charging multitude of huge fish and did not have a single second to relax . . . [surrounded by] the Alaskan smell, a nasal cocktail of rotten fish, salt, sweat, and filth."[20]

Despite the unpleasantness, the Japanese kept an eye on the prize, gaining significant upward mobility within the cannery ranks. A man might start at the gang-knife section and work up to cannery boss, or even local contractor.[21] With the rise in status, the men eventually became integrated into their respective communities and outwardly adopted American customs without abandoning the undertones of their Japanese character. Although little is known about Asian lives outside the canneries, generational stories recall a reliance on ancient philosophies of life meshed with the Alaska experience, serving to generate ethnic endurance and the ability to cope with the prejudicial attitudes they faced as "unAmerican people."

Asian cultures share similar social structures as regards class division, political alignment, and an engrained sense of ranking according to ancient feudal structure, once consisting of the aristocracy, yeomen or merchants, and farmers. Class segregation was bolstered by the Confucian sense of piety and filial duty to family, employer, and ultimately the emperor. For the Japanese this was coupled with Shintoism, stressing nationalism and the superiority of the Japanese above all others. Japanese cultural expert Edwin Reischauer determined that Confucian traits lurked under the surface even after emigration, including "the belief in the moral basis of government, the emphasis on interpersonal relations and loyalties, and the faith in education and hard work."[22] In a new environment the Samurai code of ethics and "saving face" existed amid the necessary adjustments to give the appearance of complete assimilation.[23]

Generational divisions are extremely important for understanding Asian cultures, starting with the Issei, the first immigrants. Since the Issei did not have a handle on the English language and seldom understood American customs, they often relied on their children, or the Nisei, those born in North America. The Nisei's offspring were the Sansei, and by the time of this generation, the children had become thoroughly Americanized. Elders are revered in Asian cultures, but with the Issei's dependence on their children to navigate through unfamiliar situations, mores concerning respect and politeness were inadvertently broken. In addition, those born in America were automatically citizens and would no longer be chained down by rigid Asian norms. Yet those historical bonds were not easily cast off and tended to remain just under the surface even as the younger generation became embroiled in politics and the quest for social justice.

Because of the distinct generational social status and accompanying ethnic-based standards, the elders feared that the Japanese family structure was losing its foundations. The differences between the Issei and Nisei status threatened Japanese American kinship responsibilities and respect for authority as part of the age-old Confucian structure.[24] Parents were convinced that loosening an allegiance to their Asian roots would invite a scourge upon the next generation, and for this reason "Japanese language schools" were important even in Alaska, offering an opportunity to keep the time-honored principles alive and to afford a guide for proper and ethical conduct. Because it was important to maintain the appearances of assimilation, these schools were frequently kept secret, and even today Japanese Alaskans are surprised to hear of their existence in the past.

Japanese workers were stereotyped as docile, but this was not completely true. Yes, the philosophy of Taoism was practiced, whereby a person does not fight the tide but instead meanders down the river, following nature's course in a path of least resistance. But an adaptive form of pride was prevalent when it became necessary to stand up for oneself or family, even as elders stressed the respect for heritage as armor. Today there are few reminders of this time period, except for obscure, overgrown areas of the Alexander Archipelago where grave markers still stand with either Chinese or Japanese characters and symbols from the ancient language.[25] For those poor unfortunate souls, a resting place, ritually prepared, was the only alternative to being buried in their homeland, as was the preferred custom.[26]

People do not leave their country without strong motivation. Nevertheless, when faced with the chaos in either China or Japan, it was easy for a recruiter to entice the discontented to the Pacific Coast with promises of a good life. When those dreams were replaced by hardships, immigrants built networks to buffer the anxiety caused by a foreign environment, but building a support system was not without disruptions. The early bachelor society was a prime target to fall prey to social ills. Work in the canneries was dull, dangerous, and demanding. In the few hours between work and sleep, there was often the desire to escape. The Chinese were well known for gambling and opium use, but what about the Japanese? There is little evidence that Japanese engaged in opium use to the same degree as the Chinese, although the item appeared on ship cargo lists bound for cannery bunkhouses where Japanese workers resided, despite the fact narcotics were illegal.[27] When Chris Friday discussed the use of opium among Asian workers, he emphasized that the "long days of standing in the damp conditions probably led a number of workers to lean on opium to ease their aches and pains."[28]

Opium use among the Japanese cannot be ruled out, but supporting evidence is difficult to locate; there is, however, no discounting the ample supplies of rice wine.[29] As for gambling, that activity was a bit more common. Tooru Kanazawa wrote an account based on his own experiences, illustrating how "games of chance" were played atop a spare salmon case in the bunkhouses, and one of the favorites was *shogi*, an old Japanese form of chess with pieces identified by ideographs; no doubt one of the games that separated a man from his money. A life of processing salmon from May to September in the remote wilderness frequently led to a man gambling away his wages and returning to Seattle or San Francisco penniless. "They lived for today, yielded to temptation, and did not consider the future."[30]

Whether to gamble or not may have been out of the workers' hands, and they were certainly not safeguarded against cunning traps. A 1902 labor guideline pamphlet for the Japanese warned: "You will toil from dawn to dusk with only shots of whiskey and cigarettes to enjoy. Beware of gambling."[31] It was obvious that they were sitting ducks ready for the plucking. Ironically, it was often the contractors or cannery bosses who encouraged this activity so that they could collect a cut: "Labor contractors let it be known that if a worker was to be hired for the following season, he was expected to gamble." Professional gamblers were employed to make sure the games went in favor of the contractors, "who held a complete monopoly on the gambling trade both on the ship and in the cannery."[32] These conditions reinforced the contractors' dominion whether recruiting on Seattle docks or initiating an illicit game in the bunkhouses.

The cannery owners, perhaps in an air of naïveté, often ordered the contractors to monitor narcotic use, although these same men were expert smugglers with few obstacles to their continued business arrangements. Rules stating that the ships would not carry these substances or labor contracts prohibiting their use on cannery grounds were inconsequential, and there was always a way to get the goods to someone who would pay black market prices. Even after drugs had been banned, "workers were still able to obtain a supply from the foreman." The grandson of Wong On, one of Seattle's major Chinese labor contractors, told the story of how a cannery building was torn down at one point and $30,000 worth of opium was found hidden behind a brick wall.[33] Likewise, investigative reports noted that the contraband (non-specific) found on both detained and recovered sunken ships was often concealed in the cargo hold.[34]

There were modest declines in these activities until co-ethnic labor leaders policed the gambling and narcotic smuggling. For instance, George Minato, an early Japanese labor organizer in Southeast Alaska, expressed his frustration: "The only thing that worries me is the gambling that is going on" and "no one will cooperate." He resigned himself to the fact that men would do anything for a chance to strike it big and escape their present conditions. Considering how foremen and cannery bosses were continually "pestered" to give pay advances, aspirations of wealth must have been ever present, regardless of likely outcomes.[35] At any rate, supposed enforcers turned a blind eye to keep the peace and get the salmon packed, the paramount goal.

Ships brought in other items to keep the Asians happy, including several types of rice, fish sauce, cigars, Japanese oysters, and as previously mentioned, rice wine.[36] The cargo list specified that it was for the workers, not delineating whether Japanese or Chinese. Though lumping ethnic groups together was the norm for a while, it eventually proved disastrous, and the cannery bosses learned that they must pay attention to food preferences. That was the one item that cannery workers agreed upon: a distinct desire for decent food.

During the 1920s most of the cooks were Chinese and at odds with Japanese tastes—the age-old enmity between ethnic groups producing additional tensions. The problem was gradually resolved by allowing the Japanese to have their own bunkhouse cook, who made sure to have a supply of the familiar delicacies. When each group was shown respect and catered to, there was a reduction in animosity, and that suited everyone. Rice continued to be the mainstay of Asian meals, but there was need to provide several options for the main course and to stop the practice of heavily salting meat—a ploy to ensure that the men would take smaller portions.[37] The intelligent foreman kept a diversified menu for the mess halls to avoid the "innumerable strikes in the canneries traced directly to dissatisfaction with quantity, kind, and quality of the food furnished to the men."[38]

In several instances the Japanese took it upon themselves to plant small gardens near the bunkhouses or concocted their own form of Alaska sushi, but it was never as good as back home. Regardless of narcotic use, gambling games, or more exotic meals, the men could grow melancholy, missing their families, or maybe a wife, who had to be left behind. Although many clung to the hope that they would return to their homes, others were happy in Alaska or had resigned themselves to the fact they could not leave. When faced with the knowledge that the cannery town where they lived was to be their permanent residence, they desired the companionship and family life that marriage provided, but there were few suitable partners for a traditional man, leaving only the alternative of importing a bride. For a short time there was no exclusion legislation targeted at Asian women, and they were free to become picture brides.

In the Asian cultures arranged marriages had been the standard for centuries back. The advent of picture brides, therefore, was not a strange phenomenon. Often these women were selected from a man's home region by agreement between two families. The potential groom knew his prospective spouse only through family letters and pictures.[39] One can only imagine what a difficult experience it was for the young woman to leave her family, home country, and way of living to venture on a ship, crossing the ocean to an unknown land where she did not speak the language. Yet these marriages did take place in Southeast Alaska, and according to historian David Kiffer, in Ketchikan there were at least six of these type of marriages that turned out to last a lifetime.[40]

One such marriage was that of Kichirobei "Jimmie" Tatsuda and Sen Seike. Tatsuda had arrived in Ketchikan in the early 1900s and kept himself busy working at the Fidalgo Island cannery and other odd jobs. When he turned thirty, he felt the need to settle down and wrote to his family, indicating that he was interested in marriage. His family in Yawatahama found a woman, Sen Seike, in a neighboring village, and both families agreed to the marriage, which was performed by way of the customary proxies before she sailed for America. Sen Seike arrived in Seattle in 1914 and then made the long venture north to Southeast Alaska, where the two set up housekeeping.[41] The Tatsuda family and other Japanese families made genuine contributions to their adopted communities, and their life stories are further discussed shortly in connection with the cannery towns.

Although picture brides were not uncommon, Japanese women were few in number, and several Japanese men married into Tlingit and Haida families with different levels of acceptance from the mixed community. "Japanese cannery workers most often found opportunities for companionship with Native American women, especially those in Alaska," where they might work for the same company.[42] Marriages resulting from these meetings were not always condoned by the Tlingit or other Native communities. Friday relates that if an Asian man married a Native woman, she often faced ostracism from her family, possibly because it broke clan tradition.[43] One man, a child of cannery workers, bitterly recalled that his mother had relatives "in the Indian villages, but they didn't like her for a long time because she married a Japanese."[44] In other cases families of mixed heritage were integrated into the community and frequently established well-respected businesses. In interviewing descendants of blended heritage, it emerges that they are proud of both their Japanese ancestry and their Alaska Native culture, but harmonious relations did not come easily, and alliances were difficult to solidify.

There were cases of Japanese women working with others in the canneries and forming bonds based on mutual experiences, particularly when married couples were part of the same social circles.[45] The shared immigrant experience among the Japanese women (or those married to Japanese men) tended to create deep connections or clique-like behavior and at times resulted in a sense of family. This cooperation was useful in childcare assistance or as a support system for dangerous situations, protecting against the intrusion of others. Among the group there were also understood norms that proved useful in the cannery.[46] Friday concludes that in the work environment, "Japanese women relied on ethnic bonds first when there were too few coethnics to occupy all of a filling table or section of slimers," but an all-Japanese group could not be sustained because of low numbers, so others were invited within the circle, reducing inter-ethnic tensions.[47] On the whole, however, Japanese women spent little time in the canneries.

Traditionally, a Japanese woman's place was in the home, taking care of a husband and children, according to the cultural tenet of filial piety.[48] Japanese women did find companionship with Alaska Native women, who resided in the same part of most towns, often referred to as "Indian Town," a name that illustrates the quasi-segregation. The variety of nationalities produced lively community celebrations, and on these special occasions, the entire town came out to hear brass bands and enjoy American picnic food, without differentiating between ethnic backgrounds or immigrant status. Undoubtedly this is why cannery towns like Ketchikan readily incorporated Japanese into the social matrix, whether cannery workers or shopkeepers.[49] But there were others who could not enjoy the luxury of camaraderie and were forced to adjust to much tougher circumstances.

The first Japanese immigrants arriving in Alaska had their sociocultural base tousled beyond recognition and struggled to find a nuance of normality. They were shocked by what they believed was barbarian behavior. A prime example was the belief in polite, non-direct Japanese communication, buoyed by the use of a mediator or go-between for social and business dealings in order to ensure that protocol was maintained and accordingly to lessen "the danger of an open confrontation or loss of face on either side." The exact rituals enabled the continuation of smoothness, affability, and mildness in a dialogue between two parties.[50] So when the Japanese met with a contractor in this new country they expected the familiar intermediary relationship, revealing the naïveté of men fresh off the boat. At first the contractors were "white men" or Chinese, but eventually with the growth of the Japanese labor market it became beneficial to hire Japanese men for contractor positions. *Keiyakunin* or Japanese labor go-betweens acted more in line with the traditional norms and were efficient conduits between the potential workers and employers, "recruiting laborers in the port cities, transporting them to work sites . . . and negotiating wages and labor conditions" for fees or commissions deducted from the workers' wages.[51] From the beginning the contractor system had been corrupt, and it was no less so among the Japanese. Nevertheless, there were a few exceptions.

A unique Japanese connection can be portrayed through the life story of Chinese businessman Goon Dip, a man who was antithetical to the typical corrupt contractor. Goon Dip signed up his first Chinese men for seasonal work in the Puget Sound canneries in 1905 and soon became a major labor contractor in the Pacific Northwest as well as an overall influential Chinese person in the region and renowned for his uncharacteristic benevolence.[52] When the Chinese labor pool shrank, Goon turned to the newly arrived Japanese to fill labor needs and also to act as subcontractors. To bridge the language barrier, at job sites he employed Japanese foremen, who developed a working pidgin language that could be used across the different cultures, easing difficult situations.[53] By using these Japanese go-betweens and avoiding conflict, Goon Dip was able to navigate the complex labor system along the Pacific Coast and farther north and able to bridge disputes before they got out of hand.[54] In Alaska he supplied workers to Southeast Alaska canneries and was known for his fair play and making sure the men were fed well and earned a decent wage. For example, at the Yakutat cannery, located in the northern part of the Alexander Archipelago, Goon Dip required that foremen be paid $100 a month and fines were levied for public drunkenness.[55] These wages were much higher than the norm, and his influence was evident in his ability to maintain order from a distance.

In general, however, Goon Dip or men like him were a rarity, and the Japanese were drawn to those who were not only influential but Japanese, which explained the rise of Clarence Arai and the Japanese Cannery Workers' Union (JCWU). The mention of this ethnically closed union serves as an illustration of a variance in normal or average Japanese associations. Arai's union started in Seattle, already a significant starting off place for Asian immigrants and a launching platform for Alaskan employment. Instead of a multi-ethnic membership, the JCWU was exclusively Japanese, and Arai promised that he and his labor organization were the only ones who understood the Japanese situation and would fight for equity. Arai's beliefs were rigid. He did not allow anyone other than his elite group of cultural nationalists to join, and he banned suspected Communists.

Arai confronted fierce competition in Seattle and was shunned because of his esoteric creeds. He only gained a small membership and despite his passion, it was all he could do to keep his head above water. Unlike other nascent unions at the time, he did not focus solely on Seattle. Realizing the importance of Alaska to the overall movement, he sent a few of his right-hand men up north to talk about the Japanese-only labor movement and the benefits that could be accrued, but nothing came of this recruitment trip. He continued to face cruel and relentless criticism for his Japanese nationalism, with one opposing union accusing him of being racist and "propagandizing and stigmatizing our Japanese groups to make them an isolated race. . . . Those who sided with Arai or other labor agents" were jeopardizing future relationships and business with Alaska.[56]

Another barrier to Arai's Alaska mission was that although there was some talk about unionism in Alaska, there were no aggressive campaigns, and Alaskan Japanese cannery workers tended to become members of the union their foreman encouraged them to join—that was their way of keeping the peace. The Japanese workers were already being accused by other groups of getting better pay and positions, and though this was unlikely, they did not want to stir up trouble. Arai's tunnel approach eventually gave way to the more outspoken and ethnically diverse unions, but in any discussion of Japanese workers, Arai stands out for his one-of-kind union attempt, as a risk taker, and a man way ahead of his time.

In the history of Southeast Alaska canneries there was another Japanese man who embodied both the 1930s era and World War II, in addition to the tragedies of being "other" in a suspicious world. Shoki Kayamori completed a short stint in a Seattle cannery, and in 1912 "Kayamori set out for the cannery in Yakutat, a predominantly Tlingit village, where he would spend the rest of his life and where he remains today, buried in an unmarked grave." The Yakutat residents rarely used his name but instead called him "Picture Man" based on his numerous photos in Yakutat that today provide a rare historic glimpse into the cannery life. Yakutat was already an important geopolitical site before the Russians established a fort in the late 1700s. Unlike other villages, it was a peaceful multi-ethnic settlement of Tlingit, Athabascan, and Eyak residents. When the fishing industry developed in importance, the location was favored as a good harbor for vessels and since the salmon harvest was robust, numerous companies were encouraged to start up cannery businesses. In the early 1900s C. A. Fredericks & Company of Seattle, Mulvey & Wilson, Jewell Fish Company, and Ankow Fish Company built facilities, even though for a while the principal product was salted herring. There was only minimal salmon canning until more equipment arrived along with a reliable delivery system, capable of shipping from this isolated locale. Transportation problems were solved in 1904 when the Yakutat and Southern Railway Company built a rail system that hauled fish along a special extension line. The train used an engine that had previously seen service on the elevated railroads of New York City before advancements in electricity technology. The discarded train became the heart of the Yakutat salmon business and social life even after the cannery was purchased by the mega-cannery conglomerate Libby, McNeill & Libby, a company with a growing presence in Alaska during the 1930s.[57]

To this day the Yakutat and Southern Railroad stands as the only railroad in the United States where the sole freight commodity was raw fish. Its schedule depended on the daily tides and the fishing season, requiring a certain expertise to manage processing times and a delivery schedule. The Y&S began operations with the express purpose of hauling fresh-caught fish from the Situk River to the cannery wharf in Yakutat, eleven miles to the north. After the fish were processed, the canned product was shipped straight out of Monti Bay, a deep-water port within Yakutat.[58]

Shoki Kayamori was employed in a number of cannery positions in Yakutat, and his photographs of everyday life captured the setting: Tlingit women slimed fish, a messy, dirty job and the "pay for the five month season ranged from $150 to $300, depending on the worker's race, which typically determined his (and often her) assigned task . . . the average Alaska hand could count on collecting about a third of whatever he was promised."[59] When the season was over, most of the workers returned to Seattle on a cannery vessel, but Kayamori stayed on in Yakutat. His favorite form of recreation was creating a pictorial history that included snapshots not only of cannery life but also of holidays and milestones, and to this day the elders remember weddings, Fourth of July parties, and of course, the dances. On Sunday afternoons people would meet at the cannery to take short rides on the train after church, and Kayamori's camera was there.

Though Yakutat was a remote location, residents were aware of world events. When World War I broke out there was increased demand for salmon products to feed the troops and to promote morale. It was touted that British soldiers dined on Yakutat pink salmon.[60] The "Libby company" brought in more workers, built bunkhouses, and stocked the essential cannery store. Even before the war years the Yakutat cannery was shipping sixty-two thousand cases a year, and Kayamori was right in the middle of the action.[61] For several years he was a "cooker," which most likely referred to the retorts (pressure cookers), and by the mid-1930s, as he aged, he worked in the cannery store. Not unlike many cannery settings, the workers were paid in script that was redeemable only at the "Libby" store. With a captive buying audience, the company store could set the going rate for groceries and make a profit. Nonetheless, if one was going to find a desired item, from canned peaches to colorful dress fabrics, that was the place to shop.

From the cannery store Kayamori's employment shifted to that of a night watchman with an annual salary of $500, less than half what the Scandinavian watchmen had earned.[62] Both as a hobby and to supplement his income, he invited Tlingit families into his humble apartment, where he had converted one corner into a photography studio, and offered his services for formal portraits. Tlingit elder MaryAnn Paquette remembered his family photographs and how he was always present at celebrations; she said he was a man with reading glasses and thinning gray hair and was an essential part of community life.[63] In this friendly, multi-ethnic hamlet Kayamori did not suffer the same level of ethnic discrimination that was prevalent in the bigger towns of the Pacific Northwest or even the capital city of Juneau, but eventually the long arm of hateful journalism and its prejudicial fingers reached into Southeast Alaska. Kayamori was one of the victims. His story continues in chapter 11, which describes the life and times of the Japanese during World War II.

At this juncture it is helpful to look at the few Alaska-Japanese life stories that have been recorded. Oral narratives are often the only way historians can connect the dots on events or analyze the meaning of certain passages of time in order to build an ethnohistory. Regrettably, the Chinese have virtually no documentation of their life in Alaska, but there is a bit more about the Japanese because so many of the first cannery workers stayed in Alaska, started families, and helped build communities. Through the telling of their experiences, one understands the difficulties of overcoming adversity, maintaining Japanese culture, and adjusting to a foreign country.

The research team of Ron Inouye, Carol Hoshiko, and Kazumi Heshiki interviewed Japanese Americans from southeast Alaska and summarized their narratives in "Alaska's Japanese Pioneers, Faces, Voices, Stories: A Synopsis of Selected Oral History Transcripts" in a venture that Inouye found was overdue.[64] "I find it interesting that so much of Alaska history is based on the cannery, and yet there is so little social documentation about what it was like working there, or what the structure was like. There's a lot on the statistics; how much production, which ones produced the most, but not very much on the social bases."[65] The subsequent dialogue revealed hardships based on minority status, yet also the good times. Many of the interviews took place in Ketchikan, the largest Japanese community in Southeast Alaska, and revealed an era when immigrants were careful to keep up appearances of assimilation and Americanization, yet secretly preserved the home culture though ancient rituals and language lessons, similar to William Tatsuda, who attended both Japanese language school and Ketchikan public schools.[66]

To backtrack for a moment: Tatsuda's father had immigrated in 1904, worked in Seattle, and finally settled in Ketchikan in 1910 after employment as a seasonal cannery worker for many years. From his cannery work he saved up enough money to open his own establishment, which consisted of a grocery store, tobacco store, card parlor, pool hall, and boarding house on lower Stedman Street. Eventually he consolidated his businesses into one, the Tatsuda Grocery Store, developing into a Ketchikan landmark. William's sister, Cherry Tsuruko Tatsuda Fujioka, talked about growing up in Ketchikan's Japanese community and how their family participated in the Japanese association that observed special occasions at the Japanese school building.[67] She explained that on Saturday there was Japanese School, acting to reinforce the culture and language. Later only a few talked about these schools, and there were many in the following generation who never realized such schools existed back then.[68] Cherry's contemporary, Helen Misao Shimizu Nakashima, remembers that her mother "pounded in cultural messages" and adds that she never complained about "climbing 200 stairs up the hill to get to the [Japanese] school."[69]

Not all of Cherry's friends were Japanese, and she fondly recalls playing with Alaska Native children even though they went to another school, sponsored by the Bureau of Indian Affairs (BIA). At that time the non-Native children were enrolled in territorial schools, while the Native children attended government Indian Service schools. This factor conveys an important social point that differs from the situation in other Japanese communities along the Pacific Coast, where Japanese children were excluded from "white" schools, sometimes at the point of violence. Yet Asians were excepted in Ketchikan schools, as long as they did not have a Native parent. The school board, which yielded an enormous amount of power in Southeast Alaska, did not extend the same invitation to Alaska Native children, who were not only considered inferior but also wards of the BIA in an extension of governmental paternalism.

For the children, any ethnic segregation was only during the school hours, since they lived in the same neighborhood with frequent mixed social events, and Japanese families who owned stores, like the Tatsuda family, often supplied food and beverages for town parties, and regularly delivered food and other goods out to the numerous canneries, or even out to the fishermen.[70] Everyone worked together in a cannery town, even those not working at the plant.

At the canneries, however, separate bunkhouses remained the norm, seemingly to keep ethnic crews separated from others. Cherry's husband,

Tad Fujioka, had been employed at the Taku Harbor cannery and Ketchikan canneries until graduating from University of Washington in 1942. During his summers he worked ten hours a day sorting different species of salmon and recalled that back then "the women were obviously segregated. They tended to work . . . on the slimer tables. In Ketchikan the Japanese, at least at New England, tended to be on the slimer tables. The gals seemed to be working on the so-called patching table which consisted of taking light or overweight cans and redistributing the weight so they go out proper. The so-called lye wash crew, which was, I think, sort of an elite job because you never had to touch fish except in the can" went to those having clout with the foreman.[71]

Seasoned laborers received the more desirable jobs, which were reserved for them year after year: anyone with a "little pull with the supervisor could also get on the lye wash crew" or another job that was either easier or cleaner.[72] The pay was not necessarily distributed according to experience but rather based on workers' assumed expertise level or gang membership. Gangs were crews, performing specific tasks, and usually ethnically segregated. According to Fujioka, even in the bunkhouses there was preferential treatment. He based this belief on the fact there was an "outside cannery row" with a view of the mountains reserved for higher echelon employees.

In Fujioka's experience, the social life was nonexistent, but it was not a problem for him since he often visited the "Japanese community," where there was always something on.[73] Cherry, on the other hand, disagreed and instead raved about how much she loved the summer baseball games. "We played baseball against the Ketchikan town team," she said, adding that the competition was intense, but all was forgotten in the evenings during social gatherings—everyone danced with everyone into the late hours. Cherry goes on to say that "the girls were just girls" growing up. Japanese and Native children were known to go to the library together and sometimes the movies, even though Natives were not allowed into certain theatres or, if they were, they had to stay together on the balconies, labeled "Indian Heaven," once again pointing to the distinct levels of discrimination between the Tlingit and Asians.[74] She also spoke of the protectiveness of the mothers, "who did not allow us to mix too much," but it hardly mattered because there was so little free time. If not in day school, Japanese school, or church, she was supposed to help other mothers with little ones.[75]

From other workers came another spin on the story. "I'm really thankful that we are able to go up there to Alaska when there was work . . . you're going to college . . . you need money," George Makoto Yanagimachi recalled, adding: "You made enough to pay a year's tuition and books."[76] In a common pattern many Asian immigrants went to school in the fall and winter and then back up to the canneries for about five months in late spring and summer. Yanagimachi was only thirteen when he first ventured up to Alaska to work in the canneries. When a Chinese man recruited him in Seattle, the subject of his age never came up, and after signing the paperwork, he was on his way north on a passenger steamship in third class or steerage (China Hold). Once in Alaska and despite the camaraderie, he found all aspects of cannery life dull, including the food. "Breakfast on the camp table always included rice, ysoshen root, and a kind of gourd referred to as rubber cabbage."[77] It made the introduction of salmon a real treat for a while until that too became mundane. After the war he resided in Washington in winter and then for the summer months went back up to Alaska, where he noted that each trip was "an opportunity to spend time with old friends and Japanese families."[78] He said, "You get to know a lot of Japanese people," and "we all went to the same canneries together."[79] During the 1930s the Japanese became predominant in the canneries, sustaining a thriving Japanese culture community while learning new ways.

Yanagimachi believed that Alaska Native women were the only other major ethnic group in the canneries, but there was little intermixing between the two groups. In Ketchikan the Japanese lived in "segregated bunkhouses with up to 100 in one structure" while Alaska Native women lived in the Indian section. In other places he had worked, most of the workers were single men, and he had seen gambling and other vices meant to pass the time, but at Ketchikan there was a whole Japanese neighborhood, practicing the old ways and speaking Japanese.[80] He found something in common with Nissei families and people his age, and social occasions broke the monotony of cannery work.[81]

In Yanagimachi's memories and those of many in Ketchikan today, there was a special place for the Hagiwara family and their Ketchikan grocery story and bakery. After the much-loved baseball games, the Hagiwara family gave out pies to the winners. The Japanese teams competed against the Filipino teams, who many thought took the games too seriously, but if there were genuine ethnic tensions, they were not seen on the ball field, where everyone had a good time until the clouds of war blew in and drastically reordered life. Faced with monumental challenges, some clenched to their heritage while others created new bonds to weather the storm.[82] Hagiwara recounts how similar life experiences bonded people together through struggles or ultimately, in the military.[83] Yet not all was gray, mundane, or formidable.

There were those who found ways to interject humor in an otherwise dull life, like Mack Takao Mori, who first came to Alaska in the 1920s as a seasonal worker. Mack found cannery life uncomfortable, with bed bugs and mosquitoes, and even worse, the occasions when poorly trained men suffered "getting their hands caught in the butchering machines that cut off more than fish heads."[84] On a less dangerous note but still critical: bed bugs were awful and Mori threatened the Japanese "boss" that if something was not done about the critters he would take matters into his own hands and douse the mattresses with gasoline. He was quick to add that he sure hoped nobody smoked. The boss pleaded with him not to do this, promising to remedy the problem.

One day the cannery "gang" was ordered to fill their free time by removing tree stumps left from the logging activity, but instead Mori thought his time would be better spent napping. When the cannery boss came upon him, he was not only roused from his sleep but the supervisor shouted that he was to be put on the next ship back to Japan. Mori thought that was a great idea and went back to the bunkhouse to pack. When questioned about what he was doing, he replied that he was getting ready for the incoming ship. The cannery boss, according to Mori's account, "went a little crazy" and said he could not do that because a big run of fish were coming in. The rest of this story is best told in Mori's own words: "Twenty thousand fish came in and we let that guy worry about it, you know. But, ah, my boss said, 'Go and unload that,'" but not before Mori scolded him for his rudeness and threatened to work for someone else. As the fish started to come in the cannery supervisor was placed in a difficult position and attempted to apologize, but Mori was not so easily appeased and proceeded to hit the supervisor in the chest with a fish, to show him who was really boss. The next day the supervisor bought him "a carton of cigarettes and a can of fruit."[85]

When the movie "Silver Horde" was filmed in Loring, another cannery town about fifteen miles from Ketchikan as the raven flies, Mack Mori met the stars and some of his crew were in the movie, like his friend "Lefty" Yamaguchi, whose scene included processing fresh caught salmon. The film's objective was to represent the height of the silver salmon runs back in the day and depict how important the cannery was to Alaskan communities. Most of the actors or residents never saw the movie, but they remembered when Hollywood came to Southeast Alaska. Yes, life was filled with fond reminiscences, managing the tough times, good friends, and salmon coming in, ready to butcher.

In the 1930s the territory struggled financially, unable to find buoyancy even though Alaska's salmon industry was an important element of the world market. The labor force was composed of non-Native (mostly European) residents, the Native and Asian cannery workers, and a variety of fishermen, all making deals and alliances as it suited the circumstances. In 1900 over 12,500 Japanese entered the United States seeking employment, and this perceived intrusion overwhelmed American citizens, but in Alaska immigrants were more accepted in this diverse and less populated frontier environment.[86] Japanese workers spent only a short time in canneries before branching out into other pursuits, and many only worked on a seasonal basis while finishing university degrees, prompting one Japanese media source to report: "The young man standing beside the filling machine or the butcher machine is probably a member of the local intelligentsia."[87] In terms of the economy, the Japanese were a stalwart example of entrepreneurship, adding another twist to local market economies.

The Chinese and Japanese were affected by international governments that regulated their immigration experience, ranging from legal admittance into the country to circumstances under which they could step on American soil. From that point, the government monitored Asian lives, whether the workers were in the Hawaiian sugar plantations, the agricultural fields of Salinas, California, or the Southeast Alaska canneries. The Chinese and Japanese shared common cultural values that centered on obeying authority, not making waves, and a strong work ethic, which was appealing to those in charge of the fish factories. Cannery owners built multi-million-dollar businesses based on canned salmon, and they needed these workers. Without them there would be no one to run the machines or pack the boxes, and because the immigrants tolerated lower wages and unsafe working conditions, the corporations exponentially increased profits. Politics acted as a by-product of business interests, and governmental involvement touched every aspect of cannery life. Absentee owners and their decisions, assisted by favorable legislation, created a corporate colonialism that ethnic groups worked with or around.

Though Asians were designated as "alien non-citizens" they prospered and overcame the odds, including discrimination in property ownership that threatened burgeoning business interests.[88] In Alaska, however, with its slightly different sociopolitical milieu, Asians, especially the Japanese, were integrated into the community's cadence, and instead of being locked away in a niche, they filled it so that people like Shoki Kayamori, the "Picture Man," or the Tatsuda family were vital members of the place they came to call home.

7

The Rising Voices of Alaska Natives

In 1889 the side-paddle steamer *Ancon* was docked at the Loring wharf while Chinese workers loaded four thousand cases of canned salmon. Wealthy tourists were also boarding, ready to sail south from Alaska. The *Ancon* was well known on these waters, having made this journey many times to Loring on Naha Bay, the site of an old Tlingit hunting and fishing camp. For centuries, the fishing camp had been occupied about six months out of the year, but in 1885, the Tlingit were pushed out when the cannery was built. Nonetheless, some Tlingit stayed on to work in the cannery alongside a small number of immigrants, who were housed in their own bunkhouse with gardens and penned animals.

Unfortunately, in late August 1889, the *Ancon* suffered a mishap when the lines were cast off too soon in the strong winds, and the ship drifted into a shoal, puncturing the hull. The salmon and tourists were offloaded and spent another week in Loring until another ship could make its way up north.[1] The only accommodation was the cannery facility, which was undoubtedly quite a nasal concoction for the travelers in this setting of a temporary Native village, the Chinese bunkhouse, and a few cannery foreman houses, all typical for this time period. Beyond the surface, however, the scene was another example of indigenous displacement for the purposes of Western-defined progress.[2] As this situation became increasingly widespread, a Native cadre took notice, banded together, and sought justice.

During the 1920s expanding companies invested in Alaska canneries as salmon turned into a gold mine for the absentee owners, and in the process the colonial hold on the territory was tightened while production was ramped up, creating a need for more labor. Companies not only advertised along the Pacific Coast; recruiters went to Asian countries to expound upon the glories of working in the United States and how easy it was to escape limitations in their country and earn a decent living. The pitch did not have to be true; just convincing. Once in the United States, the immigrants found it difficult to navigate in this foreign country and blindly placed their trust in the cannery foremen, producing malleable workers. Eventually foreign labor increased, displacing Alaska Native women and causing a fair amount of resentment. Simultaneously, Alaska Native communities witnessed the continued usurpation of their land and waters without compensation, motivating a call to action.

In 1912 these factors had served as a catalyst for a novel idea, the formation of the Alaska Native Brotherhood to address civil rights issues. At first the pathway to genuine American citizenship appeared to be full assimilation into the dominant culture, and correspondingly, the early members emulated the Presbyterian philosophy they had learned in boarding schools to demonstrate their uplifted state. This display, however, did not produce the desired results, and it was obvious there must be a shift in leadership to gain political leverage.

In the early years Peter Simpson, the first ANB president, drew from his experiences of working at both Metlakatla and Loring canneries to understand what was at stake in the Native cause. Realizing that arguments could not be resolved by the singing of "Onward Christian Soldiers" alone, Simpson sought a man who would not be complacent about Southeast Alaska Natives' issues and who possessed the charisma to carry off the task. At the 1929 ANB convention in Haines, Simpson challenged attorney William Paul Sr. to fight for the land, symbolically handing over the reins. In later years Paul's son Fred compared that moment to the "laying on of hands." Paul was not a patient man and entered the arena with no holds barred, fully committed to using any means to unblock obstacles in the way of his goals. Though his headstrong attitude eventually turned him into the enemy of some and factionalized the ANB, he understood the law, and the messy world of political strategy, and he had the energy to move forward. Yes, Paul collected adversaries along the way, but in retrospect, he fulfilled the leadership qualifications for the time.[3]

William Paul Sr. became widely known in Washington DC legislative circles as he joined others in the fight for Alaska fishing grounds and better cannery conditions. He understood the necessity of working with the territorial delegates Wickersham and Sutherland, and together they made the abolition of the fish trap a priority while attempting to solve the nagging problems revolving around Alaska's need for an economic base.[4] Although Wickersham was no longer working directly with legislature, he was influential and extended his wisdom to Sutherland. Sometimes there were tensions between Wickersham, Paul, and Sutherland, but for the most part they worked together for the greater good. It was a juggling act and regardless of which side the legislators and bureaucrats found themselves on, corporate interests were at the forefront with more money and the ability to manipulate situations to their advantage.

Alaskans watched "their fisheries being robbed by the alien fish trust and their tax coffers empty," while Alaskan politicians accused Congress of not fulfilling its duties based on "ignorance and venality."[5] Individual fishermen sought the help of Wickersham and Sutherland to boost Alaska's autonomy and to allow the residents to makes their own rules, but they were no match for the salmon canning lobby in tandem with the Bureau of Fisheries. Local voices went unheard as Congress continued to exert control over the territory and its resources. This attitude was summed up by Secretary of Commerce William Redfield as he claimed that Alaskans were wholly unsuitable to manage an enterprise of this magnitude and the fisheries could not be turned over "to a population of 55,000 white people."[6] It was apparent that the federal government considered Alaska in its infancy, and there was a need for a compelling force to break the stranglehold the federal government had in Alaska. The non-Native fishermen were unorganized during these early years, but for Alaska Natives the plan was clear. They counted on the ANB to regain land tenure and civil rights.

It would take more than one man to champion the Native cause, however, particularly given the division and conflicting opinions. Some favored William Paul's approach—full speed ahead—the consequences be damned. But others preferred a more moderate style that incorporated ancient ways of negotiation. Because of this split there was a need for both William and Louis Paul to work together, particularly given their complementary mind sets. William understood the underbelly of politicians and corporate maneuverings, while Louis Paul, a more patient man, took the time to seek the advice of respected older members of the Native community. William Paul was credited with moving the Native agenda forward, but it would not have been possible without Louis Paul behind him to ease the fallout produced by his brother's acerbic manner and his apparent discounting of the old ways. Together the brothers united the ANB but were careful not to be restricted in their outreach, reasoning that they could gain more support by including everyone in Alaska affected by the federal government's domination, especially the resident fishermen, who saw themselves being pushed off the fishing grounds by industrialization. In essence, the Pauls were searching for that common thread that could rally a larger, more vocal population. Above all, there was a need to get the word out.

One device that had already proved effective was the print media. Both men were graduates of the Carlisle Indian Industrial School in Pennsylvania, and as part of their curriculum they had learned to run a printing press. With this expertise, the Paul brothers built their own newspaper office and, backed by the ANB, the *Alaska Fisherman* was launched as a conduit to reveal what was happening in Alaska's fisheries, expose the repressive colonialism that existed, and express the outrage felt by all residents. As an example, in one of their early editorials they railed against ineffective legislation that did not allow "sufficient escapement to the spawning beds," and instead salmon streams were effectively blocked while other fishermen were told to "go up the creeks and get all the fish they could get," to the detriment of the fishing grounds. "We were the residents of Alaska and you were THE CANNING INDUSTRY OF ALASKA so you were not molested in your destruction. . . . We saw in Hoonah Sound a trap abreast of Emmon's Island which blocked three-fourths of the channel. . . . As philanthropists you are everything else but. As conservationists of your own interests we give you the prize. As destructionists of the Alaska fisheries you have a batting average of 1000."[7]

No one in power was paying attention though—not while the APA and other mega-companies, like Booth Fisheries and Libby, McNeill & Libby, held the purse strings in Alaska and were also responsible for employing a large group of non-Native fishermen. There was, however, a growing tide of dissent arising from the once invisible people who had been stifled too long, and together they clamored for home rule. In unison, the ANB and the *Alaska Fisherman* editorials railed against unfair employment practices and salmon theft, going right to the core of the situation: "The cannery man is never satisfied but wants to pack the last fish that swims."[8] While the Paul brothers sought fair dealings on the fishing grounds and in the canneries, Juneau lawmakers rebuffed their efforts and characterized the dissent as an omen of creeping socialism and a threat to the free enterprise system.

These attitudes had surfaced as early as 1920 when Scott Bone, a staunch Republican from Seattle, arrived in Alaska to assume his duties as governor after being appointed by President Harding. From the beginning Bone was caught in the maelstrom, between those who opposed outside interests in their fisheries and the absentee cannery owners. He categorized the complaints from Native villages as being from radical elements and wholly unpatriotic and insolent.[9] He believed: "Bolshevism is dangerous to our American institutions" and could lead to mob rule.[10] If this was not stopped, there would be a buildup of anti-Americanism, and to his way of thinking, it might already have started in the territory with the few ongoing labor conflicts in both the canneries and the mines. Wickersham and the Pauls, who were working together, had an unfavorable view of Bone and were sure he was colluding with the out-of-territory corporations not only robbing the resource but undermining Native efforts to regain their rights.[11]

William Paul criticized the profit-before-people approach as nothing less than wage slavery. In "A Paper for the Common Folk Treating Subjects of Labor and Fishing and Taxes without Fear or Favor, Depending for Its Life on the Support from the Little Fellow" he voiced his growing anger at class warfare.[12] His themes of fair pay resonated across all ethnic divisions and spoke to cannery workers, who would no longer tolerate this exploitation. The *Alaska Fisherman* stressed the message "Alaska Was for Alaskans," uniting Native fishermen with American and European immigrant fishermen in an effort to resist big business, government domination, and alleged corrupt schemes that kept them on the lowest rungs of the socioeconomic ladder.

Populist economics demanded a redistribution of the wealth and power. This was not an abstract sentiment. Plainly, a fisherman wanted a fair price for his catch so that he could support his family. In this effort fishermen and cannery workers had Progressive Party support and together formed a platform to eliminate overbearing corporations. The ANB and disgruntled laborers also sought the prohibition of fish traps, a symbol of the struggle, and the cessation of nonresident capital and labor in their fishing and cannery towns. In this process, former disagreements gave way to comity among diverse people, but could it last?[13]

As the 1920s gave way to the 1930s, the political horizon had been altered and the influence of James Wickersham and Dan Sutherland had waned, making room for new Alaska leaders. Sutherland decided he had had enough of politics, and in 1932 Wickersham lost his bid for congressional delegate, although he easily slipped into the role of elder statesman. In this new decade there was a dynamic leader who accepted the challenge of frontier government, although he came with baggage that required a good sorting through before he could be effective. Anthony "Tony" Dimond had first entered Alaska politics in 1922, winning a territorial senate seat by promoting progressive reform legislation.[14] From the start, he dove into radical and unpopular causes, such as women's property rights and the passage of an act "giving fishermen and cannery workers preferred liens on property owned by the company employing them in cases of nonpayment of wages."[15] Despite his apparent liberality, Dimond quickly gained favorable ratings as he fought for Alaska, regardless of ethnic background or social class, contending with the many obstacles along the way.

Dimond realized he could not advocate for fishermen and cannery workers until he had resolved the questions surrounding his previous involvement with the Alaska Syndicate. The notorious "Syndicate" was a conglomerate headed by financier J. P. Morgan and the Guggenheim brothers. Together they owned such enterprises as the Kennecott copper mine, the Copper River and Northwestern Railroad, steamship lines, and several salmon canneries. At one time Dimond had been the attorney for the Syndicate and other big cannery outfits that critics had labeled the "fish trust." If the Syndicate's monopolistic clutch was not bad enough, the organization was also known to employ violent methods to discourage opponents, which added to its scandalous reputation.[16] If there was a textbook example of corporate colonialism, the Syndicate would be the model: low wages, physically moving people out of their homes to make room for industry without benefit of law, and sending the profits to far away headquarters.[17]

Dimond understood how this fraudulent image might be lodged in the public's mind and that he needed to overcome the former scandal. His plan was to align himself with Paul's vision of the "common man," and ironically, the first person he needed to win over was William Paul Sr., esteem for whom was rising. The *Alaska Fisherman* was widely read, and applauded for its compelling view and daring language, while its enemies condemned the editorials as a pack of lies. Unruffled, the Paul brothers published opinion pieces, targeting the dishonesty and misappropriation of mismanaged public funds. There had been a time when Paul had directed his arrows toward Tony Dimond, reproaching his former ties with the Syndicate: "You have it in your power to elect men who will represent you and not the steamship company or the Kennecott Mine. You can put an end to the government of Alaska by carpet-baggers who look to Washington DC. But you cannot do so if you elect Tony Dimond."[18]

In the wild game of politics, circumstances and viewpoints undergo necessary and skillful modifications. Paul had a change of heart toward Dimond in 1928 when to his surprise, Dimond handily won the Alaska delegate seat, largely through appealing to the lone fisherman or lumberman trying to make a living. Succinctly, Dimond promised he was going to sever the federal government's dominance in Alaskan matters, aligning himself with settlers, homesteaders, merchants, and local commercial interests. These attitudes motivated Paul to take another view of Dimond's character and motives, yet it still took him a while to get past the fact that Dimond had been the attorney for the Alaska Packers' Association and the Booth Fisheries Company, and that it would be impossible for him to "serve both his constituents and his clients, the cannery companies, at the same time, as it would be for him to serve both God and Mammon."[19] Attitudes shifted for both men when Paul's impassioned pleas for Native rights were echoed by Dimond, a man in a position to effect real change—and the unlikely occurred: the men merged their mutual interests and formed a tight partnership. Both were interested in Native land tenure, and together they constructed a comprehensive land claims bill for Southeast Alaska Natives. The ensuing legislative and congressional battle spanned decades and, when finally decided, had a dramatic impact on Alaska.

At the 1929 ANB Convention it was resolved that the Tlingit and Haida would take all necessary steps toward legally recovering the lands and waterways that had been taken over by timber interests and canneries. As a territorial delegate Wickersham had proposed a land claims bill to the Senate Committee on Indian Affairs, but his efforts were thwarted by Secretary of the Interior Ray Wilbur, who saw no need for any legislation since the rights of Alaska Natives have always been recognized, though his assertion was without evidence.[20] Since Wilbur was an alleged proponent of American Native independence it seemed strange that he would make this statement, but it may have been aligned with his disdain for what he determined were free handouts and his leaning toward rugged individualism, as he defined it. At any rate, Wilbur, who was in the midst of reorganizing the Bureau of Indian Affairs, was an impenetrable barrier against legislation that could result in recompense for Southeast Alaska Natives, once again illustrating the power of bureaucracy.

Nonetheless Wickersham, who had inserted himself into this fight, countered this rejection, by upping the ante on the land claims bill and verbally attacking the unfair cannery employment practices and ethnic discrimination on the fishing grounds. Fully realizing the degree of tension his actions and words caused, Wickersham justified his stance: "The canneries come from San Francisco, Portland and Seattle . . . load their vessels with men, materials, and all that kind of thing, and bring what they called an Oriental crew, five or six thousand people into Alaska . . . they bring the fishermen and cannery workers; and they are only entitled to fish for a limited time, and they fish day and night during that period . . . with their double crews; and the result of it is they do not give these Tlingit and Haida Indians the assistance or work." Wickersham believed the Natives should have a hiring preference and without it they faced financial hardships "from that system which has grown up importing labor into Alaska for the canneries, thereby excluding the Indians from fishing. . . . This was one main reason which had caused those people to ask for a settlement of their rights in their lands."[21]

Wickersham, on behalf of the ANB, was relentless and further appealed to the Senate Committee on Indian Affairs and accused the "fish trust" of controlling Alaska. He declared: "Big canning interests came up here in the seventies, immediately after we purchased this country and they are a powerful organization. You can't do anything with them. They have a lobby always in Washington that is powerful, and it is almost impossible to do anything to help these Indians in the matter of fisheries, but something should done."[22] Recognizing the realities, Wickersham warned Native leaders that the road was going to be long and hard. He was well aware of how the canneries and timber companies were exerting a financial and resource extraction monopoly in Southeast Alaska and that even though land claims were appropriate, the Natives might never see compensation.[23]

Ardency aside, the Alaska Natives had to bide their time, and it was not until the winter of 1934–35 that Delegate Dimond was able to introduce a new bill to Congress, requesting permission for the Tlingit and Haida to sue the United States for compensation of the lands taken through governmental action, particularly the closing of the Tongass Forest as a result of Theodore Roosevelt's 1902 Alexander Archipelago Forest Reserve Act. Although Dimond was respected in Congress, there was a need for more urgency and authority to move the bill, and this occurred when another President Roosevelt became involved in Alaska's dilemma, simultaneous with reviving a country that had fallen off an economic ledge.

President Franklin Roosevelt had selected Paul Gordon to be the director of education for Alaska, a man who was also favored by John Collier, the outspoken head of Indian Affairs and an armchair ethnologist. For administrative purposes, Gordon was an obvious choice since he fit the pattern of paternalism begun decades before with his aspirations of assisting indigenous peoples to find full assimilation into American society. Gordon championed the assumption of Collier and others that Alaska Natives could achieve economic independence and had "been prepared to take fuller advantage of the expanding fish industry," adding that they must receive the broad backing of the federal government. Further, he used the Metlakatla Reservation as an example of what could be done if the cannery business was not only Native run, but protected from outsiders, presumably by the federal government as fiduciary agent.[24]

Gordon also believed that compensation was due to the first indigenous inhabitants, but he remained uncertain how this might be arbitrated and potentially distributed, given the fact that money seemed to disappear within the bureaucracy. Gordon suggested that all financial arrangements be managed exclusively by the Tlingit and Haida to purchase any necessary fish traps, cannery equipment, and infrastructure materials and that wages should be supplemented to ensure stability and growth in the communities.[25] Gordon was aware that the Tlingit and Haida were pursuing compensation for their lands, and should that be successful, certain adjustments would be necessary based on the final judgment. Correspondingly, he told Native leaders the ANB was too diverse in its membership for this special jurisdictional action, an assumption supported and defined by the court when it was advised that a separate organizational body be created as an advocacy group and to act as trustee in the case of a financial settlement. In 1935 Congress authorized the Tlingit-Haida Central Council to go forward with their suit. Furthermore, the council was recognized as a tribal government with the ability to negotiate on a government-to-government basis, a position that was enhanced by President Roosevelt's New Deal legislation, particularly the section regarding Native Americans.

The era of the Roaring 20s or Jazz Age was distinguished by social liberalism and lofty spending habits combined with tremendous innovation and prosperity. This high time of conspicuous consumption, however, was jerked to a screeching halt when the banks crashed in 1929. Because the Great Depression was a socioeconomic equalizer, class differences were less stark. The financial downturn did not distress Alaska as much as more urban areas, but the territory's important fishing industry was affected by dropping salmon prices and decreased wages.[26] In addition, the intrusive arm of governmental control grew further, sending its long fingers into every aspect of commercial fishing and processing, including gear types, fish trap size and ownership, and labor regulations.[27] In spite of the turbulence, Alaska continued hauling fish out of the waters and in some ways benefited from innovative federal legislation set in place to alleviate hardships.

President Franklin Roosevelt established several national programs to employ men and women in public service. The Civilian Conservation Corps (CCC) was one of the more important agencies for Alaska and was responsible for completing numerous projects, including forest maintenance, creating recreation areas, restoring Native art, and building harbor facilities. For Alaska Natives working on the fishing grounds or in canneries, the most significant New Deal policy was instigated through the Wheeler-Howard Act or Indian Reorganization Act (IRA). The 1934 IRA, also called "the Indian New Deal," was enacted to address tribal sovereignty, employment in natural resource production, and preservation of Native culture and livelihood through its economic programs. Native-owned businesses were bolstered through a revolving loan system that proved essential for starting or re-capitalizing small businesses or cottage industries. In Southeast Alaska, these capital transformations had the ability to protect indigenous fisheries and bolster Native-managed ventures, but there were immediate problems since the legislation did not correspond to Alaskan realities.

William Paul Sr. and Tony Dimond understood that these national policies were not going to succeed in Alaska, and together they hashed out modifications to the IRA that more closely met Alaska's needs by first identifying that the original legislation was dependent on tribal identity, whereas Alaska Natives were more closely aligned with a village structure. Appropriate adjustments were necessary for efficacy. After considering numerous solutions, Paul and Dimond constructed the 1936 Alaska Reorganization Act (ARA), but not without lingering questions concerning the revolving fund and its utilization. Also, would there be village sovereignty and could there be Native consensus concerning the reservation controversy? Talk of reservations, which had erupted once word got around that this was part of the legislation, triggered concern. The ARA permitted (even encouraged) designated lands to be set aside for Native use only, but the majority of Tlingit and Haida opposed such measures. There was worry that this would lead to further segregation and dependency on the federal government. Many had heard about the reservations in the states, and they did not want to be reduced to poverty or lose the rights they had worked so hard to gain.

Another group opposed reservations. The cannery owners condemned any changes that would exclude their companies from profitable fishing grounds and tie up the resource in Native hands. Despite the divisive turmoil, it was up to Secretary of the Interior Harold Ickes to administer the legislation, and he was not one to back down from a fight. Ickes, a Chicago attorney, was appointed to this position by President Roosevelt in 1933, and he was zealous in his job. As a social progressive Ickes became an ardent proponent of the New Deal and a defender of America's first peoples. To preserve indigenous land, Ickes fully supported the reservation system even though in Alaska this issue was contested. Ignoring arguments to the contrary, he was adamant that this was the only way to protect indigenous land and resources. It was going to be a hard sell, though.

Unlike many of his colleagues, Ickes was knowledgeable about Alaska and aware of the cannery monopolies and the fish trap controversy. From the onset, he exemplified the very embodiment of the New Deal liberal and worked hand-in-glove with Native leaders to ameliorate the inequities that had grown out of a colonial situation. He often sided with William and Louis Paul on issues, drawing raised brows from other factions within the ANB, notably the Peratrovich family. The Pauls from Wrangell and the Peratrovichs from Klawock had been longtime foes with diverse views of leadership, which only deepened in the 1930s as they vied for a significant role in Alaska politics.

The Peratrovich family were responsible for one of the first canneries in Alaska and enjoyed a degree of prosperity, although Louis and William Paul were convinced this chumminess had political overtones, increasing their resentment. The resulting antipathy set up a perpetual tussling match between William Paul and Frank Peratrovich, brought to a head when they both vied for the same BIA agent appointment. To weaken Peratrovich's chances of receiving the appointment Paul Sr. sent a letter to Charles Hawkesworth, the assistant superintendent of the Bureau of Indian Affairs in Juneau, complaining that Peratrovich was unfit for the job since he had conflicts of interest based on his business transactions. Of course this outraged Frank Peratrovich, but Louis Paul brushed it aside as merely an act of jealousy on Peratrovich's part.[28] In the end William Paul Sr. was hired for the position, pouring fuel on an already raging inferno. Native leadership was fractured by in-fighting at the exact moment when there was a need to present an effective and unified front, but neither party would give an inch.

In retrospect the rivalry between Frank Peratrovich and William Paul was perplexing in that both were concerned about the same matters, despite different tactics. Yet they continued their perpetual stubborn tug-of-war. Like Paul, Peratrovich had decided the out-of-territory cannery companies were responsible for the current troubles: "They have taken our own fishing grounds, closed us off from them and then controlled [the] legislature."[29] Peratrovich was firm that the cannery interests were not just a monopoly, but a complete oligarchy, with the power to set prices, drive fishermen out of their customary fishing grounds, and manipulate cannery administration with their "control of legislation, the press, and civic groups" that wanted to keep resident Alaskans down. The salmon industry lobby opposed government loans to Native fisherman (guaranteed by the ARA) while the big companies easily operated by reinvesting their Alaska profits, and according to Peratrovich, fish and wildlife agencies turned a blind eye to any problems that might exist, including the waste caused by overharvesting. In turn, lawmakers complained that their hands were tied, leaving the fish trust free to exploit the fisheries. Nonetheless, there was no argument that would convince Peratrovich that ARA reserves or the BIA were the answer to these predicaments.

The Department of the Interior had the ultimate authority to develop and administer Native reserves through the Bureau of Indian Affairs. The BIA, however, was unwelcome in Alaska, mostly because of its gripping paternalism that disregarded Native independence. In 1931 the Bureau of Education had transferred all Alaska Native services to the BIA, believing the Alaska Natives would be better served by the Department of the Interior. Initially, the ANB resisted the transfer because leaders, such as Frank Peratrovich and his brother Roy, questioned BIA ethics based on their experiences in the lower states while attending boarding school. They believed the agency squashed Native self-determination.[30] William Paul Sr., on the other hand, was certain the BIA could be molded to fit his plans with all the benefits and none of the deficits. Consequently, the philosophical split further advanced the schism within the ANB, largely propelled by the escalating feud between the Paul and Peratrovich camps.

All the while, William Paul, in his capacity as BIA agent, was an enthusiastic champion of the ARA. He traveled from village to village to promote the merits of the loan program and the positive aspects of land trusts or reservations, believing he was rousing support and doing good things. That was until the 1936 Metlakatla ANB convention and the speeches made by Frank Peratrovich and Frank G. Johnson of Kake, informing the assembly that the BIA had a deadly hold on Native operations and things were about to get worse. The two men had formed a solid partnership, cemented by their distrust of the BIA and fear of reservations. Johnson, a longtime fishermen himself, supported Peratrovich's stance, and had previously fought against the full implementation of the ARA, which he believed had the potential to isolate Alaska Native voices, rendering the Tlingit and Haida powerless.[31]

In the late 1930s, ANB politics shifted toward the Peratrovich and Johnson faction as they used methods to bring labor issues to the fore-front. Johnson was a man who "alternated between the sea and the school house. He taught and fished in Kake and Klawock." In his own words, he recalled how in 1917 his crew brought in 225,000 fish on their seine boat, which was close to the record at the time.[32] As a school teacher, he balanced the curriculum with Native stories and traditions even though this was frowned upon in some quarters since the Natives were supposed to sever their ties to the past; but Frank Johnson balanced the old culture and the current state of affairs, bringing the best of both worlds together. He remained skeptical of government and was joined by others who complained about the BIA and its encouragement of dependency based on money and programs: "Any time you give people something free you're destroying them. That's what BIA is doing to our Indian people here in Juneau."[33]

Roy Peratrovich, Frank's brother, had the same conviction concerning BIA control over the fisheries and believed governmental bureaucracy was wrong for the people, their livelihood, and Southeast Alaska condi-tions, but it seemed nothing could stop the bureaucratic machine from imposing on their way of life. Some may have thought Roy Peratrovich, who had made his living as a fisherman and was the Grand President of the ANB in 1940, would remain a critic of the BIA, but like his brother, he was conflicted about the role of government. He later joined the BIA to see how he could help the Native cause from the inside, and in the next decade, he continued to play a significant role in civil rights legislation.

Without a thorough assessment, the BIA encouraged the building of more canneries, dependent upon IRA funding, resulting in new facilities at Angoon, Kake, Klawock, and Hydaburg. Financial assistance was also available for fishery capitalization at Sitka, Wrangell, Ketchikan, Craig, and Hoonah.[34] The problem was that the BIA did not allow the canneries to be run by the Natives and instead imported non-Native and outside managers to oversee the operations. The government attempted to con-trol the fishermen as well, but that was a more challenging task given the independent nature of fishing. Regardless of the outside intrusions, there were success stories, like the Hoonah purse seine fleet. By using the ARA revolving loan, Hoonah's skilled fishermen built the largest fleet in Southeast Alaska in the 1930s. The captains were experts at navigating the treacherous waters of Icy Strait and rarely failed to deliver fresh salmon to Hoonah Packing Company, the Excursion Inlet cannery, or their families.[35]

Without fail, however, the government persisted in administering the fishing and canning industry as if they were omniscient and rarely bothered to seek information about the environment or conditions in Southeast Alaska waters. For example, the BIA sold boats to the fishermen that were supposed to be safe and efficient, yet the vessels fell apart in the local waters. Since the agency put cost over safety, there were numerous disasters and fatalities.[36] If this was not already bad enough, the BIA often restricted their leased boats to fishing only for certain canneries, and the fishermen were not allowed to harvest outside a prescribed zone, regardless of salmon run locations or current weather conditions. As Fred Paul, son of William Paul Sr., documented: "The BIA dominated the local IRA. Superintendents of canneries, federally appointed bureaucrats, held the purse strings, and unless village IRA did what they dictated, the tightening of purse strings put an end to any criticism of the local superintendent." These same managers dictated the price of fish, who would work in the canneries, and to what companies the fish could be sold in this prescribed trade situation. Millions of dollars were lost and blamed on the Native IRA organizations, whereas the government was the real culprit.[37] In essence, the BIA administration failed and the canneries lost money, while the management blamed the Native fleets or leaders.

During the 1930s the ANB and its supporters continued land reclamation efforts, as politics cultivated malevolence and greed, and the absentee fishery companies demanded an absolute monopoly. While the government and commercial interests vied for control, a foremost contestant arose in Winton C. (Bill) Arnold. Arnold had served as counsel for the canned salmon industry in Seattle and Alaska and had a private law practice in

Ketchikan. He was also a member of the Chamber of Commerce, which aided his natural inclination to support Alaskan resource development, reinforced by his connection with the Alaska Territorial Planning Council. In addition, and perhaps ironically so, he was appointed to work with military authorities on the health of Alaska's fisheries.[38] Arnold understood that salmon was a cash cow and that labor had to be managed in the context of local and national politics. Correspondingly, he played his cards close to the vest, and beyond luck, he possessed an uncanny skill of showing up at the most opportune moments to further his ambitions.

In the beginning Arnold sought Wickersham's assistance in fishery matters, particularly those sticky issues revolving around Native and Asian labor problems. Wickersham, now an elder statesman, had once called Arnold "a cunning cuss," but for some reason took his side in cannery company positions, starting with a vote for the easing of cannery trap leasing laws.[39] Perhaps it took some time for Wickersham to understand Arnold's brand of manipulation, but the ultimate recognition came about during the 1936 Alaska Republican Convention. The incident began when Arnold, understanding the necessity for aligning his political stars, schemed to "oust National Committeeman Rasmuson and Al White, the party counsel" so that he could place his own people in these commanding roles. To understand the critical nature of this maneuvering, it is helpful to know that Albert "Al" White, the head of the first division of the Republican Committee since the early 1920s, was considered an influential man in his own right. He had been Wickersham's head booster for years and was not about to let anything get in the way of this election. Since the "Indian vote or canoe vote" was important, White had also lobbied William Paul Sr. for support, baiting him with a promise to do something about the commercial fish traps. White knew how to play his chips, and so did Edward Rasmuson, who was not only an Alaska Republican National Committeeman but also a banker with significant connections. The ultimate game for White and Rasmuson revolved around appeasing William Paul while casting a wary eye toward Winton Arnold, the chief salmon lobbyist.[40] In retrospect, it was Arnold who should have been more closely scrutinized.

Arnold's plot to redirect the vote was dashed when he accidentally left his briefcase in a public area and one of Al White's supporters discovered a letter within its contents, characterized as a "dynamite shock." In this letter Arnold boasted that he could influence Wickersham's vote and gain his unequivocal support, and thereby overthrow the Republican candidates. When word got out to the Rasmuson-White delegation, extra care was taken in tallying the vote, and in the final outcome the Republicans won handily. Later Wickersham conceded that this had been a "tough blow to cannery interests, but will please Dan Sutherland while Al White will be eight feet tall when he returns to Juneau."[41] Arnold may have lost this round, but it was only a temporary setback. As Wickersham faded from public view, Arnold turned to Tony Dimond for cooperation in controlling the cannery companies and crushing William Paul Sr.'s power. Dimond, the territorial congressional delegate in 1933–45, was unmoved by Arnold's machinations and continued his advocacy for local fisheries management, a hiring preference for Alaska residents, and the abolition of fish traps. Dimond was not about to break up his partnership with Paul, even when rumors started flying that Paul may have been double-dealing.

Arnold was a stalwart opponent, however, as he argued that he alone knew how to advance Alaska's economic progress, attempting to shut down his adversaries. In congressional testimony Arnold declared that without fish traps, towns like Ketchikan would be "of no consequence"— only with the use of the traps did the cannery town become the "salmon capital of the world." Taken further out, he declared this was true for the entire Alaska fishing industry.[42] In spite of his rhetoric, money, and power, Arnold never took Dimond or the ANB down, but he did eventually head up the largest salmon industry lobby group in Alaska's history, which impacted every aspect of the territory's development.

At the beginning Dimond and Paul had grave, unresolved differences, but they sublimated their contentions to work together on important items such as the passage of Alaska's version of the IRA, Native land rights, and efforts to improve conditions in the canneries. When Paul fell into legal troubles, Dimond continued to steer the course and provided leadership for the Southeast Alaska fishermen and the cannery workers. Regrettably, the 1930s were a rocky period for William Paul Sr., and he suffered crucial impediments to his goals when his ethics were called into question, eventually leading to his disbarment in the late 1930s. Even under these circumstances Paul continued to be involved in fishery legislation and cannery interests, yet Dimond was forced to back away and start discussions with Frank Peratrovich and Frank G. Johnson. Dimond and Paul had moved through legislative circles with ease, but Peratrovich and Johnson appealed directly to the fishermen and cannery workers. This perspective gave the men an advantage in gaining support for their goals, which centered on Alaska's independence from federal control.

Since William Paul Sr. was a prominent figure in Southeast Alaska history, it is appropriate to understand his fall from grace and the legal problems that had as many controversial angles as the man himself. Drawing from Fred Paul's book, *Then Fight for It*, the story begins in 1936 when five Kake fishermen were given worthless checks from the Wrangell Narrows Packing Company and Paul, in his capacity as their attorney, traveled to Petersburg and secured three thousand cases of salmon, allegedly as ransom, although the particulars are sketchy. The fish were damaged, but Paul did not find out until later. Meanwhile, he had engaged the services of McClure and McClure in Seattle to recover the value of the salmon. Those attorneys sold the salmon for $3,286.92 and submitted their bill for $2,462.86, leaving only $825 for the five fishermen and their attorney, William Paul. In the end, no cash settlement was given to the fishermen.[43]

Another historical account centers on the political aspects of Paul's troubles, which began when he was served a subpoena at a Senate subcommittee meeting. The timing was aimed to draw the most attention possible to his predicament. The judge gave Paul a year to answer the charges, and in 1937 the district court found his response inadequate and immediately disbarred him. According to Stephen Haycox's analysis: "Legal practices were somewhat less regulated than later, and many attorneys likely could have been charged with similar offenses, but were not."[44] Paul could have been framed, but we will never know because the pertinent documents were destroyed in 1939 as a result of Juneau's Goldstein Building fire.[45]

Despite these troubles and political strife, there was no void in Native leadership during these years. The Peratrovich family stayed involved in the cannery business, organizing fishermen, and working for civil rights. William and Louis Paul did not miss a step either. These men, regardless of the sides they took on local issues, understood that Alaska fishermen were not protected from the corporations and a union was needed. In the late 1930s both Frank Peratrovich and William Paul Sr. started rival labor unions, elevating the Southeast Alaska cannery story in another direction. Unions were difficult to manage under the best circumstances, but luckily the New Deal and its corollary governmental departments and terms afforded assistance to the burgeoning sociopolitical movement and protected workers' organizations against big business. Yet governmental paternalism and racialization detracted from meaningful progress for Native jobs and business interests by limiting autonomous movements and decisions. The ANB continued to follow an indigenous pathway with some success, but could it fight the entrenched discriminatory behavior against Alaska Natives?

8

The Alaskeros

If the 1898 Spanish-American War had never taken place, the Southeast Alaska cannery experience would have been much different. Previous to U.S. involvement in the affairs of the Philippines, the islands had been under Spanish domination for three centuries. Supported by the 1823 Monroe Doctrine, sanctioning international intervention to protect American interests, in the late 1890s, the United States military assisted Philippine rebels in overthrowing the Spanish. Congress justified these actions as a tool to promote American democratic principles, and at the end of the war the Philippine Islands became a United States possession through the Treaty of Paris, resulting in cultural, economic, and educational colonization.[1]

The rebels did not consider themselves truly liberated and instead the perceived neo-domination inflamed dissidents, particularly the Tagalog, the largest Filipino ethnic group, to mount an insurrection against the American forces, which historians now brand the Philippines-American War. Given superior U.S. firearms and numerous troops, it was only a matter of time before the Filipino fighters were subdued and the United States assumed full territorial control. During the transition, the traditional educational system was replaced by a Western education model, but the students did not surrender their spirit of independence or their ancient cultural roots while absorbing American ideals.

By 1905 there was already a large population of non-English-speaking Asian foreigners along the Pacific Coast when Filipino immigrants entered the country under the patronage of the United States government. This influx caused alarm among a xenophobic populace, clearly echoed by the national press.[2] In the words of former U.S. senator Carl Schurz, Malays and Tagalogs would exacerbate the already prevalent racial problems in the country and the foreign population must be contained to preserve the peace.[3] Nonetheless, Filipino immigration to the West Coast and Hawaii escalated in the 1920s, and by 1928 many working in agricultural fields or the canning industry demanded the liberty and freedom they had learned about back in their homeland through the Western-imposed school system.

President William McKinley wrestled with the immigrant problem, particularly involving Filipino nationals, who were protected under United States territorial status. McKinley's objective and hope, as with so many of his contemporaries, was that all foreigners would assimilate to Western norms, perhaps earn a college degree, and go back to the Philippines to work for the benefit of their people.[4] With this strategy in mind the 1903 Pensionado Act was passed by Congress. Initially, the bill had been sponsored by William Taft, the McKinley-appointed governor of the Philippines, and provided federally sponsored scholarships for Philippine students based on the rationale that these educated men and women could export pro-American leadership, thereby harmonizing relations between the two countries.

Not every immigrant was granted a *pensionado*: The qualifications were stiff and students must prove unquestionable moral and physical qualifications. There was also favoritism. Recipients were predominantly connected with United States officials and came from the privileged class, a position that eased their journey through the system.[5] The college and university program, however, was not a complete ride, and a pattern developed for young men to work in the summer for cash and then return to school in the fall semester. Unfortunately, many ran out of money and were forced to accept "low-paying jobs on West coast farms and [in] Alaska canneries" for extended periods of time.[6] The growing industrialization of agriculture and marine harvests did not require educated foreigners but rather young men with strong backs.

For those without benefits it was a tough life, and many Filipino young men felt betrayed by the unfulfilled message they had received from their teachers. As activist and later martyr Gene Viernes noted, "They learned about George Washington, Abraham Lincoln, and Hollywood," but when faced with American realities, a certain dystopia set in, replacing the idealism.[7] These feelings and challenges led to frustration, resentment, and often anger. Even in the early days there was a brewing reactionary stance fueled by the memory of the past subjugation. Whether the Spanish or Americans, both powers asked them to deny their cultural roots, but they resisted and instead called each other "Pinoy," meaning they were Filipino "in thought, deed, and spirit."[8] A sense of transnationalism was not lost; the bonds remained, guiding individual actions and social networks in their new environment. Although immigrants have been characterized as perpetual foreigners or a transplanted culture, the Filipinos adopted the American ethos and the notion of getting ahead. Or, as John Bodnar surmised in his book *The Transplanted: A History of Immigration in Urban America*, "Immigrant adjustment to capitalism in America was ultimately a product of a dynamic between the expanding economic and cultural imperatives of capitalism and the life strategies of ordinary people."[9] It was a long way, however, from working the slime line to being in charge of a business.

Nonetheless, there was little time to curse their predicament. Similar to the Chinese and Japanese immigrants before them, these laborers lived by their wits. Yet a certain desperation lurked below the surface, morphing into rancor, and catalyzing into a pursuit of justice—they would not become victims.[10] For now, surviving was of utmost importance while the discontent continued to brew. Filipino men followed the employment opportunities season by season. When the work ran out in Washington State, the cannery crews headed north to the Southeast Alaska canneries, and the diaspora continued as Alaska salmon canneries recruited Filipinos from California, guaranteeing the crews excellent money, except for a slight living expense fee.[11] Many returned to the Pacific Northwest or California without a dime due to gambling and took the first job they could find, usually in agriculture, but in the next season the lure of Alaska was strong. "That's why you see so many Filipinos here during the months of May, June, and July."[12] The cycle continued through the 1920s and 1930s, and because of their predictable return to Alaska every summer, the Filipino cannery workers were dubbed "Alaskeros."

From the beginning, the Alaskeros worked at various jobs including as sorters, butchers, slimers, fillers, patchers, double seamers, and "catching can," or arranging cans on iron holders for cooking. Lowly jobs were thought to be temporary because it was assumed that through hard work and learning new skills, they would qualify for the more lucrative positions, such as foreman. At first, many of these young men may not have realized they were oppressed by contractors, the middle men who arranged for cannery labor and had a reputation for swindling. Carlos Bulosan, Filipino immigrant, author of *America Is in the Heart*, and cultural hero, worked for a stint at the Rose Inlet cannery on Prince of Wales Island. In his autobiography he described the process: "We were sold for five dollars each to work in the fish canneries in Alaska, by a Visayan from the island of Leyte to an Ilocano from the province of La Union." Bulosan called these contractors "tough"—they were predators of the naïve hopefuls in an intricate web of exploitation.[13]

Even so, a large number of Filipinos moved through ranks to become contractors or "cannery bosses" themselves. While the Japanese and Chinese were hampered by exclusion laws, the Filipinos were United States nationals with fewer restrictions, allowing for societal advancement, particularly with a practical knowledge of English and American customs. They could, in effect, straddle two worlds. From lowly salmon beheader to cannery management, the Filipinos believed they should be treated as full citizens while yearning for a piece of the American pie. Despite a precarious position and before becoming dissatisfied or restless, there were those who considered themselves lucky to have made it to the United States. In one instance, Victorio Velasco, destined to be a spokesperson for the Alaskeros, told of his early 1920 experiences working to unload salmon cans and remembering the "thrill" when he received his "first earned dollars in America," laughing at the "easy money, $7.50 for working 10 hours. In the Philippines, it takes a month for a policeman to earn what I did for barely 10 hours easy work. Such is the better prospect of life in this beautiful country."[14] Nonetheless, his attitude would change over the course of time.

Velasco displayed a complex blend of Filipino patriotism and American idealism, drastically altered when confronted by bigotry so blatant that a person could not break out without luck or connections. He continued, however, to hold onto his high ideals, which later motivated him to reject labor activist groups because he considered these organizations inherently oppressive. A prolific writer, he viewed the socioeconomic realities with an aesthetic flair, often expressed though poetry calling for social change. Other Filipino men spoke out for equity but with dissimilar stances, exemplifying a more down-to-earth approach though still grounded in comparable moral ideology.

Salvador del Fierro was such a leader as he coped with the daily grind yet strove and to extract justice and fair play out of the workplace. He would eventually become an effective advocate for cannery workers, particularly those based in Ketchikan, the heart of the Southeast Alaska cannery industry, and it is easy to see the roots of his motivation:

> They had restaurants, they gave you a meal ticket. They write it down in a book. They had stores where you can buy shoes . . . before you left the port, you were already overdrawn. And in the early days they could work you as long as they wanted to without overtime. And then, when you were in the cannery, they got you every which way. . . . They order the cooks to close the kitchen after meal hours so when you get hungry about 8–9 o'clock, you go to the store and buy some chocolate . . . perhaps crackerjacks, pilot bread or whatnot. . . . They got you both coming and going. You had no escape. You had to pay whatever they asked.[15]

And so it was for many.

Men like Del Fierro and Velasco exemplified two different approaches to cannery life, yet they did not shun their shared heritage and experiences, drawing other workers together in common cause through their passion. Determined to overcome struggles and resist the push to be melted into a pot, the Filipinos held onto their culture as a bedrock, regardless of how certain elements were remolded in this new environment. A show of Americanism was important, but the mixed Asian and Spanish heritage—readily observed in Hispanic dance and music, for instance—was an engrained part of the Alaskeros' identity. This cultural synergy was manifest in cannery towns, especially novel international celebrations that drew dissimilar people together for mutual "good times," taking a bite out of the danger and drudgery of cannery life. An infectious societal atmosphere was created, receptive to another culture whether in song, dance, or spirit. These were the building blocks that would lead to community cohesion and take some of the sting out of being branded as "other."

In terms of "racial" classification, Filipinos, who often referred to themselves as Pinoys, were not considered Mongoloid at first, similar to the Chinese and Japanese. This was a term that carried prejudicial ties, especially within miscegenation laws.[16] Washington State grouped Filipinos under Malaysian. In actuality the population of the Philippines was (and is) a diverse mix of migrants from the greater Asia-Pacific region with their own distinct identity, culture, and history. Years of Spanish colonialism, however, affected Filipinos both biologically and culturally, resulting in great diversity within the population and rendering labels erroneous, capable only of endorsing discrimination derived from stereotypes without a basis.[17]

Nevertheless, racialization and segregation were as much part of the immigrant life as the work itself. For Filipinos from California to the Pacific Northwest and Alaska, there was a hierarchy of supremacy. In fact, the cannery setting was a microcosm of that class structure from the foreman, who answered to the owner, down to those who were butchers or worked the slime line. Further, this social organization was shaped "by the colonial relationship between the United States and Philippines," and despite the Western influence in their home country, they "faced an exclusionary response from an American culture of which they were an integral part."[18] Thelma Buchholdt, a Filipina-Alaskan historian explained: "Racial discrimination against the minority workers was widespread among the white crew members. The races were hired separately and segregated during the transportation to and from the canneries. The white crew traveled in first class cabins."[19] Regardless of callous treatment, the Alaskeros were at the mercy of the steamers to get them up to Alaska and, in many cases, back down to Seattle, although the "run" could be a genuine nightmare.

On these journeys everything including water was rationed—the men were given just enough to keep them alive. In a cavalier manner, the thinking was that if the immigrants made it to Alaskan shores that was fine, but they were disposable.[20] A first-hand 1902 view described the ethnic mix in those early days. Captain Carl J. Carlson of the Alaska Packers' Association on the *Euterpe* (APA *Star of India*) wrote in his journal that when he left San Francisco there were about two hundred men aboard, and at least half of them were destined for the cannery gang; "the rest were fishermen and beach gang and cooks and so on. It was a motley crew. A chinaman was the prime contractor for the company and he recruited his men wherever he could—Chinese, Japs, Mexicans, Filipinos." The balance of the crew were "mechanics, technicians, carpenters, and about fifty fishermen who also sailed the ship."[21]

Immigrants of all nationalities were thrown into what was dubbed "the China hold" and as described by Donald Guimary, a Southeast Alaska cannery worker, as was his father before him, conditions on the cannery ships were brutal. He emphasized that the Europeans were not subject to the same harsh, closed quarters or the perilous plunging of the boat as it traveled the icy, unforgiving North Pacific waters. His description is valuable for understanding the endurance of these Filipino men. The cannery workers were quartered between decks in the bow of the ship, where there was little ventilation and where the pitch and roll of the ship seemed to be worse. Living and eating in extremely close quarters with three-tiered bunks with mattresses filled with straw—called "donkey's breakfast"—many of the workers became seasick and often the smell of the quarters was vile.[22]

These collective experiences and the oppressive conditions created a bubbling outrage. Carlos Bulosan wrote about the anger and sense of alienation among the Filipinos and "how racism and racialization were bound up in the last century's capitalist modes of production," where the cannery worker was only a mechanized unit "in the corporate system . . . we can historicize as emotional labor."[23] In socioeconomic terms the Marxian overtones were undeniable and appropriate for this situation, but philosophy was not on their minds. For the sake of personal welfare it was best to keep your head down and take the part of an industrial cog. To speak up would threaten your livelihood, much like Charles Dickens characters losing their "situation." Emotional labor drains the soul, and the corresponding racial hostility and violence against Filipinos articulated the struggle "to accommodate America's perception of Filipinos both as servile workers and as menacing racial others."[24] This angst, so passionately expressed by Bulosan, begged for an outlet.

The Filipinos talked to each other, imagining a better life, more like the one they had heard about back on their islands. A dichotomy existed between American creeds and the realities of racialization. Although the United States had designated Filipinos as a special group of "immigrant nationals," their economic plight and second-class status were a constant reminder of unfulfilled aspirations. As one immigrant lamented: "My school teachers at home were idealistic Americans [who] told me of America's promises of liberty and equality under the law, but forgot to mention the economic discrimination and racial complexes with which you interest your rainbow-hued promises."[25]

To many, the outright hypocrisy of American pledges versus actual practice was an affront to be addressed, but beyond the tensions created by discrimination there was also inter-ethnic antagonism. In Alaska, Japanese workers worried about this entrance of the Filipinos, who by the 1920s outnumbered other Asians. The Japanese sought protection from their contractors, believing they had the power to limit Filipino employment. One Japanese man summed it up: "We wanted to keep the Filipino from getting too much power . . . because then they could kick the Japanese out."[26] This was one example of many struggles in the cannery environment, and though thwarted by setbacks, barriers, and attempts to block their employment, many Filipinos countered the attacks by overlooking or denying these realities while older immigrants warned idealists not to rebel: don't stir up trouble, nothing good will come of it. Instead they advised the men to keep their heads down, but often their words went unheeded.[27] The Japanese were not the only ethnic group to worry about or resent the Filipinos, and these attitudes added to the conflict, particularly when Filipino men rose in the ranks to become foremen.

Human hostilities contrasted against the open scenic beauty of Alaska and its glaciers, pristine waters, and Tongass Forest, which had the ability to ameliorate the worst days in the fish factory. How these simple pleasures were expressed varied from one to another. There were those who took time to enjoy Alaska's splendor. Frequently, after leaving a place like urban Seattle, "many men saw Alaska as a vacation from the problems," and some started to stay on in Alaska, thinking of the cannery towns as "their territory."[28] Ketchikan was a booming district for Filipino settlement and in its heyday, the fishing town hosted as many as eight canneries, operating simultaneously, all located on the rocky southwestern shore of Revillagigedo Island, a name bestowed by eighteenth-century Spanish explorers. This quaint town, a mixture of living Tlingit culture and the pioneer past, was a natural destination for the immigrant Filipino men based on employment opportunities. Newly recruited workers observed a town with "busy streets flanked by curio shops, fruit stands and restaurants," as they slipped through town and then walked five miles out to the cannery. Their meals in the Filipino bunkhouse consisted of radish leaves, a few shrimp and slabs of pork. Meal breaks were short and there was always work to do; the pitching of fish, hooking, cleansing while others were "catching can" or loading cans onto iron holders. These were the "the coolers carrying 166 cans of salmon before going out to retort to be cooked."[29]

Except for a few breaks, cannery work was the same day in and day out. According to a 1931 account, the Filipino workers were low paid and often worked eleven hours a day or more. Despite the tedium, they continued to follow orders and abided by the contract, swearing never to come back for another season. The resolve disappeared as winter arrived "hard on the heels of autumn, then spring. And Filipinos on the Pacific Coast, young and old look toward the north and Alaska. . . . For Alaska is still the refuge."[30] But was it enough? Filipino workers were torn between their home in the Philippines and a developing fondness for the country they were in, especially because many had given up thoughts of returning. Caught between two cultures, the men (and a few women) searched for methods to bridge the gap, maintain cultural esteem, and create a recreational outlet.

With a love of traditions, Filipino men and women founded their own social and political clubs, which acted as support groups. Using the Ketchikan example again, there were several organizations formed to celebrate cultural events and as a place to discuss issues. The Filipino Social Club, located on Stedman Street in the heart of "Indian Town," was home to many nationalities, and the location of the first Filipino community center in Alaska.[31] In 1938 the organization changed its name to the Filipino Community Club but continued its mission to celebrate Filipino life and organize a platform to air grievances to public officials in hopes of better conditions. In order to display their full embracing of American sociopolitical principles, they donned the rules and regulations of other similar groups, starting with a mission statement encouraging fraternalism among members and aiding in the education of Filipino residents. With this emphasis there was a natural intersection between the social realm and that of proposed political endeavors, reinforced by the intentions and energies of the first officers, including Salvador Del Fierro, previously mentioned for his cannery work and activism, and Enrique Rodrigues, a Filipino national married to Selina Eaton, a Tsimshian woman from Metlakatla.

The blurring of social and ethnic lines was obvious from the beginning and even more so through membership in the same institutions, such as the local Catholic Church. Del Fierro and Rodrigues were members of Ketchikan's Catholic Church, as was Joe Llanos Sr., a Ketchikan business owner and also a founding member of the Filipino Social Club. The church membership and shared traditions acted as another layer of cohesion, strengthening the bonds between Filipino workers and at times, their Native wives. Together these founders encouraged more community involvement as they endeavored to lift the overall standing of Filipino workers and to participate in the budding Alaskan civil liberties movement, largely steered by the ANB. Ketchikan was an ideal location for this organization because of the cannery issues and large Filipino population, essentially developing into a model for other Filipino residents wanting to form a similar organization.

In 1929 a Juneau-based Filipino organization was initiated to celebrate such events as Rizal Day, the honoring of a cultural hero renowned for his fight against imperial powers to free the Philippines. From this inspiration, a political foundation was built by its founders: cannery workers and laborers in the local gold mine, consisting of six men and one Tlingit woman, Bessie (Jackson) Quinto, who was married to Marcelo Quinto, a miner and cannery man. Bessie Quinto balanced a dual role as a broker between her own culture and that of her husband, dividing her time between Juneau's Filipino Community, Inc. and ANB/ANS activities, and thereby assisting both bodies in becoming politically strong and fighting for employment rights.

Although humble, Bessie Quinto was a trailblazer, and other Tlingit and Haida women, often married to Filipino men, joined forces with her to combat ethnic bias. A collaboration was built consisting of the indigenous and the immigrants, which was natural considering that they lived in the same residential enclaves composed of several ethnically blended families.[32] Moreover, it was not surprising that Filipino social clubs paralleled the ANB and ANS in a similar mission of uplifting their social status in a highly discriminatory atmosphere. Like the ANS and ANB, Filipino workers were angry upon seeing signs that banned them from business establishments or the numerous impediments to starting their own businesses. Two marginalized groups, Filipinos and Alaska Natives, galvanized into a force that broke barriers while increasing membership and gaining a voice that was eventually heard in Washington DC. Yet this remarkable line of offense did not materialize instantaneously. At first there was a wide gulf between Alaska Native villages and single Asian men, and the unity had to be built brick by brick.

Before the 1930s there were not as many Filipino–Alaska Native marriages, and it is of interest to see how this social phenomenon developed during this era. Beginning in the World War I years, the influx of Filipino workers increased, but "about 95 percent of Filipinos on the west coast went to Alaska, most without families."[33] The opportunity of meeting potential marriage partners was presented through numerous social gatherings in the cannery facility, a prime site for dances, weddings, or meetings, and in time there were more mingling opportunities, resulting in an increase in immigrant-Native families. This was especially pertinent with changing migration patterns and the fact that Alaskeros were not returning to Washington State as frequently, finding Southeast Alaska a pleasant location to settle, where one could earn a living year-round and enjoy hunting and fishing. "Romances blossomed as the Filipino men worked and socialized with native women in the canneries." That did not mean bias was not present, but something about big band dances or Fourth of July fireworks brought people together.[34]

Ethnic intolerance was diminished among the children, apparently blind to differences in their playmates. Tlingit elder Marie Olson recalls her childhood summers at the cannery where her mother worked and how she loved to sneak down to the Filipino bunkhouse because they had the best rice candy. These were carefree times when the evening breezes came off the ocean and circulated the aromas coming from kitchens and dining halls in a multicultural fusion.[35] At social events cannery workers, whether Asian or Alaska Native, would often sing "God Bless America" and the "Star Spangled Banner" followed by "Philippines, My Philippines" at the end of the evening. The mixed customs "reminded whites that Filipinos belonged to American society, but also indicated Filipino refusals to accept that their heritage and being an American were mutually exclusive."[36] In this collective ethnic setting, a new allegiance was forged, ritualized in songs and dances and harmonized by Spanish guitars.

Another central focus, as previously mentioned, was the Roman Catholic Church, which drew Europeans, particularly the Italians, Spanish, French, and of course many Filipinos based on their Spanish heritage.[37] The Church provided a sanctuary for the homeless or those immigrants just arriving to a cannery town, and "offered both spiritual and material help to community members," confirming the notion of equality among people regardless of social status or origin.[38] Acting as a point of cohesion, the Catholic Church supported families and the challenges of creating a life in a foreign country. Through Church traditions, kinship connections were extended, such as *Compadrazgo*, the ritualized social relationship necessary for church baptisms, confirmations, and marriages with special emphasis on the "ties created between parents and godparents," who were now *compadres*, "bonding families closer together. Godparents were selected to help raise children who in turn were expected to treat and obey godparents as real parents."[39]

The blood and marriage bonds were of equal consequence and vital for the strength of the family unit.[40] Similar to the circumstances among Alaska Natives, group identity was more highly valued as compared to individual achievement. As one Filipina expressed it, "The most important aspect of the Filipino culture I would like to pass to my children is the family closeness. In Filipino culture, the family unit is the most important thing," as opposed to the individualistic American society.[41] Labor activist Philip Vera Cruz emphasized that family was a significant building block for community consciousness and if damaged, Vera Cruz was certain that Filipinos would be pulled apart and the unity broken.[42] In these families, the elders were revered for their wisdom, and the children were adored as the hope of the of the future.

Often both parents worked at the canneries. Perhaps a woman was a processor while her husband fished for a specific cannery under contract; or in other cases, women worked at the plants alongside their

Filipino husbands, who performed the heavier labor such as running the fish ladders or offloading scows. As in every society, the women's main concern was childcare and they depended on the support of the family.[43] Traditionally, the bulk of "insider workers" were women, and when there was a need for cash, women had to be available when the salmon runs came in, and that meant leaving the children. Although older children could act as babysitters, there were also built-in social devices through kinship networks and extended social relationships that acted as a backup system. For women cannery workers, both family and "fictive kin" were essential—an auntie, for instance, might have no biological tie, yet performed the necessary functions. This was the cultural glue that allowed families to remain intact while women worked long shifts.[44] There were times, however, when the family could not fulfill these needs and women looked outward for support from organizations or the community.[45] Cannery towns tended to have more in common than not and shunned biased behavior in favor of helping others regardless of ethnic background, thus building associations, acting as an ever present resource.[46] In summary, groups of migratory workers, filled with the ideas of Jeffersonian democracy, settled down close to the canneries, and through mutual ties social and political bonds were formed between people with a long history in Alaska and newcomers. Many of these new interactions were not necessarily formed at the cannery but also during leisure events.

Cannery shifts were long, and free time was precious. Some canneries sponsored baseball or basketball teams, where naturally there were additional opportunities for more cross-cultural understanding to occur, but they were also occasions to witness ethnic discrimination. Public gatherings often took place in movie theaters or basketball courts, but both venues remained segregated. For instance, Filipino men could play basketball on the ANB courts but not on the "white" courts. Regardless of restrictions, numerous shared occasions sowed the seeds for friendly relationships as Leon Ayson, the owner of the New York Café on Stedman Street, related: the Filipino men came up every year and interacted in the community. Eventually the men would court a woman and "that's how the families started."[47] Leon Ayson had first-hand information on this topic since he had married Elsie Brown, a Tsimshian, and he understood the problems encountered by blended families, but he spoke of more enjoyable times, such as weekend parties, clubs, and programs where everyone was invited, including the mayor and other officials. There were speeches, singing and dancing, often accompanied by a Filipino string orchestra or the local ANB band.[48] In another account Ketchikan baker Crititoto "Joseph" Llanos Sr. explained that his wife Jessie Milton, a Tsimshian woman originally from Metlakatla, was an active member of the local ANS as well as her husband's Filipino organizations. According to Llanos Sr., he and his wife operated a troller, *Debra*, and made a good living. In his later years Llanos used his expertise to become a cannery superintendent and part owner of a Ketchikan cannery, which was considered highly unusual.

Llanos was aware of the problems associated with single Filipino men and he did not envy them. The men were often lured by both gambling and prostitution—two ways to separate them from their money. This long-standing problem had been recorded earlier by fishery agents: "Orientals are inveterate gamblers, and there are usually several sharpers with each cannery gang, generally with the connivance of the contractor's agent, although it is usually an impossibility to prove this legally and they inveigle the green hands into all sorts of gambling games, and in this manner frequently succeed in winning all or part of their season's wages."[49] Even though most of the men were married, there was still a large population of transitory single men who stayed for the season in towns like Ketchikan.

Llanos recalled the fights that broke out. When money was involved, tempers could flare. In one instance a Filipino worker was gambling in a Chinese house and he disputed an eleven-dollar winning, which ended in the death of the Chinese dealer.[50] In 1922 bets were placed on a boxing match between a Filipino cannery worker and a local resident. This fight ended without incident, but the Filipino crew guaranteed they could "furnish the public any weight from bantam up to middleweight. We are ready to challenge any imported or local fighters."[51]

Llanos, for one, was sure that single men were at loose ends and that it was better if everyone was married, thus lending stability to Southeast Alaska communities. But the persistence of young men seeking adventure could not be repressed and single men, true Alaskeros, continued to travel from Seattle to Alaska every season. They came with news of what was going on in California and Washington. They talked of unions and getting a square deal. Or they spoke in haunting terms of how bad it was getting on the large waterfronts at Puget Sound or "Frisco" and that Alaska seemed like an escape. Men like Victorio Velasco, previously referred to for his activist writings, enjoyed his summers at the idyllic Waterfall, a place where he could blend his love of nature with idealism. Waterfall Cannery did not have much around, so leisure time was spent with "card games, sport fishing, hikes, beachcombing, catching crabs," but only when the fish runs were not coming in.[52] The closest town was Craig, about an hour away by boat. In the winter there were only two watchmen, but in the summer the population expanded to about two hundred workers. While the Filipino crew had their own housing, the Native crew, mainly from Hydaburg, the nearby Haida community, took boats over to the cannery when they were needed. Joy Craig, a Haida woman and a descendant of George Hamilton, founder of one of first salteries and canneries in Southeast Alaska, described the Waterfall Cannery as an organic, unrefined playground for her siblings and friends when she was young.[53] There was no formal entertainment at this cannery, and many workers passed the time by enjoying the natural landscape, transforming their experiences into song or poetry, as did Victorio Velasco. Like so many Filipino workers, he was a student at the Seattle University, and cannery work paid his tuition. In the 1920s he published the Seattle-based *Filipino Forum*, but that was only the start of his many publications. Aboard the ss *Alameda*, on his way back up to the Waterfall Cannery, he wrote a poem about Alaska, likening it to a respite for the "soul that is tired and weary" from the chaos of the city, and adding that the serenity of the landscape was of "unknown grandeur" with "joy and beauty" to those downtrodden by the drudgery.[54]

As a man of verse and social commentary, Velasco believed his people were victimized by the United States economic system and reported in the *Philippine Review* on the numerous labor disputes and discriminatory events. Even after the Filipinos were established in the Alaskan canneries, he noted that they still fought for a living wage: "The line between jobs open and not open to Orientals and Filipinos is tightly drawn. Neither work performed nor wage earned has proved attractive to American itinerant workers,"[55] and the Filipinos were at the mercy of whatever was available. Velasco, like many of his Filipino associates, sought social justice for all minorities. Whether through bucolic musings or blistering opinion pieces, he revealed the realities of surviving in a dog-eat-dog world, and his message, and other similar protests, found receptive ears and encouraged discussions revolving around equity and the need for action. Throughout his life Velasco continued to work and write from the Waterfall Cannery until his death in a bunkhouse fire in 1968.

Talk of union organization started as early as 1905 in Ketchikan, but the movement barely sputtered for a few decades before taking hold. It was not for lack of enthusiasm, but to be effective, a stable political base must be established to go against the existing monoliths. Specifically, any labor association must be adept in contending with or knowing how to benefit from connections with the American Federation of Labor (AFL) or the Congress of Industrial Organizations (CIO). The AFL was formed in 1886 as a coalition of major craft unions and quickly developed into a major political force in American economics. With money and power, the organization was able to fight for wages and better conditions all the way to Washington DC, rallying for unrepresented laborers. After its 1886 startup, a faction of the AFL, which was more interested in representing the common worker, broke away from the original organization, forming the rival Congress of Industrial Organizations. Both the AFL and CIO influenced Alaska labor relations by either conflicting or harmonizing philosophies and protest tactics.

When the Filipinos initiated unionization in the Pacific Northwest, they were ignored by the AFL and CIO and thought of as mere random upstarts, representing an inconsequential workforce, although the fishery industry was a major economic concern in the region. This snub was coupled with ideological dissension regarding ethnic membership, American nationalism, and prevailing attitudes toward Asian immigrants. The AFL was blatantly racist, and the stain of ethnic hatred was ever-present, as seen in the 1928 AFL Convention, which called for a halt to all things from the Philippines despite the desire for cheap labor that was likened to a "cancer in American private and public life, destroying American ideals and preventing the development of a nation based upon racial unity and whereas in turn this desire had exploited the Negro, the Chinese, the Japanese, the Hindus . . . there are a sufficient number of Filipinos ready and willing to come to the United States to create a race problem equal to that already here." There was a call for exclusion and legislation to prevent the Filipinos from being "imported" into the country.[56] With this prevalent mindset not only was activism not tolerated, but certain ethnic segments of the labor force were treated as a scourge to be wiped out.

During the Depression, there was greater competition for jobs and the AFL believed they knew what was at the heart of the problem. Filipinos were accused of "destroying American ideals and [preventing] the development of a nation based on racial unity."[57] The nationalism and xenophobia aimed at the Filipino immigrants was ironic since they tended to display their ties to the United States proudly, as observed through exhibiting the American flag or other national symbols at their meetings and social gatherings. While the AFL attempted to tear apart cohesion between different ethnic and economic groups, the CIO supported racial and gender diversity, becoming the protectorate of the downtrodden. The CIO, however, could "not dissolve ethnic and racial group consciousness or end cultural antagonism but they did give a highly divided work force a basis for cooperation on issues of mutual concern."[58] The CIO organizers realized the importance of Alaska and its workers, and unlike the AFL, the mega-union encouraged women to become members. Filipinos and Native women, therefore, were naturally inclined toward the CIO because it was "organized across race and ethnicity, as well as gender" and appealed to labor groups on the fringe.[59]

Within the union charters there were promises of relief from harsh economic conditions, but outsiders twisted the message so that it appeared these organizations were instead tainted by communist connections and judged to be subversive by the general public. Unions were said to be breaking the back of the capitalistic society that had been stomped upon by the Great Depression. Edward Morrissey's editorials in the *Ketchikan Chronicle*, as well as many other local papers, reinforced this charge, making it difficult to think of unionizing in Alaska with the prevailing attitude that "the Alaska canning industry had a high percentage of Filipino workers, some of whom were drawn to the Communist Party because of the Party's position against racism and imperialism."[60]

This communist charge, though overstated, was not without gravity. Influential union leader Chris Mensalvas, a former Seattle university student who had dropped out when he found out he could not be a lawyer in the United States, spoke of the discrimination that was heaped on the Filipinos and other Asians. These factors, plus his aborted student career, created a rebel, who was eloquent and fierce. That he understood the Alaskero experience helped him in his job as recruiter, and although his family was from a "landed" class in the Philippines, he was imbued with Marxian spirit after what he and his friends had gone through trying to rise in social status. When interviewed in 1975, he was proud of his radical "Stalin communist" leanings, though his beliefs had made him a target. Mensalvas was one of the more vocal messengers calling for organized labor as he brought his crusade to Southeast Alaska.[61] Later he was joined by others with the same ideals, buttressed by the news about what was happening in Seattle, yet these transitory Filipino spokesmen were never as effective in rallying support as those living the Alaska cannery life.

It was not long before Alaskan workers saw the CIO as the only union affiliation that would work for their needs despite the rumors of its alleged political stance.[62] Many considered communist charges as merely the sensationalized yellow journalism that framed organized labor or a defense against the perceived threats to status quo American institutions and values. Whether one was an ideologue or working the slime line, it was increasingly clear that the cannery owners were the true profiteers and enjoyed an untouchable oligarchy. In turn, the CIO appealed to labor because of its promise to stand by the common man. Western-schooled Filipinos were engrained with the pledge that "all men are created equal . . . pride and sensitivity will not permit [workers] to assume passively the role of an inferior."[63] These beliefs fueled the Filipino labor movement and eventually led to the formation of some of the most powerful marine workers' unions in history. In Alaska, Filipinos and Natives joined together in solidarity.

While patterns of cooperation were exemplified by cannery workers, the same could not be said for the general Alaska population. Tensions and troubles were blamed on the immigrants, and some protesters called for them to be driven out of town. One Ketchikan paper remarked that if all the immigrants were banished, "the people in Alaska do not consider it either a social or economic loss."[64] Along the Pacific Coast and into Alaska, the "white" labor force felt their jobs or status were in jeopardy and complained, eventually leading to legislation that restricted the free travel between the Philippines and the United States. With these limits, it was believed the flow of alleged undesirable elements could be halted, along with their foreign and communist doctrines. Newspaper headlines broadcast the perils of the Bolshevistic element embedded within the unions, which possessed the ability to shut down commerce in the United States.[65] Who was to blame? It was said that it was the Filipino communists who had brought the "Third Asiatic Invasion" into the country. Those drenched in nativistic attitudes took their concerns to legislators, demanding swift action. The wave of hysteria was coupled with financial concerns, such as increased Philippines imports, assumed to be putting the pinch on Midwest farmers. In its totality, it was enough impetus for Congress to react to the racial animus.[66] There could be only one answer to the burgeoning Filipino problem and that was further exclusionary legislation.

The Tydings-McDuffie Act or the Philippine Independence Act (Pub. L. 73-127) changed the Philippines Islands from an American colony to an independent country, revoking nationalist standing. In lieu of an exempt status, limitations were established for Filipino immigration to the United States. Not only were new immigrants restricted to just fifty per year, but now Filipinos already residing in the United States lost their shielded position and were considered aliens without hope of future citizenship. Further, the act extended the original 1924 Asian exclusion policy and changed the Filipino ethnic category from Malaysian to Asian, equivalent to the Chinese and the Japanese with the identical restrictions.[67] The precise language in the bill read: "For the purpose of the Immigration Act of 1917, the Immigration Act of 1924. All other laws of the United States relating to the immigration, exclusion, or expulsion of aliens, citizens of the Philippine Islands who are not citizens of the United States shall be considered as if they were aliens. For such purposes, the Philippine Islands shall be considered a separate country."[68]

Once implemented the Tydings-McDuffie Act squashed the dreams of many young Filipinos and they felt cheated, which motivated petitions to President Franklin Roosevelt. In a 1934 example, one Filipino group, demoralized by low wages and the absence of citizenship rights, wrote about racial discrimination and threats to their basic survival. The petition added: "We have all emigrated to the United States, stimulated by the high ideals of Americanism and desirous of finding a higher and more worthy means of expression, only to be disillusioned on every hand by the experiences of our unsatisfactory social status."[69] Their appeals were answered in 1935 by the Filipino Repatriation Act, which allowed the United States to deport any Filipino at will.

The field was ripe for increased labor activism. Discriminatory legislation "fueled efforts to develop a stronger and more effective union that could fight to preserve cannery jobs."[70] When people were denied basic freedoms, and this was coupled with persistent racialized legislation, unionization appeared to be the solution for taming volatile labor relations problems. The Alaskeros persisted in their efforts, striving for better paychecks and safe travel and working conditions, even though their actions brought a backlash. Deemed troublemakers, the so-called dissidents were thrown into jail or "union leaders were threatened with deportation. Verbal threats were followed by . . . violence and death."[71] Martyrs were legendized into epic heroes and their narratives were retold at union meetings throughout the Pacific Northwest, eventually traveling north to Alaska, where the movement gained purchase in a sociopolitical world of immigrants and Alaska Natives. At first glance this pairing might seem unlikely, but from a historical vantage point, the two ethnic groups were destined for a common battle.

FIG. 1. William L. Paul Sr. holding the Tee-Hit-Ton Raven Hat, 1944. The precious clan object was rescued from a thrift shop by William Paul Sr.'s mother in 1920. William L. Paul Jr. photo collection. Used by permission.

FIG. 2. Hoonah's cannery row in the 1930s. Hoonah had a number of canneries in that decade, including Hoonah Packing Company and Icy Strait Salmon Company. A significant part of this village was burned down in the 1940s. William L. Paul Jr. photo collection. Used by permission.

FIG. 3. William "Bill" Paul Jr. reading the "Johnny DoughBoy" military comic book aboard ship in 1945. William L. Paul Jr. photo collection. Used by permission.

FIG. 4. A Ketchikan cannery stacking salmon packs for shipment, 1920s. The boxes are labeled "Ketchikan Alaska Holsom Salmon Brand." Courtesy of the Michael Nore Collection.

FIG. 5. Funter Bay, located on the west side of Admiralty Island, was the site of the Thlinket Packing and Trading Company (founded in 1902) and later the site of one of the Aleut relocation camps during World War II. Courtesy of the Michael Nore Collection.

FIG. 6. Fish ready for canning at Taku Harbor. A typical example of mechanization, this was the environment for the workers for days at a time. Courtesy of the Michael Nore Collection.

Chomley, Alaska.
Olinda. 5663

FIG. 7. Chomley Cannery on Prince of Wales Island was the plant where significant Filipino activism took place aimed at improving working conditions. This cannery put out its own news bulletin. Courtesy of the Michael Nore Collection.

FIG. 8. Group photograph of Metlakatla cannery workers in uniform. Courtesy of the Michael Nore Collection.

FIG. 9. Mending nets at the Metlakatla cannery. Courtesy of the Michael Nore Collection.

FIG. 10. *Star of Greenland*, one of the Alaska Packers' Association fleet. Courtesy of the Michael Nore Collection.

9

Fighting Back with Unions in the 1930s

In President Franklin Roosevelt's 1933 inaugural address he painted a colorless portrait: "A host of unemployed citizens face the grim problem of existence, and an equally great number toil with little return. Only a foolish optimist can deny the dark realities of the moment."[1] Despite these desperate times, the worst aspects of the Great Depression were never fully realized in Alaska. Life went on as usual for the most part. Salmon were harvested, brailed, beheaded, and stuffed in a can, although there were strains on individual canneries and more competition occurred for employment. The nation was looking toward President Roosevelt's "New Deal" assurances that promised opportunities and the rebirth of industry. This was also a time of alliances, the knowledge of power in numbers, formation of labor associations, and defiance against corporatism. Laborers resisted the fact that big business made all the decisions about production and labor conditions, and a momentum energized by collective voices eventually made its way up to the rugged Southeast Alaska coves.

The cannery worker's world was a highly mechanized landscape where the individual was overlooked, but as a group, the workers' sense of helplessness was mitigated by belonging to something bigger. In this atmosphere, ethnic cleavage could be an obstacle, but with the realization of commonalities a new identity was forged, encouraging cannery workers and fishermen to band together, resulting in a strong coalition. The knowledge of potential group power had evolved slowly from discussions on the cannery docks or town meetings before it was discovered that a disparate segment of the population, fishermen and cannery workers, were attempting to attain the same goals. Because of mistrust and competition, however, inter-ethnic associations were rare, and most unions remained segregated along socially defined lines in the beginning. One outstanding example was the Alaska Fishermen's Protective Union of the Pacific Coast and Alaska, which began in 1902 with an initial membership composed of European fishermen from the San Francisco Bay area. Later the name was changed to the Alaska Fishermen's Union (AFU), and it represented both cannery and independent fishermen for the purposes of negotiating contracts, setting fish prices, and delineating the responsibilities of the fishermen and crews for up to three years in advance. It was noted that the fishermen appeared to be happy with the contracts and stuck by them, greatly reducing the number of "strikes and bickerings, which were very common some years ago."[2] "The AFU fishermen received better pay and quarters aboard the cannery ships as well as at the canneries," stirring the ire of the less fortunate.[3]

The AFU was selective in its membership and did not allow "Indians" because they were allegedly unskilled and could not compete with the non-resident fisherman. Given the history and culture of the Southeast Alaska Natives, that was an absurd conjecture, but it was the standard practice in those days, and the big cannery outfits continued to import their own non-resident fishermen and cannery workers in a "colonial pattern of exploitation where outsiders plundered the region and left locals with the ecological wreckage but not the spoils."[4] The AFU assured its members that Alaska's fishing grounds were there for harvesting without restraint, while the Tlingit and Haida, weary from seeing their usual and accustomed fishing sites impinged upon or their cannery jobs taken, looked to the ANB to prioritize their cause, aligned with the organization's goals of redeeming civil rights and regaining control of the Alaskan fishing industry.

William Paul Sr. targeted the AFU and disputed its legitimacy. He alleged that while the AFU fishermen were raking in the profits, the resident fishermen were getting a raw deal, and he described all San Francisco–based unions as migratory birds that fly "north with the cannerymen, much as the seagulls fly following the large passenger ships," ostensibly looking for leftovers granted to them by legislation favoring big business over the independent fishermen.[5] In the *Alaska Fisherman* Paul declared that "these fishermen are not Alaskans in any sense of the word . . . they come up to Alaska for the short salmon fishing season, and immediately depart for their homes" back in the Pacific Northwest or California.[6] Paul further accused them of being robbers sent to Southeast Alaska waters to "deplete our fisheries and depart for other lands when that is done."[7]

Paul was not alone in his view. There was a growing dissension between the nonresident and resident fishermen and it was said that these outsiders "were organized by the Alaska Fishermen's Union, headquartered in San Francisco. The union insisted that packers should pay the nonresident fishermen four cents more per fish than they paid the residents."[8] Resident fishermen attempted to block the nonresident fishermen, chiefly by forming their own local partnerships, but their efforts were unsuccessful because packers refused to recognize their authority or demands. While the hostility sizzled, William Paul found allies among the non-Native, independent resident fishermen, who agreed with the *Alaskan Fisherman*'s longstanding masthead slogan ALASKA FOR ALASKANS, which became a rallying cry heard from the local saloons to scows lined up at the cannery dock—it was a call for action. Back in the early years Paul had reached out to all resident fishermen, regardless of their ethnic background, and as his appeal grew along with his willingness to include everyone, the essential support was increased until it was a force to be reckoned with.

The AFU was not the only union in Alaska at the time, but it was the biggest and a natural target for the disgruntled or those shut out of the action. The crisis escalated with the entrance of mega–labor union organizations, notably the AFL and CIO, as they vied for control of the valuable Alaskan fisheries. As previously revealed, the American Federation of Labor had a rocky history in ethnically diverse Alaska, and splinter groups were created on the basis of disagreements, primarily deriving from the AFL's ethnic exclusionary policies. In Southeast Alaska the fisheries and canneries were the principal industry and employer, and Alaska Natives, whether cannery workers or independent fishermen, faced consistent discrimination from the big outfits and corporations, without recourse. This was not only an Alaskan problem but concerned all marine workers. When the CIO recognized this situation, the organization stepped in as an autonomous labor organization "at a moment of unprecedented mass upheaval and naked class conflict" and quickly gained strength because it appeared to meet the needs of disregarded workers. Union representatives rolled into action, identifying the worst problems, but could not effectively represent Southeast Alaska workers yet.[9]

During the 1930s William Paul had built a reputation in Southeast Alaska, and although it was not always positive, he was recognized for his leadership and was a frequent and passionate speaker. At the ANB and ANS conventions there were two characteristic elements: first, the meetings were opened by the much-loved Angoon brass band, playing the Brotherhood song, and second, the matter of fish traps had a high priority on the agenda. William and Louis Paul were vocal on this issue and encouraged others to join their cause of advocating for the demise of the industrial device that resulted in the outright destruction of fisheries. There was talk about physically breaking up the traps, although the impulse was tempered by more moderate views from those who did not want to risk jail time. And among the struggling fisherman, it was not only fish traps that were cutting into their livelihood. There were inequities in the pricing of Native-caught salmon. William Paul Sr. attempted to address these concerns, but to be successful he needed the full ANB and ANS backing, and due to in-fighting or more moderate viewpoints, that collaboration was not always available to him.

In frustration, some members were tired of discussions that did not accomplish the necessary changes in the industry. One of the more outspoken men on this topic was Cyril Zuboff, originally from Killisnoo, who had filled ANB office positions all the way up to president and was also a frequent guest speaker at ANS meetings. In 1933 Zuboff declared that the time had come "when we must do something. We must find other methods even if it costs blood. Nothing will happen unless we use direct action."

Chester Worthington from Wrangell and one of the original founders of the ANB considered these issues close to home since his Japanese son-in-law had worked in the canneries when he first arrived in Southeast Alaska and had faced cruel discrimination. Worthington argued, "We have indebted ourselves so much to the cannery that we can't squabble about fish prices," referring to the stranglehold cannery owners had on the Alaska fisheries. Finally, a disgruntled Louis Paul complained that they might do better in Canadian waters if allowed, although Alaska's neighbor had a spotty record in Native relations.[10]

Later in 1933, in another ANB gathering, ANB Grand President Frank Booth brought up the matter of unionization again, reminding the members that at the 1931 ANB convention he had encouraged others to "organize a sort of a union to create better labor and living conditions in the canneries." Walter Soboleff, a Presbyterian minister and champion for Natives' rights throughout his long life, supported this idea but was skeptical regarding implementation. He felt there were many pitfalls and the correct path was yet to be found. During the 1930s Soboleff was responsible for keeping the meeting minutes and often wrote his own thoughts in the margins. In one instance when the talk of unions was especially heated, he jotted down this question: "Can we really stick together?"[11] But he also added a further note: the ANS must be involved in decisions, even those concerning fish prices and especially cannery safety.

The Great Depression hurled the world into chaos, and the United States, once a vibrant financial world leader, was shaken to the core. President Franklin Roosevelt developed ambitious, radical, and effective programs that proved to be a boon to the economy and labor force. In the early years of the Depression, unions were hampered by restrictions on their activities, particularly when private companies and the government discouraged strikes. In retrospect, workers were reticent about engaging in any activity that might risk their positions and force them into soup lines, leaving them vulnerable. Because of the need to protect workers' rights, President Roosevelt responded to labor concerns by pressing for passage of the 1935 National Labor Relations Act (NLRA), which federally guaranteed the right to strike and promoted collective bargaining. Per usual, any changes were slow to be enacted in Alaska, but once the word got out about the favorable stipulations within NLRA and its accompanying labor negotiations board, it appeared to be a method to end the stagnation in labor-employer relations, and importantly, the union movement now had the backing of the government, adding high octane fuel to the mix.

One of the first Southeast Alaska unions to organize and take advantage of this New Deal legislation was the Alaska Salmon Purse Seiners' Union (ASPSU) with an auxiliary cannery workers branch. Soon after its formation, Frank Peratrovich became involved, and therefore this organization could trace a link going all the way back to the first cannery in Klawock.[12] This union was open to workers of all ethnicities, including the Scandinavians, Italians, and Slavs and also the local Tlingit and Haida fishermen and inside workers. Frank Peratrovich founded the Klawock base and became a presence in all union activities, which required his participation in fishery issues and the political scene, both locally and nationally. In this endeavor he solicited his allies in the ANB, including old ally Frank G. Johnson, and together they solidified the Alaska Salmon Purse Seiners' Union and Cannery Workers Auxiliary Union under an AFL charter with the Seafarers International Union of North America.[13] The ASPSU continued to grow in membership and influence, eventually shifting its main headquarters to Ketchikan and extending its strength throughout Southeast Alaska. These gains, however, came under scrutiny in some circles, who believed the ASPSU exhibited favoritism toward "white fishermen." The perceived discrimination and ruthless jockeying for control of the fishing grounds motivated Native fishermen and cannery workers to seek a more local or community-based body to act as an advocate in this competitive arena.[14]

William Paul Sr., who had been thinking of unionizing for many years, was quick to jump on this incoming wave, but he was not willing to start a separate organization since he was convinced the ANB was the only appropriate political body to stand with Natives. Correspondingly, by late 1935, the first Native fishermen's association and marine workers' union was begun under Paul with ANB support, but it remained a small group for several years. Later in the decade, after Paul's oldest son Bill Jr. had graduated from law school, he joined his father in the union business, and according to Fred Paul, his other son: "During the late 1930s and early 1940s my father worked at a variety of jobs. He and my brother Bill organized and operated an agency with the ANB to represent the inside workers of the Alaskan salmon canneries."[15] This addition was appropriate and greatly needed, but regrettably the fishermen's complaints were answered first, and inside workers, mostly women, were treated as secondary.

The National Labor Relations Board (NLRB) was the overseer of all labor negotiations and also approved new unions after assessing an organization's ability to represent its members fairly. With the support of the ANB, Paul Sr. claimed that the ANB union met all the requirements necessary to be approved by the NLRB and that with this stamp of approval, the union could more fully protect the interests of the fishermen and act as a bargaining agent. After a 1939 federal review the ANB-sponsored union was named the Alaska Marine Workers' Union (AMWU), but nothing was effortless. From the outset Tlingit and Haida politics gummed up the works, chiefly centered on the age-old rivalry between the Paul and Peratrovich families, both of whom were now at the helm of major Southeast Alaska unions. After years of dormancy, the old feuds were revived. Paul, known for his fiery speeches, claimed that Peratrovich's union could not represent Native interests even though Peratrovich was Native himself. Instead, William Paul Sr. claimed: "We are the only union bound together by blood, tradition, history and a real spirit of sacrifice, love for each other." He excoriated ASPSU supporters for "listening to white leaders whom you would never admit as full members of the Brotherhood," and he urged them to embrace the ANB out of ethnic loyalty. "Indians constitute ⅞ of the union membership and no matter what some might say, down underneath we are all related and . . . none of us can hold out against fathers and brothers in this civil war."[16] Despite the turbulent rhetoric there was real work to be done, and William and Louis Paul turned their focus to Native fishermen, often to the exclusion of cannery workers. The women working the line would not ignore this omission.

The Peratrovich union was ready to meet the challenge from the AMWU and went through government channels to do so. From the beginning, the NLRB had questioned the ethnic exclusivity of Paul's union and required the membership to be expanded beyond the Tlingit, Tsimshian, or Haida members in order to qualify for recognition. The ANB remedied the problem by changing the ANB constitution to admit "associate members" for those wanting to join the union but who were not Alaska Natives. As associate members they could not vote on ANB-related matters, but they were full members of the union and theoretically afforded the same bargaining and negotiation privileges. The non-Native membership was always small, yet played a role in the ensuing political maelstrom.[17]

Paul thought he had everything covered, but the AMWU was further questioned concerning the proper category for fishermen. Since fishermen were independent contractors, they could not be considered employees under the conditions of the NLRB and could not be represented as such. This seemed to be a considerable problem but was resolved by taking advantage of other newly minted legislation. A Southeast Alaska fishermen's cooperative was organized under the Fisheries Cooperative Market Act, which permitted fishermen to form an association that could legally set fish prices, thereby gaining a voice in production and marketing of their catch.[18] The ANB-sponsored fishermen's cooperative was not an official union, yet possessed equal weight in the marketplace similar to more established organizations. From the onset of this reorganization, AMWU priorities again shifted even more closely to the fishermen and their capitalization needs while overlooking the inside workers. Yet the fisherman could not manage to wield any real power either. Fred Paul believed the ANB-sponsored Alaska Marine Fishermen's Cooperative was hindered because Natives were reluctant to strike during prime fishing season.[19] Throughout its short history the AMWU struggled to maintain its position on an erratic platform, and as the union became more pro-Native fishermen, a building protest among the women workers escalated, some eying Frank Peratrovich's cannery worker auxiliary as better choice for representation.[20]

Frank Peratrovich and the ASPSU continued to confront the ANB union at every turn. Even after Paul had conformed to the requirements, his rivals remained on the offensive and targeted the Alaska Marine Fishermen's Cooperative, while tensions were heightened between the warring factions in the ANB and ANS. To counter the attacks, Paul framed the cooperative's mission in terms of resistance to those forces that would undermine Native fishermen and processors: "To throw off those abuses, usurpations, and discrimination to provide new guards for our future security and welfare, to more perfectly express our community of interest, to establish justice, promote the general welfare of the Territory of Alaska and to secure the blessings of economic and legal liberty to ourselves and our associates."[21] This premise was indeed idyllic, but could it be played out in reality? Perhaps, if the union could have striven for a more wide-ranging membership, but the genuine setback was revealed further within the charter as ethnic identity was placed on the line: "No person of Native descent can adequately and fairly be represented outside of the Brotherhood or Sisterhood. When an Indian is in a mixed group, he will find that most of the time his problems are so different that CIO and AFL will not give him help on important matters. The Business Agents should therefore endeavor to secure the membership of every person of native descent wherever they may be found."[22]

To restrict membership further in the ANB-sponsored union and the fishing cooperative, Paul announced a hiring preference for ANB and ANS members, which only included non-Native members if they were already members of the AMWU or the cooperative. Outsiders could be hired if that pool had been exhausted and only with great caution. This, of course, appeared to be favoritism, which gave the AFL and CIO cause to critique this homegrown independent union, further fueling the controversy. William and Louis Paul countered any such arguments by suggesting that the CIO and AFL were getting weaker and were desperately competing for Native members, following up with: "YOU SHOULD NOT RECOGNIZE ANY INDIAN WHO CLAIMS MEMBERSHIP IN CIO OR AFL."[23] This attitude, however, cancelled any benefits that might be derived from the CIO or AFL affiliation, and the ANB unions lost members, some joining the Peratrovich union.

Paul's Native-only philosophy polarized the ANB and the ANS, although there continued to be loyal supporters regardless of the changing times. Those faithful members weathered the criticisms of both the fishermen's cooperative and the AMWU, but this did not signify that they were indifferent to William Paul's unilateral posture or the rigid stratification within the union. Nonetheless, the AMWU remained structured in its hierarchy and, for the duration of its existence, William Paul Sr. as secretary wielded a commanding hand and it was established that he must be included in all "legal, political, scientific, and financial investigations required to secure greater bargaining power for the ANB, ANS" and the fishermen's cooperative.[24] With Paul's prolific and polemic pen, and strong oratory, he provided vibrant leadership in union affairs, and was for the most part the guiding force, although this potency did not stop those who wanted to knock him down a notch.

Despite the ongoing friction, the ANB Executive Committee successfully determined fair prices each year and secured the cooperation of the canneries. Each local ANB-ANS camp concluded individual arrangements with the canneries to which they sold salmon on a customary basis, and the process was smooth for the time being. Formal discussions addressed working conditions, living arrangements, and cannery schedules, and in these matters William Paul Sr. took on the fishermen's and workers' plight as his personal crusade, relying on his son Bill Jr. to assume more responsibility in union affairs, especially those that involved labor issues. Paul Sr. and Bill Jr. were both appalled by the physical conditions in the canneries and auxiliary housing, motivating them to make several field trips to document the circumstances, supported by a photographic record of the living quarters. As William Paul Sr. listened to the safety concerns in the dilapidated cannery facilities, he blamed both the CIO and the AFL for their disregard in addition to the absentee corporations that had historically taken advantage of the workers while harvesting salmon without proper regulation. It was no stretch of the imagination to liken the cannery facilities to a colony within a colony, but for Alaska Natives there were even more important aspects of Native American policy that impacted their lives, beyond the machinations of union activity.

The one problem Alaska Natives could not shake was BIA control. Ostensibly, the IRA-ARA legislation, crafted by William Paul Sr. and Tony Dimond to meet the realities of Alaska's lifeways, allowed a degree of Native sovereignty, but that was not how it worked for these villages. Instead the linkage between the BIA and Alaska Native endeavors acted as a chokehold in yet another pattern of paternalism. William Paul Sr. lambasted these chains that crippled attempts to make a decent living, but there were two sides to this coin. The fishing fleets owed their existence to the government-sponsored ARA revolving loan, although the BIA was an unforgiving banker. The moment the payments were late the BIA swooped in and sold the boats from right under them. In a double bind position, the fishermen could not maintain their boat mortgages due to the poor fishing, largely caused by cannery traps. The few Native-owned canneries that had been started up through ARA loans were under a similar hostage situation. "The Bureau selected the cannery managers and as an example of the disputes there was one case of a sharp disagreement when the Bureau said, 'Our man or we won't finance your cannery.'"[25]

Native-owned or -managed canneries were constantly under threat of bankruptcy. Credit was extended to the fishermen and Native cannery owners, but William Paul Sr. pointed out the fallacies in this program. The Natives did not really own the canneries outright, and Paul charged that the BIA agents would march right into the cannery offices and "take out the last dollar of any Indian delinquent in payment of his loan or interest in the community-owned cannery when the managers and fishermen should be concentrating their efforts on the fish harvest."[26] It would have been a critical matter if that were the only way the fishermen or cannery worker was separated from their wages, but there was always the cannery store and its "easy credit line." These stores were owned by the cannery companies or, at times, the government, and charged outrageous prices, further impoverishing the average Native family. It was said, "If ever people needed food at cost it is these people." If the loans or extended credit could not be paid in a timely fashion, the cannery or fishing boats went into foreclosure and the legal matter was turned over to the BIA, which showed no compassion. "The Indian Office says, 'it is out of our hands,' and the district attorney says, 'I've got my orders.'"[27]

Paul blamed the cannery losses on BIA management and its perversion of the ARA. The loans given out were inadequate for capitalization and instead left fishing captains in debt on half-outfitted fishing boats. This, it was believed, was to keep the Natives in line and dependent on the BIA. The lopsided relationship had Paul crying foul as he compared the Native plight to the Filipino's relative comfort, claiming unfair bias: "There was discrimination in employment. Filipinos were hired and paid a minimum of $1,500 a season and given the finest quarters, hot and cold water, a cook to serve them, and prepaid travel between Seattle and Alaska, while the Indian women worked for about $350.00 doing the same work."[28] As it should be, Paul emphasized the tie between the cannery workers, the canneries, and the fishermen, but he did not realize that by maligning the Filipino workers, he was also insulting blended families. Although he spoke out for Tlingit and Haida women in this instance, it appeared he did not fully realize the importance of their support or their sphere of influence in villages and among the fishermen, many of whom were their fathers, sons, or husbands.

Southeast Alaska Native women have a heritage of strength derived from ownership (stewardship) of clan property, matrilineal traditions, and egalitarian roles in their society. Men were hunters and fisherman, but the subsistence cycle could not function properly without processing, mainly done by women, thus balancing reciprocal values. Importantly, based on social esteem, women often acted as intermediaries or cultural brokers between diverse peoples.[29] Similar to the Tsimshian in Metlakatla, Western gender roles were not fully adopted, and women continued to fulfill their clan role in the village and cannery, which maintained identity and cultural esteem, and added a further mutual bond between workers, all seeking the common goals of safety and fair wages. Informal alliances benefited from this existing potency with the potential for filling a gap that had been produced due to the perceived disregard for inside workers, even as the AMWU declared it was the only union representing Native women.

William Paul was not intentionally slighting them, but his narrow focus could not fully take into account the women's predicament, although he had grown up with a model of Tlingit leadership. Matilda "Tillie" Kinnon Paul, the mother of William and Louis, was a school teacher, Christian missionary, and culture bearer, who in the past had demanded fair wages in her teaching position, something uncommon for a woman of those times.[30] Regardless, it was not only William Paul or the ANB union overlooking the big picture. Fishing issues usually took precedence over the day-to-day realities that women faced in an unsafe and unsavory environment, prompting the ANS to become involved in support of the women complaining against their bosses or about inadequate wages and dangerous conditions. But there was more to struggle against in the form of stereotypes. It was assumed that Native women were natural processors based on their cultural role, while men were seen as fit for the hard work.[31] This was the rationale for paying women less and not promoting them to managerial positions. Not only was this bias unfounded, but it ignored the fact that a woman might be the sole breadwinner for the family. Issues like this were going to become progressively more critical as time went on.

During the Depression there was an increase of women in the workforce brought about by at least two factors. First, it took two adults to maintain a household, and second, there were times when only women could get jobs, particularly because it was recognized that they would accept lower wages. These social realities affected the entire country, and the subsequent workplace diversity "laid the groundwork for a new class and gender politics among American women." Organized labor was seen as an avenue for influencing the future, and labor feminism was created by the need for "economic inclusion, for an end to paternalism, and for guaranteed rights and benefits."[32] The march for equity was more than upholding democratic principles; it was essential for feeding one's family. Through socializing and developing inner circles based on mutual interest, a collective identity was forged that included labor militancy. Women were no longer passive recipients of cannery management's production demands but instead were active agents in shaping their circumstances and destiny.[33] From the Italian women in Monterey packing sardines to the Tacoma women processing fresh apples, the political winds had been altered, and no less so for the Southeast Alaska Native woman whose work in the cannery was not necessarily prioritized over her clan duties or participation in her husband's ethnic organization.

The multi-ethnic ANS was supportive of the distinctive responsibilities women faced, and members worked together to develop strategies. In the process, the plight of the fishermen in disputes over fish prices or traps was not neglected, and so it was appropriate that the two bodies meet jointly to document various problems and develop action items. A prime example of this situation occurred at the 1933 ANS convention held in the Haida village of Hydaburg. One of the agenda items concerned cannery work, and each cannery representative submitted a report tallying wages, length of daily employment, and the number of women employed at each plant. At the Rose Inlet cannery, for instance, it was reported there were:

22 women workers
25 cents an hour at the patching table
30 cents an hour at the filling machine
35 cents as slimers[34]

The longest hours put in per day was 13 and the shortest was 2½. The average money earned for patching table workers was $53 for the season, $44 at the filling machine, and $40 as slimers. At this particular cannery, the record also noted that there were conflicts because of "too many Oriental workers."[35] Disputes were caused by competition between the Alaska Native women and so-called imported workers—ANS members believed Alaska Natives should be employed before anyone else. Regardless of inter-ethnic marriages and families, this particular rivalry seldom wavered, creating a divisiveness that was difficult to seam together.

This theme of competition can also be followed in another 1933 ANB report, which reflected the jagged line between the Filipinos and Alaska Natives. William Paul was in the thick of this, with people looking to him for leadership. In this case there was a complaint lodged against Filipinos who were allegedly taking their jobs: "The thing to which we most object is the employment of Filipinos to do all of the work at the cannery and letting the Alaska women go without work. We are asking help from Mr. William L. Paul in regard to our cannery work. Last summer most of the women went without work and stayed at their homes. A few worked the last few days of the season, but no one made more than 10 or 20 dollars during all summer. This small earning cannot pay expenses much less support a family for the winter."[36]

In turn, Paul encouraged the women to fight back if their civil liberties were threatened and to protest discrimination, but these actions came with a price tag. A woman could be fired for raising a fuss. Even so, Paul did not give up, trusting that his efforts would win out in the end: "It took four years to make the Indian Bureau see the Indians could do all the work in the cannery, iron chink and all."[37] He believed the same reckoning would come for inside workers, who were superior to any machinery, and that the BIA should match his championing efforts. The BIA rarely did though, because they were caught up in the financial angle, and therefore in conflict with the people the agency was charged to protect.[38] The government had come to the conclusion that the loans had never fulfilled the goal of creating self-sufficient Native communities. To prove this point, officials pointed to what they deemed were excessive loans to buy goods at the cannery stores without a way to recoup the money, particularly during unproductive fishing seasons.[39] In retrospect, the BIA and other government agencies were focusing on the trivial while larger problems loomed because of big corporations, fishing rivalries, trap piracy, unsafe working conditions, wage discrepancies, and resource depletion. Women cannery workers were aware of these problems, and they had had enough. There was a general feeling that something needed to happen to improve their situation, and the women stopped depending on someone or something else.

William Paul was a favorable ally, yet insufficient to the women's cause, and there came a time when they knew they must take matters into their own hands to achieve social justice. The fishermen's cooperative and its issues were important, but there were few organizations that could address their specific and unique problems, ranging from substandard housing to faulty machinery to a lack of childcare options. Besides Paul's union or even Peratrovich's cannery auxiliary, there was no group that came close to fitting the exact requirements, and the women saw that it was essential to plot their own course. To bridge the various factions there was a need for conduits to act as "cultural brokers" to speak out from their home villages and rally everyone in common cause.[40] It was not an easy journey, particularly given the extreme ethnic and gender bigotry, sometimes within their own ranks.

Louis Paul continued to blame outsiders for what was happening in Southeast Alaska and believed that Native women had been mistreated, but his vision did not always match that of the merging Tlingit, Haida, and Tsimshian women's caucus, who were not looking for agitation but for common ground. Still Louis Paul wanted to stir the pot with such rhetoric as: "You cannot be brown and white at the same time . . . it is impossible for the white people to overcome their racial prejudice; it is impossible for them to favor Indians over their own kind. . . . They will use you and when they are through, they will abuse you. And in the end you will come back to your own people."[41]

William and Louis Paul differed on several issues, but they presented a united force on the "race question" and single-mindedly assumed the ANB was the only organization that could stand by the Natives and said: "No white man will take the punishment for his efforts" like those ANB and ANS leaders.[42] Beyond politics, the "ANB was organized to give Indians an equal chance to make a living—to put bread and butter on the table for our women and children."[43] Regrettably, this appeal to a homegrown allegiance was ripped apart by in-fighting and assaults from the outside with equal vigor. The AFL and CIO attacked the ANB as merely a political fraternal organization where "certain self-seeking, power-hungry individuals in the ANB (were) seeking to pervert the organization to reduce it to a union smashing weapon," to the detriment of all the good the federations had produced for the fishermen and cannery workers. The AFL went as far as boasting that they were the true defenders of Alaska Native women.[44]

After switching between AFL and CIO affiliation and seeing no benefits, William Paul became fiercely independent, appealing to the cause of Southeast Alaska marine workers. In 1940 William Paul addressed the subject in the daily *Alaska Fishing News* out of Ketchikan by claiming that "when the ANB became strong because of leadership, the people of Wrangell, Waterfall, Kake, Petersburg were satisfied with the AFL, and would rather go down in defeat than follow the CIO," but not long after this declaration, Paul urged the workers to forget about both the AFL and CIO because they did not care about the Native fishermen or cannery workers.[45] For a while longer the Alaska Marine Workers' Union remained active and enjoyed the support of the ANB and ANS membership, but soon the long list of opponents would get the best of William Paul Sr. and his union.

In the early 1940s Paul's union had gained vigor and respect in certain villages, but the Peratrovich family, based in Klawock and Ketchikan, were a force to be reckoned with. In January 1941 an *Alaska Fishing News* headline rang out that "President Frank Peratrovich Says Business Men and Others Are Becoming Union Minded in Alaska."[46] Unionism and collective bargaining were seen as keeping industry healthy. The article went on to predict that "1941 will demonstrate more than ever the growth and values of Alaska unions. It is becoming more evident each year that the residents of Alaska are anxious to work under one organization for the benefit of all concerned."[47] Although he initially spoke of unions in the plural, when he got down to "one organization" his reference was clear—his own Alaska Salmon Purse Seiners' union, which from the beginning had accepted multi-ethnic members and formalized a women's cannery auxiliary. Perhaps, given these details, it could be said that Peratrovich had represented diverse workers better, but what neither Paul nor Peratrovich realized was that women could stand up for themselves.

Later in 1941 Frank Peratrovich predicted it would a good year and said the canneries were "absorbing all the local labor and are going ahead with their program for this season with no labor trouble expected."[48] But there was friction. Perhaps it was the inherent nature of the industry, but so often the fishermen were considered central to the industry, eclipsing the importance of the women's production output in the canneries. Further, in a typical Native household, there was often a complementary combination of cannery workers and fishermen, a strong factor in the socioeconomic matrix, supported by the traditional egalitarian nature of Southeast Alaska Native culture. There was no question that the fishing industry was the main employer of Alaska Natives, yet their livelihood was tied to the health of the resource.

The salmon run was declining largely due to federal neglect and regardless of labor disputes; without the resource there would be no canneries. Bill Paul Jr. was perplexed by the ineffectual regulatory agencies, particularly the Fisheries Board. In one instance he was invited to sit in on a meeting but refused to attend because of the hypocrisy surrounding federal oversight agencies that were "merely routine for what the Bureau wants regardless of the views expressed by the fishermen and packers."[49] In other words, they were only seeking an opportunity to tell the fishermen what the bureau had already decided. Obviously the Department of Interior, in theory the protector of Alaska Native interests and the salmon resource, was not doing its job, and this was a breach of fiduciary responsibility. William Paul Sr. also expressed disgust toward governmental incompetence and was sure the Bureau of Fisheries was in cahoots with the big canneries: "According to the Bureau forecast for 1941 Hidden Inlet was to be barren of fish this year and even the Nakat Packing Company couldn't make a pack," but Paul disputed this report. Down in Klawock "the fish are packed so tight in the streams that not another one could enter, with great swarms, still outside the streams." In responding to this report Paul Jr. believed this was yet another example of favoring certain canneries and fishing fleets at the expense of the Native-run enterprises. Concluding that complicity was involved, Paul Jr. suggested: "My idea of a hearing would be where bureau officials would be put on the stand and questioned . . . and then the proceedings sent direct to the Secretary of the Interior."[50] According to Paul Jr., the small guy could not break even against the large monopolies, but it was about to get worse when his eternal foe Winton C. Arnold entered the fray.

In the standoff between the independent Native fishermen and the packer monopolies, tension increased due to the steady pressure from lobbying groups, none more prominent than Arnold's Alaska Salmon Industry, Inc. (ASI). Arnold charted the course to destroy cannery union influence, and the ASI was in a good position to be successful in this endeavor since it represented the largest proportion of Alaskan-based canning companies and negotiated yearly contracts for fish prices and wages; at times, the scope extended to the cannery workers themselves.[51] The ANB-sponsored union, already losing strength due to loss of faith, was defenseless against this lobbying group, regardless of counter measures. Even the more popular and well-connected Frank Peratrovich was forced to endure Arnold's condescending barbs while the ASI exhibited a tentacle-like hold on the Alaskan salmon industry.

In mid-1940s congressional hearings held in Ketchikan, Arnold testified that Frank Peratrovich's viewpoint might be accepted because "in his capacity as the President of the Alaska Salmon Purse Seiners' Union, whose members are not only natives, but whites," he had garnered some respect. In addition, Arnold qualified this esteem in that "Mr. Peratrovich represents the very highest type of native or person of native origin in southeastern Alaska."[52] In this particular dispute, there was a question concerning seine use versus fish traps, and Peratrovich and Arnold were obviously on different sides of the fence. Since seiners were regulated and fish traps were not, it was easy to see who was going to win the set point in the match. In general, Arnold's opinion of Alaska Natives condemned them as backward and lifted to their current state only because of a benevolent introduction to civilization, a widespread opinion in these times. Above all, he was adamant that Native fishermen had no exclusive rights to the fisheries and would continue to argue that point into the next decade.[53] Arnold contemptuously tolerated Peratrovich, thinking Peratrovich might be advantageous to him at some point, but carried only scorn for William Paul Sr., which was fine with Paul; he had no use for Arnold either.

As a defensive strategy, the ANB-sponsored Alaska Marine Fishermen's Cooperative and cannery workers combined forces more tightly to guard against adversaries, while Paul did not mince words: "It must be remembered we bargain and work against a large, rich, strong combination of canneries, called ALASKA SALMON INDUSTRY," and the AMWU would triumph in rivaling that organization. Paul went on to echo his number one diatribe: the AFL and CIO (or any other organization) could not champion the Alaska Native cause since "no person of Native descent can adequately and fairly be represented outside of the Brotherhood or Sisterhood."[54] And the dissension continued between resident and nonresident fishermen, inside workers and cannery bosses, and the various ethnic groups, while the fish traps caught entire runs of fish beyond the view of any oversight agency.

In the early 1940s several political movements changed the course of Alaska's industrial history. The ANB cooperative became more set on the exclusion of non-Natives and immigrants, and the rivalry between the Peratrovich camp and Paul's allies heated up; harsh words spilled over into the ANB and ANS meetings, where each family held a prominent position. Peratrovich's purse seine union challenged the legality and worthiness of Paul's cooperative and cannery workers union but could neither penetrate Paul's loyal following nor downplay the fact that Paul had politicized the ANB so that it could stand up to the absentee cannery owners, the AFL, and CIO, and Washington DC. Nonetheless, by the mid-1940s Paul's union was losing members and dynamism, until finally the ANB majority turned their full attention to the land claims fight, thus sounding a death knell for the AMWU.

The ANB-sponsored union may have been short-lived, but during this period the Paul family had demonstrated their leadership and the ability to rally Alaska Native villages up and down the cannery coast. Times were changing though, and as the United States climbed out of the Great Depression, world powers were militarizing and international tensions escalated. When the United States entered World War II, the salmon industry went through drastic alterations in price and labor regulations. There were, after all, troops to feed, and housewives clutched their ration stamps, looking for the best deal for their family dinner table. Canned salmon fit the bill.

By the mid-1940s Alaska's salmon canning industry witnessed a drastic alteration as women emerged as leaders in the Pacific Coast labor movement. The segregated union of William and Louis Paul could no longer thrive in the multicultural setting of Asian workers, blended families, and the increasing interaction between the Pacific Northwest and Alaska labor force. For the nation as a whole, gender stereotypes were cast aside as the women became part of a "general upsurge nurtured by a militant, well-organized labor movement and by mobilized ethnic working class communities."[55] In seeking dignity and justice, "a labor movement must connect workers to each other and show them why they need to care about other people's issues both in their own workplace and in other places."[56] Gradually the bonds stretched further until women cannery workers found the political clout necessary to make a difference in their own lives and in the broader life of their community.

10

A Union of Their Own

Old-timers reminisce about cannery life back in the day, whether they were on the line, fishermen, or night watchmen. In 1991 longtime Angoon resident Frank W. Sharp met with archaeologist and cultural historian Charles Mobley, who was gathering information about cannery work in the 1940s. Sharp spoke to Mobley about the typical patterns of working on the line. "It starts at one end and the fish comes in whole, they've got everything on them yet. Prior to my time, they have to do it by hand. Take the heads off. Gut them. Take the blood out of the center. . . . Slime them. . . . So when they went through there, then there were women on each side. And the women then would what they call slime it. . . . And it was real fast. It just click, click, click, you know. Just moving along there."[1]

Sharp continued about the process of labeling the cans. One of his favorite labels was: "Packing with the wiggle in the tail." He recalled how the young kids' number one job was as labelers since it was safe and not near the heavy equipment. Cannery work was a family affair, but beyond close relatives, larger kinship units were created that functioned to support co-workers and those who "had your back." Everyone watched out for one another. The women were "inside workers," and the men were responsible for jobs that required greater strength, like off-loading the scows or feeding the fish elevators.[2] All these jobs were necessary for the end product, supporting a degree of egalitarianism as part of a larger sociocultural sphere despite gender segregation.

In her study of cannery workers Vicki Ruiz discovered that a common human environment existed within this type of work, characterizing it as a cannery culture, especially among the women, who had their own rituals, celebrations, and informal discussions concerning common issues. Peers became part of an extended family, capable of banding together to show collective resistance, if necessary. This bond also helped people to adapt to change. Teamwork and harmony "attested to the surprising strength of this culture and the identity was diffused along two separate parallel dimensions: interethnic and intra-ethnic."[3] That sense of oneness, however, did not eliminate all tensions. Disagreements and perceived competition still had to be worked out.

The concept of working culture has been used in several similar social settings. Anthropologist Louise Lamphere, in analyzing the shop girl environment, found that the setting involves "a complex set of relationships between cultural meanings and ideology . . . and behavioral strategies or practices."[4] Southeast Alaska's cannery culture was bound by its own oral narrative containing the ethics, mores, and at times a distinctive language or code, tending to humanize an environment restricted by steel gray walls and a dreary existence. Together the group formed strategies for coping under harsh conditions in a "we versus them" alliance, and in so doing, member roles cut across social and racial lines to generate solidarity, and natural leaders emerged from this newly created relationship and bond.[5]

While Vicki Ruiz described the cannery culture among Mexican women in the California food processing industry, Patricia Zavella found a parallel sense of connection among cannery workers in the Santa Clara Valley in northern California. The social environment was "created by workers who confront, resist, or adapt to the constraints and possibilities of their jobs. . . . Workers use work culture to guide and interpret social relations on the job."[6] These concepts were comparable to Southeast Alaska cannery life, especially the distinct inter-ethnic and intra-ethnic ties among Native women who worked side by side with men brailing the tenders, moving cans to the retort, or acting as longshoremen. Yes, there were differences, but potential discord was reduced by forming a nucleus of protection, while some attempted to transform cannery conditions as an extension of community pride, adding another level to the cannery culture.

Native women who stepped forward as spokespersons for the group understood that with authority there was responsibility and that to gather consensus each group member must be free to participate in decisions. Leadership was not about domination but instead involved "shared work" for common goals. The following short profiles demonstrate how women workers stepped forward to make sure everyone was represented and prioritized the goals of healthy homes and families in cannery towns and villages.[7] Historic accounts tend to marginalize women's roles, placing them in the background, as stories take on a more male-centric approach.[8] This does a disservice to the record since so often the women were the cogs and wheels of production. Alternatively, a historical review reveals themes centering on community development, hardball politics, and the cannery milieu through a study of these trailblazers.

Elizabeth Kinninook Baines combined family, heritage, and activism. She grew up in Ketchikan (Cape Fox) and Metlakatla understanding the importance of the natural landscape and traditions. Her grandsons say she was a quiet woman, but tough.[9] Although modest, she rose in the ranks of the ANS and fought for the rights of cannery workers when the industry was dangerous and forbidding, while keeping an eye on what was going on with the salmon runs because her husband, Joe Baines, depended upon these as a fisherman. We have insight into her life and times through a 1989 interview that was transcribed by the Alaska Woman's Leadership Program, chronicling her adherence to traditional Native customs from childhood to adult life.[10]

At first she worked at the cannery for ten cents an hour and shared her money with her family. She mentioned how strange it was to have a Chinese boss, recalling that "he used to go around and tap the can," complaining that it was too full. You had to take some off. "We had to do what others do when it comes to working. We all had to help each other." Her words convey the Native value of sharing: if another family was not having a good year, others would share with an understanding that these gestures were reciprocal. Elizabeth emphasized, "That's just what we did."[11]

During the 1930s life got rougher and material goods more expensive. Some Native families slipped down the economic ladder, but that did not stop the communities from working together for a better life. In early adulthood Elizabeth joined the ANS, both Ketchikan and Sitka camps, and to this day she is remembered for her leadership role as ANS Grand President as she campaigned for women's rights, land claims, citizenship, equality in the workplace, and issues surrounding salmon processing. With her fluency in Tsimshian, Tlingit, and English, Elizabeth served as a court interpreter and simultaneously absorbed an understanding of the Western legal system, which eventually assisted in her work with William L. Paul Sr.[12] Paul remarked that her contributions and tireless efforts not only benefited women but were beneficial for all Alaska Natives.[13]

Another Alaska Native woman who advocated for improved cannery conditions was Nellie Scott Baronovich, the first ANS Grand President in 1925. She has been described as a "strong forceful woman . . . who worked for her people . . . and knew she was right." She planned political meetings and rallies with William Paul Sr. when they called for the abolition of fish traps and the cessation of salmon wastage. During this period it was unusual for a woman to own her own business, but Nellie Baronovich did, including her own ice cream store, restaurant, and movie hall, and she encouraged other women who were thinking about being business women.[14]

Before embarking on the entrepreneurship road, Nellie had worked in canneries in the Haida villages Kasaan and Hydaburg, and from these experiences she came to understand the oppression that plagued Native cannery workers. It was said that when she spoke out against the inequities, "she had a voice that didn't hold back anything." She never lost sight of her Native roots, often addressing ANS meetings in her Haida language, but she was also aware that sitting back and waiting for justice was not going to amount to much.[15] To sustain respect in the Native community she found it necessary to understand the language of all cannery workers, politicians, and business people to be effective and relevant. For Elizabeth Baines and Nellie Baronovich, ANS membership served as a political conduit, a frequent pattern.

Margaret Jackson Wanamaker started working at the Hawk Inlet cannery near Juneau in 1910, later moving to Excursion Inlet, a large plant with a consistently high production rate. These experiences familiarized her with the problems in the fish factories. As the secretary-treasurer in the Juneau ANS and an early union official, she was a warrior on several fronts, including the fight against discrimination, supporting cannery labor, and helping to "foster the well-being of Native Alaskans."[16] In the 1940s she was a model of leadership in both the ANS and the early union movement by prioritizing the specific needs of insider workers and realizing that the fish trap was the enemy of all except the absentee cannery owners. This particular cause allowed her to combine the fishermen's and cannery workers' concerns with those of the ANB and those in local official roles who had the power to effect change.

Esteemed Tlingit elder Reverend Walter Soboleff remembered her like this: "We'd discuss the issues in our joint meetings, and some of the issues were very, very difficult. And when Margaret Cropley (Wanamaker) stood and spoke she just had words of wisdom for us."[17] She was regarded as having a genuine insight into the exigencies during a time of trenchant politics.[18] Wanamaker's daughters also carried on her tradition, but in a slightly different manner. Dorothy Wanamaker (Wallace) was born at Chatham cannery in Sitkoh Bay, first built by the Buschmann family in 1900. At the tender age of ten she was employed at the large Hawk Inlet facility until moving to Excursion Inlet. Although there was some talk about unions during this time, most of her activism was through the Juneau ANS camp, where she spoke of the issues affecting women and families. Her sister Eunice Akagi recalls working in the afternoons at the cannery in her youth and then going to pick berries, always on the watch for bears.[19] Eunice loved the ethnic diversity: "We had a League of Nations. We had the Norwegians, the Swedes, we had some Blacks, we had Hawaiians, Filipinos, Japanese, and us Native people. We all got along very well." There were many avenues for recreation, especially the dances with a wide variety of music, and when interviewed in her elder years she could still sing the Hawaiian songs.[20]

Akagi's first exposure to Native activism was through her mother's ANB-ANS meetings. She listened for hours as they discussed methods for resolving conflicts.[21] Although many issues emanated from the cannery, there were other social conflicts of the day. Amid the multi-ethnic atmosphere with songs and dances, the reality of segregated theatres and separate basketball courts was an uncompromising barrier. Akagi, and others like her, understood that recreational events were grand, but cannery towns were not always filled with harmony, and community cohesion was a hard-fought battle. There was a need to tackle the issues.

Just as Elizabeth Baines had dealt with the dual causes of labor rights and the return of indigenous land, there were others who forged through the political barriers with an understanding of the interrelated nature of these problems. One of these women was Amy Hallingstad, often referred to as the "First Lady of the First People." Her views may have appeared contradictory as she stated her case for hiring locally as opposed to using seasonal migrant workers, while at the same time campaigning for reforms in the deplorable immigrant working and living conditions found in the canneries and mines. Although inner conflict persisted, "enough women transcended the barriers of mutual distrust . . . so that at certain junctures, the parallel networks met and collective strategies . . . could be created and channeled across ethnic boundaries." While division created a competitive atmosphere, "the social aspects of their jobs contributed to a cooperative spirit."[22] In essence, despite the great differences between immigrant and indigenous labor, a new entity was formed once again through the powerful us-against-them attitude.

Hallingstad extended her efforts at Hood Bay, Excursion Bay, Pillar Bay, and Chatham Strait, seeking to improve medical facilities while revealing the urgent needs of the Southeast Alaska workers. As a cannery employee she petitioned for fair pay, particularly for women, who were consistently paid a lower wage than men. Hallingstad and other women of like mind understood that they were part of the market economy where wages and production were determined by output, and as such canneries should compensate labor fairly. When this did not occur, it encouraged the women and their allies to seek justice.

Hallingstad's knowledge and boundless energy propelled her into a position on the Fisheries Board, where a woman member was unheard of in those days. The Fisheries Board was an advisory body and extension of the United States Fish and Wildlife Bureau, serving as an integral conduit between Washington DC and Alaska. In this capacity Hallingstad was able to share vital information concerning the health of the fisheries, troubles in the canneries, and, of course, the problems surrounding fish traps, an issue that spanned all walks of life from the independent fishermen to villages dependent on salmon.

Amy Hallingstad's granddaughter Sylvia Lythgoe offers further insight about her grandmother and by extension Tlingit women leaders of the day. In Lythgoe's words, Hallingstad rose in influence during a highly discriminatory time and was determined to protest against non-Native hiring in land and waters that had belonged to the Tlingit from time immemorial. In her role as ANS Grand Camp President, she learned the political game and held her own against pro-industrial politicians, who had further ambitions for the territory and projected a rise in Alaska's financial status that would spill over onto to all residents, including Native residents; but not everyone was buying into their conclusions.[23]

In the *Petersburg Press* Hallingstad called attention to the absolute necessity for ridding the waters of fish traps, a plea that had been echoing for decades. She declared that "the fish trap is the enemy of the Native and of the independent fisherman." If people wanted to know where the real problem lay, she continued, it was not in Southeast Alaska but with the "outside big money interests who . . . drain Alaska of her greatest resource." Abolish the traps "and give fish and fisherman a chance," she exhorted.[24] She was careful not to polarize marine workers into strictly ethnic categories, with the full knowledge that a more effective alliance could be solidified through their shared difficulties.[25]

In the past, factionalism based on rigid ethnic allegiance had proven ineffective. Bessie (Jackson) Quinto stood out as an anomaly to this general trend by dividing her time between Tlingit matters and supporting her

Filipino husband's celebrations and traditions in a cross-cultural family. She heeded the call to civil action through her ANB union organizing and community activism and was referred to as "an unsung historical hero of Tlingit society."[26] Bessie might be best remembered for her message that each person had an obligation to work for all the communities, whether they were Alaska Native, Asian, or Filipino. She was originally from Haines (a Chilkat Tlingit area) but moved to Juneau when she married Marcelo Quinto Sr., the son of a Filipino immigrant, who had originally come to Alaska in search of gold. Having no luck in the mining business, Quinto turned to cannery work and eventually became a fisherman.

After the children arrived, Bessie was saddled with the common child-care predicament, but unlike many others, the Quinto family found the solution within the family structure. In both the Tlingit and Filipino cultures, one of the duties of the older children was to watch the younger ones while the mother was occupied with other tasks, including out-side employment. For Bessie it was often her in-laws who watched the children, and Bessie remarked that she felt a special kinship with her Filipino in-laws, whose culture was like her own in many aspects. When the grandparents were unavailable the duties were absorbed by other members of the extended family. Bessie's grandson Ricardo Worl recalled how taking care of children was a natural part of life: "In Tlingit culture sisters were expected to share responsibilities in raising the sister-in-law's children," and this blended well with Filipino customs.[27]

As a consequence of Bessie's involvement in Filipino cultural groups and organizations, she was seen as a "central member of the expanded Filipina–Native American community in Alaska" and easily transitioned between ethnic groups in her role as union agent.[28] This position allowed her to make a difference in the lives of immigrant Filipinos, frequently through the ANS or an established Filipino organizations, such as the Filipino Community Association (FCA).[29] Bessie was not just an active member of the FCA; she restarted the dormant organization in Juneau with the help of her friend Elizabeth "Betty" Marks Govina. Betty, born in Hoonah, was employed for many years at the Port Althorp cannery before marrying a Filipino man. She, like Bessie, had been disappointed that there was no "club" for their Filipino husbands and other relatives, motivating them to open a Filipino Community Auxiliary, but first the duo had to raise funds.

Betty's husband Rudy went into more detail: "The Native women used to hold box socials and bake sales at different canneries. They were determined to raise the money to build a community hall."[30] Rudy remarked about the enthusiasm over having a place to hold celebrations, especially for the children. "There was much racial prejudice in Juneau and there was no place where Filipinos and their Native wives could hold programs for their children without the problems of prejudice."[31] Betty compared the auxiliary to the ANS in task and focus and had no problem being a member of both organizations as a "Filipino wife."[32] Because of a sense of sisterhood and family and through her efforts, her husband and Filipino friends were able to enjoy transnational ties that were a significant aspect of their heritage.

Rosita Worl, Bessie Quinto's daughter and the current director of the Sealaska Heritage Institute, tells of the numerous occasions when she accompanied her mother to union meetings and was responsible for taking notes. "My mother was a cannery union agent. She broke from the ANB union. The one with William Paul Sr. I always wondered why she did that. Amy Hallingstad was my aunt. I grew up taking minutes for my mother as she organized unions throughout [the] southeast when I was in the 6th grade."[33] Rosita believed this was her first introduction to Alaska Native issues, but was puzzled by why Bessie Quinto "broke away" from Paul's union, especially since they were close friends. In retrospect the reason may have centered on the ANB's stance on Filipino workers and residents, or may have been because the AMWU was devoting its energies to the fishermen and not listening to the cannery workers. Furthermore, these women had issues outside of work that needed addressing, and so there was a reliance on larger organizations for support.

In Alaska, both then and now, one of the larger Native controversies concerned the traditional subsistence cycle, which was more than securing food—it permeated every aspect of the culture. The Western term *subsistence* should not be confused with eking out a living. Instead, harvesting of natural resources encompassed the social, economic, and spiritual life of the people and should more accurately be thought of as a way of life.

Women routinely tended to their fish camps and gathered natural resources according to the seasons, and nothing changed after the canneries arrived, except for increased conflict and misunderstandings. If the cannery clock did not match the Native schedule, the cannery fish were not processed, because putting up food for the winter was critical for sustaining life. The women defied orders even under threat of firing.[34]

This was the case for Sally Hopkins, a member of the ANS, culture bearer, and a woman living a subsistence lifestyle at the same time she was employed at Dundas Bay as a slimer. For Hopkins and many others, cannery employment was often at odds with her other duties and tasks that were considered essential.[35] For this reason, she carried on harvesting activities between shifts or on days off, but if she needed to miss time at the cannery, it did not matter because she was not "willing to forgo necessary and even fulfilling seasonal cycles for the sake of the canners."[36]

Women in cannery work and other similar jobs complained about toggling between their jobs and responsibilities at home, and the issue was even more acute for women practicing a subsistence lifestyle. They had an added layer or dual occupations in what could be called a domestic economy that could not be neglected because it went beyond the physical needs to nurture the spiritual side. Plainly, these activities were not merely a quest for nutrients; they encompassed a holistic relationship between the harvest and the harvesters. Another key element was that gathering their own foods boosted people's sense of self-reliance. While cannery work was mechanical and non-organic, subsistence lifeways contributed to both self and family well-being.[37] When Sally Hopkins was out collecting plants, berries, or other materials, she could take her children with her. During her cannery shift that was not possible, and "satisfaction with the quality of child-care arrangement was often crucial to women feeling good about continuing to work," typifying the discord between a woman's family responsibilities and working for wages.[38]

Sally's granddaughter, Marie Olson, a lifelong member of the ANS, remembers her grandmother attending cannery meetings and ANB-ANS gatherings with the other village women, including her own mother. She was too young to understand what was going on, but when the cannery whistle blew, she became the head babysitter for her siblings and cousins, and even now as an elder, she questioned this arrangement: "What? I [was] only nine years old." Beyond these responsibilities, Marie shared fond reminiscences of those cannery days in her youth, as did many others of her era.[39] The childcare system was managed as well as possible with the older children watching the younger ones as they spent the day creating a natural playground in their immediate environment, often right outside the cannery facility. The children were checked on during coffee breaks, called "mugging up."

During off hours subsistence activities continued, yet there was no denying that drastic changes had taken place. The women noticed that the streams, tidal pools, and berry patches did not seem as abundant with life as when they were children themselves, and more buildings were being erected on lands where traditional foods had been gathered for centuries. Amy Marvin, for one, clearly saw the problem of the burgeoning cannery operations in clan territory. She recounted the episode when a superintendent asked if he could move the graves of her family's relatives so that the cannery could build houses on the land. They promised to make it nice, so the family would feel good about it. Her father rejected this request, saying, "We've already lost too much there. I don't want you to move them."[40] This quiet indignation was spoken by people who had known cannery work from the early days but were nevertheless appalled by the intrusion. Amy herself was born at the Icy Strait Salmon Packing Company in 1912 "at the place on Icy Strait called Cannery Point in English and Gaaxw X'aayi (Duck's Point) in Tlingit." Her mother was living on their traditionally owned land in the Cannery Point area "and her father helped to build the first company-owned building at the Icy Strait Salmon Cannery."[41] In 1924, at the age of twelve, Amy Marvin became a cannery worker at Port Althorp and recalls that she was paid a minimal amount. She did not complain, most likely because of her young age, but for others it was a hardship. And the cycle persisted while grievances were buried because there was not yet an effective method for presenting what they realized were abuses of their labor and their land.

Whether in Seattle, Portland, or Southeast Alaska, Filipinos realized they were hired for the dirtiest jobs, and a collective frustration motivated them to seek a way to improve conditions.[42] The first item on the agenda was to rid themselves of the corrupt contractor system. The cannery workers understood that "the game the contractors played was forcing new employees to pay a fee (bribe) to ensure employment. Another ploy was to demand that all new employees buy their 'necessities' through the contractors as they skimmed off the top."[43] The deception had been known for years, but it seemed as if nothing could be done without a solidified alliance. In answer to these inequities and many more, in the spring of 1933 forty cannery workers established the Alaska Cannery Workers' Union (ACWU) in San Francisco. Their demands included freedom from compulsory purchases and that all seasonal labor contracts be in English to eliminate any confusion.[44] The union quickly spread, exerting political pressure in the Pacific Northwest and Washington DC, where representatives spoke with the National Recovery Administration (NRA) officials. After reviewing the evidence the NRA established the "Code of Fair Competition for the Canned Salmon Industry," which outlawed the corrupt elements of the contract system in the cannery industry.[45] Here was the beginning of workers getting some control over their working lives, but there was so much more to do.

The nascent union faced threats from other established unions and was accused of bias toward certain ethnic divisions. To improve the union's status, the leaders acted to create the appearance of a more inclusive membership by changing the union's name to the Cannery Workers and Farm Laborers Union (CWFLU), to reflect the wider scope, including a northward reach to represent the Alaskeros. In its "aggressive expansion in Seattle, Portland, and Everett," the union came to be known as the "Little International," and as its appeal rose, the membership soared.[46] Word traveled, and it was said that this Filipino-organized union could solve the problems in the industry for several diverse groups, including women.

Meanwhile, in Southeast Alaska, the APSU and the AMWU were jostling with the aggressive efforts of the AFL and CIO as the national organizations sought a monopoly on Alaska's cannery industry and its workers, but neither union was addressing the needs of all workers. When the news about the CWFLU reached Southeast Alaska there was immediate interest among the disgruntled, although starting up this new union in Alaska was difficult. There was confusion, with conflicting allegiance, tensions, and a "lack of common purpose between the CWFLU's resident and non-resident workers."[47] For Alaska Native women the CWFLU did not fit their requirements, and there was a need to look further for a strong body that could represent the diverse labor force. It was not that the CWFLU did not attempt to broaden their outreach, but they were not equipped with the right leaders or philosophy, yet there was an answer on the horizon.

The United Cannery, Agricultural Packinghouse and Allied Workers of America (UCAPAWA) was founded by former Columbia University economics professor Donald Henderson and gained official status in 1935 upon its affiliation with the CIO. This union addressed the problems that had begun during the Great Depression in terms of wage equity, and eventually the message reached Alaska, finding fertile ground among both Alaska Native women and Filipino workers.

The UCAPAWA was one of the few unions that encouraged women to fill leadership positions and supported the push for pay equality and maternity leave. From Mexican workers in California to Filipino cannery workers in Seattle, the UCAPAWA offered a solid alternative for the underrepresented groups. In the beginning it was said that "the leadership and fraternity of the union stayed strong and the men proved their loyalty to each other as Alaskeros and continued their strength through unity for years."[48] It was true that the union's top spots were controlled by Filipino men, but there was an understanding about the importance of the women's role in the labor force and union.

The UCAPAWA received a favorable boost and gained adherents through its policy of standing by workers regardless of their ethnic background, as opposed to the AFL's history of "racial discrimination and benign neglect of its few semi-skilled and unskilled unions."[49] By the late 1930s the UCAPAWA started to make inroads into Southeast Alaska, although the initial lop-sided membership consisted of many more Filipino men as opposed to Alaska Native women until this was resolved through "consolidating the leadership of Local 7 with members in Ketchikan, Juneau, Hoonah, Petersburg, and Wrangell," thereby expanding village representation in more cannery towns.[50] It was not long before the "Alaska salmon industry was dominated by the UCAPAWA," and the canneries were obligated to give exclusive contracts to the union.[51] From these small towns and villages, a female cadre developed, and they spread the word about the benefits while traveling throughout Southeast Alaska. Since the Seattle-based representatives knew so little about Alaska, they relied on this homegrown movement, and when officials traveled up to Alaska they sought out these women leaders who could assist with tricky cross-cultural exchanges.

Much of what we know about the UCAPAWA is through their own newspaper. In the 1940s there were several articles concerning Alaska canneries and the ongoing unification efforts and challenges. According to the *UCAPAWA News*, the Seattle Local 7 members had fulfilled its mission to encourage the Ketchikan Local 237 morally, physically, and financially to strike in disputes concerning wages and fair employment terms.[52] It was said the Natives were grateful for the contract signed between the UCAPAWA and the industry workers.[53] On May 4, 1938, union legitimacy was officially authorized through a National Labor Relations Board (NLRB)–supervised election and the UCAPAWA was now an unmovable fixture in Southeast Alaska.[54] Not only did this union defy the ANB-sponsored Fisherman's Cooperative and Peratrovich's purse seine union's mission and programs; it also defied the notion that the key people in the struggle had to be men.

From its roots in California fruit packing lines, the United Cannery, Agricultural Packing and Allied Workers of America remained female-centric, and this was duly recognized in the person of Rose Dellama, who played an integral part in the history of the women cannery workers in Southeast

Alaska. From humble origins she carried the spirit of activism, perhaps influenced by her life events. Her widowed mother had raised six children while working in the northern California canneries, and from a young age Rose worked in the fruit canneries. Both she and her mother had endured harsh conditions, and she was determined to do something about it. By 1939 she was serving as a lobbyist for UCAPAWA and the next year she was sent to Southeast Alaska to solicit female membership and successfully organized a base with the assistance of Marguerite Hansen, the forthright business agent for the Ketchikan CIO local. Together they were committed to negotiating for the rights of the cannery workers as they carried the message from cannery town to cannery town under the auspices of the Southeast Alaska Cannery Workers Council. The purpose of the council was to widen "union publicity; activities which will make the Alaska locals a part of the community life in the persistent fight against discrimination."[55] All four UCAPAWA locals (Juneau, Ketchikan, Hoonah, and Petersburg) contributed toward funding, building strength, and reducing conflict.

Marguerite Hansen was not of Alaska Native background, but she often acted as cultural ambassador for the naïve Dellama, who wanted to do the right thing but felt uneasy in this foreign territory.[56] Both Dellama and Hansen were successful in increasing union membership while parleying for fair wages and better hours, but it was most often Marguerite who represented the Alaska Native women at Seattle meetings, such as the one in early 1939 where she reported that the Southeast Alaska unionization efforts were "moving along in a united path in the spirit of determination" to represent the workers, who had been forgotten.[57] When the dialogue centered on the Alaskeros without a mention of the women cannery workers, Hansen emphasized that the women would switch unions if they were not promised a better outcome. Further, she warned that the AFL was "chiseling away at the turf" and that the ANB-backed union was vying for control.[58] Dellama, Hansen, and several ANS members solidified their efforts, and there was no underestimating the drive of its women warriors working together, acting as brokers or negotiators between the union officials and those working in the canneries, as they merged the worlds of cannery, village, and political platform.

Ruth Hayes was the business manager for the local UCAPAWA and well known in cannery circles and union politics. She was born at Funter Bay and knew cannery work from a young age. It was there that she met her husband, Ernest, who had been a cannery worker since 1922. Her granddaughter, Tlingit author Ernestine Hayes, remembers her with great fondness: "Grandma was a slender woman who wore her long silver and steel colored hair wrapped at the back of her head." She was held in high esteem and was proud of her heritage in addition to being a force to be reckoned with and no stranger to hard work. Ernestine talks about the hours spent in the vicinity of the cannery while her grandmother worked, and she understood that her grandmother occupied a special place in the scheme of things. As a girl, Ernestine recalls: "During our Hawk Inlet summers, [Grandma] spent long days in the cannery while I explored bear trails and nibbled on salmonberries or waded on the beach,"[59] a common avocation for the cannery kids, as they called each other.

In the 1940s Hayes organized her local union branch, served as business agent, and was a complementary asset to Rose Dellama and the UCAPAWA, as was clearly stated in a 1944 *UCAPAWA News* article: "Ruth Hayes, whose mother, father, husband and children toiled in the canneries," had a longstanding relationship with Native labor that had been instrumental "when she organized her local and remained a prominent agent for five years."[60] It is significant that in the 1940s it was rare for a married woman to be referred to by her first name. Yet the UCAPAWA never used Mrs. or her husband's first name, as was the societal custom, an indication that she was regarded as notable in her own right.

Hayes's activities and goals must be analyzed in the context of World War II, which is discussed in detail shortly, but suffice it to say here that there was an influx of military members into the Juneau area, adding another element to the social matrix. Hayes was known for her ability to smooth out the rifts between Alaska Native women and the army soldiers, particularly concerning USO functions. Prejudice was prevalent, and Hayes did not ignore the problem. When discrimination reached intolerable levels she found that "native boys in the armed forces have been prevented from walking down the street with or speaking to old friends." Subsequently, she was placed on a committee to look into the larger problem concerning the blatant discrimination practiced by the USO and together Ruth Hayes, business agent, and Rose Dellama, international representative, established a consolidated policy to eradicate bias within the military authorities and the USO.[61] It was evident this union had broadened its duties to look at regional problems that affected not only the workers but the communities they lived in, and in this endeavor Hayes and others were quite effective. As the war years progressed, there was little talk of striking or increasing wages because the government had outlawed strikes and frozen wages. The workers seemed to understand the temporary sacrifices they needed to make for the greater good, and any complaints they had could wait until peacetime, yet bigotry had no place in Southeast Alaska regardless of the times.

For Hayes and many other Native women, social problems were in the scope of workable issues. For instance, Local 269, which represented cannery workers at the Libby, McNeill & Libby cannery at Taku, spoke to Hayes about the plant's dangerously neglected condition and the need for new employee apartments to replace those that had fallen into disrepair. She accepted the challenge and through her "persistent fight," the apartments were updated and "the boys from Local 7 planted lawns and even planted a Victory Garden," a symbol of the overarching importance of the war milieu. Many similar projects were completed during this time, particularly when the government could supply the materials, but other union issues lingered unresolved.

Hoonah, a Tlingit fishing village on Chichagof Island with about nine hundred residents, was one of the original chapters of the UCAPAWA. Historically, its cannery had always packed a great quantity of salmon. Susan Brown, the lead union agent for the area, was described by the UCAPAWA News as an "Alaska Native, [who] has helped win the benefits the workers now enjoy."[62] Brown had worked in canneries since the age of thirteen, receiving twenty cents per hour for the usual ten-hour shift. Nearby Excursion Inlet mainly employed women, many of them her relatives, and in her union capacity she was called upon to figure out what was going on when the complaints starting pouring in.

A closer look at Hoonah and Excursion Inlet provides a story of how vulnerable cannery workers were exploited. Unions endeavored to protect the workers, but they could not be everywhere. In 1938 Ernest Fox, a CIO union organizer, stopped by Hoonah to investigate reports that some of the cannery workers had experienced blatant bias and had also been taken advantage of in negotiations. Although a bit condescending, he stated: "These poor Natives were deliberately misled by the Cannery owner. He informed the Natives before the season started that they were not required to join any organization as a condition of their employment, stating they were government wards."[63] The "government ward" reference was a throwback to the fiduciary relationship with Native Americans and inappropriate in this case. Fox accused the cannery of a deliberate attempt to keep women from joining the CIO, which was known for its support of minorities, and believed these women had been "compelled" to "accept what is pure and simply a company union contract" under unfavorable terms.[64] Ernest Fox, with the help of Susan Brown, sought justice and found a temporary resolution, but in the future it would be necessary to go directly to the cannery owners to convince them that issues such as proper wages were going to benefit everyone in the long run with happier and more productive workers. But that would take a great deal of effort.

In this era it was a good idea to call upon the cultural brokering expertise within the ANS, especially in the endeavors to bring relief to the "small cannery villages."[65] Rose Dellama found this organizational assistance helpful in raising awareness of what the CIO could do for women, and the circle widened when she found herself involved in the political issues of the day, including discrimination. Bigotry had been a factor from the beginning in this diverse atmosphere and was clearly seen in segregated housing, unequal pay, fewer opportunities for advancement, and the general public attitude. A prime example of the discrimination was epitomized when a Ketchikan canning company discharged six Tlingit women based on age, much to the disrespect of Tlingit mores. In response the CIO local secured old-age pensions for four of the six women, and the other two received jobs in other canneries.[66] In another example, Dellama was caught in the middle of a crisis when the associate director of the USO kicked a Native woman out of a dance. War patriotism was at a high level, and the CIO representatives pointed out that this woman's husband was serving in the army.[67] The ANS and UCAPAWA went on to settle other disputes, uplifting those facing the scourge of second-class status and its ramifications.

Despite the rise of local Native women's authority in the unions and canneries, there was still significant Filipino leadership in Alaska, and one outstanding example was Trinidad Rojo. He came through the ranks from cannery worker to union leader and, along the way, also earned his doctorate degree. In 1939 he was the UCAPAWA president and offered stability during a period of major confrontations between union management and the workers. In this pivotal time, and "with unity and perseverance the members of the Filipino labor union made their mark on the Northwest labor movement."[68] On the surface it may have appeared a strange match, but Filipino activism and cannery worker vigor forged an almost impenetrable force, assisted by charismatic leaders who understood how to rally support.

In January 1940 Trinidad Rojo gave a report to the Coastwise Conference Maritime Federation of the Pacific, held at Juneau, and stressed the unity of all workers, including the Asians and the Alaska Natives.[69] Further, acknowledging the importance of Native subsistence needs, he advocated for a decrease in the number of cannery traps since this cut into the Alaska Native livelihood. In inter-ethnic matters he spoke about Japanese efforts, stating, "Americans should encourage this pride of the Japanese by not depriving them of their jobs."[70] Rojo also complimented the Filipinos' ability to embrace all nationalities into their union: "The Cannery Workers and Farm Laborers Union in Seattle in 1933 included Japanese, Chinese, Negroes, Whites, etc. Now this union is known as Local 7 of the UCAPAWA." And it continued to make great strides, as witnessed in Alaska, "so that natives in the territory could enjoy the same wages and protection."[71] The UCAPAWA had an impact on Southeast Alaska like no other union effort, but it was greatly helped by local leaders, such as the Del Fierro family.

Salvador and Elizabeth Del Fierro were integral members of the Ketchikan community. Elizabeth, the daughter of an Italian immigrant and cannery worker, met Salvador at the local Catholic Church, but besides their religious affiliation they shared the conviction that the American dream could be attained by all who worked for it, a common ideal among immigrants, notwithstanding discouraging circumstances. "The onset of the Great Depression significantly altered Filipino perspectives on cannery work and their immigrant experience. They were transferred from youthful adventurous and romantic Alaskeros to hardened workers scratching for survival."[72] When the vision slipped from their grasp, the Filipino community intensified their efforts to realize everything America had to offer while coping with the difficulties they encountered.

Salvador recalled the working conditions: "In the early days they would work you as long as they wanted to without overtime," a frequent story. "And then when you were in the cannery they got you every which way," referring to all the hidden expenses that seemed to pop up.[73] The shifts were protracted when the salmon runs came and the hours were non-negotiable, since they had signed a labor contract stipulating that they would work as long as they were needed even if meant twenty hours a day.

Although the Del Fierros became a symbol of immigrant hope, before they could be genuinely effective they had to overcome the local bias and the national bigotry that was rampant against Asians, Filipinos, and southern Europeans, escalating during World War II. There was built-in trouble when people married outside their own ethnic circle, and it was seen as "less dangerous" for a Filipino man to marry someone of color, but in 1925 Salvador del Fierro had his eye on an Italian girl. Not only did they each risk censure from the community in general, but initially the young woman's father disapproved of the match.[74]

These attitudes and pressures compelled the young couple to escape to Seattle to avoid hostilities. During this time Salvador worked at the Olympic Hotel for a year, while Elizabeth took care of their growing family. Although they lived humbly, they often took in men down on their luck and were well acquainted with union activists, such as Chris Mensalvas and Ponce Torres. After a year, however, the Del Fierros realized they were unhappy in this urban setting and returned to Ketchikan, where they were immediately engaged in cannery problems and became known as movers and shakers against the general current. Their success can be attributed to the fact that they were well respected by the cannery workers and the fishermen. Salvador noted he was more at ease at Ketchikan meetings than he ever was among Seattle union organizers.[75] Most of all, Salvador liked to meet his fellow workers out on the basketball court to talk about the issues—the segregated Alaska Native basketball court.

Salvador, already well accepted by the Ketchikan community, increased his representation of Filipinos upon becoming the chairman of the Ketchikan Filipino Council, as he worked for equity in housing, education, and jobs.[76] Along with his natural empathy, Salvador was influential because he knew the playing field, while Elizabeth worked with Rose Dellama to encourage women to join the cio-based ucapawa. Dellama and Elizabeth Del Fierro had quickly formed a friendship based on their mutual Italian American heritage, finding they had much in common, and together they reached out to the Alaska Native community. But Elizabeth did not forget she was married to a staunch cio man and "a central figure as a local linchpin in Ketchikan for the 'community of association' for Filipinos."[77] Salvador Del Fierro remarked: "The progressive leaders of the cannery workers in Ketchikan reported that considerable headway had been made to bring about greater cooperation and unity between the workers in the Territory and those in the states."[78] With modest support, the Del Fierros brought disorganized activity under control and managed "to negotiate minimum wage guarantees for the Alaskan workers, residents and Native Alaskans alike."[79]

Elizabeth and Salvador were "race leaders who formed a social bridge among Filipinos, Natives, and whites. The mediating role operated within the unions and canning communities . . . and emphasized good fellowship between Filipinos and Americans because of their shared aims and ideals of liberty."[80] Later in his life Salvador del Fierro had a reputation as a sage elder, but perhaps it was the younger generation coming up who did not understand how much he had sacrificed for the greater good. These attitudes discouraged Salvador, and he worried about their futures in leadership roles: "Some might say that the older generation hasn't done enough to improve conditions but they have no business to say that. Because we paved the way for them, if they only realize it—what we went through, they didn't have to face. They are militant. They call it the coming age. I don't know."[81]

The Del Fierros' story illustrates the sociopolitical milieu during the 1930s and 1940s. According to labor historian Chris Friday, the married couple "served as positive public role models for interracial marriages and for cooperation between resident Alaskans—white and Native—and the 'outside' crews dominated by Filipino men from Seattle, Portland, and San Francisco."[82] This was the essence of the cannery culture and, projected on a wider screen, the "orchestrating" of soul and spirit. Whether at union meetings or social gatherings, people were brought together from all walks of life. Dances, holidays, and celebrations united the communities: the Filipinos, Italians, Japanese, Swedes, Tlingit, and Haida expanded their individual strengths through work and play, sharing experiences, and shunning the notion of class differences. Ethnic heritage and social roles might have entered the dance floor, but the dancers created their own choreography and coordinated the salsa and rumba of "labor history and its complexities and contradictions in the struggles to find dignity in the face of woefully daunting circumstances."[83] The dance spotlighted the need for cooperation against adversity, although not everyone was surrounded by the same music.

When the Depression brought the American dream to its knees and racial hatred brewed in Pacific Coast cities and then north to Alaska, there was a greater need for collaboration. In spite of the segregated houses, ethnic fraternities, and anti-Asian unions, the workers stood up against the worst abuses of the canning industry from the contract system to outright employment discrimination. To survive, there needed to be respect for differences and a more tolerant attitude to construct durable political muscle capable of guarding against the cunning ploys of major corporations and unfavorable legislation. In understanding this social, economic, and political history, as Friday suggests, we can "examine how they shaped the capitalist transformation and how they were shaped by it, how they were embattled and empowered . . . what opportunities they took and lost."[84]

For the Alaska Native, the past decades had been a time of major transformations from a bartering and communal society to a more individualist economy. Gender roles had been modified, but beyond these factors, it was no surprise that Tlingit and Haida women carved their own path. Stemming from traditional Tlingit and Haida society, the women's place was one of esteem, largely based on being the "owner" of the clan property, and they would not accept an artificial status placed on them by cannery foremen or union bosses. Women, regardless of ethnic background, were concerned about family and community, and willing to fight for a cohesive existence in the midst of alien and forbidding elements as they raised their voices against injustice.

11

The Inequities of War

World War II was an economic boon for a country struggling to climb out of the Great Depression, and the process changed the American character on several levels, particularly in terms of increased bureaucratic restraints and control. Patriotism was the pervading national hymn and generated a fervor to unmask perceived enemies and engage in scapegoating. The federal government assumed authority over major industries, including Alaskan canneries, setting the price for fish and establishing non-negotiable wages, thus striking a severe blow to union autonomy. Everyone was expected to make sacrifices for the greater good, and union activities were curbed while pay disparities were frozen in time "as if prewar inequities were unworthy of redress."[1]

Simultaneously there was a great debate over land and water ownership in Alaska, particularly concerning Native use and extraction of resources. The Native livelihood was dependent on the canneries, whether for fisherman or processor. Alaska Natives continued to engage in traditional subsistence activities, the heart of their culture since a time before memory. These factors contributed to the clashes between Alaska Native autonomy, the federal and local governments, and industrial development in Alaska, exposing the underpinnings of a skewed power hierarchy.

In June 1942 Bill Paul Jr. toured several canneries in Southeast Alaska to record the cannery conditions, housing availability, and salmon prices.

Once he delved into the situation, he found that Native fishermen were getting far less for their fish than others, and the cannery workers could barely make a living. At the same time, the cannery owners were piling up abundant returns on their investments and watching their balances increase in out-of-territory-banks.[2] It was past time for action, and Paul Jr. was determined to rectify the situation.

In the Ketchikan *Alaska Fishing News* Paul Jr. wrote an open letter to the ANB camps in the hopes of soliciting allegiance from the last few remaining AMWU members and those from the Alaska Marine Fishermen's Cooperative, promising real gains could be made if they maintained a solid front. He went on to mention that a mother from one of the villages had contacted him to let him know the young people did not believe in the ANB anymore and instead they wanted something more modern. Paul Jr., like his father and uncle, answered her concern with the assurance that the ANB was the only organization that would watch over the Tlingit and Haida to make sure they got a fair shake.[3] He submitted editorials to other Southeast Alaska newspapers with sizzling headlines like "Hot Letter by Wm. Paul, Jr. to Natives on Fish Bargaining," in which he railed against unfair fish prices, blaming unions that encouraged Native cannery workers and fishermen to sign up with them but did not nothing for these workers afterward, again arguing: "The ANB and ANS are the only ones that are going to have your back in this thing," and "The AFL and CIO do not work for the benefit of the Indians."[4]

In the 1940s the ANB-sponsored AMWU struggled to hold onto its political position, but time had run out. The grass roots union had served many, but it collapsed as its members sought other avenues to support their basic needs. The cannery workers auxiliary could not maintain strength without the Alaska Native Sisterhood and its woman warriors, who were now devoting their energies to bigger unions, predominantly the CIO-based UCAPAWA. Yet the Pauls fought for their ANB union and were not about to let it go down easily. William L. Paul Sr. accused "the whites of deserting Native Alaskans while the union silently folded up and died."[5] In retrospect, the times had changed and political priorities had been reorganized, chiefly because of the onset of World War II and its tremendous socioeconomic impacts. Additionally, the ANB was involved in the ongoing Tlingit-Haida land suit, which was pursuing compensation for the Southeast Alaska lands taken by President Theodore Roosevelt in his Tongass Forest executive reserve actions.

As energies turned to the war effort and taking care of "our boys" overseas, the government developed complex administrative agencies and departments that included a War Labor Board and the Office of Price Administration (OPA). These two offices were responsible for setting prices for canned salmon, ultimately sending out a ripple effect on wages. Alaska was the world's largest salmon packing location, and cannery owners found themselves under restrictive government contracts, but the tradeoff was that they were protected from strikes, which were deemed illegal and unpatriotic. The industry was declared a vital food defense industry and Secretary of the Interior Harold Ickes was tasked to manage the Office of Fishery Coordination, which extended complete control over Alaska's canning industry, including production quotas and which plants could operate. Capitalism and the free market economy were immobilized, and union activity was halted for the time being.[6] In the midst of these drastic changes, the fishermen increasingly complained about unfair prices, but their grievances fell on deaf ears.

Although marine workers were exempted from military service due to the critical nature of their contribution, men volunteered in large numbers, resulting in a labor shortage. To fill the void there was a greater reliance on female workers to fill the jobs once held by men, such as "the task of loading and unloading trays of cans from the retorts, which had earlier been done by two-man teams, was now done by four-women teams," and these workers demanded fair compensation and a voice in the operations.[7] Their political strength was hampered by wartime propaganda depicting women at home in aprons waiting for their husbands and sons. For those working at the plants, the canners played to the women's sense of "nationalism and self pride so they would feel they were doing their duty."[8] Women were told they were "vital to the victory over fascism" and were coached to believe they were avoiding the fate of German and Japanese women, who were "enslaved," and furthermore, they should take pleasure in "the grand feeling that they are doing their full part to help speed the day of victory."[9] Everything centered on the war's progress and "the girls gloried in their ability to handle it [the job] satisfactorily."[10] Perhaps this was what the cannery owners thought, but once the women unleashed their dynamism, there was a dramatic shift in social status.[11]

Bill Paul Jr. was a rising star in labor negotiations and was expected to protect the interests of both the fishermen and cannery workers, which pitted him against the notorious and monopolistic Alaska Salmon Industry, Inc. (ASI). This lobby group extended its clutch into every aspect of cannery operations and appeared to receive preferential treatment from the government in addition to representing 95 percent of Alaska's salmon packers. Originally the ASI mission was to act as a stabilizing force in a chaotic relationship between the packers and the more powerful unions, such as the Alaska Fishermen's Union (AFU), but in the process the ASI had grown into a giant and forceful behemoth that skirted NLRB rules and fishery regulations, and swung negotiations between the packers, the unions, and the out-of-territory cannery owners to their own advantage in the political matrix.[12] In a nutshell, while the ASI was ostensibly set up to protect the fishery resources, particularly through research facilities, in reality it could have been characterized as an oligarchy.

Arnold, as the ASI managing director, was the nemesis of the entire Paul family, further punctuated by their frequent head-to-head skirmishes over Native civil rights cases.[13] After accusations of unfair practices, heated debates were heard in June 1944 in the "matter of Alaska Salmon, Inc. and Alaska Fishermen's Union and Other Unions of the Twelfth Regional War Labor Board," a meeting held in Ketchikan. Those involved were eminent in the fishing industry, although often from opposing sides. Behind closed doors the attendees included William (Bill) Paul Jr., representing the ANB; Mr. W. C. Arnold (ASI); Frank Peratrovich, president of the Alaska Salmon Purse Seiner's Union; John Olafsen, representing the Alaska Fishermen's Union; Frank Marshall, president of the Territorial AFL; Rose Dellamo of the UCAPAWA; Tenu Haines of the CIO Cannery Workers Union; Margaret (instead of Marguerite) Hansen of the CIO

Cannery Workers Union; A. P. Hanson, representing both the Petersburg ASPSU and the Cannery Workers Auxiliary Union; and finally Joe Krause, also of the ASPSU. These men and women had a direct influence on the resource and the labor force, and although this was only one meeting, it represented the contemporary issues that were discussed during wartime, affecting the day-to-day lives of cannery workers and their families.

The hearing was called to decide jurisdictional authority over fish prices and labor wages during the unusual time, but the dialogue heated up and topics branched out to other social concerns, including working and housing conditions. Almost immediately, Arnold found himself defending his business interests and clients. Alternatively, when Frank Peratrovich and Bill Paul Jr. recognized their common cause, they united to take on the ASI—former enemies were now allies, at least for the time being.

The ASI was accused of setting salmon prices and wages unilaterally without the benefit of negotiation or collective bargaining, and the opponents of this monopolistic practice, namely the ASPSU and the ANB unions, believed this was illegal and a restraint of trade, largely based on the Sherman Anti-Trust Act.[14] Although there was certainly credence to these charges, this was a time of war and other exigencies took priority. For efficiency, the War Production Board had consolidated the canneries to weed out the less effective plants, but in effect, this set up mega-canneries having control over labor, the resource, and output. This situation played right into Arnold's hands since the ASI already managed the majority of these canneries. Moreover, wages and prices were to be monitored by the federal government under wartime requirements, but somehow the ASI had snaked its way into this matter, apparently unbeknownst to the government, and was able to set its own prices for raw salmon. When this irregularity was discovered, both Paul Jr. and Frank Peratrovich banded together to break Arnold's grip on the industry.

Intensified bureaucracy had smashed small business interests with overbearing rules and conditions, and at this meeting the first order of business was to find a way around the Office of Price Administration, which had almost completely frozen prices and wages during this time.[15] Without a fair wage, cannery or fishing families could not afford basic groceries or decent housing. To demonstrate this point, Bill Paul Jr. used Ketchikan as an example because of the number of cannery employees: "Ketchikan enjoys a higher income than any place in Southeastern Alaska, but I saw more dirty little alleys and falling down houses here than I have seen any place else." He continued his rebuke by adding: "It is a gross shame that our income should be so low that the people have to live in such terrible conditions," and he strongly hinted that this might be the cause of the tuberculosis outbreaks. He paused in his statement to ask the territorial health agent in attendance to look into this critical matter.[16]

Bill Paul explained how to get by, an entire family had to work during these strained times. The work of the wife, although seasonal, was important to the family and often this included the older children as well. It was not uncommon to have an eleven-year-old working in the canneries, even missing school in some instances. It was a way to make ends meet in these uncertain times. Regardless of what was happening in the fisheries, and whether damage derived from gluttonous fish traps or oppressive governmental regulations, the cannery workers needed a steady paycheck. Temporarily, with the wartime demand for salmon, that was guaranteed— unless the fish runs stopped, and that was a real threat.

When Arnold disputed Paul's portrayal of housing conditions, Paul entered documentary evidence as part of the public record, including photographs, showing his travels through canneries such as the one in Steamboat Bay, where he had taken pictures of the broken walkway planks and sagging lean-tos as proof to show those who might argue against his findings. Again Paul Jr. described how the substandard and crowded housing during the cannery season led to disease. At times families had no choice, but to move to another cannery because of the unsanitary conditions and dangerous insect bites, but without union support and with government restrictions, changing to an unassigned cannery was illegal, and a fine could be imposed. Paul Jr. shared the realities of this time: "Up there the cabins in which the women and children are living ought to be burnt down. I feel sure that the cabins at Tenakee are infested. Children come out of there covered from head to foot with bites. We have called upon the Territorial health authorities to make corrections, but they are unable to do so."[17]

Others in the room corroborated his story and went on to discuss the upgrades that had been completed at Hoonah, largely accomplished by the village residents. It was suggested that company property must be improved, but during the war years resources (such as lumber) were hard to come by. The substandard housing charge was challenged by the ASI representatives, who said cannery workers were free to return to their home village for meals (both mid-day and dinner) rather than stay in these houses. Considering the transportation difficulties and distance, this proposal was preposterous.

A. P. Hanson from the Petersburg Purse Seiners' Union (Alaska Salmon Purse Seiners' Union and Cannery Workers Auxiliary Union) countered the suggestion that cannery workers could be commuters—it was impossible for anyone working at the cannery to try to return to their village to prepare meals and still get back to work on time. Hanson accused "Judge Arnold" of taking a hard line that was not to the benefit of the workers, adding that he hoped the prices returned to normal or "something is going to pop," referring to the growing discontent among cannery labor and fishermen who fished for the canneries.[18]

Although this meeting had been called to discuss salmon prices and fair practices, the conversation frequently drifted back to the deplorable cannery conditions. In one instance Kake was used as an example to illustrate a location where the shacks were uninhabitable. Located on Prince of Wales Island, Kake was a large, multi-ethnic cannery with segregated housing for the Filipinos, Japanese, and Alaska Natives, which was the norm. There had been complaints about the cannery from as far back as 1937, when the Cannery Workers and Farm Labor Union (CWFLU) sent a grievance letter to officials complaining about overpriced food that was suspected of poisoning one worker, in addition to bad housing conditions and the unchecked spread of tuberculosis within the facility.[19] Seemingly, there had been few improvements in the last seven years.

Arnold denied that he was responsible for housing and unabashedly declared that his job was to look out for the cannery owners and the employees. He disagreed with Hanson and claimed there was available transportation for the Native workers to go back home in the evenings so that they did not have to stay in the cannery shacks. In response, Hanson shot back that transportation was unreliable, especially when in so many cases the women worked past 6:00 p.m. Rose Dellama, as the UCAPAWA representative and defender of the women, called Arnold negligent, reminding him the employees and their health condition were integral to any operation. Arnold shrugged off her accusations and repeated that he was unaware of any genuine problems.

Frank Peratrovich, current president of the ASAPU, emphasized the overall point that "labor unions in Alaska have to accumulate enough money to demand justice from the canning industry."[20] The time had come to effect change. and Peratrovich threatened Arnold with a federal government health inspection to determine the exact state of affairs and perhaps even to levy fines based on the findings. Arnold disregarded any allegations and instead declared that he would set fish prices at whatever level he thought right, and there was no person or agency who could rightfully interfere with this process. As far as housing or related health issues were concerned, he again dispelled any liability, stating "We feel constrained to disagree with Mr. Peratrovich's statement that in a majority of the canneries in Southeastern Alaska the housing is unsanitary." According to his assessment, the houses were built for use on a temporary basis without rent, and so basically you got what you got.[21] Further, if there were any health problems, it was not Arnold's concern but rather a matter for the Territorial Health Department. Dr. Charles Battin, the hearing officer, believed the real culprit centered on poverty conditions generated by low fish prices, but Arnold continued to blame the Health Department, claiming they were not doing their job.[22]

The poverty issue, however, could not be so easily rejected. Bill Paul Jr. entered Fish and Wildlife Service statistics into the record, which illustrated the dire state of a family's income: "an average net earning for each seine fisherman of $559.00 per year," supplemented by other members of the family, including the wife's summer work estimated at $250.00 and the children at about $125.00. Hunting and fishing were also added to the calculations to reflect about $250.00 from the wife gathering edible plants and the man (or sometimes the whole family) trolling for salmon and halibut. Formerly, deer could also be hunted, but during the war harvesting of these animals had been restricted by fish and game regulations, further burdening the family's resources.[23] This was one of the first times subsistence sources and the accompanying labor had been equated with supplemental income. In effect, these statements gave credence to the dual economy as part of the overall picture, but also worked against families in this instance, since it was inferred in a distorted conclusion that these households were better off than they actually were.

Paul added, "So long as there is any possibility during this time of war that such standards of living could be corrected, I think every effort should be made to do so."[24] Frank Peratrovich agreed with both Hanson's testimony and that of Bill Paul Jr., adding that all of them had "gone to a great deal of trouble to present conclusive evidence of the justice of our demands, and we have not heard anything to combat it."[25] Except for the Alaska Fisherman's Union, each hearing member was solidly against the monopoly enjoyed by Arnold and the ASI, and none believed he had the credentials for negotiating fish prices or fairly assessing housing conditions. Nonetheless, the inequities persisted in the 1940s.

That this meeting was contentious was an understatement. With smug replies Arnold fended off any allegation of his poor management or stinginess, while the others joined forces to oppose him and even hinted of his black market involvement or collusion in the stock market.[26] Before the meeting ended, Joe Krause of the Alaska Salmon Purse Seiners' Union also brought up concerns about wage scale inequality between residents and nonresidents, contending that the nonresidents returned south, where the living was so much cheaper and "their dollars naturally go a lot further. People up here feel they are being cheated."[27] He was not alone in this reflection; his thoughts matched the jingoistic refrain echoing throughout the territory. Krause warned that the federal government had better do something about the unfair advantage before the servicemen returned home after the war because those men were expecting good jobs.[28]

In closing, and perhaps to temper the previous harsh words, Frank

Marshall, president of the territorial American Federation of Labor, interjected that it was good that for once these hearings took place in Alaska instead of Seattle, so that local issues could be aired, since so often critical decisions were made in urban areas without consulting the fishermen or cannery workers, and these women and men were left to abide by the results, regardless of the consequences. "I don't think that anyone could fail to understand the gross discrimination that was practiced on the Alaska fishermen."[29] It was true that cannery workers and the fishermen were taken advantage of during the war years, while the corporations continued to reap a profit with the government's blessing. Many of the workers were Alaska Natives and they faced genuine hardships during this time. Those involved in the salmon industry, from women working the line to men brailing salmon on cannery docks, got by the best they could, hoping, like all of America, for an end to this war, but perhaps no one could have wished for a return to normalcy more than the Alaskan Japanese, many of them former cannery workers. Their story defies imagination and continues the tale of the inequities brought on during wartime.

No one could have predicted that this message would go out on the air waves in 1942: "A flight of about fifteen wheel-type fighting planes appeared without previous warning.... Anti-aircraft fire of great intensity opened"—Alaska was under attack.[30] Dutch Harbor in southwest Alaska had been bombed by the Japanese. There was no time to plan. Everything was grab and dash, resulting in multiple ill effects. The Unangax (Aleut) Natives were "relocated" without a plan, and the Japanese Alaskans were rounded up to be sent to internment camps. To understand what occurred during the 1940s, it is instructive to summarize the background leading to the series of events that affected Alaska Natives and Japanese Alaskans.

As early as 1910 the dominant or "white" population had labeled Asian immigrants as undesirable, goaded by newspaper stories covering Japan's growing militarism.[31] Unfortunately for the Japanese in the United States, these fears, biases, and false extrapolations targeted their very existence. Shih-shan Henry Tsai documented that "circumstances now dictated the Japanese became the focus of America's traditional irrational racist passions" and seen as a menace.[32] Japan was referred to as the "Germany of Asia."[33] In an effort to boost American preparedness against presumed Japanese aggression, immigrants and their descendants were viewed as an internal enemy that had to be eliminated. Anti-Japanese pamphlets were distributed to editorialize against Japanese Americans, and Yellow Peril fanaticism reached epidemic proportions; there were those believing it their duty to uncover "disguised truth" through the newspapers, particularly those owned by William Randolph Hearst. While the *San Francisco Chronicle* alleged the Japanese were spies, Hearst's *San Francisco Examiner* drove home the xenophobic attitudes in headlines reading: "Brown Men Have Maps and Could Land Easily."[34]

In anticipation of a possible foreign invasion, President Franklin Roosevelt had issued an executive order conferring upon the secretary of agriculture the full responsibility for the nation's food supply, and Harold Ickes, as the secretary of the interior, took over the management of Alaska's salmon canning industry. Through his administration, about 90 percent of the packs went to government purchases to feed civilians and soldiers alike.[35] No one was exempt from doing their part, right down to housewives saving cooking fat in coffee cans under their kitchen sinks.[36] Without hesitation, Alaska's bounty in fish and forests was dedicated to the defense of liberty, whether that be spruce planes or canned salmon bound for Europe.

The acceleration of mass production exposed the labor shortage, which dwindled further as more former cannery workers and fishermen joined the armed forces.[37] From the 1942 Cannery Workers and Farm Laborers Union report, it was noted that over half of the cannery workers had either been drafted or volunteered for military service. That void was filled by Alaska Native women and Filipino men.[38] Ironically, Filipinos who had been discriminated against in the past and no longer classified as U.S. nationals, now qualified for war-related jobs. The Filipinos also had an advantage in numbers. According to U.S. Fish and Wildlife Service records, working in various capacities in Southeast Alaska canneries there were 38 Negroes, 51 Puerto Ricans, 230 Chinese, 230 Mexicans, 646 Japanese, 2,917 Alaska Natives, 3,417 Filipinos, and 5,890 whites.[39]

The Japanese, as identified through statistics, were a small population in comparison to other ethnic groups in Southeast Alaska, but as the war frenzy increased and with the attempts to separate the alleged traitors from the patriots, even those numbers shrank. Many Japanese who had been employed for years were suddenly let go for security reasons and could not find other work. Simultaneously, the Filipinos went to great lengths to prove their American allegiance and certainly did not want to be confused with the suspect Chinese or Japanese. Good press helped their cause, as in the April 1942 issue of *Pacific Fisherman*, which pictured several Filipino foreman with a caption reading: "They're all set to can salmon to beat the Japs, and are determined to make it Food for MacArthur's men."[40]

With this labor shortage, managers feared they could not meet their quotas, motivating the company owners to seek special status for their workers. Consequently, by early 1943 the Alaska fishermen and cannery workers were classified as war workers and exempt from the military, since they were providing a vital service. With government loans, greater capitalization was possible, and cannery companies increased mechanization, while new airstrips were constructed so that more Alaska Native villagers could be flown from village to cannery. The APA found this economical in Southeast Alaska "where plants were closer to Native villages and towns."[41] If Alaska Natives wanted to work at the canneries they were fully employed, working side by side with Filipino men. During wartime, the status of Alaska Natives and Filipinos was altered due to production demands, and often members of both ethnic groups were promoted to higher positions, all the way up to plant manager. Their Japanese neighbors, however, were shut out of the industry, often suspected of being spies, stemming from the military situation.

In February 1942 Lieutenant General John DeWitt, head of the Western Defense Command, condemned the Japanese as a dangerous element that must be dealt with under severe terms: "In the war in which we are now engaged racial affinities are not severed by migration. The Japanese race is an enemy race and while many second and third generation Japanese born on United States soil, possessed of United States citizenship, have become Americanized, the racial strains are undiluted."[42] In retrospect, what happened next could have been predicted.

President Franklin Roosevelt, although filled with doubts, resolved that this was a military matter and gave the commanders the go ahead to proceed as they saw fit for the best interests of the nation. In essence, President Roosevelt "had signed a blank check, giving full authority to General DeWitt to take care of the matter even if that meant detention camps." According to Asian historian Ronald Takaki, "tragically for the Japanese and for the U.S. Constitution" this "racialized procedure" proceeded even though "there was actually no military necessity."[43] As far as civilians were concerned, the procedures were neither preplanned nor executed effectively, leaving many United States citizens as prisoners of war.

Ten weeks after the outbreak of war, on February 19, 1942, President Roosevelt signed Executive Order 9066 which gave to the secretary of war and the military commanders to whom he delegated authority the power to exclude any persons from designated areas in order to secure national defense objectives against sabotage and espionage. The West Coast congressional delegation knew these orders would ultimately exclude persons of Japanese ancestry, both American citizens and resident aliens.[44] Japanese citizens were given twenty-four hours to pack a few belongings and vacate their houses and businesses before being transported to internment centers.

In Alaska the FBI rounded up Japanese families from remote Deering on the Seward Peninsula above the Arctic Circle down to Ketchikan.[45] Whole families were taken aboard ships bound for Seattle. Isamu Taguchi, a former Juneau cannery worker, describes how the ship "collected Japanese Alaskans from communities such as Wrangell, Cordova, Petersburg, and Ketchikan" and added that he was surprised: "I met more Japanese than I ever realized lived in the territory."[46] From Alaska's shores, they were taken to a place with an unlikely name: Camp Harmony in Puyallup, Washington, a temporary sorting facility. Those who later spoke of the experience—and many never did—described how they sat in what was called "The Alaska Row" for several days before being sent to permanent detention camps. The War Relocation Authority was in charge of their movements.[47] This agency's records indicated that most of Alaska's internees were sent to the Minidoka Internment Facility in Hunt, Idaho.[48]

From Ketchikan fifty-nine Japanese were seized at gunpoint followed by thirty-four in Juneau, and in Petersburg twenty-nine were detained, while only one, the only Japanese man in town, was rounded up at Tenakee on Chichagof Island. The men, women, and children were jammed together in the ship's steerage and would not see their homes for several years, if ever. At the end of the war, it was reported that six Alaska Japanese internees had died at the camp, and only about thirty-five of the Japanese removed from their homes in Southeast Alaska returned to Alaska.[49]

The stories of that time offer a clear picture of inequities, yet the detainees did not give in to despair. William Tatsuda's father had immigrated to the United States in 1904 and worked at Ketchikan canneries before starting his store. When the military arrived with evacuation instructions, the Tatsudas, like so many others, were shocked when they were ordered to report to the ship that would carry them south to the Puyallup Assembly Center in Washington before relocating them to Minidoka Internment Camp.[50] Despite these hard times, William's sister Cherry had at least one fond memory of the internment camp: in 1943 she married Tad Fujioka, who had worked in the Taku Harbor and Ketchikan canneries while attending a Pacific Northwest university. They spent their wedding night in the "Honeymoon Lot, Block 44."

Not all the Alaska Japanese men were placed in the internment camps. Several men volunteered for military service and were members of the celebrated and heavily decorated Japanese-only 442nd Regiment, stationed mainly in the European theatre. Charlie Tatsuda, Bob Urata, and Jimmy Tatsuda served in the 442nd Regimental Combat Team, and Charlie Tatsuda was also sent "to military intelligence school in Minnesota, graduating as an interpreter before being assigned to the paratroopers units in the Philippines and Japan."[51] For these men, the war was a test of their American loyalties, which may have been strained because of their transnational ties.

The war changed everything for the Hagiwara family, owners of a Ketchikan grocery store. Like several Japanese Alaskan men, Patrick

Hagiwara joined the Alaska National Guard in 1940, and his Company B 297th Infantry was transferred to the Chilkoot Barracks in September 1941. These barracks, located in Haines, had been built during the gold rush period as military protection for prospectors passing through the region on their way north to the Klondike goldfields. After the buildings were no longer necessary, they were left to decay in the elements, yet they were reopened to house and train Japanese Alaskan soldiers for a short period before the men left for war hot spots or sometimes internment camps.[52] Hagiwara remembers the difficult times: "When World War II began . . . his friends Charlie Tatsuda, Bob Urata and Jimmy Tatsuda encouraged him during what he determined was an awkward and difficult period as people suspected their motives and allegiance."[53] It was tough being thought of as the enemy. Not only were the Japanese disrespected, but these men were obligated to betray their cultural mores in order to obey military commands. As a prime example, Hagiwara was told to stand guard over his Issei (first generation) neighbors, placing him in a thorny position since these were revered elders, and such actions would be viewed as unforgivable arrogance. Hagiwara went on to serve in the all–Japanese American unit, the 442nd, and left in his memoir a vivid account of war in the European theater.[54]

Not everyone came back to Alaska after the war. Several men were killed in battle, and others made a new life in more southerly regions, predominantly Washington State. Ketchikan's Ohashi family were different. They had left their business in the hands of trusted friends and had something to come back to, but not all were so lucky. Komatsu Ohashi, who had come to Alaska as a picture bride, remarked that many of these businesses had fallen into disrepair during the war years. When asked if she or her family suffered any prejudicial feelings in Ketchikan after her return, she remarked that there was a little hostility, but most people were nice. She and others were reassured by the words of "white" American citizens like Bill Baker, who called on everyone to be hospitable to the Japanese returning from the internment camps. They had not started the war and "had to sacrifice so much stuff to evacuate so why bother to pick on them [?] They are welcome."[55]

Returning to the life story of Shoki Kayamori, we can view how the war affected a prominent cannery town. He was a fixture in the Yakutat community but also subject to vicious rumors. Alaska's remoteness did not spare its residents from stories that the Japanese were going to rise up in an act of sabotage. One historian claimed the authorities were "positive that all Japanese were potential enemies, they attacked subversion where it did not exist and saw spies that never were."[56] The press was on fire with tales exclaiming that the Japanese immigrant laborers were "poised for a Trojan horse–style attack."[57] In this agitated hysteria, photographers were thought to be highly suspicious, and there was Kayamori—caught in the middle. After being fingerprinted and subjected to interrogation as part of the Alien Registration Act, Kayamori kept a low profile, but he could not escape attention. Margaret Thomas, his biographer, described how propaganda circulars were received, depicting the Japanese as "buck-toothed caricatures" resembling "the brazen wharf rats that scurried off military transports in Yakutat."[58]

The military had sent a convoy of men and supplies to Yakutat even before the 1941 Pearl Harbor bombing to defend what was believed to be a vulnerable coastline: "For a while the cannery served as barracks. Construction of a landing field was soon under way." The soldiers "invited Yakutat residents to dine at the post and paid admission to dances at the ANB Hall," sparking a few romances in this cultural exchange.[59] The ANB hall was the largest public building outside the cannery and was deemed a good place to prepare for attack. In several meetings the villagers were ordered to put blankets over their windows, cache food, and do some reconnaissance of local caves as potential hiding spots. To be prepared, soldiers staged air raids and planes "bombarded Yakutat with leaflets warning of similar Japanese sneak attacks."[60]

Kayamori's innocence was relentlessly questioned, and because of his deeply engrained Japanese ethos, these accusations, although without merit, filled him with shame.[61] His status as a marked man was vulgarly exhibited when the soldiers singled him out, beat him almost unconscious, and then rifled his pockets, presumably looking for contraband. Here was a sixty-four-year-old man employed as a night watchman for the cannery, hardly a threat to these young military officials. On December 6, 1941, Kayamori's name appeared on Hoover's War Department list and more information was requested about him as a possible suspect. Then Pearl Harbor was bombed.

The news of the attack came by radio to Yakutat and a crowd gathered to talk about what might be next. Young men were eager to enlist, but their fervor was quelled by elders cautioning them that their place was in the village. Someone noticed that Shoki was not among them, and they wondered why he had not been drawn outside by the commotion. Two men went to his house to look for him, but were not expecting what they found: "Kayamori would save them the trouble of deciding whether he was friend or enemy. According to local lore, he was found slumped over in his armchair. He died as he had lived. Alone."[62] The next day he was buried in his Japanese navy uniform while a cannery official and the military auctioned his meager belongings, which had actually been promised to his Tlingit friends.[63] A naval ramp has since erased all traces of the grave, and as John Bremner lamented: "That's the wartime. They don't worry about Kayamori."[64]

It was not only the Japanese in Alaska who were affected by the war—there is also the story of the Aleutian Islands Natives. After Dutch Harbor was bombed there were questions regarding what to do about the local Aleut (Unangax) and not much time to make decisions, resulting in evacuees being housed in Southeast Alaska's abandoned canneries for the duration of the war. One of the most notorious locations was at Funter Bay on Admiralty Island, where a large cannery operation had been functioning at the turn of the century, but its structures were inhabitable by the 1940s. Left to fend for themselves with little in the way of food or supplies, these Pribilof Islanders felt they were in an alien land.[65] The only preparation for their arrival had been the federal government's last minute lease deal for defunct cannery sites with no amenities. Unlike other evacuees, the Pribilof Islanders had been permitted to bring a few of their own boats with them, which was a life saver, because they could hunt and fish, and the nearby Tlingit residing in Angoon also regularly dropped by to check on the internees and brought fresh salmon.[66] Other than that, the Fish and Wildlife Service was in charge, as they had been with the Japanese removal, and the Alaska Natives were neglected military wards.

When winter came the residents were in trouble. The cannery buildings had never been designed for residency or harsh weather conditions. "During the past cold spell it has been impossible to heat the houses and quarters occupied by the Natives. At night they have huddled around the stoves and in the dining room getting what little sleep possible. Most of the water pipes are frozen."[67] With bad conditions and the spread of disease, one of the first sites constructed was the cemetery. The only medical care at Funter Bay consisted of two nurses who served the people housed in both the cannery and a mine on the other side of the island. Sometimes doctors would visit, but it was rare, and medical supplies were scarce. Meanwhile "epidemics raged," and the Unangax̂ families suffered from influenza, measles, and pneumonia, along with the prevalent tuberculosis. Twenty-five died at Funter Bay in 1943 and for all the evacuees, the estimate was that "at least ten percent of the Aleut died" during the relocation period.[68]

Some of the interned men found nearby work, including rebuilding the old canneries, and a few experienced men filled positions in operating canneries when they could be ferried to the location. At Killisnoo, located three miles from Angoon on the opposite tip of Admiralty Island, eighty-three Atkans were housed after arriving in June 1942. In an ironic twist, these men took the jobs of Japanese Issei men, like Matsu "Harry" Samato, who was taken from his home and shipped to the Minidoka internment camp in Idaho.[69] At Ward Lake (near Ketchikan) the evacuees helped to construct an army base at Metlakatla. They all received meager paychecks, making them no longer eligible for government-issued food or supplies. In addition, when they used their own money for camp improvements, they were not reimbursed. It would be years before any of these events and circumstances would come to light, and the evacuees rarely spoke of these difficult times, although they were not passive.

Several petitions were sent to Washington DC to complain of the conditions and inequities, and some found a path to influential Washington DC legislators. For instance, Akutan village chief Mark Petikoff wrote a letter to the *Alaska Fishing News* protesting the conditions and claimed that the Aleut were nothing more than a political football. It was time they were returned to their homes on the island chain. Nothing changed. They were told to manage their own affairs, although this situation had never been of their making. In another example, Unalaska evacuees living in the abandoned Burnett Inlet cannery on Etolin Island reported:

> Some of the houses are the red cannery buildings left standing when the great fire destroyed the cannery at Burnett Inlet a few years ago. Other houses are structures of rough board and tar paper roofs erected for the shelter of the refugees. . . . On the beach lies many tons of blackened and rusted scrap iron—the residue of the burned cannery. . . . The colony at Burnett Inlet had no doctor or trained nurse. . . . In case of emergency plane service is available from Ketchikan, although there is no means of communication save by boat.[70]

Independently, the internees at Burnett Inlet had done what they could to improve the old facility without governmental assistance while paradoxically being "managed" by Office of Indian Affairs school teachers, and as the Natives worked to refurbish the cannery buildings they were told to stop complaining, but they did not.[71] Congressional delegate Tony Dimond received a letter from Kenneth Newell, an internee at Burnett Inlet, who described the horrendous conditions under which they were living. Dimond forwarded the letter to the Claude Hirst and Fred Geeslin of the Alaska Indian Service with the presumption that immediate action would be taken, but he was wrong. The Indian Service replied: "Even though these evacuees may be receiving less than Japs in concentration camps . . . I am sure the large majority of them are satisfied under the present conditions."[72] Newell's wife was convinced she could rally support from her fellow detainees and sent a petition, signed by the whole camp, to Fred Geeslin, whose job it was to oversee the relocation. Geeslin expressed disgust with her attempts to instigate discontent, labeling her a troublemaker without substance. More than anything, Martha Newell wanted to go back home, and before the war was over she was granted her wish when she was returned to Unalaska for burial.[73]

There is no doubt that many suffered during the war years—it was a time that called for intense sacrifice—but as is common in war, there was also a boost in technology, including the aviation industry, while population dynamics and the economy were altered by the military presence. Large infrastructure projects, such as roads and airports, were completed and the nation finally realized that Alaska was located in a highly strategic position for keeping an eye on the Soviet Union as the Cold War commenced and international tensions escalated. Notwithstanding modernization, Alaska remained a frontier community with few industrial options for filling the tax coffers other than the fisheries and forest, just as it had been in Delegate Wickersham's day. Salmon was still a cash cow.

During the war years and afterward, Alaska Natives continued to face inequities over their land base, sovereignty, and citizenship. The patterns of paternalism not only persisted but dug in deeper. When Alaska Natives attempted to start their own businesses and become part of the capitalist mainstream, they were discouraged or prohibited outright from doing so. Like the Aleut evacuees and the Japanese internees, the Alaska Natives were told that federal authorities knew what was best and they should not protest. Big government controlled the economy and politics, and influenced social life and culture, as the nation reordered life after the war and welcomed in the 1950s decade with hopes of peace and prosperity.

12

The Hanna Hearings and Hydaburg

Pacific Fisherman, a journal appealing to commercial interests with a decided political bent, seldom disguised its opinion concerning "Indian fishermen" and unions. In a 1944 issue one writer claimed Alaska Natives had never proven their rights were denied or that their fishermen were qualified for any special treatment from the federal government. That is: aboriginal rights were unwarranted and any protest was groundless. In fact, the opposition claimed Native fishermen and their unions were a communist threat, and any indigenous disputes regarding commercial fishery interests could never be decided by "a policy which would set up Indian collectivist cells under the paternalistic supervision of the Office of Indian Affairs and give them assets by destroying the rights, livelihood and property of white men."[1]

These denunciations were coupled with the hyperbole started earlier through war propaganda and its aim to rouse support for ferreting out enemies. The anti-communist charges played right into these prevailing attitudes, including the argument that "Indians" needed to assimilate fully into the dominant society, and not ask for a return of any lands and waterways, but the liberal New Dealers fought on for the stipulations within the IRA, modified in Alaska to cover village residents, which offered a degree of sovereignty with the ability to form a council and write a constitution under the tutelage of the Department of the Interior. And of course there was the revolving fund enticement—a method for starting up a business or bolstering an existing one. The most controversial clause in the IRA-ARA concerned the matter of potential land and fishing grounds to be set aside for the exclusive use of Natives or a reservation. Although there was continued discord concerning the value of a reservation, Secretary Ickes had been able to convince four Southeast Alaska villages that this was the only way to secure a land base before everything was overtaken by industrial development.

The secretary's argument was challenged in what were later dubbed the "1944 hearings." Under the auspices of the Department of the Interior, the question of aboriginal ownership was brought to the forefront, and although many were afraid this would allow the government to shuffle them away to a remote area, Ickes was able to convince enough elders to testify in favor of the proposal with the hope of securing Native reserves, similar to Metlakatla. Going forward, Richard Hanna, a former chief justice of the New Mexico Supreme Court, conducted the hearings, and the attorneys for the Department of the Interior included George Folta, counsel at large for the Department of the Interior in Alaska, and Theodore M. Haas, chief counsel of the Office of Indian Affairs in the BIA. In opposition, the salmon industry was represented by thirty-three attorneys headed by Winton Arnold, and as Fred Paul, who was in attendance, sized up the lopsided teams, he characterized the proceedings: "When during the summer of 1944, Richard H. Hanna, special examiner for the Department of the Interior . . . arrived to hold hearings in Hydaburg, Klawock, and Kake, and Ketchikan . . . the editorial heat in Alaskan papers began to sizzle. At stake were more than two million acres of land and the exclusive right to fish within three thousand feet of the shore."[2]

The fishing grounds in question were located in prime territory, sending up a red flag—the cannery owners did not want a good thing spoiled. That was not the only point of divisiveness. Two influential Tlingit men, who were highly respected by the Native community, opposed any type of reservation. Frank Peratrovich of Klawock and Frank G. Johnson from Sitka agreed that Secretary Ickes had shown courage "in trying to protect us from the trespasses of white people over our aboriginal lands," but it was time for the Natives themselves to stand up for their traditional villages and fishing sites.[3] The evidence and documentation of traditional fisheries was extensive and outlined exactly when the commercial companies came in with fish traps and threatened the Native way of life. Ultimately, these hearings produced fifteen volumes of materials, including first-hand testimony, such as the words from George Edward Haldane, a Haida fishermen from Hydaburg, who explained how the White Act and other regulations had forced people off their traditional fishing grounds at considerable expense.[4] While they were closed out of the fisheries, it was also more and more apparent that the salmon runs were insufficient to sustain the demands of industrial exploitation. Ickes spoke about how a Native reservation might act as a conservation method, and there were some who believed this concept, but not enough to rally around such a far-reaching socioeconomic change in their lives.

Attorney W. C. Arnold aggressively opposed any reference to Native ownership of valuable resources and had gone head to head with Native leaders for years, particularly by defending industrial fish traps. In the mid-1940s the cannery companies operated seventy-five traps in the waters surrounding Hydaburg, Kake, and Klawock, the sites in question, and this was big money. As lead counsel for the owners, Arnold called for the hearings to be stopped immediately because the Natives' claim to the fisheries or land had "no basis in history or in law" and these actions were "unfair to the white people of Alaska and the whole United States."[5] In a September 1944 issue of *Alaska Fishing News*, Arnold denounced the proceedings: "If the Indians claims were recognized, it would result in the confiscation of a major portion of the salmon industry in southeastern Alaska. The result would be to abrogate the long recognized American principle of the common right of fisheries; extinguish the trust in tidelands and submerged lands specifically created by Congress for the benefit of the future state, and deprive the Territory of Alaska of a large part of its tax revenues."[6]

When his argument failed to gain traction, Arnold attempted to show that the Tlingit and Haida could not possibly lay claim to these vast fishing grounds because they had abandoned their rights. To substantiate his argument he had the former paymaster at the Klawock cannery testify that no "Indian" had ever protested against encroachment on the fishing grounds and never asked for compensation.[7] George Folta, as attorney for the Department of the Interior, arrived at another conclusion. In his final report, he listed several previous protest incidents to substantiate claims that Southeast Alaska Natives had attempted to stop intrusions into their traditional territories notwithstanding pressures to keep silent. A Klawock fishermen explained that some people were afraid to fight back because of potential reprisals against them, their families, or their equipment. How could they make a living? One fishermen put it succinctly: "After 1912, why then the white fishermen came, and then at that time we don't protest, because if we make a kick they always tell us this belongs to the Government, Uncle Sam, and we were ordered to shut up. Keep out of the way. You get in trouble. And they threatened us with marshals."[8]

Perhaps Judge Hanna's conclusions could have been foreseen, but in hindsight it appeared to be illogical. Prior to the end of the testimony, Hanna had confided to a friend that originally he had sided with the Natives, but later reversed his opinion when he saw nothing that indicated the Natives had been harmed by the entrance of the commercial fishing industry and that they were actually employed by the canneries.[9] Despite numerous compelling arguments, Judge Hanna's report began with the assumption that aboriginal rights existed, but it did not matter since the Natives had shown themselves to be assimilated and adapted to the life of their neighbors. Because it was believed the Tlingit and Haida had never formally protested the construction or operation of the canneries, their argument was without merit. Furthermore, it was suggested that the villagers in Hydaburg, Kake, and Klawock had "abandoned their aboriginal fishing rights by acquiescing in the use of tidal waters by commercial fishermen."[10]

What were they to do outside of armed insurrection? Historian Donald Craig Mitchell has summarized this predicament: "For the cannery companies, Richard Hanna's easy acceptance of the legal principle that to protect their aboriginal titles the Indians at Hydaburg, Kake, and Klawock should have resorted to violence to prevent whites from fishing at traditional locations and the U.S. government from patenting or otherwise disposing of or controlling land that they previously had exclusively used and occupied seemingly was a slam dunk win."[11]

A victory for commercial interests, yes indeed, and once again the veracity of a claim was predicated on "white rights" and the bureaucracy's assumed superior knowledge of how best to monitor Alaska's resources. The non-Native majority controlled the fisheries, the economic heart of Alaska, and were convinced the salmon canning industry would be ruined by turning over control "to less than one thousand natives an industry developed by white people in good faith over a period of sixty-five years." In sardonic terms: "Indian claims were founded on greed" while the "whites" were hard-working and fair-minded.[12]

At the conclusion of the 1944 hearings, the AFU, the old fishermen's union begun by European immigrants in San Francisco, applauded Arnold's efforts to confirm their claims. He had saved Alaska from "race prejudice that would have closed America to Americans." Labor, capital, fishermen and canners "were united in opposition to Indian aboriginal claims" on Alaska waters.[13] These same waters, stewarded by clans from a time immemorial, were firmly clenched in the steely grip of the federal government and corporations. But it was not over yet. Against a daunting field, Hydaburg's IRA Council decided to take up the reserve status based on the belief that they could achieve the autonomy they had sought for so many decades. Their story highlights the second-class status under which the American Natives lived, stemming from 1800s Supreme Court rulings that deemed "Indian Nations" were dependent upon the federal government and placed them perpetually under the thumb of bureaucracy. For these reasons, it is of interest to trace Hydaburg's relatively young history to understand what led up to the mid-1940s debate and the idea of reserve status as a solution to the social and economic woes of the Haida.

In the 1700s the Haida had moved from what were formerly called the Queen Charlotte Islands (now called Haida Gwaii) to the lower part of Prince of Wales Island.[14] By 1910 the villages of Klinkwan and Howkan were established along with the smaller villages of Kaigani, Koianglas, and

Sukkwan on the northern tip of Sukkwan Island. After the 1867 Alaska purchase, Euro-Americans established salmon salteries in both Klakas Inlet and Hunter Bay, and by the 1880s Klinkwan and Howkan had Western-style stores and freight and mail delivery every month. Initially the Northwest Trading Company, with a long history in Alaska, built a post in the center of these villages, but later it moved to nearby American Bay to take advantage of the deep water and protected anchorage. As more and more settlers arrived, the Haida felt the intrusion, motivating the group to seek a more isolated area, but there were major problems. Many of the families were connected to the canneries and relied on that work to provide a paycheck. In fact, the desire to participate in the cash or wage economy was high enough that entire families relocated to canneries on a seasonal basis and lived in temporary housing. The largest number of Haida worked at the Hunter Bay cannery (Northwestern Fisheries Company) or at the mild-cure salting station at Howkan, while other families traveled farther north to Klawock and Shakan on Prince of Wales Island to work or fish for those canneries. Generally this transitory labor migration began in January and the smaller villages were emptied by April until people returned in October. With the introduction of Western goods—soon to be necessities—the villagers depended on earnings to make ends meet and have enough supplies to last through the winter.

Subsistence fishing remained integral but was hampered by the packing companies' fish traps, located in strategic positions and blocking the salmon from returning to the customary streams. Families were forced either to adopt a nomadic lifestyle or live far away from their home village. Eventually the missionaries and Native education officials intervened and imposed a school schedule on the children, while the Indian Service formed a village consolidation plan and "requested" that all Haida move to the site that is modern Hydaburg.[15] The U.S. Forest Service completed the official town site survey in October 1912, and the community was fully established on Sukkwan Strait across from the Old Sukkwan village site.[16]

The paternalistic control over the Haida continued through government agencies, although somewhat disguised.[17] C. W. Hawkesworth, an agent for the Indian Service, stated that he was an advocate of Native sovereignty and assisted the residents in constructing articles of incorporation and selecting officers, which on the surface appeared to be a partial move toward self-governance. They were hopeful this would give them a solid footing to take out loans or generate revenue to build a cannery. To build a financial base, one of the first business transactions was selling lumber to nearby canneries. Backed by the local government, thirty-eight residents subscribed to 81.5 shares of stock at ten dollars per share, and the Hydaburg village store contributed another $1,800 to build the Hydaburg Lumber Company. From that point on, the Haida were fully enveloped in a capitalistic enterprise, but they still needed to comply with government rulings in a complex relationship.

In December 1912, after a year of operation, a stakeholders' meeting was held, culminating in each member receiving a dividend from the profits, indicating the Haida were entering the Western economy full throttle, and perhaps in charge of their destiny, although complications continued to exist. When large companies encroached on their lands and waters, Hydaburg residents petitioned the federal government for Indian reservation status, and the Bureau of Education recommended to President William Howard Taft that twelve square miles around Hydaburg be set aside for the exclusive use of the Haida.[18] The subsequent presidential executive order created the Hydaburg Indian Reservation. Although this seemed like a solution to the problem, the reservation did not provide the hoped-for independence since the legal trust connection between the Haida and the federal government intensified the ward status, leaving them unable to make their own decisions in business matters.[19] A little over a decade passed before the Haida fully realized they were losing their ancestral lands at the expense of becoming "reservation Indians."[20] Before forfeiting all civil rights, the Hydaburg residents sought a release from governmental control.

Missionary William Lopp, who first founded the Wales mission and reindeer station on the Seward Peninsula, was now with the Bureau of Education, and his responsibilities extended across the entire Alaskan territory. When the Haida voiced their concern about how the reservation was restricting their lives, he reassured them: "Hydaburg is in no sense an Indian reservation as we know them in the States, neither are your people reservation Indians."[21] These words did not allay their fears, and the Haida appealed to have the reservation status revoked, resulting in the rescinding of the Executive Order by President Calvin Coolidge in 1926.[22] Hydaburg residents had agreed that being released from government control would be beneficial, but it left their enterprises, particularly the potential cannery, vulnerable to ruthless actions by big companies. The Hydaburg Council sent a plea to territorial delegate Dan Sutherland, complaining about the presence of an "unreasonable number of depredatory fish traps set by merciless and self-interested concerns consequently forcing on the helpless natives an inevitable winter of hardships."[23] The Alaska Natives might have been at a disadvantage, but they were far from weak, and vehemently protested fish traps that were stifling their way of life, yet little changed until the 1930s.

When President Franklin Roosevelt's "Indian New Deal" allowed the secretary of the interior to set aside certain lands for Native Americans, including established Alaska Native villages, the Haida had used the stipulations to create the Hydaburg Cooperative Association, Alaska's first IRA Council.[24] Their first order of business was to borrow money from the IRA revolving fund to construct a salmon cannery and the infrastructure necessary to support the operation, but this was where Native self-determination was halted. The Haida were deemed unfit to run their own cannery and were ordered by the BIA to pay a "white" manager to operate the cannery, because it was believed the villagers did not have the necessary expertise. Simultaneously, a decline in the salmon runs made it difficult for the cooperative to repay the government loan, adding to both the fishing pressure and community tensions.[25] Questions started to be asked by both the Haida and the federal government about the true meaning of sovereignty within an ARA reserve, and the answer was revealed at the conclusion of the "Hanna Hearings."

In 1944 Judge Richard Hanna opened hearings in Hydaburg's federal school house and there were several days of testimony, both supporting and challenging the Haida position. The most vocal contender was W.

C. Arnold, representing the salmon packing industry and trap operators through Alaska Salmon Industry, Inc. He maintained that recognition of Haida and Tlingit land claims would devastate the salmon packing business and profits would suffer if the Natives were allowed to reserve the lands and waters. Further, he was adamant that only Congress could determine possessory rights on public domain. Predicting a financial doomsday, Arnold declared that a reservation system had the potential to halt Alaska's "rightful" development, jeopardizing the million-dollar investment in the canneries and leading to widespread unemployment.[26] He was backed by significant allies, including the spokesman for the powerful International Fishermen and Allied Workers of America (IFAWA), who feared the loss of jobs and opportunities for their workers. The Juneau and Ketchikan Chambers of Commerce declared this would be the end of the free enterprise system and falsely threatened that the "Indians" would lose their citizenship.

Alaska's pro-developers, like Governor Ernest Gruening, were up in arms and convinced Ickes had violated the spirit of the Alaska Reorganization Act and that the real purpose of the original legislation was merely to allow townsite reservations.[27] Gruening was viewed as a social liberal, but he was gung-ho on Alaska's industrial development. In 1939 he had been appointed by President Roosevelt, who no doubt felt confident he would uphold New Deal policies, including the provisions within the IRA-ARA and potential reservations. In contrast, Gruening's view was that "Indian reservations" were the wrong strategy and "savored strongly of Hitlerism."[28] He warned Ickes that if he went ahead with the reservation idea, it would mar "racial harmony" and would set the Natives back "a full generation."[29] Ickes not only had to fend off opposition such as this, but among the Tlingit and Haida concern lingered based on stories they had heard about reservations in the states.[30] At times Ickes looked as if he was standing alone in this controversy, but he did not waver from his conviction that the Native population was entitled to receive land on which they had lived for generations as well as adjacent areas necessary for economic security.

In terms of fishing grounds and traps, the original Hydaburg request sought protection against intrusion extending out three thousand feet from the shoreline, but Judge Hanna concluded that Hydaburg had not proven they had exerted full use of tidal ocean waters to that extent, except for some small areas near salmon streams.[31] Adding insult to injury, Hanna further assumed the Haida had never fully protested the cannery intrusions into their traditional waters and therefore had forsaken any rights. Historic circumstances were cited as proof of abandonment in those isolated cases where the Haida had leased out segments of their customary fishing grounds to outsiders, although this was common practice throughout the region. As if this was not enough of an attack on social justice, Hanna concluded that since the Haida had been decimated by disease they really did not need these resources any longer. In summary, Hanna construed, "the Haidas and Tlingit had, for the most part abandoned their aboriginal rights to streams flowing into tidal waters, inland lakes, forests, and uplands used for hunting and trapping."[32]

The gravity of Hanna's declaration on aboriginal title could not be taken lightly since it meant that outsiders could now legally put up anything they wanted, including fish traps, on traditional Haida lands and waters. In a rather offhand manner, it was declared that if there was credible reason to suspect the Haida had been separated from their land or rights, then Congress could investigate the matter at a later date and authorize a cash settlement, if appropriate, but for now the cannery fish trap stayed![33] Secretary Ickes was frustrated but would not give up the cause.

In 1945 Ickes consulted with the associate solicitor Felix Cohen.[34] Together they wrote up a proposal whereby the Haida might reserve up to 101,000 acres for Hydaburg, a land base much smaller than they initially asked for, though perhaps feasible for sustaining a living; but the Hydaburg residents were unsatisfied with this judgment. In September 1945 Hydaburg representatives formally requested a rehearing in front of the Interior Department, and in January 1946, after a delay, Ickes agreed there was reason to believe the Haida had not received an equitable deal after all, and in his authority awarded the Haida, Kake, and Klawock villages 800 additional acres. The basis for Ickes's dissent was his belief that the Natives had proven exclusive land occupation, and he could not in good conscience wait for the bureaucrats to set the record straight, prompting him to take matters into his own hands. Ickes further defied previous rulings by deciding that the original three villages, Kake, Hydaburg and Klawock, were Native property from the nearby beaches down to the low tide mark, and that meant any fish trap currently anchored on "Indian land" could not be operated without the consent of the Natives. This development appeared to strengthen Native leverage in these affairs, but could it endure? Ickes firmly believed that Native property rights had suffered "an invasion" that must be rectified, but the court was going to scrutinize his actions carefully. The next step was the judicial system.

When the Hydaburg Cooperative Association was formed, it needed to make a profit or go under, and there was stiff competition from the big companies. In the late 1930s the Haida had relied on an early decision that guaranteed an extension of Haida aboriginal fishing rights out to three thousand feet, giving Hydaburg a temporary advantage. In addition, P. E. Harris and his cannery company "agreed to install a trap south of the village and deliver the entire production" to the Hydaburg cannery.[35] This agreement was advantageous until the contract expired at the end of the 1947 season and Libby, McNeill & Libby refused to extend their consideration. The Haida had to make a deal. In the end the Nakat Packing agreed to deliver fish to the Haida cannery for the next five seasons if allowed to install traps near the village.

All was well and good until Hydaburg decided to accept the terms under the IRA reserve status, and Nakat Packing and Libby, McNeill & Libby were informed they would now be charged rental fees for their traps because they were in reservation waters. Nakat Packing responded by presenting the agreement that had been made with Hydaburg to continue their traps, free of any charges, until 1952. Bill Paul Jr., who had stayed current with Hydaburg matters despite attempts to push him out of the way, figured if Nakat got its way, regardless of the original contract, Hydaburg fishermen "will be effectually deprived of the use of three traps . . . amounting to a loss . . . of approximately $3,000,000."[36] Sides were drawn between the Hydaburg fisherman and cannery management, and the government was the ultimate referee.

The contract in question was highly irregular, and it did not take long for the local newspapers to get wind of this controversy. In March 1950 "Restriction Stops Indian Reservations" headlined the front page of Juneau's *Daily Alaska Empire*.[37] The article outlined that Alaska Natives wanted to be treated as Americans and not second class citizens, yet would not necessarily give up the advantages of their reservation system. Regardless of these arguments, the Tlingit and Haida were sitting on a money-making business and because of favorable legislation were in a position to call the shots. This shift in Native political standing not only affected Southeast Alaska but also had ramifications for Washington State.

Washington's congressional representative Henry "Scoop" Jackson, a self-described "Cold War Liberal," was well aware of the economic lifeline Alaska had traditionally provided for his state and did not want any changes to the status quo. As a witness to the 1944 Hearings, he had already formed an opinion of the legitimacy of Tlingit and Haida assertions: if the Southeast Alaska Natives were found to hold aboriginal title "to waters in which fish traps annually were earning Jackson's constituents in the state of Washington substantial incomes, Congress should invalidate the determination."[38] He further appealed that "a policy of placing Alaska Indians, Eskimos and Aleuts on reservations appears to be devoid of merit, retrogressive, unnecessary, and indefensible from the standpoint of settling native land claims," and he did not want any BIA funds going toward reservation orders. Jackson extended his argument by saying: "It is high time to stop treating the Indian as a second class citizen. Indians should be treated just as other citizens and assimilated into our population. Why talk about a civil rights program if we are not going to apply it to the first Americans?"[39]

Obviously, these issues were diverse. If there was something valuable up for sale, then the Alaska Natives did not need "special treatment" because they were just like anyone else, but if there was a pang of conscience and nothing was at stake, the villages were sheltered by the federal government and its fiduciary obligations, however that might be interpreted at that moment. Nothing altered Jackson's message as he continued to opine that: "It is just a Jim Crow program for the Indians and should be ended. I believe the Indians should be given the same status as other Americans and where necessary the government should make loans and grants to help them reach their proper place in our civilization."[40]

All the while, the Hydaburg cannery was in jeopardy and without legal representation. For a while this presented a problem, because it was obvious that a judicial decision was necessary. They could not rely on the ANB because its resources and energy had been directed toward the Archipelago-wide land claims suit. At that moment, however, a new actor arrived on the scene in the person of attorney James Curry, an Irish socialist and one of the legal assistants for the National Congress of American Indians (NCAI), which had been founded in November 1944 to represent Native Americans in their quest for civil liberties. He had been alerted to the controversy, motivating him to fly from Washington DC to Hydaburg to meet with the town council and the IRA Council. From this meeting, it was determined that the Haida would demand the BIA seek an injunction so that the Nakat Packing and Libby, McNeill & Libby traps would have to be removed for non-payment of the rental fees. This was a volatile step, and Curry knew he needed the help of the big guns. He asked the influential John Collier, former commissioner of Indian Affairs, to act on the situation any way he saw fit. Collier's decision was to publish a letter in the *New York Times*, declaring the Hydaburg situation was nothing short of a scandal and the matter deserved the attention of citizens, who might carry their protests to the Interior Department.[41] Upon hearing of these troubles, the Interior Department asked the Department of Justice to file a lawsuit with the Alaska District Court on behalf of the United States, the legal owner of the Hydaburg reservation, requiring the Libby, McNeill & Libby company to remove their trap.

In *United States v. Libby, McNeil, and Libby*, the Hydaburg plaintiffs sought to enjoin the cannery company from operating the salmon trap on a site within the boundaries of the Hydaburg Indian Reservation and to collect damages from previous activity. The defendants countered by citing the fact that the trap had operated at this site since 1927 under a War

Department license, a special permit of the U.S. Forest Service. According to the law, therefore, they were compliant with statutory requirements. The attorney for the defense, Winton "Bill" Arnold, took the point further, claiming there was no evidence the reservation was valid.[42]

Up to this point Alaska Native legal cases had been rare, and precedents were virtually nonexistent, except for the Alaska Organic Acts, one of the few pieces of previous legislation that referred to Alaska Natives' rights. The 1884 Organic Act guaranteed that Alaska Natives would not be disturbed in those lands and waters under their occupation, use, or otherwise claimed, but the definition of what constituted these areas was vigorously debated, particularly considering the wide chasm between Western land title in fee simple and the Native view of lands and waters as clan-owned and protected for a subsistence livelihood, covering miles and miles.

In the 1940s the Organic Act had been used as evidence for aboriginal title and occupation in two Tlingit legal cases concerning the military usurpation of traditional subsistence waters near Juneau, but the court had found no proof there had been continuous use dating back to 1884, which was required to prove ownership under the legislation. Judge George Folta had presided in both cases as well as the 1944 hearings, and he was consistent in his decisions.[43] Representing the Hydaburg residents in these two cases had been Bill and Fred Paul, sons of William Paul Sr., and Judge Folta may have held a prejudicial view since he had been largely responsible for the elder Paul's disbarment back in 1939. Regardless of the hint of bias, the former proceedings were fresh in the mind of the judge. When Fred Paul, who was watching the Hydaburg trial, saw Judge Folta take the bench, he was convinced the proceedings would not go in favor of the Haida, but he could not have imagined the final turn of events.[44]

In the Hydaburg fish trap legal case, the burden of proof was on the Hydaburg residents to show uninterrupted settlement under the provisions of the Organic Act. Arnold hammered the idea that the Haida could not claim use of these waters since the only yardstick, the stipulations and language within the 1884 Organic Act, was inconclusive due to the "lapse of time, communal tenure, lack of continuity of use or possession, abandonment, and the profound changes in the mode of life of the Haida after the turn of the century."[45] To prove the Haida never occupied the land and waters in question, Arnold entered into evidence an old 1900 account by James Taylor, who had claimed that at Sukkwan Island, the old Haida village and where the trap in question was located, there had been only one white man and his Tlingit wife "living on the entire island which is the size of Manhattan Island."[46] At this late date, Sukkwan remained an important Haida historical site, but for Arnold it had always been a strategic trap location. In fact, Arnold had previously warned cannery owners to watch Sukkwan and to keep the Haida away from the area.[47] Further, Arnold added that even though the Haida had formerly lived at Howkan and Klinkwan, he believed they had abandoned these traditional sites upon establishing Hydaburg in 1912.

Ultimately the Haida had been no match for the double barrels of Arnold's wiles and the agenda of Judge Folta, whose opinion relied on the premise that the Haida must show continual use of property to maintain ownership—merely hunting and fishing on the land did not ascertain possessory rights, and once again the debate volleyed between the Western concept of land owned in fee simple title and the Native regard for the land and waters under their stewardship.[48] When the reservation system was questioned, the judge concluded that "Congress did not intend to give the Secretary of the Interior authority to reserve vast areas of Alaska" and further that Congress would never have tied up that much land since it was "the policy of Congress to encourage settlement and development of the territory," to maintain the drive of civilization.[49]

As a result, the Haida's plea was dismissed by Judge Folta, who reasoned that there was limited proof of actual use and occupancy. Further, it was conceded that Secretary of the Interior Julius Krug, who had replaced Harold Ickes in 1946, had exceeded his authority when "he established a reservation whose boundaries encircled land and waters, that the Haidas had not actually occupied."[50] Notwithstanding discussions and testimony concerning land occupation, former legal decisions, aboriginal title, and the meaning of extant legislation, there was more that sealed the fate of the

Haida's petition. The final decision did not rely on morals, ethics, or the merits of the case but rather on Krug's failure to process the designated reserve status documents properly. In essence, the signing of the order creating the reservation, which had been rushed by Secretary Krug on the last day of his incumbency, had failed to follow the proper methods as prescribed by the Administrative Procedure Act, by not notifying the defendant of the potential formation of a reservation at Hydaburg and not allowing a platform for those who might object, namely the non-Native fishermen or cannery interests. A simple disregard for bureaucratic process ended the controversy and voided the Haida claim.[51]

In summary, regardless of the sociological grounds, it was decided that Native people could not run their own business affairs, but even more to the point: "The Secretary did not comply with the Administrative Procedure Act nor receive the prior approval of the Director of the Bureau of the Budget, the Attorney General and the Secretary of Agriculture" to proceed with his actions. The Haida lost their land, fishing grounds, and protected status on a technicality.[52] After years of being held down by the federal government's thumb, the Haida were now to be treated like any other United States citizen without aboriginal title or protection. Arnold had been adamant that "racial discrimination is virtually nonexistent" and equality was only a matter of the "emancipation of the Indian from wardship restrictions."[53] That convenient reasoning served Arnold's purposes and was in step with the political atmosphere. In Judge Folta's final statement he concluded that beginning with the Klondike gold rush, it was the duty of Congress to encourage the settlement and development of Alaska and "since World War II the importance of increased population to national defense has been stressed repeatedly in Congress, in military circles, and by administration's spokesmen. In the ensuing 54 years the Indians of Southeastern Alaska and particularly the Haidas, have abandoned their primitive ways and adopted the ways of civilized life." Now, he declared, they were "fully capable of competing with the whites in every field of endeavor. . . . It is a matter of common knowledge that today the Indians of Southeastern Alaska prefer the white man's life despite its evils and shortcomings."[54]

Although there were clear reasons to dispute Judge Folta's decision, no appeal was forthcoming, possibly because of lack of funds and the lingering disdain for any type of reservation that might segregate Alaska Natives from mainstream life and demote them to second class citizens. Instead, Alaska Natives wanted to assume their rightful place in the postwar society, and in the end, the outcome of *United States v. Libby, McNeil, and Libby* was that the reservation system was illegal. By 1954 the Department of the Interior recorded a notice in the public land records that invalidated the Hydaburg reservation land withdrawal completely.[55] The Hydaburg cannery never operated at peak capacity again, but it mattered little in the big picture. The salmon cannery era was waning based on the lack of salmon, seafood diversification, and Alaska's populist movement focused on the statehood drive. The Haida's setback, however, did not deter their quest for civil rights, a recognition of aboriginal title to the lands and waters, and achieving the benefits of full American citizenship.

While fighting to sustain their socioeconomic position, the Alaska Natives watched as industry took over their lands and fished in their waters, but they could do nothing without legal recourse. Those circumstances, however, did not dissuade Alaska Native individuals and groups from continuing the struggle against the barriers. Two legal scholars summarized the conditions: "Since Native nations were not believed to hold absolute legal title to their lands, the national government claimed the power to administer their property," and the government only acted on the benefit of Natives when "it needed to take or exploit the remainder of their lands."[56] Anthropologist Caroline Brown advised that Alaska Native political and legal status was "characterized by fragmentation and ambiguity . . . and disparities between federal and territorial priorities that would continue into Alaska's statehood era," most of this due to the "historical contingencies of the lands' economic value connected to the uneven integration of Alaska Natives into the national polity."[57]

In reality, it did not matter that the Metlakatlan Tsimshian or Haida understood the workings of cannery equipment, salmon runs, processing, and marketing; they were deemed unqualified to run their own operations based on ethnic categorization. Charles Wilkinson, another prominent expert on indigenous legal history, believes that genuine Native sovereignty was interrupted by a "century of assimilationist policies and their effect," which barred the expression of sovereignty and the practice of free enterprise without government involvement.[58] Donning the veneer of an acculturated Native never proved to be an asset, and an unsolicited legacy, dating back to missionary control, congealed the racialized precept that the original owners of the land could not be trusted to manage resources or engage in commerce, while the American legal system backed up the verdict.

13

The Cannery Period Heyday Wanes

In the early 1940s Roy and Elizabeth Peratrovich found the Juneau house they wanted to buy, but the couple were turned away because they were "Indians." This prejudicial act angered them and they were determined to right the wrong. Roy, the son of the Croatian immigrant who had built the first cannery in Klawock and brother to the influential Frank Peratrovich, had been active in Native issues all his adult life. He worked as a BIA agent with a specialty in natural resource management, giving him a bird's-eye view of the fisheries. Elizabeth was a college-educated woman and high-ranking member of the ANS. With their expertise and influence, Roy and Elizabeth acted as a team to fight against this blatant discrimination, with the assistance of Governor Ernest Gruening, a proponent of Native causes. In fact, Gruening had encouraged Frank Peratrovich to run for office in order to represent Alaska Native interests more fully. In turn, Frank, still maintaining his interest in the Southeast Alaska purse seine union, had been elected to the territorial house of representatives in 1944, and in 1946 he was elected to the territorial senate. The Peratrovich name became synonymous with the movement to wipe out bigotry in Alaska, leading to the passage of the 1945 Alaska civil rights bill, decades before its equivalent in the states. The civil rights battle demonstrated Alaska's political atmosphere in the late 1940s, which affected cannery workers and fishermen.

When the bill was first introduced the territorial legislators scarcely gave the matter a glance and of course, the bill did not pass. The Alaska Congress believed they had more pressing matters to address, such as Alaska's responsibilities as a strategic locale after the war. When Ernest Gruening and others pressed for passage of the discrimination bill, it was negatively received, as observed through the words of Senator Allen Shattuck of Juneau, who opined that Alaska Natives "had not attained the level of the white man's civilization." Upon hearing this statement, Roy Peratrovich countered: "I am wondering just what they call civilization[;] looking over the court record in Alaska, one wonders if the white man is really civilized."[1] The Peratrovich family were no strangers to adversity and did not shy away from combat. In 1945 Roy and Elizabeth again brought their proposal to the Alaska Territorial Legislature and then listened to the floor debate from the gallery. Once again Senator Shattuck raised objections: "This legislation is wrong. Rather than being brought together, the races should be kept further apart. Who are these people, barely out of savagery, who want to associate with us whites, with 5,000 years of recorded civilization behind us?"[2]

Governor Gruening was an eyewitness to the debate and described how Elizabeth Peratrovich rose in the gallery and asked to be heard. As she came to the floor, the audience was silent and filled with anticipation as she spoke: "I would not have expected that I, who am barely out of savagery, would have to remind the gentlemen with 5,000 years of recorded civilization behind them of our Bill of Rights." Her eloquence was unmistakable and received exuberant applause. The Senate passed the bill, eleven to five, and Gruening believed a "new era in Alaska's racial relations had begun" at that moment.[3] That was, of course, optimistic— engrained public sentiment was not so easily swayed.

The next afternoon newspapers reported that Elizabeth Peratrovich had attacked the "super race theory" and won.[4] Signs on businesses that had previously read: "No Natives Allowed" disappeared overnight. The symbolic importance of the 1945 Alaska Civil Rights Act was irrefutable and an essential piece of Alaska's postwar milieu. The Peratrovichs had risked censure, but through their efforts they provided an example for the rest of the nation. It was significant that this campaign had been implemented by the direct descendant of an immigrant, who had established one of Alaska's first canneries only a generation before, and his wife, the Grand President of the Alaska Native Sisterhood. The legislation was a testimonial to the power of minorities and demonstrated how women had gained a voice in the public forum. Whether it was articulate women like Elizabeth Peratrovich or Amy Hallingstad, or the quieter but equally effective Ruth Hayes, there was no turning back the momentum of these movers and shakers as they reshaped public opinion.

After the war several canneries in Southeast Alaska remained consolidated or closed, largely based on decreased employment and less demand for canned fish. Although there was a reduced need for governmental control, the lifting of labor regulations and strike bans was slow to come, and even when the canneries reopened the day-to-day operations were molded by local and international economics. Furthermore, there were renewed efforts in fishery conservation, a concept and program the packers opposed, although they outwardly displayed interest to bolster their public image. Eventually, however, wartime restrictions were lifted, and the price of canned salmon rose so rapidly that there was fear the product might be out of the reach of the average consumer. In part the price hike was due to the sudden governmental restrictions on salmon harvest, producing an artificial shortage. During the war the escalation in packing salmon was perceived as a patriotic duty, accompanied by the theme "we are feeding our boys overseas." After the war a new rallying cry was necessary to perk up business, and consequently the packers claimed they were providing protein "during a period of acute world food shortage."[5] This manufactured benevolence served as a sales ploy and defensive strategy against an increasingly stringent conservation force, which also played havoc with a misshapen supply and demand relationship.

    While commerce attempted to regain its former autonomous potency, the Fish and Wildlife Service looked closely at Alaska's resources and planned regulations that would ultimately affect output. Packers gave the impression that they supported conservation efforts but were aware of potential hardships to the industry, and indeed some of these new policies led to "miserable failures." Faced with profit reduction, cannery companies blamed government agencies for ill-conceived conservation measures, particularly limitations on fish traps, calling these actions the heavy hand of bureaucracy.[6] Simultaneously, the fishermen were accused of harvesting every salmon out of Alaska waters, prompting the United States Senate to become involved, and in 1944 an Alaska fisheries bill was proposed that would define Alaska's fishing boundaries and allowable gear types. The cannery owners, fearing the loss of fish traps, lobbied for a grandfather clause that would establish property rights for existing traps and applauded efforts within the bill to shut out foreigners, such as Japanese fleets that were accused of encroaching on the salmon stock. Alternatively, a provision was requested requiring that fishing grounds to be open to all U.S. citizens free of exclusive claims or occupancy rights, aboriginal or otherwise. Obviously, this would shut out Alaska Natives from any special privileges in the fisheries while allowing the big canneries to fish without restriction.

In the ensuing contest Delegate Anthony Dimond went up against W. C. Arnold and his colleagues with the goal of getting rid of "absentee landlordism and we have it with a vengeance in Alaska." In the final analysis, the Alaska Fisheries Act and the proposed bills that followed, which attempted to define ownership within the fishing grounds and curb overharvesting, were laced with language that would "deprive the natives of Alaska of aboriginal rights, antedating the establishment of commercial fishing in that region and on which they were largely dependent for their sustenance."[7] There was growing apprehension that these legal barriers would produce increased Native dependency on government sources to avert total poverty. But that was not the only issue.

With the unstable market and unpredictable fish runs, people were concerned about their jobs. The air of economic uncertainty spilled over into the political arena, eventually instigating a rise of activism in the Pacific Northwest. Workers from all walks of life could not wait for Congress to fix their problems, while intense labor competition drove suspicions about national allegiance, particularly in the budding years of the Cold War. The perceived enemies must be watched, and fingers were pointed directly at the "bad sort" found among union members, who were accused of being communist agents, aiming to take down America. The labor unions were an easy target since they could not hide their link to the Communist Party, but in reality, politics were merely a side issue for most workers. They wanted better wages and working conditions—everybody was trying to get by. Could the unions help them achieve those goals?

Regardless of whether it was through newspaper editorials or radio programs, the message was received that the labor unions held excessive and destructive muscle. In the Pacific Northwest, union critics and businessmen recalled what had occurred in previous decades, most notably the 1934 strike by the International Longshore and Warehouse Union (ILWU), which had resulted in several deaths on what was termed "Bloody Thursday." That strike had ground commerce to a halt and paralyzed the country, and there was fear it could happen again.[8] The combined hostile actions had evolved over attempts by big corporations to smash unions and control wages and working conditions. One of the most dramatic confrontations of this week-long strike took place in San Francisco when employers interfered with the longshoremen's walkout and placed strike breakers on the dock. In answer "militant men" stormed the area, and "two thousand men battered down pier doors, swept police aside, and halted work on eleven ships. . . . The strikers took over entire control of the waterfront. The high point of this uprising came on Bloody Thursday, when an army of San Francisco police tried to reopen the port by terrorizing the maritime strikers into submission."[9] In retrospect, these skirmishes, many of them fatal, were not unique but rather a continuation of class warfare that had "punctuated the American industrial landscape for more than a century."[10]

It is beneficial to pause for a moment in this narrative to take another look at this strike and the ILWU because of its immediate effects on the Pacific Northwest Coast and also for the future ties of the ILWU in Alaska. The ILWU, an offshoot of the International Longshoremen's Association

(ILA), was solidified after the 1934 uprising, and although it represented longshoremen and dockworkers, it expanded in the 1950s to advocate for fishermen and eventually cannery workers in Alaska. Bruce Nelson, author of *Workers on the Waterfront*, has described the conditions that led to maritime unionism as spontaneous radicalism that came together like "parched grasslands waiting for a spark to ignite them." In context, there were several socioeconomic factors, including the desperation created by the Great Depression, the optimism of the New Deal, and the growing presence of the Communist Party and its promises of equality. Nelson believed the movement drew upon those factors that "were deeply rooted in a longstanding way of life and work on the waterfront."[11] Although it was true that Southeast Alaska had not experienced parallels to "Bloody Thursday" nor been a part of the Pacific Northwest ferment, there was the same spirit of activism, and the ILWU was gaining a foothold in Southeast Alaska cannery towns.

The packing companies were aware of the power these workers had in numbers and in conviction, which catapulted corporations to plead with the federal government for legislative relief from unions and their activities. Along the Pacific Coast the longshoremen, the fishing fleets, and the Filipino-controlled cannery unions were targeted by an aggressive backlash condemning their alleged red hue of communism as the nation was absorbed in an undeclared war against foreigners and immigrants. In all of this, Alaska was in a critical geopolitical position with its proximity to the Ice Curtain.[12] There were incendiary rumors asserting that the territory housed sympathetic spies, but regardless of the furor, the salmon industry carried on.[13] Unlike in the Pacific Northwest, in Southeast Alaska the threat of labor slowdowns was almost nonexistent. and as Fred Paul recalls, even after the ban was lifted the fishermen and the cannery workers were afraid to strike and miss out on a sorely needed paycheck.[14] It would have mattered little since strikes were smashed.

The government had promised the American people that if they sacrificed during the war years, after a treaty was signed, there would be peace and prosperity for all. When this did not occur right away the culpability had to be placed on someone or something. Before the main feature at movie theatres, propaganda newsreels included animated film clips depicting unions as the culprit for the higher prices found at the supermarket.[15] Inflation was creeping up and causing hardship for the American consumer until tensions begged for a release. In 1947 President Harry Truman, a Democrat, who described himself as a political eunuch, not only had to follow President Franklin Roosevelt's legacy but was also faced with an anti-labor, conservative Congress that was set on breaking the back of unions.[16] In short order, the Labor Management Relations Act, more commonly referred to as the Taft-Hartley Act, was passed, outlawing preferential hiring for union members and strikes over jurisdictional issues. The legislation eroded the authority of the National Labor Relations Board to settle labor issues, and now boycotts or strikes were deemed illegal and a threat to the national interest.

One of the most controversial provisos in the act required elected union leaders to sign affidavits stating they were not communists before they could hold office in their own unions. There was no mistake about it—the Taft-Hartley Act was designed to bust unions, and President Truman seemed unable to do anything about it, but it did not stop him from opposing corporate America, a monolith he deemed the real culprit in this chaos.[17] Nonetheless, the Taft-Hartley Act orchestrated the funeral scene for the New Deal. Against the rising conservative pro–big business groundswell, Truman scrambled to propose his ultra-progressive Fair Deal platform to mitigate what he believed was a crusade against the working class.[18] He was supported by big labor and shunned by big business.

Immediately, labor leaders experienced the burden of the massive federal oversight created by the Taft-Hartley Act and called for a halt to its implementation, but instead the National Labor Relations Act was amended to curtail the hard-won workers' rights that had been earned through collective bargaining. What was the impetus for such a move? In the postwar environment there was a concern that America could not rebuild industry and manufacturing if the business sector was bombarded by strikes or production slowdowns. For labor, including Alaska cannery workers, the legislation was oppressive, and in some quarters this act was referred to as the slave act, a term first coined by President

Truman, due to the apparent loss of freedoms and the attack on democratic principles. The opponents attempted to show that the act could not stand up to constitutional scrutiny, but after numerous nationwide demonstrations, the majority of American citizens believed unions were part of a foreign-driven plot to bring the United States to its knees in this Cold War environment.

The strength of the Taft-Hartley Act cannot be overlooked—it changed American labor policy forever, even along Southeast Alaska's coastline. Although there were no significant strikes in Alaska, the fishermen and cannery workers were closely linked with what was happening in Seattle, particularly with so many Alaskan Filipino families, who maintained a relationship with their extended kin in the Pacific Northwest. Now the workers were unable to protest without fear of being arrested. During union agent Rose Dellamo's time, the UCAPAWA (CIO affiliation) was robust in Southeast Alaska, and a large proportion of its membership consisted of Alaska Native women. The union and its members had made real strides in equitable wages and increased safety in the workplace, but the leadership core needed to be widespread to be effective. When Dellamo left Alaska to attend to business in California, she longed to go back, but the CIO advised that there was not enough at stake up north.[19] With the organizational confusion that plagued unions in postwar society, energies could only be directed toward the hotspots along the Pacific Coast where there was a great deal of mayhem, including outright murder. The UCAPAWA had acted as a beacon in those early years, but when world events changed realities, its outreach gradually faded out of existence in Alaska, with many workers joining the International Longshore and Warehouse Union.

While the UCAPAWA was at its apex of activity, it had integrated "women into important slots and avoided paternalistic policies while striving to develop local leadership . . . women who were not afraid to go out and organize their local, women who [found] time to take on duties as officers, shop stewards, and as untitled rank and filers to help carry on Union work." One of its pillars, and this was certainly true in Southeast Alaska, was assembled from kin and friend networks, and across ethnic lines "unionization gave an activist edge to the cannery culture as people joined together to improve their working conditions." In explaining the strength and scope of the UCAPAWA, Vicki Ruiz found that Native women "at Alaska salmon firms, substantially contributed to union success," even though they split their time between the workplace and family and community interests.[20]

In Alaska the fisheries remained significant in the overall political economy, but more fishermen were independent and not necessarily tied to a specific cannery. In this way they were free to sell to the highest bidder and did not necessarily need representation. For Native fishermen and workers, the AMWU had lost its former vigor and Peratrovich's union also declined.[21] Inevitably, the UCAPAWA was eclipsed by the more prominent Pacific Northwest Filipino-run unions, and the Alaska Native women were forgotten in the recasting of social organizations. Meanwhile in Seattle, Local 7 (still affiliated with Alaska cannery workers) was accused of communistic tendencies and was under surveillance by governmental agencies scoping out their activities and even attempting to infiltrate union hall meetings.[22] Filipino workers, activists, and union organizers were singled out by the opposition with the hope that these "enemies" would be deported as criminal aliens and communist agents, and there was a general plea to the government to pass legislation to support these allegations.

The public outcry was answered by the passage of the 1952 McCarran Act, authorizing a halt to immigration of suspected subversive types, and the Filipino union organizers realized the legislature was a definite barrier to future union numbers.[23] The act was a product of the American frenzy against the "other" and was intended to stomp out all un-American influence. It was also meant to uphold a clause from 1924 immigration legislation that restricted entry into the country based on national origin. Truman vetoed the bill initially, believing it was an infringement on first amendment rights, but no objection could drown out those who believed the country could not return to normalcy until the foreigners were eliminated.

Despite the maelstrom, Southeast Alaska fishermen and cannery workers made sure the fish were caught and packed, even though they had fewer advocates to fight for their cause. W. C. Arnold was now labeled the "most powerful man in Alaska," and any changes in wages or conditions had to be negotiated through the Alaska Salmon Industry, Inc.[24] Armed with the Taft-Hartley Act, Arnold moved through the inner circles from Juneau to Seattle to Washington DC, doing what he could to undermine the unions, and in the process he sculpted Alaska politics in his favor. In his quest to solidify his monopoly, he was assisted by the organizational disunity in the unions, the confusing entry of other smaller unions, and in-fighting along the Pacific Coast, eventually filtering into Alaska.

The fierce rivalry between seafood worker unions in the Pacific North-west followed the Alaskeros to the north, while their foes characterized them as "puppets of the Communist International Local 7." These charges, regardless of veracity, spurred resident Alaskans to take matters into their own hands with the belief "the time was ripe to wrest union control from outsiders to Alaskans anxious to work in the canneries," so as not be dominated by Seattle or San Francisco conglomerates or seasonal workers.[25] In other words, they wanted an Alaska-based union for cannery workers, and Alaska residents looked for one body, one voice, that might unite their concerns. It was found in the compelling and homegrown chant: "Alaska for Alaskans," as it fell on rich soil and took root. Alaskans would no longer tolerate victimization by big business and distant government. From the beginning, the populist movement targeted fish traps, the symbol of economic colonialism, and this theme was merged with the statehood movement. Statehood, it was believed, would free people from the shackles that bound the territory and open the door to a new era in self-determination.

While all of this was taking place, the ANB and ANS remained viable bodies with a commanding presence and continued to support Native causes. At one time the Pauls had been at the helm of this leadership, but that time had passed. The rise of Frank Peratrovich through the ranks and the introduction of Sitka's Andrew Hope to territorial influence were as storied as the men. Governor Ernest Gruening was familiar with their qualifications and determined to tap into this dynamism with the hopes of creating a fairer Alaskan society. Accordingly, Gruening encouraged

Peratrovich and Hope to throw their hats into the political ring, and in 1944 both men were elected to the territorial legislature, ultimately following a trail first blazed by William Paul Sr. Now it was time for these men to extend that legacy. Frank Peratrovich had gained a good deal of experience as the president of the Alaska purse seine union and Andrew Hope's background included his many years as a Sitka fishermen and boat builder. Together, they understood how to stand up against unfair government regulations, which influenced wage growth and the Alaskan economy.

Defiantly, Alaska residents ramped up their campaign for the abolition of fish traps, using their own office holders, such as Frank Peratrovich and Andrew Hope, to boost the cause. These Alaskans fervently sought the opportunity to name their own destiny, and although the Alaska Native population was divided on the potential benefits of statehood, they agreed with the abolition of the fish trap, first condemned in print by William Paul Sr. Although disbarred, Paul had never stopped advocating for Native rights and declared that "after many years of effort to abolish all special privileges and reservations enjoyed by a few special interests, the Indians finally concluded that the federal government is governed by those enjoying special privileges and that every fish trap is a reservation."[26] Paul continued by pointing out that because of corporate fish traps, Alaska's circumstances were dire: "Klukwan, Haines, Juneau, Wrangell and Kasaan no longer catch salmon" near their villages, but must instead travel "over 100 miles away," consuming precious fuel on the way. The cannery companies and their technology had impoverished the fishermen and destroyed their property worth "millions of dollars at Chilkat, Tee Harbor, Taku Harbor, Icy Straits, Wrangell, Santa Ana, Yes Bay, Loring and many other places."[27] Native-owned enterprises were especially in jeopardy and there appeared to be no remedy in sight for the continual crippling of village economies. Conditions, however, were about to become worse for Alaska Natives, particularly those who had worked to build their own canneries or fishing fleet.

The Taft-Hartley Act was unpopular and ineffective. In retrospect, there was little evidence the legislation accomplished what it proposed to do besides oppress labor activities, and by the late forties union leaders campaigned for Truman based upon his promise to repeal the Taft-Hartley Act, but they were a minority and their ideas were contrary to the attitude of the general public. Union membership had been declining, and in the early 1950s only about one-third of the total United States labor force remained unionized. To gain employment, often a potential employee had to produce a sworn affidavit stating that he or she was not affiliated with a union.[28] In Alaska, however, there were even more problems within the fishing industry that transcended national politics.

Salmon was a waning resource, a situation brought on by years of overfishing and lack of effective regulation. Often discussions were overwhelmed by biology politics, or using the most favorable studies to back up one's position on salmon health, regardless of facts, while the men who made the rules denied that a crisis existed. According to economist Richard Cooley, "the absentee canners had extraordinary leverage in Congress," and since Washington DC had no idea of the Alaska conditions, the company spokesman's word was accepted as the genuine state of affairs. The packers served as lobbyists, and "political and economic strength was centered in the hands of a few absentee corporate presidents and managers . . . who were interested primarily, if not exclusively, in maintaining profits and dividends from their investment in the remote northern region of Alaska."[29] Alaska Native leaders spoke out about these problems, but no one in power seemed to listen, while subsistence fishermen were unable to harvest enough fish for their family needs, and all this was followed by the federal government's resolve to break its fiduciary tie with Native Americans, largely based on fiscal concerns.

Back in 1946 President Truman had signed the Indian Claims Commission bill, which created a claims court for American Native legal and land cases that had not been previously heard, but what the president might not have anticipated was the backlash that would occur when the tribes were awarded money from the Treasury Department. After establishing the Indian Claims Commission court, Truman had hoped the "lingering discrimination against First Americans" would be alleviated, and he predicted a new era for Indian citizens. He had been motivated in this action by the contributions made by Native World War II veterans, and he urged their full inclusion into mainstream American society. Beyond that, like so many politicians before and after him, he anticipated that by recognizing and settling indigenous land and resource questions, his administration could encourage a shift in stance from tribal allegiance to that of full participant in "America's postwar capitalist market economy."[30]

During his presidency Truman had fought for workingman's equality, American Native rights, and even Alaska's bid for statehood, but he faced a conservative barricade, strengthened by an American public suffering with the vulnerabilities of a nation recovering from World War II, a volatile economy, and the weight of inflation reducing the value of their pay checks.[31] Little was resolved until the next president assumed responsibility for the socioeconomic woes, and his design reshaped every aspect of American society, including Native communities. In response to the complaint that Natives were recovering too much money from the Indian Claims Commission, President Dwight D. Eisenhower called for a halt to this perceived leniency and appointed Glenn Emmons, a banker, as commissioner of Indian Affairs. Emmons was a staunch supporter of the idea that the federal government should sever all ties with Native Americans, and it did not take long for the Eighty-third Congress to adopt House Concurrent Resolution 108, which halted the former special treatment of "Indians" based on treaties; instead Native Americans and Alaska Natives were subject to the same laws and privileges as other citizens. In effect, this strategy was to go further than previous attempts to break up tribal communities with the hope that the "Indian problem" would dissolve. To add to the confusion, the government did not offer a transition plan for what was called the "termination policy."

In addition, the Indian Reorganization Act, which provided financial incentives and support for economic endeavors, was attacked because it was viewed as making it the government's responsibility to oversee the welfare of tribes and uphold land trust status, potentially tying up valuable land that could be used to make money.[32] To reduce government involvement in Indian affairs, Congress halted Indian Claims Commission payments until a tribe agreed to termination proceedings with the ultimate goal of saving federal funds.[33] Ultimately, American Native rights and their sovereignty, first established under President Franklin Roosevelt's New Deal policies, were eclipsed by a nation grappling with an unsteady economy and an avarice for indigenous resources.

For Alaska, the legislation obviously could not terminate reservations that did not exist, but the policy acted to thwart the Indian New Deal and the Alaska Reorganization Act, which had been so carefully architected by William Paul Sr. and Tony Dimond. The Native-owned canneries were in jeopardy and vulnerable to the loss of federal subsidies and loans. ANS President Amy Hallingstad railed against the termination policy and the demise of the revolving fund that acted as a safety net for Native-owned fishing fleets and canneries, particularly those at Kake and Klawock, although there were certainly more sites. Only Metlakatla was safe, based on a previous executive order that could not be easily rescinded. To save these canneries and the Native purse seine fleets, ANB President Cyril Peck joined Hallingstad's crusade and wrote over six hundred letters to newspapers and legislators across the nation, protesting the end of the Alaska Reorganization Act (a modified IRA). All was for naught—the New Deal era died, and there was a return to the tribal pulverizing that Theodore Roosevelt had first sought during his administration at the turn of the century.[34]

In this transitional period with so many doubts and anxieties, Alaska Natives who owned businesses waited to see what the outcome would be, while the Tlingit and Haida lands case continued gathering testimony in the hope of salvaging their primordial land, waterways, salmon, and settlements. Regardless of what was going on in Alaska Native villages, Juneau political leaders attempted to break free from federal shackles and a colonial existence. Governor Ernest Gruening, the self-proclaimed embodiment of Alaska's resistance, pitted himself against his arch rival, W. C. Arnold, whose view was that Alaska's statehood and further taxation must be avoided, and it was no surprise when the dissension between Gruening and Arnold heated up to a white hot flame.

In a nutshell, Arnold wanted no further encumbrances placed on the absentee cannery owners or the fish traps that were harvesting thousands of salmon. Gruening, however, needed a tax base and a productive economy to enhance the territory's pursuit of statehood with its promise of sovereignty. A solid illustration of the conflict can be observed through the 1950s Territorial Federation of Labor hearings, where one dispute concerned the hiring preference between resident fishermen and cannery workers versus the seasonal men, who were transported from the Pacific Coast by cannery ships. Frank Peratrovich, serving in the Alaska Territorial Senate, and Gruening were in favor of hiring locally, but Arnold objected on the grounds it was discriminatory and un-American. When the issue was settled in Arnold's favor, Gruening declared "the canned-salmon lobby had won a tremendous victory against public sentiment."[35]

The battle was one of many involving Gruening, the territorial legislature, and Arnold. In "Message to the People of Alaska," Gruening rallied Alaskan residents to the cause of independence, stating: "In my view, it was improper and undignified for the Territory to put itself in the position of accepting as a gift a crumb which the canned salmon industry graciously offers the people of Alaska from its sumptuous banquet table."[36] Gruening understood that Arnold and the ASI stood in the way of statehood, profitable local industry, healthy Alaskan banks, and an overall prosperous outlook for Alaskans. For this vision to become a reality, Gruening was convinced outsiders must be repulsed, an attitude that played into the populist movement of "Alaska for Alaskans," where the territory's destiny could be freed from the landlords who held sway over the forests and fisheries. For decades the symbol of this freedom quest had been the fish trap, and now it was conceded that this device was a "menace to a continued successful operation of fisheries in Alaska," contributing to the "destruction of the major industry of Alaska and jeopardizing the livelihood of the many resident workers . . . [with] the continued exploitation of Alaska resources by an absentee monopoly that must have a profit far in excess of that of any other business."[37]

Governor Gruening continued to campaign for statehood, putting up Alaska's natural bounty as collateral and claiming that this wealth would be an asset to the nation. He also asked for increased taxes on industry, and when it looked as though the measure might pass, Arnold retorted: "We're not going to pay those taxes. They're outrageous, they're confiscatory, we're going to take all of them to court and we will hit you with so many injunctions you will be paralyzed."[38] Despite his protests, however, the statehood drive grew—there were parades in the streets, and in local bars glasses were raised to toast the possibility that Alaska could be on equal footing with the rest of the country. Faced with adversity, Arnold changed his strategy on the statehood question and attempted to show that all this talk was premature. In a curious fashion, he argued that Alaska could not seriously go forward with statehood until the question of Alaska Native claims had been settled. After years of declaring that Alaska Natives had no legal ownership of lands, waterways, or resources, his skeptics cried foul and scoffed at his obvious stalling tactic. Nevertheless, Arnold was unwilling to discontinue the fight since he realized that Alaska statehood would not only increase local taxes, but there would be federal taxes to deal with and possibly more regulation on his industry—nothing was going to topple his empire.

In ongoing testimony he extended his arguments against statehood, claiming it would doom Alaska to "perpetual pauperism and bureaucratic control," mainly due to the hodge-podge land selection process that would result in Alaska only receiving federal leftovers, incapable of drawing a profit. Ironically, the hearing committee took his line of reasoning seriously and incorporated a solution to this potential problem within the eventual state constitution that acted to protect not only state lands but also traditional Alaska Native resources, including the valuable fisheries.[39] In the end W. C. Arnold unwittingly became the grand architect of Alaska's optimal land selection policy.[40] To extend the irony, Senator Frank Peratrovich, as part of Alaska's Constitutional Convention, assisted in the implementation of land selection based on the most favorable areas for Alaskan growth.

Outside of newspaper coverage, the average Southeast Alaskan cannery worker probably had no idea of the arguments flying between Gruening and Arnold, nor how the conflict affected their day-to-day life, and in the meantime another major problem was getting worse. Due to the lack of effective federal oversight, the salmon stocks were barely being monitored, and the lack of fish runs was affecting the still functioning canneries. Arnold and the ASI may have noticed the resource depletion, but they had lost their leverage and could no longer make a difference. The publisher of the *Anchorage Daily Times*, the influential Bob Atwood, described the aftermath: "He (Arnold) was the only apparent opponent of statehood that was backed by an organization that raised money and spent it liberally to fight statehood. . . . We were bitter enemies. . . . At the time statehood (1958) was achieved, the salmon industry collapsed and disappeared, he came to Anchorage and practiced law here, and became a local citizen."[41] After statehood the fishing industry changed drastically, as did cannery life, but before this time there had already been great alterations in ethnic relations and gender attitudes, chiefly brought on by the war's aftermath.

Civil right issues were brought to a head when the soldiers returned from the war. Many Alaska Natives and Asians believed they were entitled to solid jobs, and those expectations were not always met. Although Asian men had fought on the battlefield in a highly decorated battalion, the prejudice against the "enemy" was slow to relent, and even the Filipino families, who were considered a bit more American than others, faced discrimination in housing and employment. Under strained circumstances, the Japanese had to re-enter society after the banishment to relocation camps and were unsure of their position in this transformed world. The American conscience had rationalized imprisoning Japanese families, many of them citizens, for security reasons. Although these men had fought overseas for democracy and the American way, there was no stopping the national hysteria that had mushroomed through unfounded xenophobia and the fear of communism. The 1950s were characterized by these attitudes, forming an invisible wall that blocked the upward path for ethnic minorities. Simultaneously, Alaska Natives were anticipating the outcome of the Tlingit and Haida land claims issue and what it would mean for their status. Additionally, by this time, Native Americans had joined together in common cause to form a pan-Indian movement.

Beyond racial attitudes, however, there had been another change brought on by World War II. Since many women had fulfilled the necessary roles that had been left abandoned as men went to war, they knew the jobs, and had kept up with new technology, and employees understood their capabilities. The women would no longer go back to fulfilling a subservient role. This defiant stance caused tension when "the boys came back from war" and employees were under public pressure to fire women and give their jobs to men. The women were not passive and "collective action in the interests of gender equity took place . . . to protest wholesale dismissal," while decisions were challenged if they were made solely on the basis of gender.[42] A trend had taken hold, and "women sought to defend their wartime gains through strategies designed to bring together the interests of women and men through working-class unity," even calling each other sister.[43] This style of address meshed well with members of the ANS, who were already not only using the terminology but embodying the spirit behind its meaning. And of course the term had been used for years in the unions regardless of perceived communistic overtones. The cannery setting, however, was not based on one gender—men and women continued to work together, and the cannery worker on the line was as important as the fishermen filling his scow with fresh salmon.

When canneries had closed or consolidated, women moved to other packing houses, often far from home, but were happy to return to their old jobs after the war, when many canneries reopened. They brought with them years of experience, which was appealing to the management. With the demise of the salmon runs, however, the canneries diversified into processing other types of seafood, and in the 1950s it was not uncommon for women to be employed in the Petersburg shrimp factory or crab canneries in Hoonah, for instance.[44] The venue might have changed, but not the cannery culture, and camaraderie was strengthened because of shared experiences.[45] As far as union activities went, the larger organizations appeared to have splintered, and small unions or associations were established by the local cannery companies themselves to fill the void. For example, a woman who worked in a Hoonah crab plant in the 1950s had a union card that only said Juneau Union. She didn't recall exactly what the union did, but she remembered paying dues.[46]

Beyond the importance of a paycheck, women had grown more confident in their political prowess—whether this emanated from union hall meetings, ANS conventions, or the Filipino social clubs—and these modifications enabled community members to cope in a multifaceted socioeconomic environment. Cooperative strategies promoted alliances between ethnic groups, particularly the social and political relationships that transpired between Filipinos and Native women. Native women had "joined unions to fight discrimination, earn better wages, and to maintain a position within their communities. The union became an equal rights organization." The women joined the ANS and unions in a type of dual membership, meant to push stridently for racial empowerment largely in relationship to Euro-American colonization of their homelands and to secure their place within the social order that "white policy had imposed upon them."[47] In real terms this was defiance against the complex web that held Native women in an inferior class.[48] It must be remembered, however, the Alaska Natives were not victims. They made conscious choices whether to fish or work the slime line, although they protested blatant inequities. In sum, Tlingit, Haida, and Tsimshian cannery women were not props but major actors on the labor stage, maintaining "their rights to employment and political activity."[49]

By the early 1950s Alaska salmon numbers had taken an unrecoverable hit, although the depletion had been ongoing for years. With the statehood drive, however, boosting industrial growth was paramount, coupled with a nostalgic longing to return to the once healthy fisheries. As though it were a one-act play, the *Pacific Fisherman* described the scenario as a suspense drama: "There was a race—against time, against sturdy competitors. There was a motive—money running into millions. There was love-interest—developing in uncounted herds of salmon. There was conflict—of men jockeying and wrestling for position and advantage. . . . There was a game—experts playing poker, trying to wait each other out until one should weaken—playing for gigantic stakes in profit or loss; in big shares or none; in pay-checks or rocking chair money."[50]

Beyond theatrics, by 1953 the total Alaska canned salmon pack was down to less than three million cases, the lowest in forty-two years.[51] The

Alaska fisheries were in such distress that President Eisenhower declared an industrial disaster, eligible for relief funds. Ernest Gruening, who had believed in Alaska's progress for so many years, reviewed this state of affairs, and considered it the epitome of fishery failure.

"A disaster designation customarily followed major calamities such as flood, drought, hurricane, tornado, earthquake, conflagration or pestilence, usually referred to as an act of God. In this case, it had been the failure of a federally managed resource, attributable rather to the acts of man." There was little question of the disaster's gravity or the need for help.[52]

Through a series of conservation measures, the salmon runs were gradually increased and today Alaska's fisheries remain profitable, though the fish stocks never fully recovered from the pre–fish trap days. After statehood, fisheries management by the U.S. Fish and Wildlife Service was replaced by that of the Alaska Department of Fish and Game, which struggled to prove itself in those early days. Field agents were acutely aware of the problems associated with lack of salmon escapement, and attempts at reform included limitations on gear types and restrictions on the times and locations of fishing. Fish traps were finally banned. Profitable canneries continued to operate and employed a full crew of multi-ethnic workers, while other canneries were abandoned and left to the elements, signaling the end of Southeast Alaska's cannery heyday.

In the first half of the twentieth century a cultural revolution had begun the moment immigrants arrived on the Pacific Northwest shores. Eventually these foreign pioneers filled the spaces left by gold seekers, miners, saloon keepers, and homesteaders. At first foreign labor was welcomed: Chinese workers were followed by the Japanese, and in the end the fish factories were dominated by Filipino men. Each new group brought their own work ethic and customs. It was a tough life. Partnerships and social events made that drudgery a bit easier, including parties, celebrations, and sharing good times, ultimately blending varied traditions into an innovative social phenomenon—the cannery culture—acting as a support group and social network with membership open to all.

Southeast Alaska canneries were a historical test tube filled with distinct elements, capable of producing an observational study of multidimensional ethnocentrism and racialization, inherent conflicts, and class warfare. A naïve immigrant without a grasp of the English language or understanding of Americanism might arrive and work himself up the hierarchy, but the Chinese and Japanese did not stay in cannery work long, preferring to return to their homeland, start their own businesses, or relocate to a more urban setting like Seattle or Portland, Oregon. In contrast, the Filipino-centric unions identified closely with civil rights and labor issues and stayed in the fight. The UCAPAWA served as a common link for a number of years, generating gains in wage growth and fish factory conditions. Beyond union organizations and despite the pull of Americanization, Alaska Natives kept their age-old lifeways and sought their own political avenue or indigenous pathway, guided by a cadre of leaders, exerting pressure to capture the rights guaranteed to all citizens by the Constitution.

After World War II the Alaska Territory emerged as a global entity, increasing its innovative technology in all industries to become more efficient and diversified. Although this was a new age, the old-timers looked back, remembering the long hours spent on slippery floors in dimmed light, but also remembering a full life with festive gatherings or union meetings in a highly charged atmosphere. Decades had passed since the first canneries were built, and in the Southeast Alaska climate, many abandoned plants had deteriorated, with perhaps only the bunkhouses or mess hall left standing. For some, this seasonal housing had been their first introduction to indoor plumbing and electricity, and "cannery camps were places where Western novelties like movies, new foods, music" were sources of entertainment in the off hours.[53] Many of the men and women from this era have left this temporal world, but their children and grandchildren, often referring to themselves as "cannery kids," have kept the stories alive and narrate the tales of what went on in those weather-worn buildings constructed on piles and how the dock workers waited for the incoming scows laden with salmon still wiggling with life. Time stands still for a moment and one can hear the endless rain resonating on the metal roof in rhythm to the cacophony of gears and cogs.

14

When Cannery Children Remember

Social history is composed of the attitudes, emotions, beliefs, and outlooks of those who lived in the past. For this reason, there is great value in looking at an era through their eyes as they wove their destiny. The narrative then becomes more than a litany of great leaders and achievements or diatribes of the notorious; it is the story of everyday people who made up the society and transformed a culture to make it their own. Statistics and demographics have their place as supporting data, but a researcher or reader cannot get the feel of the story without learning of the experiences of others. In essence, this approach incorporates a cultural history composed of behaviors influenced by inherited mores that were further shaped by encounters, exigencies, and influential people and times. Recollections add missing details for how the workers, their families and extended kin maneuvered through the racialized and genderized aspects of the environment.[1] Affinity with the land and to each other provides more "than just a setting for an account"; it frames and shapes the narrative.[2] And the future is molded by the responses and reactions to change while culture remains ever dynamic.

Hawk Inlet cannery, situated on Admiralty Island near Juneau, was a place that Betty Allen remembered well. During work breaks there were "older Tlingit women sitting on benches in their yellow oilskin aprons and handkerchief head coverings, thoroughly enjoyed each other's company, they had such a good time, they were always laughing, most of them spoke Tlingit, we couldn't understand their jokes, but they were sure having fun." The young people thought nothing of a long workday followed by socializing at the end of the day. Because the Filipino bunkhouse was the largest floor space available, social events took place there—an intercultural mix of food, music, and dance. In those days teens did not worry much about wages; it was just pocket change to them. After all, they did not have to support a family and could afford to be leisurely.[3] These children grew up at a time when differences seemed to be accepted, and everyone shared common experiences. Interestingly enough, the adults who were children back then recall many incidents and events that mirror the themes within this narrative, further magnifying the view of Southeast Alaska's cannery culture during the first half of the twentieth century—a time of struggles, yet camaraderie, and great growth in a territory that eventually became the forty-ninth state.

Life was not always idyllic. There was lots of work to be done to keep body and soul together. Besides fishing, it was customary to tend a summer garden. Rebecca Rose describes these activities from her time at the Kake cannery: "Every day after school, we'd row over there to work in the garden. It was mainly potatoes, we hardly had rice. We used to live on potatoes and turnips mostly, instead of rice."[4] The gardens supplemented the traditional subsistence lifestyle and helped take care of the family's needs during the winter with enough left over to share. Rebecca (Davis) Rose started working in the Kake cannery in 1937 when she was just thirteen years old, earning fifteen cents an hour doing minor tasks. She was too young to work around the heavy machinery, so her job, like those many of her peers held, was "to stack cans on the floor, piling cans, they used to call it. At the end of the summer, my paycheck was over $30.00 and I thought that was a lot." The living situation was an endless challenge: "Everybody used to have to move to those little shacks down by the cannery. You see some standing there where the Dements are staying. They used to call them company houses and that is where everybody moved." Rose continued, "There was no road going down there. . . . We'd have to use rowboats and that's something we used to enjoy. My brother George and I, we had to do the moving back and forth, until everything was moved to those little houses. It was the same when summer was over, we'd move everything back again."[5]

For the Tlingit and Haida seasonal cannery housing mimicked the old summer camps that had traditionally been maintained year after year by the clans. The Native housing was set off a distance from the Asian bunkhouses, which were located at the opposite end of the cannery, whereas the "white man's bunkhouse was centrally located near the main cannery building," in a common pattern for all the canneries.[6] Those bunkhouses, though isolated, could form a community of their own. Even in bachelor societies there was a need to feel part of something. However, as Friday reminds us, "the bunkhouse was built for the advantage of the cannery owner, not the social well-being of the workers."[7] The living arrangements might have been segregated, but the social events and recreational times were not.

The children grew up in a multicultural world even as Southeast Alaska retained a frontier atmosphere where every role was important to the communities, from the Japanese storeowner to the Native fisherman to the Filipino union organizer and, of course, the women who were inside workers. The Native children of this era had never known a time when there were not Asian children or immigrants in their town or village; that was the way it was from 1900.[8] The pioneer emigrants who decided to make Alaska their home established families and participated in town events, even though neighborhoods tended to remain partially segregated. In spite of the physical divisions, children cut through the racial barriers. As one Japanese girl explained: "We went to school together, we went to church together, we visited each other's homes and played together. I can remember there was always a group of us girls and we would go to the movies together, the library together, like that."[9] Cherry Tatsuda emphasized the friendliness among all the girls, and as a young child she did not experience extreme problems. Although she grew up in the relatively larger town of Ketchikan, the schools were separated into territorial facilities and Native-only BIA schools, but even if the children did not all go to the same school, everyone came around to her family's store to make purchases and socialize: "We were in what you call the Native section or also called Indian Town and so its customers were on the whole mostly Natives."[10]

Though Japanese and Native children gathered together for special occasions, each culture valued their own customs and holidays. For the Japanese an important nationalistic event was "Tenchosetsu," with its undertones of age-old Buddhism. Cherry explained that the holiday was observed at the Japanese Association building, located high up on a hill: "We ate lots. Oh and we had programs. The kids sang and put on little programs for such occasions. And we all seemed to enjoy that."[11] For a Japanese child, life was grand until the 1940s when World War II changed everything. The propaganda and hate campaign could not be concealed, and parents worried about their children, who were discouraged from openly displaying their cultural traditions. To this day, many of the descendants are unaware of the former Saturday Japanese school and its emphasis on preserving the ancient language. The young people were instead taught to make the appearance of full-fledged patriots to avoid any sign of disloyalty. As the old Asian adage advised, don't be the nail that sticks up and gets pounded.[12]

Back in the day, however, community gatherings did not discriminate based on ethnic origin, age, or gender, and in modern times this was mirrored in "Cannery Days," a celebration organized by those who had grown up in the canneries. These get-togethers provided a place for the elders to share their stories with the younger generation—a past filled with hard work, adversarial relationships, lifetime friendships, and adventures. Communities were an "extension of family and friend networks . . . [that] nurtured the development of a closely-knit work environment."[13] Andrea Ebona-Michel, who headed up the event, described her motivation: "We're doing it for the elders because that is a time of their lives that they cherish. . . . They still talk about those days at Hawk Inlet, in Hood Bay, in Chatham, in Tenakee, and how hard they worked. It was a part of their life that they will never forget, and I will never forget because it's dear to our hearts."[14]

Annie Ebona, grandmother of Andrea Ebona-Michel, was originally from the Killisnoo-Angoon area and the clan leader "matriarch" of the Dei Shu Hit (Beaver Clan). She came from an old cannery family who worked at the Tyee and Todd canneries, and as an adult she worked at Hood Bay Cannery and New England Fish Company at Chatham, not retiring until she was seventy-five years old. In 1920 she married a Filipino fisherman named Martin Ebona, who later worked for the U.S. Immigration and Naturalization Service.[15] Their life may have been unusual, but that did not stop the mixing of cultural associations, ranging from involvement in Juneau's Filipino organizations to Annie's leadership in the ANS for Camp 2 in Juneau, along with her membership in the Tlingit-Haida Central Council. Just as Martin was working with immigration problems, Annie was a delegate to the AFL-CIO (they merged in 1955) during a critical time for the cannery workers.[16]

At the "Cannery Days" celebration, Annie Ebona told how the boredom and fatigue were almost overwhelming, so they would sing songs way into the night to keep their spirits up. Often these songs were old Tlingit legends set to a modern melodies, or at other times, music and dance were a fusion of indigenous cultures from around the world— Japan, Scandinavia, or the Polynesian islands. Eunice Akagi, who was eighty-five years old at the time, also shared her stories, describing how all nationalities gathered for dances and other social events. And she especially appreciated that fact that there were "songs to sing each day" from many cultures and lands far away. She was young when she went to work at the cannery, but there were recreational opportunities after the shifts: "We had so many wonderful memories no matter how hard the work was. . . . Sometimes we had to work 18 hours a day and then you got to get up in the morning and go right back to work." The whole family followed that routine. Eunice continued, "So we used to sing to keep awake so we wouldn't collapse. We would sing really loud, but of course nobody could hear us because a cannery is really loud."[17]

Music was a consistent theme in the memories of workers, but everything was not rosy among the workers and they were not sheltered from the outside world. Akagi added that there were tough times when they had to endure negative slurs and prejudicial attitudes. In her opinion, the

Asians had it easier since room and board for non-Native workers "was free, but we had to stop at the company store and buy our food and try to cook it in a short amount of time. Sometimes you have only a half-hour for lunch and that was no time at all." If you were late back to the shift there would be real trouble.[18] Nonetheless, inherent tribulations from fatigue to monotony were interspersed with both planned celebrations and the more spontaneous events. "Our generation were dancers," Akagi mused. "Even the young people. We used to sneak around and pretend we had Indian regalia. They wouldn't let us have any real things, but the folks used to manage something whenever we would have an Indian party."[19] Andrea Ebona-Michel emphasized that this was an important part of the history. "The men fished on the boats, the women worked in the canneries, and the kids played in the woods and [on] the beach all summer. Our mothers and fathers, grandmas and grandpas all worked in the canneries."[20]

During the summer the Hawk Inlet cannery population expanded to about five hundred people, developing into a cosmopolitan village with "Japanese supervisors, Caucasian college boys, Filipino and Hawaiian workers," and Southeast Alaska Natives—all glad when the long shifts were over and the deafening machinery was turned off. The young people seemed to never be tired, and if was not too late, the cannery transformed into a playground under the midnight sun. For the children, most days were spent outside, and it was the perfect escape from the customary two-room cabin with a small stove and no running water, which despite these hardships, the dwellers proudly called their "summer home."[21] Sandi Benzel thought back to her carefree youthful years from seven to twelve, living her "happiest memories" at Hawk Inlet. "The kids would hike up to the dam for fresh spring water, the coolest, clearest, and sweetest in [the] Southeast. A rope hung from the boat house, where the children could swing out over the water." Boats or other water vessels were an important recreational component, and Benzel described how up to ten kids piled into the company skiff, and the boys rowed in pursuit of the whales known to frequent the waters.[22]

Marie Olson, granddaughter of Sally Hopkins, recalled sneaking over to the Filipino bunkhouses because "they had the best rice candy, we all liked it so much."[23] Everyone played together and with boundless imagination and energy, the children fashioned playthings from fallen timber or discarded items. "We entertained ourselves playing and if a skiff was not handy we used to row along the shore with a huge wash tub . . . at coffee times our mothers would look at us from the cannery which wasn't really so far from the family cabins."[24] It was not surprising how all the kids took care of each other while parents worked; sometimes the oldest girl in a family was in charge or at other times a teenager might be hired. At any rate, the whole cannery was a play yard and the bunkhouses were an international experience.[25]

Marie explained that ethnic lines were not tightly drawn among the children, who just saw each other as having the common goal of fun. "We amused ourselves and loved to build boats out of scraps. Sometimes the oldest boy had a long pole with a huge nail tied to the tip. We would take turns trying to spear a Dungeness crab and kept that crab in an old abandoned wash tub. When we had at least one half tub full, we boiled the crab on shore over a driftwood fire. Imagine eating a whole Dungeness crab by yourself. You can imagine our disappointment when we ordered a crab salad at Fisherman's Wharf [San Francisco] years later."[26]

Marie attended the Wrangell Institute, a boarding school in Southeast Alaska for Native children, but problems forced her to drop out and get a cannery job, the only work available for a high school student with no experience. For a while she stayed at the Tyee cannery "at the very tip of Admiralty Island—[a] cove right next to it called Murderer's Cove, and Point Gardiner."[27] Although she enjoyed having money of her own, her earnings also went toward new clothes, particularly during her school days. She added that this was true of her sister as well.[28] Eventually she left Alaska and went to work for a Bay area telephone company in California. It was there that she became involved with unions, proudly declaring she would always be a union woman just like the Southeast Alaska women with whom she had grown up: "the National Labor Relations Board was the best thing that ever happened for union people."[29] In California she was interested in taking labor history courses, but none were available until the Ford Foundation funded the Institute of Industrial Relations at Berkeley. Studying on a scholarship, she learned more about the current social movements and boasted about the incongruous situation where "I was hobnobbing with the Black Panthers."[30] In later years she returned to Southeast Alaska and renewed her cultural ties, especially through her membership in the Alaska Native Sisterhood, where she is today a revered elder and culture bearer.

During those old cannery days on the Alexander Archipelago, the largest temperate rainforest in the world, these kids had their fair share of rainy days, but the weather conditions did not stand in the way of pursuing their brand of fun. When there was a need to make a dry play area, the "children would pull the mattresses off the bunks to line the floor for gymnastics and put on plays for each other."[31] Additionally, there were the ever popular basketball games, and in the evenings they built fires to cook clams and crabs they had collected during the day. These young people lived by their wits and loved it.

In contrast, Helen Sarabia recalled the long hours in her teen years at the Excursion Inlet packing house near Hoonah. The job was so tedious that everyone was on "auto pilot," trying to fight off exhaustion.[32] Naturally, that was when accidents happened, and to be cautious everyone watched out for the others in an environment split between cannery drudgery and children's carefree days. There was also serious business in those days. Several of the children remember their mothers going to both labor union and ANS meetings. They tagged along and knew it was a great time to see one's friends, but they probably had no idea what the meetings were about or what their mothers confronted in the workplace.

When Alaska Native women started to organize unions in the 1930s, motivated by the promise of a reduction in lengthy shifts, an increase in pay, and general relief from the most difficult aspects of cannery work, there were numerous roadblocks in the way.

"They didn't want it here in Juneau. They called it (the unions) all kinds of name, like AFL-all full of liquor and CIO-crazy Indian organization," Akagi said. The pro-union workers stayed firm and unionized. "We had a lot of difficulty, but it came out all right," Dorothy Walker said. "For a while there was harsh feelings on both sides," but after the union came, the cannery workers were paid more, "working all summer for $600," Rosa Miller recalled, and among the changes during that time, the cannery put in washing machines to replace the tub and washboards the families had been using for years. That was one of the improvements and, again referring to the eventual union, she was sure that although "it took a long time coming . . . it was better for us."[33]

Now as adults, the youthful years seemed idealistic, but not far below the surface was the reality of the racial tensions they faced, and that was why Martin "Snooky" Goenett called the cannery a safe haven. In 1914 his parents worked at Hawk Inlet, and it was enjoyable for him because there was no one calling them "Indians" in derogatory terms, mostly because the Tlingit and Haida were in the majority. The single men (mostly Asians) stayed in separate quarters, and the Alaska Native families had their own temporary villages. Goenett called it a working vacation and a good place for kids to be kids. At the end of the season, Filipino and Tlingit families gathered together to celebrate and share local foods in what was described by some as a "child's paradise."[34]

The children of the cannery workers grew up understanding the inter-cultural nature of the cannery landscape: there were the Japanese "bosses," white college boys, and Filipino and Hawaiian workers. Eunice Akagi often talked about how much she loved the Hawaiian music, but she also appreciated "swing" and "big band" music, evoking the enduring sounds of Benny Goodman or Frank Sinatra. Music was the one constant during the Great Depression, World War II, the Cold War, and postwar society.[35] There were times when the cannery women would pool their money to buy a radio to listen to the sounds of the "Hit Parade" during break time. When Dorothy Walker spoke of her endless hours in front of the filler machine, she also remembered that one way to relieve tedium was singing "You are My Sunshine" or "Goody, Goody" until the notes were the only thing she heard amid the cranking machines, and hours later, the melody still reverberated in her head.[36]

Not every day was filled with work; there was time for recreational pursuits. Rosa Miller, daughter of Bessie Visaya, the founder of the Juneau ANS chapter, missed the picnics most of all. They enjoyed gathering berries, seaweed, or Indian asparagus and producing a magnificent spread for the "mini potlatches," where children imitated the age-old rituals by fashioning their own regalia, often out of paper because there were so few materials for creating apparel. Of course, it was exciting when the ferry came in with novel goods to choose from, like fabric to make a new dress for the cannery party. Using old borrowed sewing machines and pictures cut out from catalogs, the girls created grand dresses, each hoping to look special on the dance floor. Days before, the planners had made sure the warehouse was secured for the event, and the night watchman kept the lights burning. Everyone mingled in an inter-ethnic celebration of life, and as Eunice Akagi shared: "The music would take over and suddenly everyone, the children and the elders, the Filipinos, Natives, Norwegians, Hawaiians, and Japanese were all dancing together." She learned the "schottische and hambo" from the Norwegians and practiced the jitterbug with her Japanese co-workers, while sampling "salmon caviar" in the company of her lifetime friends.[37]

Through struggles and good times the most important part of the cannery culture was the sense of community, which displayed a microcosm of a pluralistic America that could not be denied. The cannery culture was even more than "special foods and recipes, of traditional dress and music and dances like the polka and schottische," because meaning was found in the "value placed on kinship, traditions of mutual assistance, manifested through ethnic fraternal and benevolent societies," actively shaping daily life and bolstering the esteem necessary to create a better future.[38] Through unity and cohesion, members resisted oppression and reoriented life experiences whether through the individual or group, thereby manifesting a voice in their destiny. Over the decades, cannery life changed due to different social forces, a growing economy, and technology, but the core of the workers' bond endured.

In March 1957 Salvador del Fierro Sr. traveled from Ketchikan, where he was a foreman at the Sunny Point Cannery plant, to be one of the judges at the nineteenth Annual Canned Salmon Cutting Demonstration at the Olympic Hotel in Seattle. The Olympic Hotel had been his employer when he and his wife, Elizabeth, had decided to escape Southeast Alaska because of the bigotry they faced, and while in Seattle they encountered and embraced Filipino activists and union organizers building a budding union movement. Through the UCAPAWA, Salvador and Elizabeth were able to represent those who labored in the Alaskan cannery industry, the largest salmon fishing grounds in the world at that time. When the UCA-PAWA faded out of existence and was eclipsed by stronger unions in the early 1950s, he and others joined the powerful International Longshore and Warehouse Union (Local No. 37) based in Seattle, an organization with a rocky history.

In 1957 it was reported that cannery workers of the ILWU (Local 37) "made an aggregated gain of about $60,000.00 over the 1956 wages in a recently negotiated contract with the canned salmon industry," but not everything was optimum. The cannery workers' union was able to send only five hundred men to Alaska, representing the largest cutback of Filipino workers since the Alaskeros first arrived on the shores of Southeast Alaska. Formerly, more "than 4,000 men used to man the operation in the salmon canneries," but now the union was undergoing a financial crisis.[39] This was not the only change since the cannery heyday. Technological advances had enabled larger fishing harvests, better methods of preserving fresh fish had been developed, and there was increased automation inside the processing plants, thus reducing the need for a large workforce. The bulk of inside workers were now college students up for summer break and had no investment in Alaska, which by 1959 had reached statehood status and was trying out its wobbly legs, including a brand new Alaska Department of Fish and Game (ADF&G) assuming duties previously in federal hands. With this bureaucratic change there were power struggles between the agency, fishermen, and canneries, increasing as more regulations were placed on salmon fishing to counteract decades of resource depletion.

These changes motivated owners and corporations to escalate diversification efforts in a shift to processing crab, shrimp, and other marine catch. Women whose mothers once worked in the old salmon canneries were now likely to be employed by a Petersburg shrimp plant or cleaning crabs in Hoonah. They still enjoyed the independence of working out of the home, but things had altered drastically in the postwar years. There was an increase in the cost of living, resulting in a demand for higher wages, while corporations strove to maintain a profit margin. With increased costs, corporations shipped fresh salmon to China for processing, the product was then sent back to the United States, and company owners saw their profits rise. For instance, much of the work to debone salmon must be done by hand. In the United States that cost is about a dollar per pound, whereas in China the same work is $0.20 per pound. Further, there were fewer canneries maintained in certain areas because wealthy home buyers wanted to purchase shorefront property, and a salmon processing plant was regarded as unsightly.[40] But nothing was going to transform the economy faster or more dramatically than the discovery of oil in northern Alaska.

In 1968 a major oilfield was discovered in northern Alaska's Prudhoe Bay, and suddenly oil companies were flooding Alaska, all trying to get a piece of the action. There was one problem though—who owned this land? While oil companies were trying to figure out how to transport oil from the frozen and desolate north, devoid of any infrastructure, to an ice-free port, the federal, state, and Native governments met to hash out the problems of aboriginal title. After a deal was reached the pipeline was built, slicing through the state. Alaska's politicians and residents were convinced black gold would solve all fiscal problems and there was great excitement, although in the end, no one received exactly what they wanted, and the final arrangement resulted in one of the largest socioeconomic impacts Alaska Natives had ever experienced, remaining a subject of debate to this day.

This progression started with a mammoth piece of legislation that has never been duplicated anywhere. In order to settle indigenous land claims so that the oil companies could move in, President Richard Nixon signed the Alaska Native Claims Settlement Act (ANCSA) in 1971. Designated Native lands were divided into twelve regional for-profit Native corporations with about two hundred village corporations. Overnight Alaska Natives were thrust into corporate America and had to make a profit or face bankruptcy. The cultural shock was enormous and turned the traditional social order upside down. After ANCSA, village dwellers became shareholders, while a whaling captain could be elected CEO in a do-or-die position. If they did not make money, mostly based on their own local natural resources, they faced bankruptcy and losing their children's inheritance.

In Southeast Alaska the regional corporation was Sealaska, and as with the other Native corporations, it was time-consuming to start up a business of this nature. At first, the new corporate administration had to rely on imported expertise for assistance, which ate away at their portion of the ANCSA cash settlement.[41] During the 1970s and 1980 Sealaska engaged in controversial practices in order to earn the money they needed to sustain the corporation and provide dividends to their shareholders, placing a burden on the surrounding Tongass Forest and the fisheries in the region. A case in point comes from Hoonah, a Tlingit village on Chichagof Island. The village corporation, Huna Totem, hired an outside logging company to harvest the dense stands of timber on the hills around the village, and the subsequent clear-cutting led to massive erosion and the clogging of salmon streams. The resultant lack of oxygen forced the fish to throw themselves out of the water in a desperate act of survival.[42] The likelihood of further ecological and economic disasters had been predicted for years, and to this day fishery controversies continue.

In addition, because of the effects of globalization, international issues emerged that had to be managed and resolved. After World War II Japan concentrated resources on restoring its former strength and looked to fish processing for an economic base. This Japanese industry received a boost in 1964 when Alaska Governor Egan "invited Japanese buyers to purchase unprocessed salmon and the Japanese accepted at 10.5 cents a pound." Egan was trying to avoid losing out on harvest monies because of the actions of cannery companies closing their doors in defiance of the fishermen's demands. Egan thought they would at least make a bit of money that summer, and he was determined to see that Alaska, after spending approximately $20 million for its Fish and Game Department since 1959 to regulate these crises, would prevent salmon from rotting.[43] In turn, Japanese buyers and investors expanded their interests in Alaska fishery products, and freshly caught salmon is routinely sent to Asia for processing at a lower cost, intensifying business ties between Asia and Alaska.

At the turn of the century and after gold fever had ceased to sizzle, it was the salmon industry that distinguished Alaska from other similar territories, and in the process Alaska became a colony outpost. After oil was discovered, the fishing industry remained an important element of the economy and one of the top employers, but in addition, Alaska was struggling to define itself and pondering whether it was a wilderness or a modern industrial state. ANCSA corporations have augmented the economy to a significant level while striving to keep the cultural heritage alive for the next generation and for all Alaskans to share. Although the Alaska Native–managed companies were predicted to fail by the foes and skeptics alike, for the most part they have not only thrived but evolved into a fundamental piece of Alaska's economy and future. The fishing industry, however, is subject to a number of regulations.

After Alaska statehood, the Department of Fish and Game took over management of the salmon runs and it was no shocking revelation that the resource was in dire need of appropriate and unbiased oversight. Several methods were tried to increase the salmon stocks, such as limiting the openings or restricting the hours of commercial fishing, but the results were inadequate. In 1973 the Alaska legislature approved the Limited Entry Act, deemed to be the answer to the fishery problem. The Limited Entry Act required qualified fishermen to purchase a special license to fish in certain waters. The qualifications were based on history in the fishing grounds and need for harvesting (commercially and/or subsistence). There were those Native fishermen who refused to go through the filing procedure because they felt they already had a right to the fishery without any state approval. Others were confused by the bureaucracy and paperwork and failed to act before the deadline. Decades later it was demonstrated that limited entry was not the cure the state had hoped for and that it had instead impoverished fishermen and at times whole fleets. In some cases, villages dependent on commercial fishing were left without an economic base. Desperation set in, and as the price for existing limited entry permits increased, fishermen sold their permits to make quick cash. By the late 1980s, the fishing fleets had been severely reduced, resulting in traditional fishermen being banished from the fishery grounds they had known since childhood. Again using Hoonah as an example, the salmon fishing fleet once known as the largest in Southeast Alaska, had been reduced by two-thirds in 1989.[44]

To this day Alaska is still struggling to find and maintain the balance between being a resource market and preserving the landscape. Historian Stephen Haycox termed Alaska an American colony, and for good reason given its history. Yet Alaskans, whether rural or urban, have forged their own path and think of themselves as exceptional in the land of tundra and Pleistocene ice caps, boasting of both the largest temperate rainforest in the world and the highest mountain peak in North America, the majestic Denali, the great one. It is "a spirit characterized by individualism, self-reliance and initiative," much of that originating from its isolated placement as the one Arctic state in the union. Although Alaska is a non-contiguous part of the United States with its own time zone, the population faces the same problems as any other state, frequently centered on economic sustainability. At the time he wrote *Alaska, an American Colony* (2006), Haycox believed that Alaska's future economy would "continue to be based on resource extraction, and Alaska is likely to continue to function as a colony for corporate investment in its resources." His expectations were realized until more recent times, when oil started to run out and the related troubles threatened to dim the future. Even with a call to open up exploratory regions, will it be enough to sustain the economy? Large oil companies are pulling out based on the bleak cost-benefit ratio, shifting energy needs, and unease about building costly new infrastructure with only a hunch there might be oil. Furthermore, due to dramatic climate changes in the Arctic and elsewhere, there is a scramble to find alternate forms of energy and to break the hold that fossil fuels have on the nation—the sociopolitical climate has been drastically modified and is undergoing unprecedented reorganization without a firm plan of action.

Nevertheless, the salmon industry continues to be a multi-million-dollar industry, supplying fresh and processed fish internationally, but great caution must be taken to maintain sustainability. Immense burdens, many human caused, plague Southeast Alaska's ragged coast and rugged coves. The oceans and streams have never fully recovered from the over-harvesting of the early 1900s with its shameful wastage, but now these problems are coupled with further environmental threats—warming of the oceans has introduced fatal problems that must be resolved. The acid level has increased in the oceans, killing off several species, and so has the water temperature increased, resulting in an ecosystem where salmon can no longer survive.[45] In fact, during the record-breaking summer of 2019, some salmon water bodies exceeded eighty degrees and the fish suffered heart attacks.[46] Without scientific measures, the resource is threatened beyond repair.

Cannery industry dynamics, with its accompanying strife and cultural adaptations, shaped Alaska's history and its ethnic relationships. The need for labor brought people from many nations, and as Filipino worker Donald Guimary emphasized, it was dirty work; but it was enough to keep body and soul together. Most immigrants left the industry after a short stint, but those who stayed in the cannery towns were integral in building egalitarian communities where each person played a role in the well-being and continuing health of the place they called home. Diversity and overlapping lifeways augmented the beauty and richness of the Last Frontier. Ultimately, their story illustrates how collective energy stimulates innovative ideas without disregarding traditional knowledge. This same vigor is essential for meeting the future environmental and sociopolitical challenges of an ever-expanding, yet fragile world.

NOTES

INTRODUCTION

1. White, *It's Your Misfortune*, 3.
2. Armitage, "From the Inside Out," 32–47.
3. Robbins, *Capitalist Transformation*, 7.
4. DeVoto, *Western Paradox*, 39.
5. Miner, *Corporation and the Indian*, 214.
6. Omi and Winant, *Racial Formation*.
7. Omi and Winant, "Racial Formations," 9.
8. Raibmon, *Authentic Indians*, 13.
9. Whymper, *Travel and Adventure*, 78.
10. Kent, *America in 1900*, 105.
11. Friday, *Organizing Asian-American Labor*, 38.
12. Takaki, *Strangers*, 30.
13. Tilly, "Transplanted Networks," 88–89.
14. Asian Women United of California, *Making Waves*, 25–26.
15. Guimary, *Marumina Trabaho*, 77.
16. Ruiz, *Cannery Women*, 31.
17. Zavella, *Women's Work*, 100.
18. Foner, *Women and the American Labor Movement*, x.
19. Scott, "Gender."
20. Milkman, *Gender at Work*, 2–3.
21. Tsosie, "Changing Women," 567.
22. Klein, "Mother as Clanswoman."
23. Miller, "Contemporary Native Women," 70.
24. Durrenberger and Reichart, *The Anthropology of Labor Unions*, 1.

25. Cobble, *Other Women's Movement*, 15.

26. Faue, "Paths of Unionization," 298–99.

27. Bordewich, *Killing the White Man's Indian*, 19.

28. White, *Roots of Dependency*.

29. Robertson, *Conquest by Law*, ix.

30. Arnesen, *Human Tradition*, xv.

31. Churchill, *Marxism and Native Americans*.

32. Friday, *Organizing Asian-American Labor*, 1, 5–6.

1. A TIME BEFORE THE SALMON CANS

1. Black, *Russians in Alaska*, 40–41.

2. Boneman, *Alaska*, 62.

3. Sheet'ka K̲waan: Sheet'ka loosely translates to land behind the island, and K̲waan refers to a regional designation.

4. Black, *Russians in Alaska*, 161.

5. Kan, *Memory Eternal*, 50.

6. Hanable, "New Russia."

7. Khlebnikov, *Colonial Russian America*, 51.

8. Khlebnikov, *Colonial Russian America*, 54.

9. Gibson, "Russian Dependence," 29.

10. Grinev, *Tlingit Indians*, 118.

11. Price, *Great Father in Alaska*, 48.

12. Grinev, *Tlingit Indians*, 209.

13. Gibson, "Russian Dependence," 33.

14. Arndt and Pierce *Construction History*, 71.

15. Arndt and Pierce, *Construction History*, 137.

16. Arndt and Pierce, *Construction History*, 200.

17. Cooley, *Politics and Conservation*, 24.

18. Black, *Russians in Alaska*, 265.

19. Gibson, "Russian Dependence," 39.

20. Worl, "Tlingit *At.oow*."

21. Whitehead, *Completing the Union*, 35.

22. Arnold, *Fishermen's Frontier*, 56.

23. Friday, *Organizing Asian-American Labor*, 28.

24. Friday, *Organizing Asian-American Labor*, 29.

25. Friday, *Organizing Asian-American Labor*, 29.

26. Friday, *Organizing Asian-American Labor*, 2.

27. Alekseev, *Destiny of Russian America*, 280.

28. Grinev, *Tlingit Indians*, 278–80.

29. Case and Voluck, *Alaska Natives*, 47.
30. Price, *Great Father in Alaska*, 19.

2. THE TIN CAN MEN

1. Story told to author by elder Jake White in Hoonah, Alaska, July 1990.
2. William Gouvernor Morris, letter to the Department of the Treasury, July 23, 1878, in 45th Cong. 3d Sess., 1879, S. Exec. Doc. 59.
3. Hinckley, *Americanization of Alaska*, 125.
4. Hinckley, *Americanization of Alaska*, 135.
5. Hume, *Fresh Columbia Salmon*.
6. Hinckley, *Americanization of Alaska*, 126, backed up in the eyewitness account by Kutchin, *Report on the Salmon Fisheries of Alaska, 1896–1898* (1899).
7. Ballou, *New Eldorado*, 192. Coopers were necessary for many years to make barrels for shipping salted or brined fish.
8. Scidmore, *Appleton's Guide-Book*, 58.
9. Replogle, *Among the Indians*, 63; Peratrovich Family Book, compiled and kept by Gina Peratrovich.
10. Peratrovich Family Book, courtesy of Gina Peratrovich.
11. Hinckley, *Canoe Rocks*, 171.
12. Cross, *Financing an Empire*.
13. *Alaska Appeal*, September 30, 1879, 1.
14. Information and story from the Peratrovich Family Book, provided by Gina Peratrovich.
15. The term *Ḵwáan* is from the traditional Tlingit social division and refers to a large area or region that was home to several clans. An example of a *Ḵwáan* might be Sitka or Yakutat.
16. Olson and Hubbard, *Fishing*, 20–21; Moser, *Salmon and Salmon Fisheries*, 24, 25.
17. Klein, "Mother as Clanswoman," 30.
18. Guimary, *Marumina Trabaho*, 62. Donald Guimary and his father were both cannery workers in Southeast Alaska. Much of his information and many of stories come from passed down sources.
19. Klein, "Mother as Clanswoman," 30.
20. Jones, *Report of Alaska Investigations in 1914*, 102.
21. Dauenhauer and Dauenhauer, *Haa Kusteeyí, Our Culture*, 40. The Dauenhauers have compiled numerous biographies of Tlingit, Haida, and Tsimshian culture bearers, including the founding members of the Alaska Native Brotherhood (ANB).
22. Hinckley, *Canoe Rocks*, 231.
23. Moser, *Salmon and Salmon Fisheries*.

24. Moser, *Salmon and Salmon Fisheries*.

25. Moser, "Alaska Salmon Investigations in 1900 and 1901."

26. Arnold, *Fishermen's Frontier*, 69.

27. Moser, *Salmon and Salmon Fisheries*, 24, 25.

28. *Koo.eex'*, the Tlingit term for the potlatch, is translated as to invite, referring to the call out to appropriate guests. The ceremonial aspects are not only ceremonial but touch every aspect of the Tlingit society.

29. Coppers called *tinaa* by the Tlingit were finely decorated pieces of pounded copper. Their value was extended by what they meant to the people and transcended anything that could be measured in monetary amounts.

30. Wyatt, "Alaskan Indian Wage Earners," 46.

31. Wyatt, "Alaskan Indian Wage Earners." This amount was an enormous amount of money at the time and could have been amassed from several sources, including when the men worked as packers for the miners during the Klondike gold rush.

32. Originally from Governor John Brady to the Secretary of the Interior, January 6, 1902, cited in Wyatt, "Alaska Indian Wage Earners."

33. Willard, in McCoy, *Life in Alaska*, 345–46; Fred Falconer supports the contention of poverty in "Yailth-Kock," *Assembly Herald*, vol. 10 (1904): 513–14.

34. McCoy, *Life in Alaska*. Douglas Cole and Ira Chaikin present the argument that missionary efforts were the demise of the Tlingit potlatch and state: "While it persisted in remote Yakutat and even at Hoonah for a time, the Tlingit potlatch was disappearing, its passing unaffected by any law prohibiting it." The authors focused on the Northwest Coast and Canada where the potlatch was prohibited by law, but no law was ever enacted in Alaska. Further, culture bearers to this day speak of the continuation of the potlatch, which may have gone underground at times to make the missionaries happy, but never relinquished strength (testimony of Harold Jacobs). See also Cole and Chaikin, *Iron Hand*.

35. Thornton, *Being and Place*, 18.

36. Kutchin, "Report on the Salmon Fisheries," 20; Wyatt, "Alaska Indian Wage Earners," 43–49.

37. Roy Bean, interview, in "The Southeast Alaska Salmon Fishery: Interviews with Men and Women Engaged in Commercial Fishing, 1913–1978," tapes in author's possession.

38. Roy Bean interview.

39. Thornton, *Being and Place*, 4.

40. Thornton, *Haa Leellk'w*, xi.

41. Thornton, *Being and Place*, 3.

42. Banner, *How the Indians Lost*; author's general thesis.

43. Dombrowski, *Against Culture*, 94.

44. Cooley, *Politics and Conservation*, 65.

45. Arnold, "Putting Up Fish"; Arnold, personal communication, June 2010.

46. Stahl, "Theories of International Labor Migration."

47. Hinckley, *Americanization*, 127.

48. Scidmore, quoted in Hinckley, *Americanization*, 128.

49. "The Influx of Chinese in Alaska," *Alaska Mining News*, November 1888.

50. "The Influx of Chinese in Alaska."

51. Geary Act of 1892 27 Stat. 25, Sec. 7, and McCreary Amendment 28 Stat. 7, Sec. 2.

52. Nash, "The 'China Gangs,'" 257–58.

53. Guimary, *Marumina Trabaho*, 135. Far from "looking out" for the hapless Asian cannery workers, the cannery bosses were more or less in collusion with separating a man from his money.

54. Guimary, *Marumina Trabaho*, 160.

55. Takaki, *Strangers*, 35.

56. Moser, "Salmon Investigations of the Steamer Albatross in the Summer of 1900," 183–84.

57. Orosa, "An Investigation," 52.

58. Moser, "Salmon Investigations," 185.

59. Masson and Guimary, "Asian Labor Contractors."

60. *Alaska Journal*, September 23, 1893; *The Alaskan*, April 7, 1894.

61. *Alaska Journal*, April 7, 1894.

62. Immigrants retained their culture in the new land regardless of change and new situations. For the Chinese, the belief in Taoism was strong and allowed the Chinese to meet challenges as though they were a meandering river. A pleasant life could "be attained through simplicity, tranquility, and harmony." In Alaska there are few if any records of the early Chinese. From other areas such as Washington State and California, it can be assumed the Chinese approach to life was similar and a foundation for survival. Tsai, *Chinese Experience*, 43.

63. Jones, *Report of Alaska Investigations in 1914*, 30; Kirk, "Labor Forces of the Alaska Coast," 354.

64. George Ramos, interview, February 2, 2000, Project Jukebox, University of Alaska, Fairbanks, Tape H 2002-07, http://jukebox.uaf.edu/WRST/ramos/gera.html.

65. Cooley, *Politics and Conservation*, 83–85.

66. Scows are boats used to haul fish from nets or traps to the cannery dock. They are smaller than tenders that have large holds to carry tons of fish.

67. Journal of Fisheries Agent S. J. Kirkwood, 1909, quoted in Steve Colt, "Salmon Fish Traps in Alaska: An Economic History Perspective," 35, Anchorage:

Institute for Social and Economic Research report, February 15, 2000, http://www.alaskool.org/projects/traditionallife/fishtrap/FISHTRAP.htm.

68. Paul, *Then Fight for It*, 37.

69. Paul, *Then Fight for It*.

70. Robert "Bob" DeArmond, personal communication, Sitka Alaska, July 1995.

71. Hardin, "Tragedy of Commons."

72. U.S. Department of Commerce and Labor, Bureau of Statistics, *Commercial Alaska, 1867–1903*, 43.

73. Although Alaska was the major salmon supply region, the headquarters, decisions, and capital were centered in San Francisco and Seattle. According to economist Richard Cooley, "the pattern of economic absenteeism had given rise to numerous problems, conflicts, disagreements, and misunderstandings, which have greatly compounded the difficulties of conserving the resource" (*Politics and Conservation*, 26).

74. Cooley, *Politics and Conservation*, 26.

75. Hinckley, *Americanization*, 195.

76. See Niblack, *Coast Indians*, 299, 386.

77. "Salmon Is Wasted," *Alaska Dispatch*, November 3, 1903, 1.

78. Grinnell, *Alaska 1899*, 351.

79. Scidmore, *Appleton's Guide-Book*, 127.

80. Haycox, *Alaska, an American Colony*, 243.

81. The term "fish trust" was first coined by early Alaska politicians such as Judge James Wickersham and Delegate Dan Sutherland. In the 1920s it was a common term in congressional hearings and newspaper alike.

82. Liljeblad, *Filipino, Alaska*, 16.

83. Mitchell, *Sold American*, 108, originally published in the *Thlingit*, a student newspaper from the Sheldon Jackson school.

84. Arnold, "Work and Culture," 232.

85. Letter from Willoughby Clark to President Benjamin Harrison, January 21, 1890, Appendix of *Tlingit and Haida Indians of Alaska v. United States*, Docket 47900, U.S. Court of Claims.

86. John J. Healy Letter (1891), "Report within the Proceeding of the Alaska Boundary Tribunal." Part 1. Final Report of the Boundary Tribunal, 459, 1900.

87. The Organic Act of May 17, 1884 at 25 Stat. 24.

88. Purvis, *Drive of Civilization*.

89. Plaintiff's Exhibit, no. 84 in the records of *Tlingit and Haida Indians of Alaska v. United States*.

90. Mitchell, *Sold American*.

1. Drucker, *Native Brotherhoods*, 81.
2. Jonaitas, *Chiefly Feasts*; Mitchell, *Sold American*.
3. *Taak'w Aan* is the modern orthography for the Taakan Clan land, in this case a site. As noted in chapter 1, *Lingit Aani* is all Tlingit land, the whole Alexander Archipelago, all clan territories combined. *Ta'quan* is how a totem pole, discussed later in the present chapter, was referred to in the missionary orthography of the time.
4. Elder Embert James (presently residing in Ketchikan) relates that this was the traditional land of the Tongass clans and that a deal was struck between the Tsimshian and the Tlingit for this site. James argues that the story of the United States government giving permission for settlement is not at the core of Native history. Embert James, online interview with author, July 2016.
5. Hosmer, *American Indians*, 198–200.
6. Conditions in Alaska: Report of the Subcommittee of Committee of Territories Appointed to Investigate Conditions in Alaska, Hearings Before the Subcommittee of Committee on Territories, 58th Cong. 2d Sess. (Washington DC: Government Printing Office, 1904).
7. Talking with Tsimshian descendants today, it is amazing how the stories have been passed down about holding potlatches in secret or hiding totem poles. Although the Tsimshian were under the thumb of the Church and then the federal government, they remained proud people and always refer to themselves as special, not unlike other Native groups in what they believe is well-deserved ethnocentrism.
8. Knight, *Indians at Work*, 22.
9. Of interest is that Father Duncan did not strictly adhere to getting rid of all Tsimshian symbols. In front of the first structures in the late 1880s, totem poles were still displayed. One remains of particular significance to this day. The Ta'quan pole was displayed in front of one house in Port Chester, now called Metlakatla. Steve Henrikson, curator of the Alaska State Museum informed me that it is now located at the Sheldon Jackson Museum in Sitka.
10. Hinckley, *Canoe Rocks*, 138.
11. Case and Voluck, *Alaska Natives*, 11. Contemporaries recount their elders speaking of this time and they are adamant that Duncan did not have a hold on them or their occupations.
12. Conditions in Alaska, Hearings Before the Subcommittee on Territories. Senate document, no. 195, 50th Congress, 2d (Washington DC: Government Printing Office, 1901).
13. Case and Voluck, *Alaska Natives*, 70.

14. Moser, *Salmon and Salmon Fisheries of Alaska*, 66–67.
15. Fiske, "Colonization and Decline."
16. Progressives were those who adopted or proselytized the Christian faith and Western customs.
17. Cooper, "Native Women," 45–47.
18. Beattie, *Marsden of Alaska*, 65.
19. Committee of Indian Affairs, "Statement of Mr. Duncan's Work among the Tsimpsheean Indians of British Columbia and Alaska," 53d Cong. 2d, Senate Doc. 144, Committee of Indian Affairs (Washington DC Government Printing Office, 1894).
20. Indian Citizenship Act, http://www.thecanadianencyclopedia.ca/en/article /indian-act/, Canadian Encyclopedia Online.
21. Beattie, *Marsden of Alaska*, 64, 68.
22. Kohlstedt, "William Duncan."
23. Murray, *The Devil and Mr. Duncan*. In retrospect, President Theodore Roosevelt might have agreed on this point because of his interest in the Tongass Forest, which he wanted to preserve and yet open for development. The original Tsimshian Alaskan reservation had been approved based on the "Act to Repeal Timber Culture Laws" with the rationale that the Tsimshian would develop the forest resources. "Statement of Mr. Duncan's Work Among the Tsimpsheean Indians of British Columbia and Alaska," 53d Cong. 2d Doc. 144, Senate, 1894 to the Committee of Indian Affairs.
24. In 1901 President Theodore Roosevelt addressed the public regarding the General Allotment Act and indicated that this would fully assimilate Native Americans by pulverizing the tribal masses.
25. Hinckley, *Canoe Rocks*, 332–33. Material originally found in Letter from John G. Brady to Charles I. Thompson, February 17, 1902; Beattie, *Marsden of Alaska*; Letter from William Duncan to William T. Harris, February 15, 1901, Governor's Annual Report for 1901, John G. Brady.
26. Reynon, "The Tsimshians," 85–89.
27. Joseph Murray, "Report on the Salmon Fisheries in Alaska," Department of the Treasury, Special Agents Division, 1895, 356–72 (1896).
28. Stevens, *Sheldon Jackson*.
29. Price, *Great Father in Alaska*, 171.
30. Murray, *The Devil and Mr. Duncan*, 229.
31. Metlakatla Indian Community, Constitution and By-Laws, Annette Islands Reserve, Alaska, Article I, Jurisdiction, 1919.
32. Moser, "The Salmon and Salmon Fisheries of Alaska," 66.
33. Moser, "The Salmon and Salmon Fisheries in Alaska," 66.

34. Hinckley, *Canoe Rocks*, 386.

35. Price, *Great Father in Alaska*, 79.

36. Case and Voluck, *Alaska Natives*, 65.

37. *Alaska Pacific Fisheries v. United States*, No. 212, December 9, 1918, argued in front of the United States Supreme Court.

38. Case and Voluck, *Alaska Natives*, 9.

39. Case and Voluck, *Alaska Natives*, 9.

40. "Metlakahtla Indian Fishing Rights Upheld," *Pacific Fisherman*, April 1917, 16.

41. Radke, *Pacific American Fisheries*, 125.

42. *Territory of Alaska v. Annette Island Packing Company*, 289 F. 671–73 (9th Cir. 1923). Also included was a stipulation to purchase lumber from the Indians at market value, including boxes for the shipping of salmon cans.

43. American Trust Company, "Monthly Review," no. 7, March 15, 1922, 230.

44. U.S. Department of Commerce, Bureau of Fisheries, "Report of the U.S. Commissioner of Fisheries, 1922," Document No. 913 (Washington DC: U.S. Government Printing Office, 1923), 39–42.

45. June Allen, "A President's Ill-Fated Trek to Alaska," *SitNews*, Ketchikan, July 23, 2003, http://www.sitnews.net/JuneAllen/Harding/072303_warren _harding.html.

46. "President Harding Visit in Alaska," *The Alaska Fisherman*, 1923, 1.

47. "President Harding Visit in Alaska," 1.

48. Allen, "A President's Ill-Fated Trek to Alaska."

49. The term "fish trust" was used by critics to condemn the absentee canneries that had a hold on the fisheries, but it grew in prominence through the Native-published newspaper *The Alaska Fisherman*. One example comes from "Native Fishermen Vigorously Protest Reservations," *The Alaska Fisherman*, February 1923, 1.

50. Paul, *Then Fight for It*, 36–37.

51. Murray, *The Devil and Mr. Duncan*, 320.

52. Mitchell, *Sold American*, 277.

53. Hosmer, *American Indians*.

54. Berkhofer, *White Man's Indian*, 56.

55. Hosmer, *American Indians*, 219.

56. Hosmer, *American Indians*, 224.

4. FROM FJORDS TO GLACIERS

1. "National Landmark Nomination: Kake Cannery," United States Department of the Interior, National Park Service, 1997, https://npgallery.nps.gov /GetAsset/2a648905-b792-4480-9116-f8b62865376f.

2. Petersburg today has a Chief Lott street, but when residents are questioned about this historical figure, no one seems to know about him. Through Tlingit and Haida Genealogy RootsWeb it emerges that he was born about 1859 in the Wrangell Narrows area (Kake territory) and married to Mary Lott.

3. Because the rainforest climate results in rapid deterioration of wood products, many of the totem poles and other artifacts today indicating indigenous presence are not the originals but carefully crafted duplicates from Native artists.

4. U.S. Bureau of Fisheries, *Pacific Salmon Fisheries*, Merchant Marine and Fisheries, 1938.

5. *Congressional Record*, 57th Cong. 2nd Sess., House Report on Fisheries of Alaska, 1903, p. 1089.

6. Pat Roppel, "Southeast History: Petersburg's First Cannery," *Capital City Weekly*.com, originally printed February 9, 2011.

7. I am not sure if "Paul" was a first or last name, but the surname is common among the Tlingit. The Trade and Manufacturing Act covered forestlands to make sure the timber was not exploited by big companies but instead only by homesteaders. The requirement was to improve the land through building livable structures. The act was adopted by Alaska in 1891.

8. August Buschmann, "Peter Thams Buschmann Life History," paper presented to the Norwegian Commercial Club in Seattle, Washington, 1941.

9. Bower, *Alaska Fishery and Fur-Seal Industries* (1925), 358.

10. Alaska Historical Society, "August Buschmann Speaks," blog post, July 5, 2013, alaskahistoricalsociety.org/tag/Petersburg.

11. By 1900 the APA had combined several canning operations and controlled two-thirds of the salmon canning on the West Coast. Donald H. Dyal, "Alaska Packers Association," Texas Digital Library, https://ttu-ir.tdl.org/handle/2346/47365?show%20full2local-attribute.de.

12. The APA *Star* fleet refers to a group of sailing ships that were at the disposal of APA canneries to take cargo back and forth from Alaska to other parts of the West Coast. They were named the *Star of India*, *Star of Norway*, *Star of Russia*, and so on. The *Star of Greenland* is featured in the photograph gallery.

13. Duncan, quoted in Hosmer, *American Indians*, 206; Cooley, *Politics and Conservation*.

14. See National Park Service, https://www.nps.gov/articles/aleu-mobley-ch-4-pt-1.htm.

15. Alaska Historical Society, "August Buschmann Speaks."

16. Roppel, "Southeast History: Petersburg's First Cannery."

17. Roppel, "Southeast History: Petersburg's First Cannery."

18. Moser, "Alaska Salmon Investigations in 1900 and 1901."
19. Roy Bean of Kake, interview, in "The Southeast Alaska Fishery: Interviews with Men and Women Engaged in Commercial Fishing, 1913–1978," tapes in author's possession.
20. David Arnold, interview with author regarding his book about the Southeast Alaska salmon fishery, June 2010.
21. Arnold, *Fisherman's Frontier*, 131, repeated in Thornton, *Haa Leelk'w Has Aani Saaxu'*.
22. Thornton, *Haa Leelk'w Has Aani Saax'u*, xii.
23. Arnold, *Fisherman's Frontier*, 108.
24. White, *Evolution of Culture*.
25. Alaska Historical Society, "August Buschmann Speaks," AHS blog online, July 2013.
26. Alaska Historical Society, "August Buschmann Speaks."
27. Kutchin, *Report on the Salmon Fisheries of Alaska, 1903* (1904), 2.
28. Jones, *Report of Alaska Investigations in 1914*.
29. Couture, "Leverage Legitimacy," 19–20. Natural resource economist Richard A. Cooley intimates that such corruption was present, especially in the late 1920s, but does not indict any particular hatchery.
30. Kutchin, *Report on the Salmon Fisheries*; Bower, "Fish Cultures in Alaska," 66–68; Cobb, "Fishing Grounds and History of Fishing in Alaska," 247–53, in Cobb, *Pacific Salmon Fisheries*.
31. Alaska Historical Society, "August Buschmann Speaks."
32. Semmingsen, *Norway to America*.
33. Quoted in Arnold, *Fisherman's Frontier*, 126; Cooley, *Politics and Conservation*, 94–95.
34. Oscar Otness, quoted in Arnold, *Fisherman's Frontier*, 131; discussions with fisherman John Hillman, captain of the *Johnnie-O*, Hoonah, Alaska, July 1990.
35. Although there was a mutual and cooperative relationship between the Native fishermen and cannery workers, that did not hold true for the fishermen in general on a cross-cultural level. Interviews with Jake White, retired purse seine fleet captain, Hoonah, July 1990, and Embert James of Kuiu Island, June 2017; James was especially vocal about the competition between the Native fishermen and those he believed were interlopers.
36. White, *It's Your Misfortune*.
37. Arnold, *Fishermen's Frontier*, 138–39.
38. Embert James, interview, June 2017.
39. Arnold, *Fishermen's Frontier*, 140.

40. Moser, "The Salmon and Salmon Fisheries of Alaska: Report of the Operations of the United States Fish Commission Steamer Albatross for the Year Ending June 30, 1898," 23–24.
41. *San Francisco Daily News*, quoted in Jones, *Report of Alaska Investigations in 1914*, 7–8; W. T. Lopp, "Native Labor in Alaskan Fisheries," *Pacific Fisherman*, November 1914.
42. Jones, *Report of Alaska Investigations in 1914*, 23–24.
43. U.S. Department of Commerce, Annual Report of the Secretary of Commerce, 1915, 117; *Pacific Fisherman*, January 1915, 11.
44. Freeburn, *Silver Years*, 9.

5. SALMON AND CORPORATE CAPITALISM

1. Haycox, *Alaska, an American Colony*, 221.
2. As noted in the preceding chapter, the APA controlled most West Coast salmon; see note 11 to chapter 4.
3. Martin, *Banana Cowboys*.
4. Atwood, *Frontier Politics*.
5. U.S. House of Representatives, *Salmon Fisheries of Alaska Reports of Special Agents Pracht, Luttrell, and Murray*, 406, quoted in Arnold, *Fisherman's Frontier*, 59.
6. Atwood, *Frontier Politics*, 263.
7. James Wickersham, "Address to the People of Alaska," copied into the Diary of James Wickersham, Alaska, July 23rd 1916 to March 4th 1917. Election of 1916, Wickersham Family, Historical Collections, Alaska State Library, Juneau, MS 107, box 4 (Diary 2).
8. James Wickersham Diary, entry for August 20–28, 1912, Alaska History Library.
9. President William Howard Taft spent time and energy on Alaska issues, including setting aside lands for the Haida in 1912.
10. Atwood, *Frontier Politics*, 348–50.
11. *Congressional Record*, 63rd Cong. 3rd Sess., 698–708.
12. James Wickersham Diary, entry for July 12, 1915, Alaska Historical Library.
13. Atwood, *Frontier Politics*, 362.
14. Prucha, *Great Father*, 264.
15. James Wickersham Diary, additional entry for October 11, 1915.
16. *Alaska Pacific Fisheries v. Territory of Alaska*, 249 US 53, Juneau, 1919.
17. The language in judicial proceedings might be difficult to understand for ay readers. In *Alaska Pacific Fisheries v. Alaska* (1919) the United States Supreme

Court refused to make a ruling because "when a case involving constitutional as well as other issues is taken from the District Court for Alaska to the Circuit Court of Appeals for the Ninth Circuit, the judgment of the latter court is not reviewable in the Court by writ of error, but only by certiorari." In other words, a case cannot be brought to the Supreme Court based solely on the appellant's claim that the original court made a mistake, but instead can only be reviewed by this higher court if they agree to hear the case. If they do not, the case stands based on the last court's judgment. At *prima facie* the cannery owner would have been hard-pressed to prove that his constitutional rights had been undermined based on taxation of his salmon harvest.

18. *Alaska Pacific Fisheries v. Territory of Alaska*, 249 US 53, Juneau, 1919.
19. Kirk, "Labor Forces of the Alaska Coast." This article is an ideal snapshot of the times and mirrors many of the themes of this narrative. Kirk carefully explains the ethnic diversity by showing that most workers were Alaska Native and Chinese in 1915, but there were also Hawaiians, Mexicans, and African Americans working for the canneries across Alaska.
20. Cooley, *Politics and Conservation*, 103. It was known at this time that there was a trading relationship between Japan, Siberia, and the Kurile Islands. The subject of Japanese canneries in Siberia during this early period appears to be a topic for more historical research.
21. *Pacific Fisherman*, September 1920, 21.
22. Higham, *Strangers in the Land*, 222.
23. The Bolshevik or October Revolution took place in 1917 when a group of Bolsheviks led an armed insurrection in Petrograd, resulting in the overthrow of the aristocratic autocracy. This was a shock to the world and turned the course of World War I.
24. Higham, *Strangers in the Land*, 226.
25. Kazin and McCartin, *Americanism*, 84.
26. Allen, *Spirit*, 3–5.
27. "Our Platform," *Ketchikan Alaska Chronicle*, July 19, 1919.
28. Edward Morrissey, "First editorial page for the Ketchikan Alaska Chronicle," July 19, 1919.
29. Pearl Buck's classic and Pulitzer Prize–winning *The Good Earth* is an excellent fiction narrative depicting China in pre–World War I times, demonstrating the class system.
30. W. M. Shields, "A Historical Sketch," *The Thlinget* (Sitka, Alaska) 1, no. 8 (March 1909): 1.
31. Hope, *Founders*.

32. Beatrice Yamamota-Pitt, interview, in "Persons Engaged in Fishing for Canneries" Southeast Alaska, *Pacific Fisherman* 12, no. 1 (January 1913): 55, speaking of her grandfather's settlement in the Tlingit village of Angoon.

33. William Paul, "Candidates for the Legislature, Argument against Wm. L. Paul," *Alaska Fisherman* (Ketchikan, Alaska), October 1924.

34. Metcalfe, *In Sisterhood*, 15.

35. Drucker, *Native Brotherhoods*, 29. This sentiment concerning the importance of the ANS was often noted in the ANB meeting procedural narratives.

36. Drucker, *Native Brotherhoods*, 29.

37. Beverly, "The Alaska Fisherman," 2–11.

38. The Alaska Fisheries: Hearings on HR 2394 Before the Subcommittee of the Committee on the Merchant Marine and Fisheries on Fish and Fish Hatcheries, Pt. 2, 67th Cong. 2d. Sess., 93–100 (1922).

39. Alaska Fisheries Hearings, 1922.

40. Alaska Fisheries Hearings, 1922.

41. Haycox, *Alaska, an American Colony*, 239.

42. The 1915 Citizenship Act allowed Alaska Natives local voting rights if they could prove they had disavowed all tribal cleavages and lived like a "white man." They also needed seven non-Native witnesses to sign the application and then have it verified by a school teacher. Although this was stringent, many went through the steps and paperwork to qualify. For more on how this applied to voting and political campaigns in Southeast Alaska, see Purvis, *Drive of Civilization*, 69–70.

43. *Juneau Daily Empire*, April 14, 1924, 1.

44. The *Juneau Daily Empire* article was signed "A Citizen."

45. *Alaska Fisherman*, February 1924, 5, 7.

46. William Paul Sr., *Alaska Fisherman*, March 1924, 6.

47. Paul, *Then Fight for It*, 28.

48. "Statement of William L. Paul, Wrangell, Alaska, Representing the Native Fishermen of Southeastern Alaska," Subcommittee of the Committee on the Merchant Marine and Fisheries on Fish and Fish Hatcheries, House of Representatives, Sixty-Seventh Congress (January 17, 1922), 94.

49. William Paul, *Alaska Fisherman*, September 1923, 3.

50. "Hoover Denounces Fisheries Charges," *New York Times*, April 28, 1924, 1.

51. Case and Voluck, *Alaska Natives*, 87–88.

52. Cooley, *Politics and Conservation*, 125–26.

53. Cooley, *Politics and Conservation*, 125–26.

54. House Committee on Merchant Marine and Fisheries, "Alaskan Canneries," 71 Cong. 3 sess. Pt. 1, 56, 1923.

55. "Sourdoughs Had a Great Time in Seattle," *Dawson Daily News*, January 7, 1921.

56. Taylor, "Well-Thinking Men and Women," 366.

57. Paul, *Then Fight for It*, 36.

58. Louis Paul, "Statesmanship," *Alaska Fisherman*, May 1924.

59. Henry O'Malley was commissioner of fisheries during this tumultuous period and fluctuated in his opinion by stating that artificial propagation (hatcheries) were not effective in supporting fishery reserves. He regularly butted heads with Sutherland and William Paul Sr.

60. Paul, *Then Fight for It*, 37.

61. *Congressional Record*, 68th Congress, 1st Sess. 5976.

62. William Paul Sr., "The White Bill," *Alaska Fisherman*, April 1924, 16.

63. Purvis, "When Eagle and Raven Fly with the Dove."

64. Morrissey, "Our Platform," *Ketchikan Alaska Chronicle*, July 19, 1919.

65. William Paul Sr., "The White Bill: How Real Alaskans Regard the Latest White Fish Bill," *Alaska Fisherman*, May 1924, 9.

66. William Paul Sr., "The White Fish Bill: Hoover New Duke of Alaska," *Alaska Fisherman*, September 1924.

67. *Congressional Record*, 68th Cong. 1st Sess. 5977.

68. Cooley, *Politics and Conservation*, 123; *Congressional Record*, 68th 1st Sess. P. 7160, 9519–20.

69. Naske and Slotnick, *Alaska*, 97.

70. Paul, *Then Fight for It*, 37.

71. Paul, *Then Fight for It*, 38.

72. Bower, *Alaska Fishery and Fur-Seal Industries in 1923*, 88–89.

73. Crutchfield and Pontecorvo, "The Pacific Salmon Fisheries," 241.

74. Crutchfield and Pontecorvo, "The Pacific Salmon Fisheries," 241.

6. THE IMMIGRANTS ARE NECESSARY

1. Davis, *Social and Cultural Life*, 7.

2. Guimary, *Marumina Trabaho*, 15.

3. "Mob Law in Alaska: How the Chinese Were Driven from the Douglas Island Mines," *New York Times*, August 23, 1886, https://www.nytimes.com/1886/08/24/archives/mob-law-in-alaska-how-the-chinese-were-driven-from-the-douglas.html.

4. United States Department of the Interior Report on Population and Resources of Alaska, 54.

5. Hinckley, "Prospectors, Profits, and Prejudice," 59.

6. Friday, *Organizing Asian-American Labor*, 95.

7. Friday, *Organizing Asian-American Labor*, 100, 103.

8. *Personal Justice Denied*, Report of the Commission on Wartime Relocation and Internment of Civilians, 37.

9. U.S. Congress, House, Committee on Immigration and Naturalization, "Japanese Immigration," 1023.

10. Takaki, *Strangers*, 209.

11. Hosokawa, *Nisei*, 108.

12. The Meiji Restoration period (1868–1912) marked a dramatic break with the feudal system including the disintegration of the shogunates (war lord fiefdoms) and the phasing out of the Samurai class in favor of development in the Western economic model. The political slogan emphasized Western learning and Eastern ethics. As with all major social disruptions, the status quo was shaken up in terms of economic systems, social relationships, and national character, and yet the cultural roots lingered.

13. Takaki, *Strangers*, 42, 43.

14. Takaki, *Strangers*, 46.

15. The term "racialized" is charged with meaning and must be carefully used to be exacting and objective. More and more as this story develops, the term is applicable and is defined as: any individual or group actions (including words) that negatively focus on a certain group of people, whether they be Native American, Latino, Asian, or Euro-American (to name only a few ethnic groups pertinent to this narrative). See Sears, Sidanius, and Bobo, *Racialized Politics*.

16. U.S. Commission on Immigration, *Japanese and Other Immigrant Races* 393.

17. Roosevelt, "National Life and Character," *Sewanee Review*, August 1894, quoted in Takaki, *Strangers*, 102.

18. The gentlemen's agreement of 1907 was a pact made between the Japanese government and President Theodore Roosevelt. The Japanese agreed to issue passports only to non-labor migrants, and the president said he would attempt to reduce school discrimination in California.

19. Quoted in *Oyama v. California*, 332 US 633. 654, footnote 4 (1948); *In re Naka's License*, 9 Alaska 1 (1934), discussed in Deloria and Wilkins, *Legal Universe*.

20. Takaki, *Strangers*, 184.

21. Takaki, *Strangers*, 184, 518.

22. Reischauer, *The Japanese*, 214.

23. Socialization or the process of learning societal norms and customs is engrained even if one rejects the values as an adult because they have been internalized. If one's upbringing has provided a framework to live by, it becomes a support system and point of reference in difficult circumstances. Gergen and Gergen, *Social Psychology*, 358.

24. Yanagisako, *Transforming the Past*, 6.
25. Bob Sam, caretaker of the Sitka cemeteries and cultural bearer, told me of the graves he has found that have either Chinese or Japanese writing. The Chinese ones are few because it was believed that the soul could not rest unless the bones were transported back to the homeland. There are, however, gravesites that are distinctly Chinese or Japanese in Southeast Alaska, but Bob Sam says they are difficult to find because they are overgrown with weeds.
26. Chinese workers coming to the United States or Canada believed that for a comfortable afterlife, their bones must be returned to the mother country. For obvious reasons, this rarely took place.
27. In 1889 San Francisco enacted a law against shipping opium to the Pacific Northwest and Alaska. Other local laws were also made in addition to international agreements. These laws were ignored, and there was little oversight on the seas to enforce any such laws.
28. Friday, *Organizing Asian-American Labor*, 55.
29. Ship list from the *Star of India*, in Cobb, "Report on the Fisheries of Alaska," 1907, 19.
30. Kanazawa, *Sushi and Sourdough*, 194, 184.
31. Friday, *Organizing Asian-American Labor*, 185.
32. U.S. Commission on Immigration, *Reports, Emigration and Immigration, 1907–1910*, 407.
33. Mason and Guimary, "Asian Labor Contractors," 391.
34. Pat Roppel, "Southeast History: Opium at Canneries and other Narcotic Use," *Capital City Weekly*, December 8, 2010, http://www.capitalcityweekly .com/stories/120810/bus_751896243.shtml.
35. Friday, *Organizing Asian-American Labor*, 178.
36. Cargo list from APA *Star of India*, 1909.
37. Alaska Historical Society, Alaska Cannery Project, Alaska Cannery History, http://alaskahistoricalsociety.org/category/alaska-canneries.
38. Cobb, *Pacific Salmon Fisheries*, 452.
39. Takaki, *Strangers*, 47.
40. David Kiffer, pers. comm., Ketchikan, June 2017.
41. David Kiffer, "Tatsuda's Grocery Celebrates Centennial," *SitNews: Stories in the News*, Ketchikan, Alaska, May 19, 2016.
42. Kan, *Russian-American Photographer*, 22–23; and Kei Tanaka, "Japanese Picture Marriages," 115–35. Tanaka offers several cross-cultural examples including those in Washington state and Alaska.
43. Kan, *Russian-American Photographer*.
44. Kan, *Russian-American Photographer*.

45. Kan, *Russian-American Photographer*.

46. Friday, *Organizing Asian-American Labor*, 120. Friday has an excellent analysis of Japanese employment in the canneries and ethnic discrimination. Of
interest are his citations from journalist James Omura, who worked for the
canneries and was shut out by those in power who did not want him to start
trouble. Omura does refer to himself as militant.

47. Friday, *Organizing Asian-American Labor*, 119.

48. Christopher, *The Japanese Mind*, 101–3.

49. U.S. Immigration Commission, "Immigration in Industries," 379.

50. Reischauer, *The Japanese*, 137.

51. Takaki, *Strangers*, 182.

52. Frank Chesley, "Goon Dip," HistoryLink.org, May 26, 2009, www
.historylink.org/File/9026.

53. Takaki, *Strangers*, 168.

54. Takaki, *Strangers*, 182, 183.

55. Libby, McNeill & Libby records, "Summary: 1916–1960," University of
Washington Archives, Special Collections.

56. Friday, *Organizing Asian-American Labor*, 162.

57. Cobb, *Pacific Salmon Fisheries*, 448.

58. Norm Israelson, whose family has a longtime connection with the Yakutat
cannery, talks about his work on the Yakutat and Southern Railroad hauling
fish and people as his father did before him. Norm Israelson, pers. comm,
January 2017.

59. Thomas, *Picture Man*, 42.

60. Thomas, *Picture Man*, 41.

61. Thomas, *Picture Man*, 60.

62. Thomas, *Picture Man*, 60.

63. Thomas, *Picture Man*, 60.

64. The Alaska Japanese project contains a few transcripts but all the tapes. Both
were used in this research.

65. Thomas, *Picture Man*, 60.

66. Inouye, Hoshiko, and Heshiki, "Alaska's Japanese Pioneers," 42.

67. Inouye, Hoshiko, and Heshiki, "Alaska's Japanese Pioneers," 20.

68. David Kiffer, a Ketchikan resident and historian, mentioned that contemporary Japanese descendants had no idea about a Japanese school nor the
continuation of the language. For the most part, they had been told that they
were not to speak the language. David Kiffer, pers. comm., June 2017. His
descriptions were in response to my request to interview the local people
with whom he grew up.

69. Inouye, Hoshiko, and Heshiki, "Alaska's Japanese Pioneers," 30.

70. Inouye, Hoshiko, and Heshiki, "Alaska's Japanese Pioneers," 30.

71. Inouye, Hoshiko, and Heshiki, "Alaska's Japanese Pioneers," 10–11.

72. Inouye, Hoshiko, and Heshiki, "Alaska's Japanese Pioneers," 10–11.

73. Interview between Tad, Heshiki, and Inouye, Alaska's Japanese Pioneers Research Project, 1990, transcripts from the projects on file at the University of Alaska Archives, 1990 (separate copy from the archive selection).

74. Eric Morrison, Tlingit leader from Sitka, pers. comm., March 2007.

75. Ronald Inouye, Alaska's Japanese Pioneers Research Project, transcribed interviews from Seattle Washington, October 1991. Typed transcripts from the Oral History Office, copies in the Archive records, University of Alaska, Anchorage, 14.

76. Inouye, Hoshiko, and Heshiki, "Alaska's Japanese Pioneers," 46.

77. Inouye, Hoshiko, and Heshiki, "Alaska's Japanese Pioneers," 46.

78. Inouye, Hoshiko, and Heshiki, "Alaska's Japanese Pioneers," 46.

79. Inouye, transcribed oral histories, 23–24.

80. Inouye, Hoshiko, and Heshiki, "Alaska's Japanese Pioneers," 46–47.

81. Inouye, Alaska's Japanese Pioneers Research Project, transcribed oral histories, typewritten, 17.

82. Inouye, Alaska Japanese Pioneers Research Project, oral histories, 17.

83. Inouye, Alaska Japanese Pioneers Research Project, oral histories, 44.

84. Inouye, Alaska Japanese Pioneers Research Project, oral histories, 28.

85. Inouye, Alaska Japanese Pioneers Research Project, oral histories, 33.

86. U.S. Immigration Commission, "Immigrants in Industries," 48–49.

87. *Japanese-American Courier*, June 2, 1928.

88. Bob Wing, "Crossing Race and Nationality: The Racial Formation of Asian-Americans, 1852–1963," *Monthly Review*, December 1, 2005, https://monthlyreview.org/2005/12/01/race-and-nationality-the-racial-formation-of-asian-americans-1852-1965/.

7. THE RISING VOICES OF ALASKA NATIVES

1. June Allen, "Loring: Once a Serious Rival to Ketchikan," *Stories in the News*, Ketchikan, Alaska, September 14, 2002. For more information on Tlingit names and territories see Thornton, *Haa Leelk'w Has Aani Saax'u.*

2. In Tlingit property law, even if the area is used primarily for a seasonal fish camp, it is still "owned" by certain clans, and when the land is usurped it is the equivalent of theft.

3. Fred Paul and Judson Brown, interviews, in *The Land Is Ours*, documentary produced by Laurence A. Goldin, January 14, 1997.

4. The fish trap situation was long and drawn out, lasting until Alaska achieved statehood. During the 1930s Tony Dimond introduced several bills to limit fish traps in Alaskan waters. The lines were drawn between residents and non-residents with the latter populated by the absentee cannery companies. The cannery companies defended the traps by saying that salmon would be wasted without the efficiency of the devices. A. W. Brindle, president of the Ward Cove Canning Company, testified in front of Congress that the fish would overcrowd and pollute the streams. He blamed the pressure to abolish the fish traps on "professional agitators and radicals" sent to the north to stir up trouble. U.S. House, Merchant Marine and Fisheries Committee, *Fish Traps in Alaska*, Hearings on H.R. 4254 and H.R. 8213, 74th Cong. 2nd Sess., 193–95.

5. Atwood, *Frontier Politics*, 304.

6. Wickersham, "Slaughter of the Silver Horde," 243.

7. William Paul, "The Canning Industry of Alaska," *Alaska Fisherman*, March 1925, 14.

8. *Alaska Fisherman*, January 1924, 1.

9. *Alaska Daily Empire*, July 13, 1921.

10. *Alaska Fisherman*, April 1924, 1.

11. Haycox, *Alaska, an American Colony*, 244.

12. William L. Paul Sr., "A Paper for the Common Folk Treating Subjects of Labor and Fishing and Taxes without Fear or Favor, Depending for Its Life on the Support from the Little Fellow," typewritten copy in author's possession, provided by Ben Paul, undated.

13. *Alaska Fisherman*, May 1923, 1–2.

14. Mangusso, "Anthony J. Dimond," 250.

15. Mangusso, "Anthony J. Dimond," 250.

16. Naske and Slotnick, *Alaska*, 90.

17. When the copper mining interests moved into south-central Alaska, near the Cordova area, they seized land from the Ahtna Athabascans without legal means. The Kennecott Mine was built on that land. The issue has never been successfully addressed. On the Alaska Syndicate in the early 1900s, see https://en.wikipedia.org/wiki/Alaska_Syndicate.

18. *Alaska Fishermen*, October 1928, 2.

19. *Alaska Fisherman*, November 1928, 1.

20. Senate Report, no. 462, 72d Cong. 1st Sess. (1932), 4.

21. Senate Hearing on S. 1196, 7.

22. Lipps, "Laws and Regulations."

23. Brown and Everson, *Documents*, "Minutes of the 1929 ANB Convention," Wickersham 1929 speech.

24. Memorandum of March 16, 1934, from Paul E. Gordon to John Collier, Plaintiff's Exhibit No. 114 of the records of the *Tlingit and Haida Indians of Alaska v. United States*.

25. Letter to Harold Ickes from Will Rogers, March 8, 1935, in 74th Cong. 1st Sess., 1935, H. Rep. 621, 3. The role of the Alaska Department of Education and Paul Gordon cannot be underestimated. Because the education officials were tasked to "control" the Natives, they had much to say about the state of affairs. This influence stemmed from the early missionaries and is an indication of the paternalistic treatment of indigenous peoples.

26. Naske and Slotnick, *Alaska*, 109.

27. Cooley, *Politics and Conservation*, 49.

28. "Louis F. Paul Makes Reply to Hambler over ANB Controversy," *Alaska Fishing News* (Ketchikan), February 5, 1936.

29. Testimony of Frank Peratrovich in Alaska Statehood Hearings Before the Committee on Interior and Insular Affairs, United States Senate, Eighty First Cong, 2d Sess. On HR 331, an Act to Provide For Admission of Alaska into the Union, April 1950. Of interest, Winton Arnold testified during the same hearings and was against statehood because of his position in the cannery industry (p. 286). The testimony gave the history of the problem during the 1930s.

30. Haycox, *Alaska, an American Colony*, 252.

31. Testimony of Frank Peratrovich in "To Conduct a Study and Investigation of the Various Questions and Problems Relating to the Territory of Alaska," Hearings on H. Res. 236 Before the Committee of Territories, 79th Cong. 1st Sess. 33–37, 1940. This was only one of the venues to hear Peratrovich and Johnson's words about the BIA and possible Alaska reservations. It was a common topic in ANB and ANS meetings during this time period.

32. Dauenhauer and Dauenhauer, *Haa Kusteeyi, Our Culture*, 311–12.

33. Metcalfe, *In Sisterhood*, 78.

34. Paul, *Then Fight for It*, 79–80.

35. Jake White, pers. comm., Hoonah, Alaska, July 1990. Mr. White, a purse seine captain as well, was speaking of his father's generation.

36. Act of June 18, 1934, 48 Stat. 984; Readjustment of Indian Affairs: Hearings on H.R. 7902 before the Committee on Indian Affairs, 73d Cong. 2d Sess., 498–99, 1934.

37. Paul, *Then Fight for It*, 79–80.

38. Mitchell, *Sold American*, 241.

39. Atwood, *Frontier Politics*, 381–82.

40. Mitchell, *Sold American*, 237–38; the Rasmuson family goes back to the turn of the century when the first Rasmusons, Swedish immigrants, were missionaries in Yakutat.

41. *Anchorage Times*, June 10, 1936; Wickersham Diary, June 5, 1936.

42. United States House of Representatives, Committee on the Merchant Marine and Fisheries, *Alaskan Fisheries Hearings*, part 3 (1939), 710, 745.

43. Paul, *Then Fight for It*, 7.

44. Dauenhauer and Dauenhauer, *Haa Kusteeyi, Our Culture*, 517.

45. Ben Paul, William Paul's grandson, interview with author, 2007. Ben related to me that at the time William Paul had come under a continual barrage of slings and arrows and believed no matter what evidence he turned up, he would have been a condemned man. He was "tired," Ben said, and added, "None of us were there. We don't really know what happened."

8. THE ALASKEROS

1. Cuba was the initial target for this "war," and upon Spanish defeat, Guam and Puerto Rico were ceded to the United States, Cuba became a protectorate (for the time being), and the Philippines was bought.

2. McPherson, "Americanism against American Empire," 172.

3. Sterngass, *Filipino Americans*, 28.

4. Remini, *Short History*, 192.

5. Salamanca, *Filipino Reaction*, 28.

6. Sterngass, *Filipino Americans*, 41.

7. Viernes, "Alaskeros History," 128.

8. Sterngass, *Filipino Americans*, 13.

9. Bodnar, *The Transplanted*, 107.

10. Crystal Fresco, "Cannery Workers' and Farm Laborers' Union, 1933–39: Their Strength in Unity," Seattle Civil Rights and Labor History Project, 1999, http://depts.washington.edu/civilr/cwflu.htm.

11. Sterngass, *Filipino Americans*, 45.

12. Fujita-Rony, *American Workers*, 104.

13. Bulosan, *America Is in the Heart*, 101.

14. Erik Luthy, "Victorio Velasco: Pioneer of Filipino-American Journalism," Seattle Civil Rights and Labor History Project, 2006, https://depts.washington.edu/civilr/victorio_velasco.htm#note6. Originally from Diary, Victorio A. Velasco Collection, University of Washington Archives, Special Collections, Seattle.

15. Buchholdt, *Filipinos in Alaska*, 50–51.

16. Corinne Strandjord, "Filipino Resistance to Anti-Miscegenation Laws in Washington State," The Great Depression in Washington State Project, Civil Rights and Labor History Consortium, http://depts.washington.edu /depress/filipino_anti_miscegenation.shtml.

17. "Race Reconciled," in "Living Anthropologically," https:// livinganthropologically.com/biological-anthropology/race-reconciled -debunks-race/.

18. Fujita-Rony, *American Workers*, 16.

19. Buchholdt, *Filipinos in Alaska*, 52–53.

20. Guimary and Masson, "Getting There," 104.

21. Guimary and Masson, "Getting There," 104.

22. Guimary, *Marumina Trabaho*, 91.

23. Santa Ana, "Emotional Labor of Racialization."

24. Santa Ana, "Emotional Labor of Racialization."

25. Buaken, "Where Is the Heart of America?" 410.

26. Friday, *Organizing Asian-American Labor*, 123.

27. Professor David E. J. Ramos, author of *We Have Not Stopped Trembling Yet: Letters to My Filipino-Athabascan Family*, interview with author.

28. Liljeblad, "The Filipinos," 4.

29. Velasco, "Alaska—A Filipino Refuge," 439.

30. Velasco, "Alaska—A Filipino Refuge," 439.

31. National Park Service, Stedman-Thomas Historic District, Ketchikan, Alaska, https://www.nps.gov/places/stedman-thomas-historic-district.htm.

32. Buchholdt, *Filipinos in Alaska*, 133.

33. Masson and Guimary, "Asian Labor Contractors," 386, originally from an interview with Ponce Torres, December 7, 1977. Torres, like Chris Mensalvas, was a major player in union activities in Seattle and Ketchikan.

34. Liljeblad, "The Filipinos," 4.

35. Marie Olson, pers. comm, Sitka, Alaska, September 2008.

36. Friday, "Orchestrating Race," 1, 3, 4.

37. David Kiffer, pers. comm., Ketchikan, June 2017.

38. Julie Byrne, "Roman Catholics and Immigration in Nineteenth-Century America," National Humanities Center, November 2000, http:// nationalhumanitiescenter.org/tserve/nineteen/nkeyinfo/nromcath.htm.

39. Fujita-Rony, *American Workers*, 97.

40. *Fictive kin* is the anthropological term for those people not related by blood or marriage who take on the functions of a family member.

41. Revilla, "Brown and Proud," 119.

42. Scharlin and Villanueva, *Philip Vera Cruz*, 94.

43. Fujita-Rony, *American Workers*, 196–98.

44. Fujita-Rony, *American Workers*, 197.

45. Fujita-Rony, *American Workers*, 97.

46. Fujita-Rony, *American Workers*, 104.

47. Fujita-Rony, *American Workers*, 104.

48. Fujita-Rony, *American Workers*, 104.

49. Cobb, *Pacific Salmon Fisheries*, 452.

50. "Murder in Gambling House," *Ketchikan Alaska Chronicle*, June 18, 1920.

51. "Challenge from Beeble Cannery," *Ketchikan Alaska Chronicle*, June 7, 1922.

52. Obert Orrenstad, pers. comm., June 2007.

53. Joy Hamilton Craig, interview with author, Ketchikan, August 2016.

54. Kim and Mejia, *Filipinos in America*, 31.

55. Velasco, "The Philippines," 10.

56. *Reports of the Proceedings of the American Federation of Labor*, Washington DC: Law Report Publishing, 1928, 217.

57. Scharlin and Villanueva, *Philip Vera Cruz*, xx.

58. Green, *World of the Workers*, 161.

59. Green, *World of the Workers*, 161.

60. Brian Grijalva, "Organizing Unions: The 30's and 40's," Communism in Washington State: History and Memory Project, https://depts.washington.edu/labhist/cpproject/grijalva.shtml.

61. Chris D. Mensalvas, interview by Apolonia Buyagawan, University of Washington, Special Collections, digital archives, 1974, https://digitalcollections.lib.washington.edu/digital/collection/ohc/id/243.

62. The AFL and CIO are federations of smaller unions. Historically, when a small union joined forces with either the AFL or CIO, which had different politics and philosophies, these bodies were said to be affiliated with either the AFL or CIO. In 1955 the AFL and CIO merged.

63. Burma, *Spanish Speaking Groups*, 53.

64. *Ketchikan Alaska Chronicle*, November 11, 1921.

65. Fujita-Rony, *American Workers*, 164–66. Professor Chris Friday, pers. comm., Western Washington University, September 2007.

66. Baldoz, *Third Asiatic Invasion*.

67. Posadas, *Filipino Americans*, 29–30.

68. Tydings-McDuffie Bill 1934, *Congressional Record*, 73rd Congress, 2nd Sess., 1934, Vol. 78, Part 12, Public Law no. 127.

69. "Petition to President Roosevelt, 1934," *Philippines Mail*, October 8, 1934.

70. Viernes, "Alaskeros History," 133.

71. Buchholdt, *Filipinos in Alaska*, 53.

1. "Franklin D. Roosevelt's First Inaugural Address, 1933," 368.
2. Cobb, *Pacific Salmon Fisheries*, 446.
3. Arnold, *Fisherman's Frontier*, 14.
4. Arnold, *Fisherman's Frontier*, 14.
5. William Paul, "Politics vs. Business." In response to an editorial published on October 3, 1924, in the *Alaska Weekly*, published in Seattle, Washington. Reprinted and rebutted in the *Alaska Fisherman*, November 1924.
6. "So-Called Alaska Fishermen's Union," *Alaska Fisherman*, March 1925.
7. *Alaska Fisherman*, March 1925.
8. Naske and Slotnick, *Alaska*, 111.
9. Bernstein, *Turbulent Years*, 217.
10. Soboleff notes from November 1933 ANB meeting. These are copies of handwritten notes. William and Louis Paul believed that the Canadian Natives fared better in their fisheries, but in reality based on the repressive Indian Act, they had few rights. Canadian historian Dianne Newell came to the same conclusion in her book *The Development of the Pacific Salmon-Canning Industry* (1989).
11. Soboleff notes from November 1933.
12. Arnold, *Fisherman's Frontier*, 149; Drucker, *Native Brotherhoods*, 58.
13. The Seafarers International Union was a huge organization and so the question naturally arises: Why would they be interested in a little purse seine union in Southeast Alaska. The answer lies in Alaska's geopolitical proximity to the Soviet Union. There was actual interest in trade with the closed-off country, but beyond this there was also a question of national security. As more and more communist elements were part of all unions, there was an interest in spreading that influence and creating a foothold. Nelson, *Workers on the Waterfront*, 242–43.
14. Drucker, *Native Brotherhoods*, 59.
15. Paul, *Then Fight for It*, 75.
16. Arnold, "Putting Up Fish"; Arnold, extended conversations on how William Paul attacked these issues, June 2009.
17. Most fishermen testimony was in the form of written depositions taken to Congress by representatives such as William Paul Sr. or the secretary of commerce. It was too expensive for fishermen to travel to the other side of the nation.
18. Drucker, *Native Brotherhoods*, 43.
19. Paul, *Then Fight for It*, 75.

20. In 1940 the Alaska Fishermen's Cooperative Association was established under the Cooperative Marketing Act, and the charter members included well-known Native leaders and fishermen such as Frank Price, Peter Simpson, Andrew Hope, S. G. Davis, Frank Booth, Louis Paul, C. Zuboff, Robert Perkins, Ralph Young, William Paul (secretary), and A. J. Wanamaker. It was no surprise that these men were also affiliated with the ANB, many were charter members of the organization, and their wives and daughters were members of the ANS.

21. William Paul, notes from the AMWU (handwritten), Sealaska Heritage Institute Archives.

22. By Laws of Fisherman's Collective Market Agency, Resolutions and Instructions Authorizing Bargaining Agency (enacted by Alaska Native Brotherhood, Alaska Native Sisterhood, and Alaska Fishermen's Cooperative Association), Office of the Secretary, Juneau, Alaska.

23. By Laws of Fisherman's Collective Market Agency, all capitals as in the original document.

24. By Laws of Fisherman's Collective Market Agency.

25. William L. Paul Sr., in his capacity as Grand President, Alaska Native Brotherhood, "Alaska Native Service, Too Proud to Serve: Comment on W. H. Olsen's Proud to Serve," Area Director, Alaska Native Service, Juneau, Alaska, undated but possibly 1944.

26. Paul, "Alaska Native Service."

27. Paul, "Alaska Native Service."

28. Paul, "Alaska Native Service."

29. Klein and Ackerman, *Women and Power*, 262 and in general.

30. Klein and Ackerman, *Women and Power*, 262.

31. Durrenberger and Reichart, *Anthropology of Labor Unions*.

32. Cobble, *Other Women's Movement*, 15.

33. Lamphere, "Bringing the Family"; Tilly, "Paths of Proletarianization."

34. Fish are covered in a protective slime that must be removed, along with the scales, before further processing. Alaska Native women were known as top slimers, a merit of dubious distinction.

35. Alaska Native Sisterhood, Hydaburg, Alaska, 1933. *Oriental* mostly applied to either the Japanese or Chinese and is now a defunct term.

36. Report for the Annual Convention of the Alaska Native Brotherhood in its session in Juneau, November 11, 1933, President of the Alaska Native Sisterhood, Hoonah, Alaska.

37. Report for the Annual Convention of the Alaska Native Brotherhood, November 11, 1933.

38. Even though William Paul Sr. had worked as a BIA agent to disseminate information about the ARA, in the late 1930s he made a notation on the back of a picture of a BIA agent that read "diabolical," referring to the federal organization.

39. United States Department of the Interior, *Alaska's Health: A Survey Report*, compiled by Alaska Health Survey Team (Thomas Parran, Chef), Report for June 2, 1954, 33–34; commonly called the Parran Report.

40. The term "cultural brokers" is appropriate at this point to indicate the role of the women as intermediaries between fishermen, cannery companies, and government, both federal and local. In some meetings it was the women who could speak English fluently, and therefore their roles were indispensable. This is a subject that could be expanded into its own narrative form. See Szasz, *Between Indian and White Worlds*.

41. *Alaska Fishing News* (Ketchikan), April 15, 1940, 6.

42. *Alaska Fishing News*, April 15, 1940.

43. *Alaska Fishing News*, November 27, 1939, 6.

44. *Alaska Fishing News*, November 29, 1943, 3.

45. Letter from William L. Paul Sr. to Bill Paul, January 1944, from the Ben Paul collection.

46. *Alaska Fishing News*, January 1941, 6.

47. Friday, "Competing Communities," 312.

48. *Alaska Fishing News*, June 1941, 1.

49. *Alaska Fishing News*, September 1941, 3. See chapter 10 for more about the Fisheries Board.

50. "Paul Comments on Hearing of Fish Bureau," *Alaska Fishing News*, June 1941, 3.

51. Schairer, "A Survey."

52. "To Conduct a Study and Investigation of the Various Questions and Problems Relating to the Territory of Alaska," Hearings on H. Res. 236 Before the Committee on the Territories.

53. "Without Benefit of Courts or Congress," *Pacific Fisherman*, December 1944.

54. Alaska Native Brotherhood and Alaska Native Sisterhood, "Alaska Fisherman's Cooperative Association," Office of the Secretary, box 81, Juneau, Alaska, no. 209, 1940. Of interest the cover page reads: "Under no circumstances is this document to fall into the hands of CIO or AFL even temporarily."

55. Barrett, "Women's Work," 266.

56. Savage, "Small Places," 131–55.

1. Frank W. Sharp, interview with Charles Mobley for the Fish and Wildlife Service, Angoon, 1999.
2. *Southeast Alaska Salmon Canneries*, documentary produced by John Saballa and Associates, Anacortes, Washington, 1984.
3. Ruiz, *Cannery Women*, 32.
4. Lamphere, "Bringing the Family," 521.
5. Leonardo, "Women's Work."
6. Zavella, *Women's Work*, 100.
7. Friday, "Orchestrating Race," 20.
8. Cruikshank, *Life Lived*, 3.
9. Robert Baines, grandson of Elizabeth Baines, pers. comm.
10. Maria Brooks transcript, "Alaska Women's Oral History Project," Anchorage Community College, 1983.
11. Elizabeth Baines, interview, tape 1, side 1, transcript in Maria Brooks, "Alaska Women's Oral History Project," Anchorage Community College, 1983.
12. Elizabeth Baines interview.
13. Paul, *Then Fight For It*, 43.
14. Koester and Widmark, "By the Words of Thy Mouth." Unfortunately there is little current information about the "movie hall," but it must have been interesting during the time of ethnic segregation.
15. Koester and Widmark, "By the Words of Thy Mouth," 36.
16. UCAPAWA *News*, May 15, 1944, 4.
17. Metcalfe, *In Sisterhood*, 42.
18. UCAPAWA *News*, May 15, 1944, 4.
19. Joseph "Joe" Akagi was born in Japan and lived in Killisnoo. There was a Japanese group who made their homes in Killisnoo. Joe Akagi served in World War II, which is significant because this was the time of the Japanese internment.
20. Metcalfe, *In Sisterhood*, 91–92.
21. Metcalfe, *In Sisterhood*, 92–93.
22. Ruiz, *Cannery Women*, 35. Friday, *Organizing Asian-American Labor*, 118–19.
23. Gruening, *Many Battles*, 418.
24. Amy Hallingstad, *Petersburg Press* (Petersburg, Alaska), September 1948.
25. Philp, *Termination Revisited*, 35.
26. Testimony from Sylvia Lythgoe, in Philp, *Termination Revisited*.
27. Dauenhauer and Dauenhauer, *Haa Kusteeyí, Our Culture*, 271.
28. Fujita-Rony, *American Workers*, 197.

29. Ricardo Worl, son of Rosita Worl and grandson to Bessie Jackson Quinto, interview, in Fujita-Rony, *American Workers*, 197.

30. Buchholdt, *Filipinos in Alaska*, 106.

31. Buchholdt, *Filipinos in Alaska*, 106.

32. Metcalf, *In Sisterhood*, 201.

33. Rosita Worl, pers. comm., April 13, 2012.

34. Subsistence refers to a way of life and must be understood in those terms. Rosita Worl, daughter of Bessie Quinto and an advocate of subsistence rights, testified before Congress in 2002: "Beyond its economic importance, she believed that subsistence played a powerful spiritual role in Native lives. . . . This relationship requires native people to adhere to certain codes of conduct and to treat animals in prescriptive ways to ensure success in future hunts." Arnold, *Fishermen's Frontier*, 179.

35. Dauenhauer and Dauenhauer, *Haa Kusteeyi, Our Culture*, 272.

36. Dauenhauer and Dauenhauer, *Haa Kusteeyi, Our Culture*, 272.

37. Kuokkanen, "Indigenous Economies"; Wolfe and Walker, "Subsistence Economics in Alaska."

38. Zavella, *Women's Work*, 95.

39. Marie Olson, pers. comm., May 2012.

40. Dauenhauer and Dauenhauer, *Haa Kusteeyi, Our Culture*, 464.

41. Dauenhauer and Dauenhauer, *Haa Kusteeyi, Our Culture*, 463.

42. Crystal Fresco, "Cannery Workers' and Farm Laborers' Union, 1933–39: Their Strength in Unity," Seattle Civil Rights and Labor History Project, 1999, http://depts.washington.edu/civilr/cwflu.htm.

43. Fresco, "Cannery Workers.'"

44. *Western Worker*, May 8, 1933.

45. Masson and Guimary, "Asian Labor Contractors."

46. U.S. Bureau of Labor Statistics, *Labor Unionism in American Agriculture*, 218.

47. Guimary, *Marumina Trabaho*, 231.

48. Fresco, "Cannery Workers."

49. Guimary, *Marumina Trabaho*, 205.

50. Victor Nelson-Cisneros, "UCAPAWA and Chicanos in California," 464.

51. UCAPAWA Yearbook, December 1939.

52. Rojo, "Salmon Cannery Workers and the Cannery Industry," *UCAPAWA News*, January 9, 1940, 9–10.

53. Rojo, "Salmon Cannery Workers," 9–10.

54. The certification election is a vote among workers to signify which union they want to belong to in order to form a collective bargaining unit. Once the

vote is tallied, the "winner" becomes the exclusive union for the workers and is expected to bargain in good faith.

55. Friday, "Competing Communities," 317. This information comes from Chris Friday's interview with Rose Dellama. When I spoke with Vicki Ruiz in 2012, she corroborated these ideas and historic details, saying this was true for both California (UCAPAWA outreach) and Alaska.
56. Friday, "Competing Communities," 317.
57. Marguerite Hansen attended the January 1939 UCAPAWA Seattle meeting representing Alaska Local 237 and the "Southern Alaska Cannery Union," no doubt referring to the Council. She attended with her Norwegian-born husband, Ragnar Hansen, who was representing Alaska fishermen. *Voice of the Federation*, January 19, 1939.
58. *Voice of the Federation*, January 19, 1939.
59. Hayes, *Blonde Indian*, 8. The USO was the United Service Organization, founded by FDR in 1941 for troop entertainment.
60. "Win Better Quarters at Libby Plant," *UCAPAWA News*, May 15, 1944, 4.
61. Hayes, *Blonde Indian*, 8.
62. "Win Better Quarters at Libby Plant," *UCAPAWA News*, May 15, 1944, 4.
63. Friday, "Orchestrating Race," 22. The term "government ward" is derived from the trust relationship between the American federal government and indigenous peoples.
64. Friday, "Orchestrating Race," 22.
65. *UCAPAWA News*, May 15, 1944.
66. Friday, "Orchestrating Race," 26.
67. *Alaska Fishing News*, April 10, 1944, 6.
68. Fresco, "Cannery Workers."
69. Fresco, "Cannery Workers."
70. Fresco, "Cannery Workers."
71. Fresco, "Cannery Workers."
72. Friday, "Orchestrating Race."
73. Chris Friday, Western Washington University, pers. comm. (e-mail), June 2012.
74. Fujita-Rony, *American Workers*, 136.
75. Fujita-Rony, *American Workers*, 136.
76. Friday, "Orchestrating Race," 11.
77. *Voice of the Federation*, June 29, 1939, 2–3; December 22, 1938, 3; July 7, 1939, 4–5.
78. *Voice of the Federation*, June 29, 1939, 2–3.
79. *Voice of the Federation*, December 22, 1938, 3.
80. Friday, "Orchestrating Race," 16.
81. Salvadore del Fierro, interview, June 1, 1977, cited in Liljeblad, *Filipino, Alaska*, 9.

82. Friday, "Orchestrating Race," 89–90.
83. Friday, "Orchestrating Race," 92.
84. Friday, "Orchestrating Race," 8.

11. THE INEQUITIES OF WAR

1. Mann, *Our Daily Bread*, 67.
2. "Wm. Paul Jr. Negotiating for Brotherhood," *Alaska Fishing News*, June 1942.
3. "Hot Letter by Wm. Paul, Jr. to Natives on Fish Bargaining," *Alaska Fishing News*, June 24, 1942. The article also mentions that the government will take a share at their price.
4. "Hot Letter by Wm Paul, Jr."
5. Friday, "Competing Communities," 318.
6. Order No. 1925, U.S. Department of Interior, Secretary Harold Ickes, March 6, 1943, Washington DC.
7. Friday, *Organizing Asian-American Labor*, 189.
8. Friday, *Organizing Asian-American Labor*, 190.
9. Foner, *Women and the American Labor Movement*, 339.
10. "Women at War—Doing the Work of Men," *Pacific Fisherman*, September 1943.
11. Milkman, *Gender at Work*.
12. Randali, "Labor Agreements."
13. Alaska Salmon Industry, Inc., University of Washington Archives, http://digitalcollections.lib.washington.edu/cdm/ref/collection/pioneerlife/id/5211.
14. AFL-CIO Records, Hearing Transcript, Alaska Salmon, Inc., and Alaska Fisherman's Union, Case No. 111-7617 of the Twelfth Regional War Labor Board. Testimony of William Lewis Paul and others, June 1944 (hereafter cited as 1944 Hearing Transcript).
15. Cooley, *Politics and Conservation*. Cooley was under the impression that because of the price controls exerted by the OPA, the salmon resource was protected from overexploitation.
16. 1944 Hearing Transcript, 11.
17. 1944 Hearing Transcript, 12.
18. 1944 Hearing Transcript, 21. Winton Arnold also served as a judge from time to time and for this reason was often called Judge Arnold.
19. Kake Cannery Crew, Letter to the Grievance Committee of Cannery Workers' and Farm Labor Union 18257, August 26, 1937, University of Washington Digital Archives, Pacific Northwest Historical Documents. In many cases, cannery workers were expected to pay for their own meals.
20. 1944 Hearing Transcript, 37.
21. 1944 Hearing Transcript, 40.

22. 1944 Hearing Transcript, 40.
23. 1944 Hearing Transcript, 40–41.
24. 1944 Hearing Transcript, 11.
25. 1944 Hearing Transcript, 43.
26. 1944 Hearing Transcript, 4.
27. 1944 Hearing Transcript, 50.
28. 1944 Hearing Transcript, 50.
29. 1944 Hearing Transcript, 54.
30. "Bombing of Dutch Harbor—Report On," from the Commanding Officer of the Northwest Sea Frontier Pacific Fleet, to the U.S. Pacific Fleet, Alaska Sector, July 6, 1942, National Archives and Records Administration (NARA), Seattle Branch, RG 81, 514889-906, Commandant Office.
31. Takakai, *Strangers*, 268.
32. Tsai, *Chinese Experience*, 104.
33. Tsai, *Chinese Experience*, 104.
34. Limerick, *Legacy of Conquest*, 271.
35. Guimary, *Marumina Trabaho*, 238.
36. Saved cooking fat was turned in to the appropriate station and later used to make glycerin for gunpowder.
37. *Personal Justice Denied*, 37.
38. Guimary, *Marumina Trabaho*, 240.
39. Bower, *Alaska Fishery and Fur-Seal Industries*, 1942, 30.
40. *Pacific Fisherman*, July 1942, 14.
41. Guimary, *Marumina Trabaho*, 244.
42. Takaki, *Strangers*, 391.
43. Takaki, *Strangers*, 392.
44. *Personal Justice Denied*, 49, in reference to Executive Order 9066.
45. George Moto (shortened from Yamamoto) arrived in Deering on the Seward Peninsula in the late 1800s after traveling on a whaling ship. He married a local Inupiat woman and lived a subsistence lifestyle until sent to a relocation camp. After the war he returned to Deering. Today the Moto family is prominent in southwest Alaska. Deering, however, is quite remote and can only be accessed by ferry or plane in favorable weather, and that is why the "capture" of this particular Japanese immigrant stands out as an anomaly, considering the trouble the FBI went to for just one man. When taken into custody neither George nor his family knew anything about the war.
46. Inouye, Hoshiko, and Heshiki, "Alaska's Japanese Pioneers," 38–39.

47. The War Relocation Authority was responsible for all aspects of relocation from transportation to guards. The authority moved out all persons of Japanese ancestry from the West Coast and Alaska and placed them in various internment camps, often separating families. They were also responsible for moving the Aleut (Unangan) to the Southeast Alaska locations.

48. The Minidoka Internment Camp in Hunt, Idaho, was not as bad as some of the camps, although it was surrounded by barbed wire to keep the internees in and deter others from coming in. During the war there were celebrations, weddings, and Buddhist services, and several of the internees were allowed to leave the camp during the day for outside jobs.

49. *Personal Justice Denied*, 10.

50. *Personal Justice Denied*, 21.

51. David Kiffer, "Tatsuda's Grocery Celebrates Centennial," *SitNews: Stories in the News*, Ketchikan, Alaska, May 19, 2016.

52. Some of the men who received training at the Chilkoot Barracks included former cannery worker Tad Fujioka, who was interned at the Minidoka camp before volunteering to join the 442nd and serving in Italy. William "Bill" Tatsuda, Charlie's brother, was already at Haines National Guard Chilkoot Barracks, awaiting his orders, which led him to the South Pacific as an interpreter. In 1941 his younger brother had been drafted and was a member of the 442nd in Europe. Shortly after, Bill Tatsuda was also drafted and also served in the European theatre.

53. "Alaska's Japanese Pioneers," 26.

54. "Alaska's Japanese Pioneers," 26.

55. "Alaska's Japanese Pioneers," 35.

56. Thomas, *Picture Man*, 59.

57. Thomas, *Picture Man*, 87.

58. Thomas, *Picture Man*, 87.

59. Elaine Abraham and MaryAnn Paquette, Project Jukebox, Oral History Program, University of Alaska, Fairbanks, www.jukebox.uaf.edu.

60. John Bremner, quoted in Thomas, *Picture Man*, 78.

61. Japanese culture has been described as a "shame culture" as opposed to the Western concept of guilt. Going back to the fact that Japanese society is bound up in the family rather than the individual, there is a great fear of bringing shame to the family or the ancestors through bad acts or even innocent actions that can be perceived as wrong. The abstract ethical principles are based on the failure to meet expectations. In extreme cases, the end result of this "shame" may be to end one's life. Reischauer, *The Japanese*, 14.

62. Thomas, *Picture Man*, 78.

63. Judy Daxootsu Ramos, Yakutat resident, pers. comm., June 2017. Her grand-mother Elaine (referenced in note 59 in Project Jukebox) was a personal friend of Shoki Kayamori and was often photographed by him.

64. Bremner, quoted in Thomas, *Picture Man*, 79.

65. Gabe Emerson, "Funter Bay History: Aleut Evacuation and Internment," Saveitforparts blog, July 7, 2013, https://saveitforparts.wordpress.com/2013/07/07/funter-bay-history-aleut-evacuation-and-internment/.

66. Testimony in *Aleut Relocation: The Untold Story* (DVD), documentary produced by the Aleutian–Pribilof Island Association, 1992.

67. Emerson, "Funter Bay History"; Gabe Emerson, several conversations with author.

68. *Personal Justice Denied*, 21.

69. William and Loretta Samato (descendants of Harry Samato), pers. comm., July 2017. Harry lived in Killisnoo and was married to a Tlingit woman.

70. Mayberry, "Call of the Williwas," *Alaska Life*, 48–49.

71. Mayberry, "Call of the Williwas," 48–49.

72. *Personal Justice Denied*, 351.

73. *Personal Justice Denied*, 352.

12. THE HANNA HEARINGS AND HYDABURG

1. "Paternalism for Profit," *Pacific Fisherman*, November 1944, 45. This is the same editorial that William Paul Sr. disputed in the past.

2. Paul, *Then Fight for It*, 104.

3. Price, *Great Father in Alaska*, 113.

4. Price, *Great Father in Alaska*, 114.

5. Mitchell, *Sold American*, 288.

6. Paul, *Then Fight for It*. 107.

7. Mitchell, *Sold American*, 289.

8. George W. Folta, Theodore H. Haas, and Kenneth R. L. Simmons, Brief Proposed Findings of Fact, Conclusions of Law and Recommendation of the Petitioners, 22, in Department of the Interior of the United States, Hearings on Claims of Natives of the towns of Hydaburg, Klawock, and Kake, Alaska, Pursuant to the Provisions of Section 201, 21b of the Regulation for Protection of the Commercial Fisheries of Alaska, 1944.

9. Mitchell, *Sold American*, 289.

10. Price, *Great Father in Alaska*. 115.

11. Mitchell, *Sold American*, 290.

12. Arnold, *Fishermen's Frontier*, 150.

13. Arnold, *Fishermen's Frontier*, 151.

14. In 1787 English Captain George Dixon named these islands after Queen Charlotte. The main islands are Graham and Moresby, also named by Englishmen. The location, however, is the traditional home of the indigenous Haida on the north coast of British Columbia. In 2009 the Haida took their case to court to have the name changed back to the original Haida Gwaii, islands of the Haida.

15. It was said by the missionaries and Bureau of Education that the elders had voiced their opinions, but at this late date it is difficult to verify if this was fact.

16. Pat Roppel, "Southeast Alaska History: The Founding of Hydaburg," *Capital City Weekly*, April 10, 2013; the weekly was taken over by the Morris Agency and *Capital City Weekly* became part of the *Juneau Empire*, https://www.juneau empire.com.

17. There is confusion between the terms "Indian Service" and "Bureau of Education" stemming from the interchanging of terms in historical documents. There never was an "Indian Service" in Alaska. The agency consisted mainly of Indian agents in the continental United States. The Bureau of Education was a federal agency but heavily influenced by missionary activity in the early days. In 1931 the Bureau of Education was replaced by the Bureau of Indian Affairs.

18. Mitchell, *Sold American*, 264; Executive Order 1856, June 19, 1912; Case and Voluck, *Alaska Natives*, 74.

19. As a reminder, Federal Indian Trust status and wardship were begun in 1823 after the Supreme Court decisions that considered the indigenous people as domestic nations under the fiduciary protection and control of the federal government. These cases, sometimes dubbed the Cherokee Cases, were decided by Chief Justice John Marshall.

20. "To Conduct a Study and Investigation of the Various Questions and Problems Relating to the Territory of Alaska," Hearings on H. Res. 236 Before the Committee on Territories, 78th Cong. 1st Sess. 33–37 (1944).

21. W. T. Lopp to Hydaburg Town Council, November 28, 1912, in Bureau of Indian Affairs pamphlet "Hydaburg, Alaska—Its History, Population and Economy"; Planning Support Group Report 257 (July 1978), 295.

22. Executive Order 4421, April 17, 1926.

23. *Alaska Fisherman*, August 30, 1927.

24. An IRA or Indian Reorganization Council was formed in a town or village after local consensus, and a federally approved constitution was developed and published. The council had some degree of sovereignty but remained under federal government auspices.

25. United States Senate Committee on Interstate and Foreign Commerce and House Committee on Merchant Marine and Fisheries, Hearings on S.R. 1446 and H.R. 3859, Salmon Trap Sites, 195–97. The fishing pressure was due to wastage coming from the big cannery interests in Southeast Alaska, and the resource was not monitored by federal or local authorities.
26. Folta, Haas, and Simmons, Brief Proposed Findings.
27. The 1926 Townsite Act was meant to secure property ownership of Alaska Native towns and villages but met with limited success. According to legal experts David Case and David Voluck, "The 1926 Alaska Native Townsite Act provided an opportunity for individual Natives to obtain title to lands in public domain. However, federal administration of the Townsite Act was plagued by bureaucratic and statutory confusion" (Case and Voluck, *Alaska Natives*, 130). In the Hydaburg case, the confusion was evident in that documented discussions or legal testimony mentioned Hydaburg Townsite, but there is no evidence that any part of Hydaburg was ever qualified under the Town Site Act.
28. Philp, "The New Deal."
29. Philp, "The New Deal," 278.
30. Frank Peratrovich was adamantly opposed to any reservation and based his opinion on his experience in boarding school in the states. He was recorded saying, "I am against any form of reservation. I don't think that is the solution to our problems here in Alaska." See "To Conduct a Study and Investigation of the Various Questions and Problems Relating to the Territory of Alaska," Hearings on H. Res. 236 Before the Committee on Territories, 79th Cong. 1st Sess. 33–37 (1946). This hearing was carried over from a similar set of hearing in the previous Congress.
31. "To Conduct a Study and Investigation of the Various Questions and Problems Relating to the Territory of Alaska."
32. "To Conduct a Study and Investigation of the Various Questions and Problems Relating to the Territory of Alaska."
33. Folta, Haas, and Simmons, Brief Proposed Findings, 22 and general, including Part II.
34. Felix Cohen, often referred to as the architect of American Indian law for his work with *Handbook of American Indian Law*, worked for the Department of Interior for many years until leaving government service in 1947 to pursue private practice. He was the quintessential expert in Native American legal cases, including those in Alaska. He left his private practice for a year to work with the Hanna Hearings of the 1940s. Although he was well respected at the

time, he did have his enemies. One of those adversaries was Governor Ernest Gruening.

35. Mitchell, *Sold American*, 304; BIA monitored the transaction, 420.
36. Mitchell, *Sold American*, 305.
37. *Daily Alaska Empire*, January 15, 1950.
38. Mitchell, *Take My Land*, 206–9.
39. Mitchell, *Take My Land*, 294.
40. "Restriction Stops Indian Reservation," *Daily Alaska Empire*, March 20, 1950, 1.
41. "Letter to the Editor," *New York Times*, January 30, 1951.
42. "Hydaburg Testimony Ends, No Decision Expected Soon," *Daily Alaska Empire*, July 17, 1932.
43. "Paul Facing Disbarment Charges," *Daily Alaska Empire*, May 23, 1936; *United States ex rel G.W. Folta v William L. Paul*, U.S. District Court, March 1, 1937; Mitchell, *Sold American*, 246–47.
44. Paul, *Then Fight for It*, 106.
45. Paul, *Then Fight for It*, 106–7.
46. Paul, *Then Fight for It*, 106–7.
47. Arnold, "The Hydaburg Indian Reservation."
48. In the final verdict District Judge George Folta, who was unsympathetic to the "Indian cause" and had recently ruled against another Alaska Native group during the Hanna Hearings, upheld that the Haida had abandoned their former lands and waters, the final blow for the Natives' plea. Folta should have recused himself from the case because of a conflict of interest, but there was not a large pool of judges in those days, and impartiality was not always a requirement.
49. *United States v. Libby, McNeil, and Libby*, 1952 (the company is called Libby, McNeill & Libby in its records in the University of Washington Archives, Special Collections).
50. Mitchell, *Sold American*, 307.
51. *United States v. Libby, McNeil, and Libby*, 107 F. Suppl 697 (D. Alaska 1952).
52. *United States v. Libby, McNeil, and Libby*.
53. *United States v. Libby, McNeil, and Libby*.
54. *United States v. Libby, McNeil, and Libby*.
55. "Order Designating Reservations for Indians of Hydaburg, Alaska: Notice of Invalidation," *Federal Register* 20 (168), 1955.
56. Deloria Jr. and Wilkins, *Legal Universe*, 8.
57. Brown, "Political and Legal Status," 254.
58. Wilkinson, *American Indians*, 122.

1. Richard Stitt, "A Tribute to Roy Peratrovich," Address to the Central Council of Tlingit and Haida Indian Tribes of Alaska, April 15, 1987, 9.

2. Dauenhauer and Dauenhauer, *Haa Kusteeyi, Our Culture*, 46.

3. Gruening, *Many Battles*, 330–31.

4. "Superior Race Theory Hit in Hearing," Alaska State Library, copy from the original *Daily Alaska Empire* article, http://vilda.alaska.edu/cdm/singleitem/collection/cdmg21/id/2058.

5. Cooley, *Politics and Conservation*, 158.

6. Cooley, *Politics and Conservation*, 162.

7. Cooley, *Politics and Conservation*, 170.

8. The International Longshore and Warehouse Union (ILWU) represented West Coast dock workers in Hawaii, Alaska, and British Columbia. It was founded in 1937 after a consolidation of several unions that were not fulfilling the needs of their members. Through its history this union was known for its communist ties and violent strikes. For more information, see "The ILWU Story," International Longshore and Warehouse Union website, http://www.ilwu.org/history/the-ilwu-story.

9. Nelson, *Workers on the Waterfront*, 129.

10. Nelson, *Workers on the Waterfront*, 130.

11. Nelson, *Workers on the Waterfront*, 4.

12. Nelson, *Workers on the Waterfront*, 32.

13. Crutchfield and Pontecorvo, "Pacific Salmon Fisheries," 95–103.

14. Paul, *Then Fight for It*, 26.

15. Fielding, *The American Newsreel, 1911–1967*, 392.

16. Stanley K. Schultz, "From New Deal to Fair Deal: New Game?," American History 102 course website, https://courses.dcs.wisc.edu/showcase/hist102/lec22/22_01.html. Truman's characterization of himself as a political eunuch no doubt stemmed from the lack of information that he was allowed even though he was the president. The apparent mistrust followed him throughout his presidency and was a great handicap.

17. *The Great Swindle*, documentary produced by United Electric, 1948; reproduction by Quality Information Publisher, Inc.

18. Fair Deal was Truman's progressive agenda, which he unfolded in his 1949 address; it included national health insurance, civil rights, and a minimum wage. Truman also supported Alaska's statehood, which was unpopular at the time.

19. Vicki Ruiz discussed her 1980 interview with Rose Dellamo in our 2009 discussion.

20. Ruiz, *Cannery Women*, 120–21.

21. Drucker, *Native Brotherhoods*, 31.
22. Micah Ellison, "The Local 7/Local 37 Story: Filipino American Cannery Unionism in Seattle, 1940–1959," The Seattle Civil Rights and Labor History Project, https://depts.washington.edu/civilr/local_7.htm.
23. The Immigration and Nationality Act Pub. L. 82–414 66 Stat. 16, also known as the McCarran-Walters Act. According to Alaska labor historian Donald Guimary, the act allowed the Immigration Department the "authority to bar unsatisfactory aliens as well as certain classes of citizens from re-entering the United States from its territories." Felons who had not been pardoned by the president could not come back to the United States. Guimary, *Marumina Trabaho*, 265.
24. Gruening, *Many Battles*, 331.
25. Guimary, *Marumina Trabaho*, 256.
26. William Paul Sr., "Fish and Fish Traps: The Indian View," *Alaska Life*, July 1948, 11.
27. Paul, "Fish and Fish Traps," 12.
28. Hewitt, Homer H. III, "The Right to Membership in a Labor Union," *University of Pennsylvania Law Review*, http://scholarship.law.upenn.edu/cgi/viewcontent.cgi?article=8214&context=penn_law_review.
29. Cooley, *Politics and Conservation*, 202.
30. Koppes, "From New Deal to Termination," quoted from a speech in the Truman papers.
31. Whitehead, *Completing the Union*, 204.
32. Debo, *History of the Indians*, 352.
33. Deloria and Lytle, *American Indians, American Justice*, 18.
34. Alysa Landry, "Dwight D. Eisenhower Tried to Knock Out Jim Thorpe and Assimilate Indians," August 23, 2016, presidential series, Indian Country Today, https://indiancountrytoday.com/archive/dwight-d-eisenhower-tried-to-knock-out-jim-thorpe-and-assimilate-indians-yO_OTO3TckimtROrJbNEPQ.
35. Gruening, *Many Battles*, 331.
36. Gruening, *Many Battles*, 318.
37. R. Warren, Alaska resident, testifying before the U.S. Senate on a bill to form all lease fish trap sites to persons, U.S. Senate, Hearings on S. 1446, 1948, 246.
38. Gruening, *Many Battles*, 231.
39. U.S. Congress, Senate, Committee on Interior and Insular Affairs, Alaska Statehood Hearings on H.R. 331 and S. 2036, 81st Congress, 1st Sess. (April 24–29, 1950), 317–18.
40. Naske, *History of Alaska Statehood*, 145.

41. Robert Atwood, publisher of the *Anchorage Times*, transcript from the Alaska Historical Society meeting, November 4, 1984.
42. Baron, *Work Engendered*, 353.
43. Milkman, *Gender at Work*, 152.
44. Lilly James, interview with author, Hoonah, 2017.
45. Lilly James interview.
46. Lilly James, speaking of her mother's past employment. Copy of the union card in the author's possession.
47. Milkman, *Gender at Work*, 41.
48. Klein, "Contending with Colonization."
49. Klein, "Contending with Colonization," 106.
50. *Pacific Fisherman*, November 1952, 19.
51. Cooley, *Politics and Conservation*, 186.
52. Gruening, *State of Alaska*, 405.
53. Dombroski, *Culture Politics*, 26.

14. WHEN CANNERY CHILDREN REMEMBER

1. Sadie Bergen, "Telling Labor History through Stories: An Interview with Historian Premilla Nadasen," September 7, 2015, https://www.historians .org/publications-and-directories/perspectives-on-history/september-2015 /telling-labor-history-through-stories-an-interview-with-historian-premilla -nadasen.
2. Cruikshank, *Life Lived*, 3.
3. Metcalfe, *Bob and Betty Allen's Alaska*.
4. Kake Elders, *In Our Words*, "The Kake Cannery," United States Department of the Interior, National Park Service, report by the Organized Village of Kake, interviews from Kake Elders, 1989, 18–19.
5. Kake Elders, *In Our Words*, 18–19.
6. Kake Elders, *In Our Words*, 19. Rebecca Rose speaks about the housing arrangement using the Kake cannery as a familiar reference, but the layout was similar at each cannery in Southeast Alaska.
7. Friday, *Organizing Asian-American Labor*, 52.
8. This narrative concentrates on the largest ethnic populations in the Southeast Alaska canneries, which include the Tlingit, Haida, Chinese, Japanese, and Filipinos. That is not to discount other nationalities such as Mexicans from Mexico and California; African Americans, especially after World War II; and Polynesians. Stories are also told from the Anchorage and southwest Alaska canneries of the many Korean immigrants who worked alongside everyone. The Hawaiians have a long history in Southeast Alaska, starting

with their Hudson's Bay Company employment. Even today the elders talk about how much they loved the Hawaiian music and instruments.

9. Inouye, Hoshiko, and Heshiki, *Alaska's Japanese Pioneers*, interviews and transcripts, 46.
10. Kake Elders, *In Our Words*, 18–19.
11. Inouye, Hoshiko, and Heshiki, *Alaska's Japanese Pioneers*, 43.
12. Dave Kiffer, pers. comm., Ketchikan June 2017.
13. Ruiz, *Cannery Women*, 19–20.
14. Andrea Ebona-Michel, in Marianne Mills, "Cannery History Remembered at Annual Reunion Days Banquet," *Juneau Empire*, September 1, 2006.
15. It was unusual for an immigrant to work for the Immigration Service, but it did occur. Martin worked there for two years until he went back to fishing full time, according to Annie's granddaughter Andrea Ebona-Michel, July 2017 (Tlingit spellings from news article subject to new orthography).
16. "Annie James," Tlingit, Haida and Tsimshian Genealogy of Canada and Alaska, last update August 23, 2017, for Annie James (sometimes Paul) Ebona.
17. Eunice Akagi, quoted in Kristin Hutchison, "To Hear the Reminiscing at a Reunion Last Week, Hawk Inlet Cannery was as Much Summer Camp as Work Camp," *Juneau Empire*, 2002.
18. This was a similar situation to the one reported by Bill Paul Jr. as regards the Alaska Salmon Industry, Inc. hearings before the War Labor Board in the early 1940s.
19. Eunice Akagi, quoted in Mills, "Cannery History Remembered."
20. Hutchison, "To Hear the Reminiscing."
21. Mills, "Cannery History Remembered."
22. Sandi Benzel, quoted in Mills, "Cannery History Remembered."
23. Marie Olson, interview with author, Sitka, Alaska, March 2012.
24. Marie Olson, pers. comm. (e-mail), May 2, 2012.
25. Marie Olson e-mail, May 2, 2012.
26. Marie Olson e-mail, May 2, 2012.
27. Metcalfe, *In Sisterhood*, 109. Murder's Cove or Murder Cove is located on the southernmost corner of Admiralty Island and is so named because an alleged revenge murder of two prospectors took place there during Alaska's military period.
28. Marie Olson, pers. comm., July 15, 2020.
29. Marie Olson e-mail, May 2, 2012.
30. Metcalfe, *In Sisterhood*, 109; Hutchison, "To Hear the Reminiscing."
31. Metcalfe, *In Sisterhood*, 109.

32. Helen Sarabia, quoted in Mills, "Cannery History Remembered."
33. Eunice Akagi, Dorothy Walker, and Rosa Miller, quoted in Hutchison, "To Hear the Reminiscing."
34. Martin "Snooky" Goenett, quoted in Hutchinson, "To Hear the Reminiscing."
35. Eunice Akagi, interview, in Mills, "Cannery History Remembered."
36. Dorothy Walker, quoted in Mills, "Cannery History Remembered."
37. Chris Friday sums up the Alaska cannery period well and what the old-timers might have been thinking: "We need to recognize this is much more than a small vignette played out in distant Alaska or the U.S. West: it encompasses issues of interethnic relations that reach far beyond the region, it reveals how world markets shuffled people and resources around the globe; and more importantly it demonstrates how people struggled at individual and community levels to make a reasonable life for themselves in the face of much larger constraints." Friday, "Competing Communities," 328.
38. Chambers, "New Social History."
39. Kim and Mejia, *Filipinos in America*, 54, 57.
40. Andrew Weil, "Alaskan Salmon from China?," drweil.com, May 4, 2017, https://www.drweil.com/diet-nutrition/food-safety/alaskan-salmon-from-china/.
41. In the ANCSA legislation, almost one billion dollars was authorized to be distributed among the regional corporations as part of the settlement.
42. Purvis, "When Eagle and Raven Fly with the Dove."
43. Guimary, *Marumina Trabaho*, 276.
44. Purvis, "When Eagle and Raven Fly with the Dove."
45. Corey Binns, "Pacific Ocean Grows More Acidic," Live Science, April 6, 2006, https://www.livescience.com/4032-pacific-ocean-grows-acidic.html.
46. Anna Rose MacArthur, "Record Warm Water in Lower Kuskokwim River Likely Caused Heart Attacks in Salmon, Biologist Says," *Anchorage Daily News*, July 15, 2019, https://www.adn.com/alaska-news/rural-alaska/2019/07/15/record-warm-water-likely-gave-kuskokwim-salmon-heart-attacks-biologist-says/.

BIBLIOGRAPHY

ARCHIVES AND MANUSCRIPTS

Abraham, Elaine, and MaryAnn Paquette. Alaska Oral History Project Jukebox. University of Alaska, Fairbanks. www.jukebox.uaf.edu.

AFL-CIO Records. Hearing Transcript, Alaska Salmon, Inc., and Alaska Fisherman's Union, Case No. 111-7617 of the Twelfth Regional War Labor Board. Testimony of William Lewis Paul and others, June 1944. Alaska State AFL-CIO Records, Archives and Special Collections, Consortium Library, University of Alaska, Anchorage.

Alaska Fisheries: Hearings on HR 2394 Before the Subcommittee of the Committee on the Merchant Marine and Fisheries on Fish and Fish Hatcheries, Pt. 2, 67th Cong. 2d. Sess. 93–100 (1922).

Alaska Native Brotherhood. Report for the Annual Convention of the Alaska Native Brotherhood in its session in Juneau. November 11, 1933, President of the Alaska Native Sisterhood, Hoonah, Alaska.

Alaska Native Brotherhood and Alaska Native Sisterhood. "Alaska Fisherman's Cooperative Association." Office of the Secretary, Box 81, Juneau, Alaska, no. 209. 1940.

Alaska Native Brotherhood and Alaska Native Sisterhood. Alaska Fishermen's Cooperative Association, Office of the Secretary, Juneau, Alaska. Resolutions and Instructions Authorizing Bargaining Agency. By Laws of Fisherman's Collective Market Agency. 1941.

Alaska Native Sisterhood, Hydaburg, Alaska, 1933, MSS 7 Series, box 6, folder 1, Walter A. Soboleff Papers, Alaska State Library, Juneau.

Alaska Salmon Industry, Inc. University of Washington Archives. http://digitalcollections.lib.washington.edu/cdm/ref/collection/pioneerlife/id/5211.

American Trust Company. "Monthly Review." No. 7, March 15, 1922.

Arnold, W. C. "The Hydaburg Indian Reservation: Its Background, Validity, and Effect." December 21, 1950. Department of the Interior, ARLIS collection, University of Alaska, Anchorage.

"Bombing of Dutch Harbor—Report On." From the Commanding Officer of the Northwest Sea Frontier Pacific Fleet, to the U.S. Pacific Fleet, Alaska Sector. July 6, 1942. National Archives and Records Administration (NARA), Seattle Branch. RG/81, 514889-906, Commandant Office.

Brooks, Maria. "Alaska Women's Oral History Project." Transcripts. Anchorage Community College, 1983.

Brown, Judson B., and Donelle Everson. Edited by John Hope and Dannis Demmert. *Documents from the 1929 Alaska Native Brotherhood and Sisterhood Convention, Haines, Alaska.* "Minutes of the 1929 ANB Convention."

Buschmann, August. "Peter Thams Buschmann Life History." Paper presented to the Norwegian Commercial Club in Seattle, Washington, 1941. Copy in author's possession.

Clark, Willoughby, to the President Benjamin Harrison, January 21, 1890. Transmittal located in the Appendix of *Tlingit and Haida Indians of Alaska v. United States,* Docket 47900, U.S. Court of Claims, 177 F. Supp. 452, 1959.

Committee of Indian Affairs. "Statement of Mr. Duncan's Work among the Tsimpsheean Indians of British Columbia and Alaska," 53d Cong. 2d, Senate Doc. 144. Washington DC: Government Printing Office, 1894.

Congressional Record, 57th Cong. 2nd Sess. House Report on Fisheries of Alaska, 1903.

Folta, George W., Theodore H. Haas, and Kenneth R. L. Simmons. Brief Proposed Findings of Fact, Conclusions of Law and Recommendation of the Petitioners. In the Department of the Interior of the United States. Hearings on Claims of Natives of the towns of Hydaburg, Klawock, and Kake, Alaska, Pursuant to the Provisions of Section 201, 21b of the Regulation for Protection of the Commercial Fisheries of Alaska, 1944.

Friday, Chris. "Orchestrating Race, Gender, and the Meaning of Work in Pacific Northwest Salmon Canneries." Draft in author's possession with permission. 2000.

Gordon, Paul E., to John Collier. Memorandum of March 16, 1934, Plaintiff's Exhibit No. 114 of the records of the *Tlingit and Haida Indians of Alaska v. United States.*

Healy, John J. Letter (1891) "Report within the Proceeding of the Alaska Boundary Tribunal." Part 1. Final Report of the Boundary Tribunal, 459. 1900.

Inouye, Ronald. Alaska's Japanese Pioneers Research Project. Transcribed interviews from Seattle, Washington, October 1991. Typed transcripts from the Oral History Office, copies in the Archive records, University of Alaska, Anchorage.

Kake Cannery Crew Letter to the Grievance Committee of Cannery Worker's and Farm Labor Union 18257, August 26, 1937, University of Washington Digital Archives, Pacific Northwest Historical Documents.

Kake Elders. *In Our Words.* "The Kake Cannery." United States Department of the Interior, National Park Service, report by the Organized Village of Kake. Interviews from Kake Elders, 18–19. 1989.

Libby, McNeill, & Libby records. "Summary: 1916–1960." University of Washington Archives, Special Collections.

Lipps, Oscar H. *Laws and Regulations Relating to Indians and Their Lands.* United States Indian Service, Department of Justice. Boise, Idaho: 1914.

Lopp, W. T., to Hydaburg Town Council, November 28, 1912. In Bureau of Indian Affairs pamphlet "Hydaburg, Alaska—Its History, Population and Economy." Bureau of Indian Affairs, Planning Support Group Report 257 (July 1978), 295. See Hydaburg_Its_History_Population_and_Econ.html.

Metlakatla Indian Community, Constitution and By-Laws. Article I, Jurisdiction [1919]. See *Constitution and By-laws of the Metlakatla Indian Community, Annette Islands Reserve, Alaska.* Approved August 23, 1944. Washington DC: Government Printing Office, 1946.

Morris, William Gouvernor. Letter to the Department of the Treasury, July 23, 1878. In 45th Cong. 3d Sess., 1879, S. Exec. Doc. 59.

Paul, William L., Sr. "A Paper for the Common Folk Treating Subjects of Labor and Fishing and Taxes without Fear or Favor, Depending for Its Life on the Support from the Little Fellow." Typewritten copy in author's possession, provided by Ben Paul. Undated.

Paul, William L., Sr., in his capacity as Grand President, Alaska Native Brotherhood. "Alaska Native Service, Too Proud to Serve: Comment on W. H. Olsen's Proud to Serve," Area Director, Alaska Native Service, Juneau, Alaska. 1944. Copy from Ben Paul, William L. Paul Papers, University of Washington.

Sharp, Frank W. Angoon, interview with Charles Mobley for the Fish and Wildlife Service. 1999. USFWS National Digital Library, document ID 1139.

"The Southeast Alaska Salmon Fishery: Interviews with Men and Women Engaged in Commercial Fishing, 1913–1978." Interviewed by Stephan B. Levy and George Figdor. Tapes in author's possession, copied courtesy of Historical Collections, Alaska State Library, Juneau, 1991.

Stitt, Richard. "A Tribute to Roy Peratrovich." Address to the Central Council of Tlingit and Haida Indian Tribes of Alaska, April 15, 1987. Copy from Rosita Worl, Sealaska Heritage Institute.

Tlingit and Haida Indians. Plaintiff's Exhibit, no. 84 in the records of *Tlingit and Haida Indians of Alaska v. United States*, 1959 (United States Court of Federal Claims, 177 F. Supp. 452, Fed. Cl. 1959).

"To Conduct a Study and Investigation of the Various Questions and Problems Relating to the Territory of Alaska," Hearings on H. Res. 236 Before the Committee on Territories, 78th Cong. 1st Sess. 33–37 (1944); 79th Cong. 1st Sess. 33–37 (1946).

Transcript from the Alaska Historical Society meeting November 4, 1984, Robert Atwood, publisher of the *Anchorage Times* Newspaper. Bob A. Wood Papers 1907–1997, Archives and Special Collections, Consortium Library, University of Alaska, Anchorage.

Wickersham, James. "Address to the People of Alaska." Copied into the Diary of James Wickersham, Alaska, July 23rd 1916 to March 4th 1917. Election of 1916. Wickersham Family. Historical Collections, Alaska State Library, Juneau, MS 107, box 4 (Diary 2).

——. Wickersham Diary, Entry for July 12, 1915. Historical Collections, Alaska State Library, Juneau.

PUBLISHED WORKS

Alekseev, A. L. *The Destiny of Russian America, 1741–1867*. Translated by Marina Ramsay. Edited by R. A. Pierce. Fairbanks: Limestone Press, 1990.

Allen, June. *Spirit, Historic Ketchikan Alaska*. Ketchikan AK: Historic Ketchikan, 1992.

Armitage, Susan H. "From the Inside Out." *Frontiers: A Journal of Western Studies* 22, no. 3 (2001): 32–47.

Arndt, Katherine L., and Richard A. Pierce. *A Construction History of Sitka, Alaska as Documented in the Records of the Russian-American Company*. Sitka: National Park Service, 2003.

Arnesen, Eric. *The Human Tradition in American Labor History*. Wilmington DE: Scholarly Resources, 2004.

Arnold, David. *The Fishermen's Frontier: People and Salmon in Southeast Alaska*. Seattle: University of Washington Press, 2008.

——. "Putting Up Fish: Environment, Work, and Culture in Tlingit Society, 1790s–1940s." PhD diss., University of California, Los Angeles, 1997.

——. "Work and Culture in Southeastern Alaska: Tlingit and Salmon Fisheries." In *Native Pathways: American Indian Culture and Economic Development in the Twentieth Century*, 156–83. Boulder: University Press of Colorado, 2004.

Asian Women United of California. *Making Waves: An Anthology of Writings by and About Asian American Women*. Boston: Beacon Press, 1989.

Atwood, Evangeline. *Frontier Politics: Alaska's James Wickersham*. Portland OR: Binford and Mort, 1979.

Baldoz, Rick. *The Third Asiatic Invasion: Empire and Migration in Filipino America, 1898–1946*. New York: New York University Press, 2011.

Ballou, Maturin M. *The New Eldorado: A Summer Journey in Alaska*. Boston: Houghton, Mifflin and Company, 1890.

Banner, Stuart. *How the Indians Lost Their Land: Law and Power on the Frontier*. Cambridge MA: Belknap Press of Harvard University, 2005.

Baron, Ava. *Work Engendered: Toward a New History of American Labor*. Ithaca NY: Cornell University Press, 1991.

Barrett, James R. "Women's Work, Family Economy, and Labor Militancy: The Case of Chicago's Immigrant Packinghouse Workers, 1900–1922." In *Labor Divided: Race and Ethnicity in United States Labor Struggles, 1835–1960*, edited by Robert Asher and Charles Stephenson, 249–66. Albany: State University of New York Press, 1990.

Beattie, William Gilbert. *Marsden of Alaska*. New York: Vantage Press, 1955.

Berkhofer, Robert F., Jr. *The White Man's Indian*. New York: Vintage Books, 1978.

Bernstein, Irving. *Turbulent Years: A History of the American Worker, 1933–1941*. Boston: Houghton Mifflin, 1970.

Beverly, James. "The Alaska Fisherman and the Paradox of Assimilation: Progress, Power, and the Preservation of Culture." *Native Press Research Journal* 5 (1987): 2–15.

Black, Lydia. *Russians in Alaska, 1732–1867*. Fairbanks: University of Alaska Press, 2004.

Bodnar, John. *The Transplanted: A History of Immigrants in Urban America*. Bloomington: Indiana University Press, 1985.

Boneman, Walter R. *Alaska, Saga of a Bold Land*. New York: Harper Collins, 2003.

Bordewich, Fergus M. *Killing the White Man's Indian: Reinventing Native Americans at the End of the Twentieth Century*. New York: Anchor Books, 1997.

Bower, Ward. *Alaska Fishery and Fur-Seal Industries in 1923*. Washington DC: U.S. Fish and Wildlife Service, 1925.

———. *Alaska Fishery and Fur-Seal Industries*. Publication no. 30. Washington DC: U.S. Fish and Wildlife Service, 1942.

———. "Fish Cultures in Alaska." In *Alaska Fisheries and Fur Industries in 1911*. Bureau of Fisheries Document no. 766. Washington DC: Government Printing Office, 1912.

Brown, Caroline L. "Political and Legal Status of Alaska Natives." In *A Companion to the Anthropology of American Indians*, edited by Thomas Biolsi, 248–67. Malden MA: Blackwell Publishing, 2008.

Buaken, Manuel. "Where Is the Heart of America?" *New Republic*, September 1940.

Buchholdt, Thelma. *Filipinos in Alaska, 1788–1958*. Anchorage: Asian Alaskan Cultural Center, Aboriginal Press, 1996.

Bulosan, Carlos. *America Is in the Heart*. Seattle: University of Washington Press, 1943.

Burma, John H. *Spanish-Speaking Groups in the United States*. Durham NC: Duke University Press, 1954.

Case, David S., and David A. Voluck. *Alaska Natives and American Laws*. 2nd ed. Fairbanks: University of Alaska Press, 2002.

Chambers, Clarke A. "The New Social History, Local History, and Community Empowerment." *Minnesota History* 49 (Spring 1984): 14–18.

Christopher, Robert C. *The Japanese Mind: The Goliath Explained*. New York: Linden Press–Simon and Schuster, 1983.

Churchill, Ward. *Marxism and Native Americans*. Boston: South End Press, 1983.

Cobb, John N. *Pacific Salmon Fisheries*. U.S. Department of Commerce, Bureau of Fisheries document no. 1092. Washington DC: Government Printing Office, 1930.

—— . "Report on the Fisheries of Alaska in 1906." Special Paper, Bureau of Fisheries document 618. Washington DC: Government Printing Office, 1907.

Cobble, Dorothy Sue. *The Other Women's Movement: Workplace Justice and Social Rights in Modern America*. Princeton NJ: Princeton University Press, 2004.

Cole, Douglas, and Ira Chaikin. *The Iron Hand upon the People: The Law against the Potlatch on the Northwest Coast*. Seattle: University of Washington Press, 1990.

Cooley, Richard A. *Politics and Conservation: The Decline of the Alaska Salmon*. New York: Harper and Row, 1963.

Cooper, Carol. "Native Women on the Northern Pacific Coast: An Historical Perspective, 1820–1920." *Journal of Canadian Studies* 24, no. 4 (1992): 44–75.

Couture, Monique. "Leverage Legitimacy: How Alaska Circumvented Salmon Sustainability." Master's thesis, Western Washington University, 2016.

Cross, Ira B. *Financing an Empire: History of Banking in California*. Chicago: S. J. Clarke, 1927.

Cruikshank, Julie. *Life Lived Like a Story: Life Stories of Three Yukon Native Elders*. Lincoln: University of Nebraska Press, 1992.

Crutchfield, James, and Giullo Pontecorvo. "The Pacific Salmon Fisheries: A Study of Irrational Conservation." In *An Alaska Anthology: Interpreting the*

Past, edited by Stephen W. Haycox and Mary Childers Mangusso, 238–45. Seattle: University of Washington Press, 1996.

Dauenhauer, Nora Marks, and Richard Dauenhauer. *Haa Kusteeyí, Our Culture: Tlingit Life Stories*. Seattle: University of Washington Press, 1994.

David, E. J. Ramos. *We Have Not Stopped Trembling Yet: Letters to my Filipino-Athabascan Family*. Albany: State University of New York Press, 2018.

Davis, Mary Lee. *We Are Alaskans*. Boston: W. A. Wilde, 1931.

Davis, Ronald L. *The Social and Cultural Life of the 1920s*. New York: Holt, Rinehart and Winston, 1972.

Debo, Angie. *A History of the Indians of the United States*. Norman: University of Oklahoma Press, 1970.

Deloria, Vine, Jr., and Clifford M. Lytle. *American Indians, American Justice*. Austin: University of Texas Press, 1983.

Deloria, Vine, Jr., and David E. Wilkins. *The Legal Universe: Observations on the Foundations of American Law*. Golden CO: Fulcrum Press, 2011.

DeVoto, Bernard. *The Western Paradox: A Conservation Reader*. Edited by Douglas Brinkley and Patricia Nelson. Ithaca NY: Cornell University Press, 2004.

Dombrowski, Kirk. *Against Culture: Development, Politics and Religion in Indian Alaska*. Lincoln: University of Nebraska Press, 2001.

——. *Culture Politics: The Story of Native Land Claims in Alaska*. Lincoln NE: Syron Design, 2014.

Drucker, Philip. *The Native Brotherhoods: Modern Intertribal Organizations on the Northwest Coast*. Washington DC: Government Printing Office, 1958.

Durrenberger, E. Paul, and Karaleah S. Reichart. *The Anthropology of Labor Unions*. Boulder: University of Colorado Press, 2012.

Faue, Elizabeth. "Paths of Unionization: Community, Bureaucracy, and Gender in the Minneapolis Labor Movement of the 1930s." In *Work Engendered: Toward a New History of American Labor*, edited by Ava Baron, 296–319. Ithaca NY: Cornell University Press, 2004.

Fielding, Raymond. *The American Newsreel: A Complete History, 1911–1976*. 2nd ed. Jefferson NC: MacFarland and Company, 2006.

Fiske, JoAnne. "Colonization and Decline of Women's Status: The Tsimshian Case." *Feminist Studies* 17, no. 3 (1991): 509–35.

Foner, Philip S. *Women and the American Labor Movement*. New York: Free Press, 1979.

"Franklin D. Roosevelt's First Inaugural Address, 1933." In *A Documentary History of the United States*, edited by Richard Heffner and Alexander Heffner, 367–72. 8th ed. New York: Signet Books, 2002.

Freeburn, Laurence. *The Silver Years of the Alaska Canned Salmon Industry.* Anchorage: Alaska Northwest Publishing Company, 1976.

Friday, Chris. "Competing Communities at Work: Asian-Americans, European Americans, and Native Alaskans in the Pacific Northwest, 1938–1947." In *Over the Edge: Remapping the American West,* edited by Valerie J. Matsumoto and Blake Allmendinger, 303–28. Berkeley: University of California Press, 1999.

———. *Organizing Asian-American Labor: The Pacific Coast Canned-Salmon Industry, 1870–1942.* Philadelphia: Temple University Press, 1994.

Fujita-Rony, Dorothy B. *American Workers, Colonial Power: Philippine Seattle and the Transpacific West, 1919–1941.* Berkeley: University of California Press, 2003.

Gergen, Kenneth J., and Mary M. Gergen. *Social Psychology.* New York: Harcourt, Brace Jovanovich, 1988.

Gibson, James R. "Russian Dependence on the Natives of Alaska." In *An Alaska Anthology: Interpreting the Past,* edited by Stephen W. Haycox and Mary Childers Mangusso, 21–42. Seattle: University of Washington Press, 1996.

Green, James R. *The World of the Workers: Labor in Twentieth-Century America.* New York: Hill and Wang, 1980.

Grinev, Andrei Val'Terovich. *The Tlingit Indians in Russian America, 1741–1867.* Lincoln: University of Nebraska Press, 2005.

Grinnell, George Bird. *Alaska 1899: Essays from the Harriman Expedition.* Seattle: University of Washington Press, 1995.

Gruening, Ernest. *Many Battles: The Autobiography of Ernest Gruening.* New York: Liveright, 1973.

———. *The State of Alaska.* New York: Random House, 1954.

Guimary, Donald L. *Marumina Trabaho: A History of Labor in Alaska's Salmon Canning Industry.* New York: iUniverse, 2006.

Guimary, Donald L., and Jack R. Masson. "Getting There Was . . . er, Half the Fun." *Alaska Journal: A 1981 Collection* (March 1981): 102–6.

Hanable, William S. "New Russia." *Alaska Journal* 77 (Spring 1973): 77–80.

Hardin, Garrett. "Tragedy of Commons." *Science* 62 (December 13, 1968): 1243–48.

Haycox, Stephen. *Alaska, an American Colony.* Seattle: University of Washington Press, 2006.

Hayes, Ernestine. *Blonde Indian: An Alaskan Native Memoir.* Tucson: University of Arizona Press, 2006.

Higham, John. *Strangers in the Land: Patterns of American Nativism, 1860–1925.* New Brunswick NJ: Rutgers University Press, 2002.

Hinckley, Ted C. *The Americanization of Alaska, 1867–1897*. Palo Alto: Pacific Books, 1972.

———. *The Canoe Rocks: Alaska's Tlingit and the Euramerican Frontier, 1800–1912*. Lanham MD: University Press of America, 1996.

———. "Prospectors, Profits, and Prejudice." *American West* 2 (Spring 1965): 59–66.

Hope, Andrew, III. *Founders of the Alaska Native Brotherhood*. Sitka AK: David Howard Memorial Fund, 1975.

Hosmer, Brian G. *American Indians in the Marketplace: Persistence and Innovation among the Menominees and Metlakatlans, 1870–1920*. Lawrence: University of Kansas Press, 1999.

Hosokawa, Bill. *Nisei: The Quiet Americans*. Denver: University of Colorado Press, 1969.

Hume, William. *Fresh Columbia Salmon*. New York: William Hume, 1890.

Inouye, Ron, Carol Hoshiko, and Kazumi Heshiki. *Alaska's Japanese Pioneers: Faces, Voices, Stories—A Synopsis*. Alaska's Japanese Pioneers Research Project Team, 1994.

Jonaitas, Aldona. *Chiefly Feasts: The Enduring Kwakiutl Potlatch*. Seattle: University of Washington Press, 1991.

Jones, E. Lester. *Report of Alaska Investigations in 1914*. Department of Commerce, Bureau of Fisheries. Washington DC: Government Printing Office, 1915. http://www.archive.org/stream/reportofalaskain00unit /reportofalaskain00unit_djvu.txt.

Lipps, Oscar H. "Laws and Regulations Relating to Indians and Their Lands." United States Indian Service, Department of Justice: Boise ID, 1914.

Kan, Sergei. *Memory Eternal: Tlingit Culture and Russian Orthodox Christianity through Two Centuries*. Seattle: University of Washington Press, 1999.

———. *Russian-American Photographer in Tlingit Country: Vincent Soboleff in Alaska*. Norman: University of Oklahoma Press, 2013.

Kanazawa, Tooru J. *Sushi and Sourdough*. Seattle: University of Washington Press, 1989.

Kazin, Michael, and Joseph A. McCatin, eds. *Americanism: New Perspectives on an Ideal*. Chapel Hill: University of North Carolina Press, 2006.

Kent, Noel Jacob. *America in 1900*. New York: M. E. Sharpe, 2000.

Khlebnikov, Kyrill T. *Colonial Russian America: Kyrill T. Khlebnikov's Reports, 1817–1832*. Translated by Basil Dmytryshyn and E. A. P. Crownhart-Vaughan. Portland: Oregon Historical Society, 1976.

Kim, Hyung-Chan, and Cynthia Mejia. *The Filipinos in America, 1898–1974: A Chronology and Fact Book*. New York: Oceana Publications, 1976.

Kirk, William. "Labor Forces of the Alaska Coast." *Survey* 35, no. 1 (July 1, 1916): 352–57.

Klein, Laura. "Contending with Colonization: Tlingit Men and Women in Change." In *Women and Colonization, Anthropological Perspectives*, edited by Mona Etienne and Eleanor Leacock, 118–29. Westport CT: Praeger, 1980.

——. "Mother as Clanswoman, Rank and Gender in Tlingit Society." In *Woman and Power in Native North America*, edited by Laura Klein and Lillian Ackerman, 28–45. Norman: University of Oklahoma Press, 2000.

Klein, Laura F., and Lillian A. Ackerman, eds. *Women and Power in Native North America*. Norman: University of Oklahoma Press, 1995.

Knight, Rolf. *Indians at Work: An Informal History of Native Indian Labour in British Columbia, 1858–1930*. Vancouver: New Star Books, 1978.

Koester, Susan H., with assistance from Emma Widmark. "By the Words of Thy Mouth Let They Be Judged: The Alaska Native Sisterhood Speaks." *Journal of the West* 7 (1974): 35–44.

Kohlstedt, Edward D. *William Duncan, Founder and Developer of Alaska's Metlakatla Christian Mission*. Palo Alto CA: National Press, 1957.

Koppes, Clayton R. "From New Deal to Termination: Liberalism and Indian Policy, 1933–1953." *Pacific Historical Review* 46 (November 1977) 543–66.

Kuokkanen, Rauna. "Indigenous Economies, Theories of Subsistence, and Women: Exploring the Social Economy Model for Indigenous Governance." *American Indian Quarterly* 35, no. 2 (Spring 2011): 215–40.

Kutchin, Howard M. *Report on the Salmon Fisheries of Alaska, 1896–1898*. Department of the Treasury, Special Agents Division. Washington DC: Government Printing Office, 1899.

——. *Report on the Salmon Fisheries of Alaska, 1901*. Washington DC: Government Printing Office, 1902.

——. *Report on the Salmon Fisheries of Alaska, 1903*. Department of Commerce and Labor, no. 12. Washington DC: Government Printing Office, 1904.

Lamphere, Louise. "Bringing the Family to Work: Women's Culture on the Shop Floor." *Feminist Studies* 11 (Fall 1985): 519–40.

Leonardo, Micaela di. "Women's Work, Work Culture, and Consciousness." *Feminist Studies* 11, no. 3 (Autumn 1985): 490–96.

Liljeblad, Sue Ellen. *Filipino, Alaska: A Heritage*. Anchorage: Alaska Historical Commission, 1986.

——. "The Filipinos and the Alaska Salmon Industry." *Alaska in Perspective* 1, no. 2 (1978): 1–9.

Limerick, Patricia Nelson. *The Legacy of Conquest: The Unbroken Past of the American West*. New York: Norton, 1987.

Mann, Geoff. *Our Daily Bread: Wages, Workers, and the Political Economy of the American West*. Chapel Hill: University of North Carolina Press, 2007.

Martin, James W. *Banana Cowboys: The United Fruit Company and Culture of Corporate Colonialism*. Albuquerque: University of New Mexico Press, 2018.

Mangusso, Mary Childers. "Anthony J. Dimond and the Politics of Integrity." In *An Alaska Anthology*, edited by Stephen W. Haycox and Mary Childers Mangusso, 246–66. Seattle: University of Washington Press, 1996.

Masson, Jack, and Donald Guimary. "Asian Labor Contractors in the Alaskan Canned Salmon Industry: 1880–1937." *Labor History* 22, no. 3 (1981): 377–97.

Mayberry, Genevieve. "Call of the Williwas." *Alaska Life* 7, no. 8 (1943): 48–49.

McCoy, Caroline, ed. *Life in Alaska: Letters of Mrs. Eugene S. Willard*. Philadelphia: Presbyterian Board of Publication, 1884.

McPherson, Alan. "Americanism against American Empire." In *Americanism: New Perspectives on an Ideal*, edited by Michael Kazin and Joseph A. McCartin, 169–91. Chapel Hill: University of North Carolina Press, 2006.

Metcalfe, Kimberly L. *In Sisterhood: The History of Camp 2 of the Alaska Native Sisterhood*. Juneau: Hazy Island Books, 2008.

Metcalfe, Peter. *Bob and Betty Allen's Alaska: A Miracle of Hotcakes, a Fleet of Saints, and Rising Tide of Visitors*. Juneau AK: Silver Bay Books, 2011.

Milkman, Ruth. *Gender at Work: The Dynamics of Job Segregation by Sex during World War II*. Urbana: University of Illinois Press, 1987.

Miller, Bruce G. "Contemporary Native Women: Role Flexibility and Politics." *Anthropologica* 36, no. 1 (1994): 57–72.

Miner, H. Craig. *The Corporation and the Indian: Tribal Sovereignty and Industrial Civilization in Indian Territory, 1865–1907*. Norman: University of Oklahoma Press, 1976.

Mitchell, Donald Craig. *Sold American: The Story of Alaska Natives and Their Land, 1867–1959*. Fairbanks: University of Alaska Press, 2003.

———. *Take My Land, Take My Life: The Story of Congress' Historic Settlement Claims Act*. Fairbanks: University of Alaska Press, 2001.

Moser, Jefferson F. "Alaska Salmon Investigations in 1900 and 1901." In *Bulletin of the U.S. Fish Commission*, vol. 21 (for 1901), 173–398. Washington DC: Government Printing Office, 1902.

———. *The Salmon and Salmon Fisheries of Alaska*. Bulletin of the Salmon Fisheries of Alaska, 1895. Washington DC: Government Printing Office, 1896.

———. "The Salmon and Salmon Fisheries of Alaska: Report of the Operations of the United States Fish Commission Steamer Albatross for the Year Ending June 30, 1898." In *Bulletin of the United States Fish Commission*, vol. 18 (for 1898), 1–178. Washington DC: Government Printing Office, 1900.

Murray, Joseph. "Report on the Salmon Fisheries in Alaska." Department of the Treasury, Special Agents Division, 1895 (1896): 356–72.

Murray, Peter. *The Devil and Mr. Duncan: A History of the Two Metlakatlas*. Victoria BC: Sono Nis Press, 1985.

Nash, Robert A. "The 'China Gangs' in the Alaska Packers Association Canneries: 1892–1935." In *The Life, Influence and the Role of the Chinese in the United States, 1776–1960*. San Francisco: Chinese Historical Society, 1976.

Naske, Claus M. *A History of Alaska Statehood*. Lanham MD: University Press of America, 1985.

Naske, Claus M., and Herman E. Slotnick. *Alaska: A History of the 49th State*. 2nd ed. Norman: University of Oklahoma Press, 1987.

Nelson, Bruce. *Workers on the Waterfront: Seamen, Longshoremen, and Unionism in the 1930s*. Urbana: University of Illinois Press, 1990.

Nelson-Cisneros, Victor. "UCAPAWA and Chicanos in California: The Farm Worker Period, 1937–1940." *Aztlán* 7, no. 3 (Fall 1976): 453–77.

Niblack, Alfred P. *The Coast Indians of Southern Alaska and Northern British Columbia*. Report of U.S. National Museum Under the Direction of the Smithsonian Institute, 1890.

Olson, Wallace M., and Lyle T. Hubbard Jr. *Fishing, the Key to Tlingit Culture*. Juneau AK: Juneau-Douglas Community College, 1975.

Omi, Michael, and Howard Winant. *Racial Formation in the United States: From the 1960s to the 1990s*. New York: Routledge, 1994.

——. "Racial Formations." In *Social Construction of Race, Ethnicity and Diversity*, edited by Michael Omi, Beverly Daniel Tatum, and Howard Winant, 23–27. Northeast Wisconsin Technical College. New York: Pearson Custom Printing, 2009.

Orosa, Jose Rizalino. "An Investigation of the Non-Resident Personnel Management Problems and Practices in the Alaska Canned Salmon Industry." Master's thesis, University of Washington, 1948.

Paul, Fred. *Then Fight for It*. Victoria BC: Trafford Publishing, 2003.

Personal Justice Denied. Report of the Commission on Wartime Relocation and Internment of Civilians. 1983; repr. Seattle: University of Washington Press, 1997.

Philp, Kenneth R. "The New Deal and Alaskan Natives, 1936–1945." *Pacific Historical Review* 50 (1981): 309–27.

——. *Termination Revisited: American Indians on the Trail to Self-Determination, 1933–1953*. Lincoln: University of Nebraska Press, 1999.

Posadas, Barbara Mercedes. *The Filipino Americans*. Westport CT: Greenwood Press, 1999.

Price, Robert E. *The Great Father in Alaska: The Case of the Tlingit and Haida Salmon Fishery*. Douglas AK: First Street Press, 1990.

Prucha, Francis Paul. *The Great Father: The United States Government and the American Indians*. Lincoln: University of Nebraska Press, 1986.

Purvis, Diane J. *The Drive of Civilization: The Stikine Forest versus Americanism*. North Charleston SC: Createspace Independent Press, 2016.

Purvis, Diane. "When Eagle and Raven Fly with the Dove: The Historical Hoonah, Alaska Purse Seine Fleet versus the Alaska Department of Fish and Game." Master's thesis, Alaska Pacific University, 1991.

Radke, August C. *Pacific American Fisheries, Inc.: History of a Washington State Salmon Packing Company, 1890–1966*. Jefferson NC: McFarland, 2001.

Raibmon, Paige. *Authentic Indians: Episodes of Encounter from the Late Nineteenth Century Northwest Coast*. Durham NC: Duke University Press, 2005.

Randali, Roger. "Labor Agreements: The West Coast Fishing Industry Restraint of Trade on Basis of Industrial Stability." *Industrial and Labor Relations Review* 3, no. 4 (July 1950): 514–41.

Reischauer, Edwin O. *The Japanese*. Cambridge MA: Belknap Press of Harvard University Press, 1977.

Remini, Robert V. *A Short History of the United States*. New York: Harper Perennial, 2008.

Reports of the Proceedings of the American Federation of Labor. Washington DC: Law Report Publishing, 1928.

Replogle, Charles. *Among the Indians of Alaska*. London: Headly Brothers, 1904.

Revilla, Linda A. "Brown and Proud: The Ethnic Identity of Filipino American College Students." In *Bearing Dreams, Shaping Visions: Asian Pacific American Perspectives*, edited by Linda A. Revilla, Gail M. Nomura, Shawn Wong, and Shirley Hune, 107–24. Pullman: Washington State Press, 1993.

Reynon, William. "The Tsimshians of Metlakatla Alaska." *American Anthropologist* 43 (1941): 85–89.

Robbins, William C. *The Capitalist Transformation of the American West: Colony and Empire*. Lawrence: University of Kansas Press, 1994.

Robertson, Lindsay G. *Conquest by Law: How the Discovery of America Dispossessed Indigenous Peoples of Their Lands*. Oxford: Oxford University Press, 2005.

Ruiz, Vicki. *Cannery Women, Cannery Lives*. Albuquerque: University of New Mexico Press, 1987.

Salamanca, Bonifacio C. *The Filipino Reaction to American Rule, 1901–1913*. Hamden CT: Shoe String Press, 1968.

Santa Ana, Jeffrey. "Emotional Labor of Racialization: Carlos Bulosan's Anger as a Critique of Filipino Alienation in America." *Journal of Asian-American Studies* 19, no. 1 (February 2016): 75–100.

Savage, Lydia. "Small Places, Close to Home: The Importance of Place in Organizing Workers." In *The Anthropology of Labor Unions*, edited by E. Paul Durrenberger and Karaleah S. Reichart, 131–55. Boulder: University of Colorado Press, 2010.

Schairer, Rosemary Agnes. "A Survey of the Alaska Salmon-Canning Industry in the Post-War Period." Master's thesis, University of Washington, 1956.

Scharlin, Craig, and Lilia V. Villanueva. *Philip Vera Cruz: A Personal History of Filipino Immigrants and the Farmworkers Movement*. Seattle: University of Washington Press, 2000.

Scidmore, Eliza Ruhamah. *Appleton's Guide-Book to Alaska and the Northwest Coast*. New York: D. Appleton and Company, 1893.

———. *Alaska: Its Southern Coast and the Sitkan Archipelago*. Boston: D. Lothrop and Company, 1885.

Scott, Joan W. "Gender: A Useful Category of Historical Analysis." *American Historical Review* 9, no. 5 (December 1986): 1053–75.

Sears, David O., Jim Sidanius, and Lawrence Bobo, eds. *Racialized Politics: The Debate about Racism in America*. Chicago: University of Chicago Press, 2000.

Semmingsen, Ingrid. *Norway to America: A History of the Migration*. Minneapolis: University of Minnesota Press, 1978.

Stahl, Charles W. "Theories of International Labor Migration Overview." *Asian and Pacific Migration Journal* 4, no. 2 (June 1, 1995): 211–32.

Sterngass, Jon. *Filipino Americans*. New York: Chelsea House, 2007.

Stevens, Robert Laird. *Sheldon Jackson: Pathfinder and Prospector of the Missionary Vanguard in the Rocky Mountains and Alaska*. New York: Fleming H. Revell Company, 1908.

Szasz, Margaret Connell, ed. *Between Indian and White Worlds: The Cultural Broker*. Norman: University of Oklahoma Press, 1994.

Takaki, Ronald. *Strangers from a Different Shore: A History of Asian Americans*. Boston: Little, Brown, and Company, 1989.

Tanaka, Kei. "Japanese Picture Marriages and the Image of Immigrant Women in Early Twentieth-Century California." *Japanese Journal of American Studies* 15 (2004): 115–35.

Taylor, Joseph E. "Well-Thinking Men and Women: The Battle for the White Act and the Meaning of Conservation in the 1920s." *Pacific Historical Review* 71 (August 2002): 356–87.

Thomas, Margaret. *Picture Man: The Legacy of Southeast Alaska Photographer Shoki Kayamori*. Fairbanks: University of Alaska Press, 2015.

Thornton, Thomas F. *Being and Place among the Tlingit*. Seattle: University of Washington Press, 2008.

———. *Haa Leelk'w Has Aani Saax'u: Our Grandparents' Names on the Land*. Seattle: University of Washington Press, 2012.

Tilly, Charles. "Transplanted Networks." In *Immigration Reconsidered: History, Sociology, and Politics*. New York: Oxford University Press, 1990.

Tilly, Louise. "Paths of Proletarianization: Organizations of Production, Sexual Division of Labor, and Women's Collective Action." *Signs* 7 (Winter 1981): 400–417.

Tsai, Shih-shan Henry. *The Chinese Experience in America*. Bloomington: Indiana University Press, 1986.

Tsosie, Rebecca. "Changing Women: The Crosscurrents of American Indian Feminine Identity." In *Unequal Sister: A Multicultural Reader in U.S. Women's History*, edited by Vicki L. Ruiz and Ellen Carol DuBois. 3rd ed. New York: Routledge, 2000.

United States Department of the Interior Report on Population and Resources of Alaska. Washington DC: Government Printing Office, 1893.

United States House of Representatives, Committee on the Merchant Marine and Fisheries. *Alaskan Fisheries Hearings*, part 3 (1939).

United States Senate Committee on Interstate and Foreign Commerce and House Committee on Merchant Marine and Fisheries. Hearings on S.R. 1446 and H.R. 3859, Salmon Trap Sites.

U.S. Bureau of Fisheries. *Pacific Salmon Fisheries*. Merchant Marine and Fisheries, 1938.

U.S. Bureau of Labor Statistics. *Labor Unionism in American Agriculture*. Bulletin no. 836. Washington DC: Government Printing Office, 1945.

U.S. Commission on Immigration. *Reports, Emigration and Immigration, 1907–1910*, 1907–1910. Washington DC: Government Printing Office, 1911.

U.S. Commission on Immigration. *Japanese and Other Immigrant Races in the Pacific and Rocky Mountain States*. 3 vols. Immigrants in Industries, no. 25, Washington DC: Government Printing Office, 1911.

U.S. Congress, House, Committee on Immigration and Naturalization. "Japanese Immigration."

U.S. Department of Commerce, Bureau of Fisheries. "Report of the U.S. Commissioner of Fisheries, 1922." Document No. 913. Washington DC: U.S. Government Printing Office, 1923.

U.S. Department Commerce and Labor, Bureau of Statistics. *Commercial Alaska, 1867–1903.*

U.S. House, Merchant Marine and Fisheries Committee (Congress). *Fish Traps in Alaska.* Hearings on H.R. 4254 and H.R. 8213, 74th Cong. 2nd Sess.

U.S. Immigration Commission. *Immigrants in Industries: Japanese and Other Immigrant Races in the Pacific Coast and Rocky Mountain States,* 1911.

Velasco, Victorio A. "Alaska—A Filipino Refuge." *Mid-Pacific Magazine,* November 1931.

———. "The Philippines." *Philippine Review,* February 1931.

Viernes, Gene. "Alaskeros History." Vignette in Ron Chew, *Remembering Silme Domingo and Gene Viernes: The Legacy of Filipino American Labor Activism,* 120–45. Seattle: University of Washington Press, 2012.

White, Leslie A. *The Evolution of Culture: The Development of Civilization in the Fall of Rome.* New York: McGraw-Hill, 1959.

White, Richard. *It's Your Misfortune and None of My Own: A New History of the American West.* Norman: University of Oklahoma Press, 1991.

———. *The Roots of Dependency: Subsistence, Environment, and Social Change among the Choctaw, Pawnee, and Navajo.* Lincoln: University of Nebraska, 1983.

Whitehead, John S. *Completing the Union: Alaska, Hawai'i and the Battle for Statehood.* Albuquerque: University of New Mexico Press, 2004.

Whymper, Frederick. *Travel and Adventure in the Territory of Alaska.* London: John Murray, Albermarle Street, 1868.

Wickersham, James. "Slaughter of the Silver Horde." *American Conservation* 1, no. 7 (August 1911): 243–52.

Wilkinson, Charles F. *American Indians, Time, and the Law.* New Haven: Yale University Press, 1987.

Wolfe, Robert J., and Robert J. Walker. "Subsistence Economics in Alaska: Productivity, Geography, and Developmental Impact." *Arctic Anthropology* 24, no. 2 (1987): 56–81.

Worl, Rosita. "Tlingit *At.oow*: Tangible and Intangible Property." PhD diss., Harvard University, 1998.

Wyatt, Victoria. "Alaskan Indian Wage Earners in the 19th Century: Economic Identity on Southeast Alaska's Frontier." *Pacific Northwest Quarterly* 78, nos. 1–2 (1987): 43–49.

Yanagisako, Sylvia Junko. *Transforming the Past: Tradition and Kinship among Japanese Americans.* Palo Alto CA: Stanford University Press, 1985.

Zavella, Patricia. *Women's Work and Chicano Families: Cannery Workers of the Santa Clara Valley.* Ithaca NY: Cornell University Press, 1987.

INDEX

populism, 98, 144
Port Althorp, 209, 212
potlatch (*Koo.eex*), 34–35, 304n28, 304n34, 307n7
Prince William Sound, 51, 86
Progressive Era, 89, 93, 95
Pyramid Harbor, 46

Quinto, Bessie, 169, 208–10, 329n34
Quinto, Marcel, 169, 209

race, 26, 164, 166, 262, 284
racial formation theory, 4
red scare, 97–98
regional history, 1–2
Rizal Day, 169
Rojo, Trinidad, 220–21
Roman Catholic Church, 171
Roosevelt, Franklin D., 148, 149, 181, 237, 252
Roosevelt, Theodore, 60, 142, 308nn23–24, 316n18
Rose Inlet cannery, 162, 194
Russian American Company (RAC), 3, 15–21, 19, 20, 25
Russians, 15–21, 25, 171

San Francisco, 3, 29, 38, 41, 45, 74, 82, 83, 92, 93, 147, 181, 213, 249, 267
Sarabia, Helen, 291
Scidmore, Eliza Ruhamah, 38
Shelikhov-Golikov Company, 16
Siberia, 16, 96
Silver Horde (film), 132
Simpson, Peter, 68, 101, 140
Soboleff, Walter, 185, 206
Southeast Alaska Cannery Workers Council, 216
Spanish-American War, 6, 159
subsistence, 10, 210–11, 220, 329n34
Sutherland, Daniel (Dan), 108–9, 112

Taft, William, 160, 251
Taft-Hartley Act, 269, 274
Takamori, Mack, 136, 137
Tatsuda, Charlie, 238, 239, 333n52
Tatsuda, Cherry (Fujioka), 133–34, 238, 286
Tatsuda, Jimmie, 125, 238, 239
Tatsuda, William, 132, 238, 333n52
termination policy, 275, 276
Tlingit, 16–19, 21, 36, 48–49, 72
Tlingit-Haida Central Council, 148–49, 288
Tlingit-Haida lawsuit, 227
Tores, Ponce, 221
totem poles, 56, 307n3, 307n7, 307n9, 310n3
tragedy of the commons, 45
Troy, John, 99, 104
Truman, Harry, 269–70, 274, 338n16, 338n18
Tsimshian, 4, 53–73, 307n7, 307n9, 308n23
Tydings-Duffie Act, 179

Unangan (Aleut), 18–19, 234, 241–43, 333n47
United Cannery, Agricultural Packing and Allied Workers of America (UCA-PAWA), 214–17, 220, 270, 294
United States Fish and Wildlife Service (USFWS), 31, 208, 242, 265, 282

Velasco, Victorio, 162–63, 173–75
Viernes, Gene, 161
Visaya, Bessie, 293

Wallace, Dorothy Wanamaker, 206
Wanamaker, Margaret Jackson, 206–7
War Labor Board, 227, 228
Waterfall cannery, 174
White Act, 107–8, 111
Wickersham, James, 89–97, 146, 147, 155